SAFEGUARDING FEDERALISM

SAFEGUARDING FEDERALISM

How States Protect Their Interests
in National Policymaking

JOHN D. NUGENT

UNIVERSITY OF OKLAHOMA PRESS : NORMAN

Publication of this book is made possible through the generous support of Edith Kinney Gaylord.

Library of Congress Cataloging-in-Publication Data

Nugent, John Douglas, 1969–
   Safeguarding federalism : how states protect their interests in national policy-making / John D. Nugent.
        p.   cm.
   Includes bibliographical references and index.
   ISBN 978-0-8061-4003-2 (hardcover : alk. paper)
   1. Federal government—United States—History. 2. State governments—United States—History. 3. United States—Politics and government. I. Title.
   JK311.N84   2009
   320.473'049—dc22

                                                                2008033599

The paper in this book meets the guidelines for permanence and durability of the Committee on Production Guidelines for Book Longevity of the Council on Library Resources. ∞

1 2 3 4 5 6 7 8 9 10

For Tristan

CONTENTS

Figures and Tables

Figures

Tables

ACKNOWLEDGMENTS

I t is my pleasure to publicly acknowledge my intellectual and personal debts to my teachers, graduate school colleagues, friends, and family as well as to numerous state and federal staffers who took time to speak with me about their work.

This book's earliest origins are a graduate seminar paper on the Seventeenth Amendment written for Professor Jeffrey Tulis at the University of Texas at Austin. My understanding of state-governmental interests and my first inklings that they were probably not promoted today primarily by U.S. senators began to develop as I wrote that paper. More generally, Jeff's writing and teaching heavily influenced my understanding of American political and constitutional development. I was also greatly influenced by course work and conversations with Walter Dean Burnham, who cochaired my dissertation committee. Other professors at the University of Texas whose courses and scholarship particularly inspired my thinking about government and politics include Sanford Levinson, H. W. Perry, Jr., David Edwards, J. Budziszewski, and Gretchen Ritter. Closer to the dissertation stage, a brief but important hallway conversation at the Midwest Political Science Association conference with Ross Baker of Rutgers University put me on the path that ultimately led to this book. He mentioned a building called the Hall of the States just off Capitol

Hill that houses most of the governors' Washington offices. I was intrigued by why governors would have offices in Washington, D.C., and the interviews I later conducted there serve as the foundation of this book's conception of state-governmental interests.

Noting how much one learns from fellow students, Thoreau mused in *Walden* that "tuition . . . is an important item in the term bill, while for the far more valuable education which [the student] gets by associating with the most cultivated of his contemporaries no charge is made" (p. 34). In this vein, I owe many intellectual debts to my fellow students at the University of Texas Department of Government, which in the mid-1990s had a large and talented cohort of graduate students studying American politics and political development. In particular, I learned a great deal from Jasmine Farrier, Suzanne Globetti, Azza Layton, Marc Hetherington, Jay Mason, Shannan Mattiace, Jay McCullough, Bruce Peabody, Clare Sheridan, and Joe Smith. I should also note that a wide range of extracurricular activities at numerous central Texas watering holes, barbecue joints, and state and national parks with these people kept me sane throughout graduate school.

At important points in the development of my ideas about federalism and intergovernmental relations, I benefited from serving on conference panels with several other budding federalism scholars, Steve Bragaw, Jennifer Jensen, and Troy Smith.

At Connecticut College, I taught a senior seminar organized along the same lines as this book, which gave me an opportunity to think through and present as a coherent whole the basic ideas presented herein. I thank the students for tackling an eclectic set of materials with me and for putting up with what was, at the time, quite a number of only partially developed ideas regarding state–federal relations.

Keith Whittington provided helpful feedback and encouragement on the book prospectus, and I wish to thank Matthew Bokovoy for his enthusiasm about the project and his encouragement and suggestions as the manuscript went through the revision process while he was at the University of Oklahoma Press. Two reviewers for the Press gave the manuscript a very close reading and provided dozens of valuable suggestions that greatly improved the final product, and Kimberly Kinne's careful editing made the book better in numerous ways.

I want to thank my parents, Lee and Edna Nugent, for their love, encouragement, and support of all the scholarly endeavors that ultimately led to this book.

The impending June 2006 arrival of Skye Mourne Nugent provided the impetus for completing the manuscript and sending it out to reviewers. As rewarding as it is to put this research project to bed, nothing compares with the joys of putting Skye to bed after a day of fun and watching her sink into a peaceful slumber.

My deepest thanks go to my wife, Dr. Tristan Anne Borer. As a fellow political scientist, best friend, and life partner, she has supported me in innumerable ways as I have worked on this book, and I have dedicated it to her. For her sake, I hope its completion will begin the phasing out of my running commentary on how federalism and intergovernmental relations pervade and explain just about everything we happen to be doing, talking about, or driving by.

SAFEGUARDING FEDERALISM

INTRODUCTION

The Constitution and the "Construction" of American Federalism

Even after four decades of talk about the "political safeguards of federalism," there is a lot we do not know about the formal and even informal ways in which states' interests influence congressional decisionmaking. What seems clear, however, is that there are avenues of influence, often very strong ones.
—Evan Caminker, *Columbia Law Review*[1]

Imagine the following conversation with a friend:

You: You probably have a basic idea of how the U.S. Constitution's checks and balances are supposed to work, right?
Friend: I think so.
You: OK. So, what sorts of "weapons" can the president and Congress use against one another when they disagree?
Friend: Let's see. The president can veto a bill that Congress passes. Congress can override a veto and can reject a president's nominee for a judgeship or cabinet position. A president could also instruct the executive branch departments to interpret and implement a law in ways that Congress didn't intend. And didn't Congress pass the War Powers Act after Vietnam to try to reassert its foreign policy powers?

3

You: Right. OK, that's a good start. Now, the Constitution's authors also envisioned a set of checks and balances between the federal government and the state governments so *they* could exercise limits on another's authority over time. Can you explain how some of those work nowadays?

Friend: Um . . . er . . .

Taking as my premise that the friend in this conversation represents a wide variety of well-educated people who have taken (or even taught!) a college political science course, I pose and answer three questions in this book: How do state governments protect and promote their interests vis-à-vis the federal government today? What exactly *are* those interests? How do state officials' efforts to protect and promote the various interests of their states affect our understanding of the U.S. Constitution's division of authority between the states and the federal government?

The primary advocates of the 1787 Constitution believed federal and state officials would check and balance each other in ways broadly similar to those used by officials in the three branches of the national government.[2] Indeed, James Madison's famous essay on interbranch checks and balances—"No. 51" in *The Federalist*—identifies federalism as the Constitution's primary separation of power: "In the compound republic of America, the power surrendered by the people is *first* divided between two distinct governments, and then the portion allotted to each subdivided among distinct and separate departments. Hence a double security arises to the rights of the people. The different governments will control each other, at the same time that each will be controlled by itself."[3]

In this book, I explain how the first half of this double security works today. Constitutional scholars have long been interested in whether state governments can adequately protect their interests and prerogatives[4] against perceived federal encroachments. The most vivid examples in American history of states' attempts to check and balance the federal government have taken forms such as states seceding and governors standing in schoolhouse doors, but state governments protect their interests today in ways that typically involve constructive engagement rather than brinksmanship. In this book, my close examination of the national policymaking process reveals numerous ways that state officials protect their interests by participating in the development and implementation of federal laws and regulations.

The checks used most frequently by states are not necessarily ones that the framers of the Constitution anticipated or wrote about, but they nonetheless afford state officials leverage against their federal counterparts at each stage of the federal policymaking and policy-implementation processes. In the course of their daily work, state officials continuously perceive and promote the legalistic, fiscal, and administrative interests of their states relative to the federal government. These three general interests involve states' legal authority to act independently of the federal government, states' desire for adequate and predictable federal funding, and states' desire for at least some flexibility and autonomy when they implement federal policies. As state officials pursue such interests in specific policymaking episodes, they frequently succeed in parrying perceived federal encroachments on state authority and state interests. Collectively and over time, such state–federal interactions across a range of policy areas not only yield workable solutions to pressing public problems, but they also clarify and extend our understanding of the constitutional balance of authority between the states and the federal government. In recent years, a growing scholarly literature has illustrated how ordinary and extraordinary political and policymaking efforts clarify the ambiguities and silences of the Constitution's text—a process sometimes called constitutional "construction."[5] That literature has focused on separation of powers and civil liberties questions much more than federalism questions, and the present work fills that gap by describing and explaining the many nonjudicial determinants of the state–federal balance of authority.

• • •

A great deal has been written about the constitutional relationships between the three branches of the federal government and how political skirmishes among elected and appointed officials of each branch have affected their respective constitutional prerogatives over time.[6] These works have fruitfully conjoined constitutional and policy analysis, yielding theoretically grounded assessments of how this element of the Constitution's separation of powers is faring in the contemporary United

States. However, the literature on how the federal and state governments check and balance one another today is comparatively underdeveloped. Some scholars have examined particular state–federal checks individually, but no work connects the dots to reveal a complete picture of how state officials currently promote and protect their interests in the national policymaking process.

Given that the text of the Constitution specifies few formal means by which states can check the federal government, the most useful means available to state officials—governors, state legislators, and state administrators—are a set of informal powers and practices that they have developed over time. Although none of these means resembles anything as decisive as a formal states' veto over federal action, they nonetheless provide state officials with ongoing opportunities for constructive involvement in making and carrying out federal policy. In any particular policy area (welfare, taxation, environmental protection, and so forth), state officials may attempt to retain policymaking authority for themselves by passing quality legislation that obviates the need for federal policymaking in that area. If Congress does decide to act, state officials can attempt to influence the content of federal policies as they are being written by Congress. Finally, state officials can attempt to influence the rulemaking process through which federal agencies often flesh out federal law, and states can also use their role in the federal implementation process to enforce federal policies in ways that promote their own interests. State officials thus have opportunities to check the federal government at the prelegislative, legislative, and postlegislative stages of the federal policymaking process.

• • •

Although political scientists and legal scholars have written much about federalism and intergovernmental relations, their research for the most part proceeds on separate tracks.[7] Political scientists studying the historical development and policy implications of state–federal relations have taught us much about how the country has progressed through eras of dual federalism, cooperative federalism, and competitive federalism.[8] Legal scholars have typically focused on the broader constitutional issues stemming from judicial efforts to draw clear, workable lines between state-governmental authority and the federal government's authority.[9] As a result, rather than a single scholarly literature on federalism, there are actually at least two literatures. Political scientists almost never cite law review articles on the constitutional aspects of American federalism, and legal scholars rarely give more than cursory citations of the political science literature on federalism, intergovernmental relations, and public administration. It is thus rare to get more than half the picture from either group of scholars.

In this book, I synthesize the constitutional and policymaking approaches into an explanation of how state officials currently perform a constitutional function by attempting to check and balance their federal counterparts. The constitutional and policy-related aspects of federalism are not developed in isolation; rather, they are mutually reinforcing in a variety of ways. Indeed, it is imprecise to use the passive verb tense and say that federalism "is developed"; instead, state officials, federal officials, and (less frequently) state and federal judges do their jobs in ways that raise questions about the boundaries separating state and federal authority and prompt searches for resolutions. Through this process, a variety of intergovernmental political activities at the various policymaking stages constitute American federalism, and these activities yield relatively settled agreements about which policy decisions will be made by state governments, which will be made by the federal government, and which will be made jointly. Policy debates over federal programs that are largely administered by state governments, such as welfare or Medicaid, generate two sorts of resolutions. In the short term, they result in distributions of decisionmaking authority, money, and administrative responsibility for these programs. Over the longer term, they yield more general understandings about which level of government ought to have primary authority to devise, pay for, and implement programs in broad policy areas like social services, health care, and environmental protection. Synthesizing the insights of political scientists and legal scholars thus indicates the microlevel political causes of macrolevel constitutional changes in the balance of state–federal authority. Leonard White wrote in 1953 that the debate over the proper balance between the federal government and the states "was once primarily on constitutional grounds, but the matter now has become a political and an administrative issue."[10] In fact, federalism debates continue to have both of these aspects, and they need to be examined in tandem.

This study draws on and in turn contributes to four streams of research by legal scholars and political scientists. The first is the literature concerning the "political safeguards of federalism." This line of research has its modern origins in a 1954 *Columbia Law Review* article by Herbert Wechsler, and the debate has been carried on mainly in law reviews since then.[11] Echoing essays 45 and 46 of *The Federalist*, in which Madison anticipates the various powers that state and federal government officials might use "to resist and frustrate the measures of each other,"[12] Wechsler argues that the constitutional system, with features such as state-governmental control over congressional redistricting, the determination of voter qualifications, and the selection of slates of electors to the electoral college, "is intrinsically well adapted to retarding or restraining new intrusions by the center on the domain of the states. Far from a national authority that is expansionist by nature, the inherent tendency in our system is precisely the reverse, necessitating the widest support before intrusive measures of importance can receive consideration, reacting readily to opposition grounded in resistance within the states."[13] Wechsler's position was developed more thoroughly by legal scholar Jesse Choper in a 1980 book titled *Judicial Review and the National Political Process*, and the political safeguards thesis was explicitly endorsed by the Supreme Court in 1985 in *Garcia v. San Antonio Metropolitan Transit Authority*.[14]

One implication of Wechsler's and Choper's reasoning—stated more forcefully by Choper than by Wechsler—is that the federal courts ought *not* to serve as the referee of state–federal relations but should leave such questions to be resolved through the political process. (As such, this general view is sometimes referred to as "process federalism.") Those who worry that state governments have lost a great deal of their authority to the federal government over time tend to reject Wechsler's and Choper's view and call for the federal courts to referee state–federal relations by restraining the federal government (particularly Congress) when it encroaches on state authority.[15] Since 1995, the federal courts have responded to the invitation by restraining federal authority in some of its manifestations, although the results have been uneven at best.[16]

Scholars continue to debate whether the various political safeguards are in fact adequate to protect state-governmental interests, and in the present work I contribute to this literature by arguing that Wechsler and those who have echoed his views are correct that there are effective political safeguards of federalism but that they have generally not identified the most important ones, which are mostly informal and extraconstitutional rather than the formal, constitutional provisions that Wechsler and Choper focused on.[17] Although Congress and the president are still the ultimate architects of federalism (because of their control of the federal purse strings and ability to pass legislation that constrains or preempts state lawmaking efforts, for example), the key pressures to design, pass, and implement more state-friendly federal legislation come from sources other than the president, senators, and members of the House of Representatives. Thus, I hope to redirect scholarly attention away from federal officeholders and toward a congeries of state officials, institutions, and processes that influence federal decisionmaking and policy-implementation processes in less visible—but no less important—ways. Chapters 3 through 5 present case studies of three of these informal political safeguards of federalism.

Although I believe that various political safeguards are more effective than some scholars have recognized, I do not endorse Choper's view that the judiciary should therefore decline to hear cases about the boundaries of state–federal relations. Legal scholars have tended to frame the debate as a forced choice between political or judicial safeguards. Saikrishna Prakash and John Yoo, for example, preface one of their discussions by noting the following:

> When we refer to the political safeguards of federalism we mean the theory that because the states are represented in the national political process, judicial review of federalism questions is either unnecessary or unwarranted. In other words, the political safeguards of federalism refers to the theory that the political safeguards are the exclusive means of safeguarding the states. Under this approach, federal courts are not to exercise review over questions that involve the balance of power between the federal government and the states.[18]

In this book, I reject this needlessly narrow view of the political safe-guards of federalism, which places scholarly blinders on efforts to determine the effectiveness of state officials' attempts to influence federal policymaking and policy implementation. In this book, I am interested in answering the empirical question of whether there are political safeguards that succeed today rather than the normative question of whether federal courts should view federalism disputes as nonjusticiable. Although this second question is not unimportant, scholars who focus on it seem destined to overlook enormous swaths of evidence of how state officials successfully protect and promote their interests in the federal policymaking process today.

A second stream of scholarship I draw on in this book concerns the ways in which the political branches (Congress and the executive) participate over time in the interpretation and clarification of ambiguities in the Constitution's text. This process has been referred to as nonjudicial interpretation, constitutionalism outside the courts, constitutional construction, coordinate construction, and departmentalism, but the basic point is the same: the Constitution is ambiguous or incomplete in many regards, and its meaning cannot be—and in practice is not—determined exclusively by federal judges. When presidents and the Congress engage in what Susan Burgess calls "contests for constitutional authority," the results are relatively settled understandings of the boundaries of institutional powers that were left ambiguous by the Constitution's text. Decades ago, noted constitutional scholar Edward S. Corwin explained that the purpose of a constitution is "to lay down the general features of a system of government and to define to a greater or less extent the power of such government, in relation to the rights of persons on the one hand, and on the other—in our system at any rate—in relation to certain other political entities which are incorporated in the system."[19] According to Corwin, "the" American Constitution consists of the written text of the document, a "vast bulk of judicial decisions," "certain important statutes, for example, The Judiciary Act of 1789, as amended to date, The Presidential Succession Act of 1886, The Inter-State Commerce Act, or portions of it," and "certain usages of government which have developed since the formal constitution first went into effect, and some of which indeed, have virtually repealed portions of the latter."[20]

Constitutional authority regarding matters such as impeachment, the Louisiana Purchase, budgeting, and war powers has been clarified by debates between Congress and the executive branch, with little or no judicial involvement. The dimensions of many other federal powers, such as executive privilege and congressional authority to charter a national bank, have been clarified through a combination of political and judicial construction. Nonjudicial constitutional construction is a necessary feature of American political development because the institutions and processes created by the Constitution generate disagreements about its provisions that cannot be resolved simply by resorting to interpretations of the constitutional text.[21] Political and administrative action must supplement judicial interpretations of the text.

From the standpoint of federalism, the role of constitutional construction in defining and redefining the respective spheres of state and national authority is particularly important because of the text's ambiguity concerning the extent of those spheres.[22] The Constitution

> does not state any principle that might be used to determine the powers that are available to national and state governments. With each proposal for a new program to deal with some perceived problem, therefore, an opportunity is created to reopen the debate over whether government should be involved at all and, if so, which level of government should be responsible for the new activity. . . . Yet the debate is never resolved because it cannot be resolved in the absence of clear principle. Instead of principled resolution, the issue is pragmatically temporized, over and over again.[23]

State and federal officials engage in specific debates over public policy that yield both short-term allocations of money and decisionmaking authority as well as longer term settled understandings of the state–federal division of labor under the Constitution. An example that will be discussed in greater detail in chapter 4 is the debate over the 1996 welfare-reform law, which redefined—without the involvement of the courts—the proper level of government at which primary responsibility for designing welfare programs should reside. The law (the Personal Responsibility and Work Opportunity Reconciliation Act) obviously held great near-term significance for state agencies and low-income Americans, but it is important to note also its longer term constitutive importance as a political means by which state governments fought for and won additional decisionmaking authority in the realm of social welfare policy.

In this book, then, I present an account of the sorts of political activities that state officials use to actuate their views on the limits of national power. Some of these limits are legally enforceable, and others are politically enforceable, but both sorts are central to the construction of American federalism through the national policymaking process.

The third body of literature that informs this study is the political science and public administration work on federalism and intergovernmental relations. The question of the relationship between state governments, the national government, and the American people (who are dual citizens of both levels of government) has occupied scholars since at least the 1780s. These questions have theoretical, legal, political, policymaking, fiscal, and administrative implications, and all have received extensive scholarly treatment. Until the late 1950s, the bulk of scholarship on such issues adopted a dual federalism perspective that emphasized the *separate* policymaking responsibilities and legal authority of state governments and the national government. Around 1960, Morton Grodzins and his student Daniel Elazar began publishing a series of works advancing the opposite view—that American federalism is and has been characterized by a great deal of shared responsibility for a wide range of policymaking and policy implementation.[24] Other scholars adopting this viewpoint, notably Deil Wright and Michael Reagan,[25] shifted the emphasis in the scholarly literature to intergovernmental relations—the joint efforts of federal, state, and local officials to devise, finance, and implement federal programs. Reagan concluded that the constitutional dual federalism envisioned by James Madison was dead, having been replaced by a so-called permissive federalism in which "there is a sharing of power and authority between the national and state governments, but that the state's share rests upon the permission and permissiveness of the national government."[26]

The death of federalism has been proclaimed prematurely on a number of occasions, particularly since New Deal–era observers like Harold Laski and Luther Gulick eulogized its passing,[27] but phoenix-like revivals of federalism were in fact regular features of twentieth-century American

politics. Accordingly, although the much-heralded "devolution revolution" of the 1990s was always more rhetoric than reality,[28] the past
decade *has* been marked by a greater emphasis on the value of clarifying or sorting out the respective responsibilities of government at each
level.[29] In addition, the Supreme Court has helped foster a scholarly
reexamination of the boundaries separating state and federal authority
since 1995, when it reassumed (albeit haltingly and inconsistently) its
long-dormant role in enforcing certain limits on congressional policymaking.[30] The most thorough chronicler of federalism at the dawn of
the twenty-first century is David Walker, who has painstakingly documented the conflicted and ambivalent nature of American federalism
today but is guardedly optimistic about the full emergence of a "protected federalism" in which state prerogatives are not at the mercy of
federal politicians.[31]

In the present work, I draw on both of these two scholarly approaches,
coupling detailed descriptions of intergovernmental policymaking efforts
and a general theoretical view of the dynamics of American federalism.
As Elazar demonstrated, despite the extensive sharing of policymaking
duties between state governments and the federal government, states
remain political societies whose distinct legal standing vis-à-vis the
federal government has not been seriously threatened. This situation is
not for lack of federal efforts to reduce the autonomy of the states,
however, and the case studies in later chapters illustrate how state
governments today resist the "reduction of all the states into a consolidated government,"[32] which a steady stream of observers has been
warning about since the founding era.

The fourth body of literature I draw on concerns public policymaking
and public administration. This study contributes to scholarly understandings of how state and federal officials (elected and appointed)
come into contact with one another on a daily basis as they attempt to
resolve near-term policymaking challenges in the wide variety of areas
in which the states and federal governments share responsibility for
designing and implementing programs—social services, environmental
protection, transportation, and law enforcement, to name just a few.
Political scientists and legal scholars have written a great deal about these
issue areas but usually not with an eye toward how state governments

use their implementation powers to promote their interests vis-à-vis the federal government.

In sum, legal scholars have, I believe, done the best job at stating the central constitutional question of American federalism: are there political safeguards of federalism that permit state governments today to protect their interests relative to the federal government? Despite framing the question so concisely, however, legal scholars' substantive and methodological training does not typically incline them to look closely at the details of policymaking and street-level implementation, where compelling evidence of the safeguards' effectiveness can be found. Rather, they focus on judicial attempts to find "bright lines" demarcating the putatively "proper" zones of state and federal authority. Because several centuries of judicial effort have failed to generate anything like neutral doctrinal principles of federalism that enjoy the sustained approval of judges and legal scholars,[33] scholars need to know as much as possible about how federalism is contested in the political and policymaking realms.

• • •

Rather little will be said in subsequent chapters about the role of the judiciary in protecting the interests of state governments. I have taken this approach intentionally, for two reasons. First, a great deal of scholarly attention has already focused on the ways that the federal courts have or have not restrained federal decisionmakers in the name of preserving state-governmental authority. However, there is little work that closely examines how state officials—governors, state legislators, heads of state agencies, and staff members working on their behalf—attempt to influence federal policymaking and when, how, and why they succeed. This imbalance in the literature is a problem because it may lead observers to conclude—incorrectly, I think—that the interests of state governments today are largely at the mercy of the federal government and that only judicial intervention can protect them.[34] Therefore, in this book I present a wide range of empirical evidence regarding political safeguards of federalism so that observers can better weigh the respective possibilities and limits of political and judicial safeguards.

Second, as a practical matter, the contestation between state and federal officials determines the nature of American federalism as much as or more than judicial decisions for practical reasons, such as resource and time constraints on the courts' ability to referee every dispute between levels of government.[35] This situation is due to the fact that, "although judicial review in federalism cases invalidates statutes that exceed the outer bounds of federal power, it does nothing to constrain the exercise of power *within* those bounds,"[36] and we must therefore examine what states can do to protect their interests vis-à-vis the federal government even when perceived federal encroachments do not rise to the level of constitutional violations. Moreover, as noted above, the Constitution simply does not contain enough detail about the respective scope of state and federal authority to clarify decisively and for all time the states' role in our system of government. Judicial rulings have generated some clarity in this regard, but those decisions cover only a small swath of state–federal relations and frequently raise more questions than they answer. Daily state–federal interactions in the political and policymaking realms generate additional understandings about the roles of state governments and the federal government in addressing public concerns related to poverty, environmental degradation, education and job training, health care, and many others. In this way, the development and implementation of joint state–federal public policy yield constitutional understandings of federalism that are just as important in practical terms as the more overt rearticulations of American federalism periodically handed down by federal courts. This link between political practices and constitutional understanding was characterized well by Arthur Schlesinger: "The Constitution was an extraordinary document. But a document is only a document, and what the Constitution 'really' meant—i.e., meant in practice—only practice could disclose. It therefore fell to the daily experience of government under the Constitution to explore the document's possibilities, reconcile its contradictions, and repair its omissions."[37]

In this book, I look at the daily experiences of state and federal officials under a magnifying glass to see how their cooperation and conflicts generate both public policy outcomes and constitutional meaning.

None of this should be taken to mean that the Supreme Court's recent jurisprudence regarding the Commerce Clause and the Tenth and Eleventh Amendments is unimportant or that the federal courts ought not adjudicate state–federal disputes. There will always be a role for the federal courts to play in refereeing the respective scope of state and federal authority.[38] As noted earlier, though, whereas Jesse Choper's and other scholars' goal is to catalog the political safeguards of federalism in order to make the case that judicial review of federalism disputes is unwarranted, my goal is to provide an intensive look at how and why these safeguards work today. In doing so, I acknowledge the recent work of scholars who have pointed out that the political versus judicial safeguards debate relies to some degree on a false either–or dichotomy between the political and judicial spheres. J. Mitchell Pickerill and Cornell Clayton, for example, have documented the ways that the Supreme Court's recent federalism jurisprudence has reflected existing trends within the elected branches of the federal government rather than developing independently in a countermajoritarian fashion.[39] Citing earlier scholarship that reveals how the courts are more political than political scientists' traditional political–judicial dichotomy implies, Pickerill and Clayton instead offer a political-regimes approach premised on the idea that developments in the judiciary and the elected branches of government are much more intertwined than they are often thought to be. Because the present book is not a call for the federal courts to stay out of state–federal disputes, my account is consistent with Pickerill and Clayton's view that state–federal relations are contested through mutually influential political and judicial means rather than proceeding on separate tracks. Indeed, if the judiciary is viewed at least in part as a political branch of government and it holds at least some promise of restraining congressional or presidential incursions on state authority, then the full range of political safeguards I outline in chapter 2 may be even larger than I have stated.

• • •

The theoretical and empirical insights I present in this book rest on several dozen semistructured interviews with staff members of numerous state and national officials, original content analyses of policy positions adopted by the National Governors' Association and the National Conference of State Legislatures and of governors' state-of-the-state addresses, and a wide variety of primary and secondary source materials. Further details of the methods used in this study are presented in the appendix.

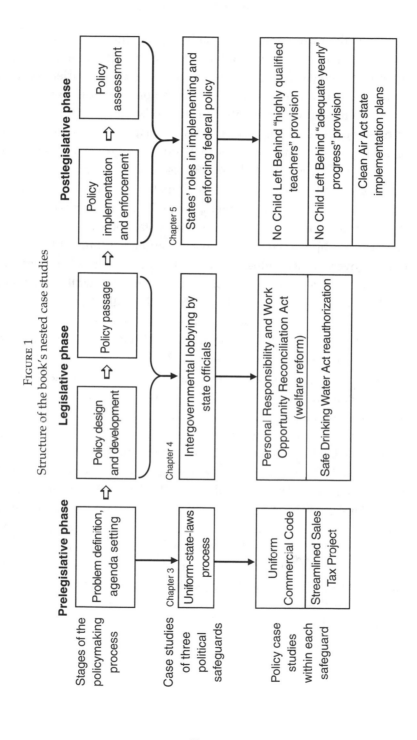

FIGURE 1
Structure of the book's nested case studies

Prelegislative phase

Legislative phase

Postlegislative phase

Stages of the policymaking process

Problem definition, agenda setting → Policy design and development → Policy passage → Policy implementation and enforcement → Policy assessment

Case studies of three political safeguards

Chapter 3: Uniform-state-laws process

Chapter 4: Intergovernmental lobbying by state officials

Chapter 5: States' roles in implementing and enforcing federal policy

Policy case studies within each safeguard

Uniform Commercial Code

Streamlined Sales Tax Project

Personal Responsibility and Work Opportunity Reconciliation Act (welfare reform)

Safe Drinking Water Act reauthorization

No Child Left Behind "highly qualified teachers" provision

No Child Left Behind "adequate yearly progress" provision

Clean Air Act state implementation plans

Rather than presenting a normative grand theory of how state and federal authority *ought* to be divided, I describe and explain the ongoing intergovernmental policy battles that *are* waged in a variety of arenas. To analyze these battles, we need terminology for describing what the state and federal governments perceive to be their respective interests in these policymaking episodes. Thus, in chapter 1 I outline a typology of state–governmental interests that indicates the general lines along which state officials and federal officials tend to disagree. To provide a sense of the full range of strategies available to state officials pursuing those interests, I catalog in chapter 2 the political safeguards of federalism that exist today. Empirical evidence of how state officials use these means appears in chapters 3 through 5 in case studies of three of these modes of intergovernmental influence. I describe and explain the uniform-state-laws process, intergovernmental lobbying, and the states' roles in the implementation of federal policy, each of which illustrates states' efforts at a different stage of the federal policymaking process. These case studies are used to test the idea that state officials today achieve meaningful successes in defending against perceived federal encroachments on their decisionmaking authority, their fiscal well-being, and their administrative flexibility. As shown in figure 1, the case studies of these three safeguards are buttressed by several additional nested policy case studies exemplifying the workings of each safeguard. These policy case studies include the Uniform Commercial Code, the Streamlined Sales Tax Project, the Personal Responsibility and Work Opportunity Reconciliation Act, the Safe Drinking Water Act, the No Child Left Behind law, and the Clean Air Act. As a whole, these case studies reveal how the activities of state officials work to influence the development, passage, and implementation of federal policy. They reveal vibrant and dynamic relationships between state governments and the national government that provide state officials with frequent and sequential opportunities to resist, frustrate, and—above all—constructively influence the design and implementation of federal policies.

CHAPTER 1

What's at Stake?

State-Governmental Interests vis-à-vis the Federal Government

The true essence of federalism is that the States as States have legitimate interests which the National Government is bound to respect even though its laws are supreme.

—Justice Sandra Day O'Connor,
Garcia v. San Antonio Metropolitan Transit Authority[1]

Although their personal motives may vary, governors, state legislators, and other state officials seek public office to try to remedy what they perceive to be public problems in their states. Once in office, however, many learn that they are not entirely free to tackle state problems in any way they would like. The federal government has legislated or issued regulations in many areas of public concern, and over time those federal policies have circumscribed or eliminated state authority in some policy areas. A new state legislator eager to do something about air polluters in his or her district quickly learns that the federal Clean Air Act and its subsequent amendments and regulations define numerous state and federal responsibilities for designing, paying for, implementing, and enforcing clean air regulations. These and other conjoint governing arrangements cause state and federal officials to view policy issues in certain ways and to perceive their respective political interests accordingly. Some of the interests perceived by state officials as they do their jobs concern what is best for their states as states (i.e., as "corporate" entities) in their dealings with the federal government. It is these state-governmental interests that are at stake in the state–federal contests for authority that collectively determine the nature of American federalism.

Developing a terminology for talking about state-governmental interests is a critical first step toward my ultimate aim in this book: evaluating the degree to which state governments succeed today in safeguarding their interests vis-à-vis the federal government.[2] It is surprising that the federalism and intergovernmental relations literatures lack a concise statement of these interests. Although many people generally understand that state officials bristle at federal constraints on their autonomy, we need to know much more than this to fully understand how and why state officials try to check and balance the federal government today.

In the introduction, I noted the similar ways that the leading framers of the U.S. Constitution viewed the dynamics of the so-called horizontal separation of powers (among the three branches) and the so-called vertical separation of powers (between state governments and the federal government). According to Madisonian logic (best articulated in *The Federalist*, "No. 51"), the institutional interests of Congress, the executive branch, and the federal courts are promoted by the exercise of powers exerted in service of the personal, political, and policy ambitions of the individuals within those institutions.[3] According to the political science literature on congressional decisionmaking, for example, members of Congress are primarily interested in increasing their own power, winning reelection, and making sound public policy.[4] With this in mind, it initially seems patently incorrect (if not absurd) to say that "the Congress" has a single, identifiable set of collective interests or preferences that it pursues in its dealings with "the executive branch" and "the federal courts." At the very least, such an argument requires some explanation because it seems to ignore the fact that individuals with many competing goals and motivations comprise these institutions.

However, if self-promotional and policy-related concerns were the *only* interests members of the national political branches perceived, it would be impossible to explain recurrent congressional and presidential behavior aimed at protecting the institutional authority of their respective branches. As Madison expected, in addition to their daily political and policy-related concerns, officeholders within these institutions also develop broader institutional interests stemming from their roles as temporary stewards of their respective institutions.[5] When these interests diverge, we have seen political and legal battles by presidents and executive officials to defend assertions of executive privilege, to resist the inquiries of independent counsels, to prevent public disclosure of the deliberations of presidents and their political and policy advisors, to challenge congressional assertions of war powers, and to acquire "fast-track" authority to negotiate international trade agreements.[6] Such battles have similarly included congressional challenges to presidential pocket vetoes during intrasession adjournments, presidential exercises of the line-item veto, recess appointments of judicial and executive branch officials, executive branch rulemaking, the use of presidential signing statements to undercut Congress's legislative intent, and the exercise of judicial review by the Supreme Court.[7] Such actions cannot be explained solely by reelection goals, policymaking aspirations, or partisan or personal animus (although those factors may be important); instead, they reflect the jealous guarding of institutional prerogatives that transcends the interests of individuals or political parties. When push comes to shove, the three branches of government are usually reluctant to cede institutional authority to the others—even when the branches of government in question are controlled by the same political party.[8] In this sense, one can plausibly think, as Madison and others did, in terms of the branches having discrete, identifiable institutional interests. *Constitutional* analysis of this sort thus brackets, but does not deny, the personal and partisan interests of officials within these branches in order to focus on the institutional interests that periodically take center stage.

To extend the separation of powers analysis to state–federal relations, we need a similar understanding of the interests and motives of state officials and particularly the generic so-called corporate interests of state governments.[9] When and why do state officials and federal officials square off in contests pitting state authority against federal authority? What precisely is at stake?

Although federalism scholarship frequently refers to "the states" as if they all shared the same set of interests when dealing with the federal

Figure 2
A typology of state-governmental interests vis-à-vis
the federal government

Content	Scope: Universal	Scope: Categorical	Scope: Particularistic
Legalistic	Universal legalistic interests	Categorical legalistic interests	Particularistic legalistic interests
Fiscal	Universal fiscal interests	Categorical fiscal interests	Particularistic fiscal interests
Administrative	Universal administrative interests	Categorical administrative interests	Particularistic administrative interests

government, many federal policies result in new or renewed alignments of like-minded states. Sometimes all fifty governors agree on a policy position and sign a letter to Congress or the president reflecting their unanimity. Other policies may be supported by regional or other groupings of states, and sometimes only one or two states are affected by a particular federal policy. A typology of state-agreement interests should reflect such variations in the scope of state agreement, and I will refer to these different interests as "universal" (perceived by all states), "categorical" (perceived by certain categories of states), and "particularistic" (perceived by just one or a few states).

A typology should also distinguish the content of state-governmental interests. The content of a state-governmental interest is the benefit or advantage that state officials want to preserve or secure for their governments. To simplify somewhat, state officials typically want three things when dealing with the federal government: legally decisive decision-making authority that can't be easily trumped by Washington, sufficient and predictable federal funds to cover costs states incur from federal programs, and flexibility to implement and enforce federal programs. I refer to these varying types of content as "legalistic," "fiscal," and "administrative."[10]

These variations in the scope and content of state-governmental interests yield the nine-celled typology shown in figure 2. Although the individual parts of this typology provide few startling new insights into what state governments want from Washington, in combination, they provide a powerful means of characterizing the full range of interests state officials perceive with regard to federal policymaking efforts. The typology underlies the explanations in subsequent chapters of how and why state officials pursue various interests in different federal policy-making contexts. Before examining the typology in more detail, however, more should be said about the theoretical bases of state-governmental interests in general, because it is not immediately obvious how or why state governments can be said to have interests.

Do State Governments Really *Have* Interests?

As with members of Congress and the executive branch, in the realm of federalism, state officials perceive a set of state-governmental interests that precede and outlast the career of any particular official. And like members of Congress and presidents, state officials also perceive a wide variety of political, policymaking, and personal interests. Many of these interests are not directly relevant to the study of federalism, however, and we need not be concerned in this study with every matter that occupies the attention of governors, state legislators, and state administrators. Foreign policy issues are generally not major topics of gubernatorial deliberations nor are other federal issues that do not affect the legalistic, fiscal, or administrative interests of state governments. As a staff member for the governor of New Jersey explained:

> There are [federal] bills that don't matter to us. . . . There will be a
> bill that you will think is really going to impact the world. You

know, you're really kind of excited about it. [But] when you look at it, there's no money to the state. There's nothing the state has to do to change or not change for this measure to go through. And so you start thinking like that, rather than: "Campaign finance reform: doesn't that sound like an interesting thing?" We could care less about [it]. Now, there are those in New Jersey who certainly care about campaign finance reform, but it will not change how the government works in New Jersey at this point. So, while politically, you'd think we might cover it, we don't. . . . It's not the kind of thing we would watch.[11]

Despite frequent scholarly and journalistic use of the term "state interests," political scientists and legal scholars have not provided a precise typology of those interests. (The phrase "states' rights" also continues to be used today to mean roughly the same thing. As discussed in more detail below, I use the term "interests" because it is more analytically precise as well as easier to operationalize.) For example, one author who analyzed the influence of state-governmental officials in national policy-making during the 104th Congress used the term "state interests" (or "their interests" where the referent was clearly state governments) a total of 36 times without defining or explaining the term.[12] Likewise, in *Judicial Review and the National Political Process*, one of the most important contributions to the political safeguards of federalism literature, Jesse Choper uses interchangeably the terms "states' rights," "the viewpoint of a state," "the state's view," "states' true positions," and the "states' opinion." He asserts—correctly—that the "viewpoint of a state's government" may be different from "that of the people of the state," but he does not explain the difference or indicate which of these he thinks is at stake in state–federal relations.[13] Choper is right to note that state officials have preferences, but he stops well short of specifying what those preferences are.

The analysis of state-governmental interests in this book rests on the premise that state governments have identifiable institutional (or corporate) interests vis-à-vis the federal government. This view rests on theories of state autonomy and institutionalism. Scholarship in these areas has established two theoretical premises that are valuable in explaining how officials of state governments view policymaking in Washington. First, scholarship on state autonomy has demonstrated that governments are more than neutral arenas that organize and channel conflict among various organized private interests. Rather, government itself (sometimes referred to as "the state") "may formulate and pursue goals that are not simply reflective of the demands or interests of social groups, classes, or society."[14] As such, "collectivities of administrative officials can have pervasive direct and indirect effects on the content and development of major government policies."[15] Although one must be cautious in applying theories of the state to the United States, where decisionmaking authority is highly fragmented among and within governments,[16] the concept of state autonomy helps explain why state-governmental officials (like governors and state legislators) are continuously interested in federal policymaking efforts in areas like environmental protection and human services despite the fact that voters and interest groups within these officials' states may have no idea, for example, that their governor participates in meetings of the National Governors' Association or that their state representative or senator periodically travels to Washington to testify at congressional hearings. A second line of research by scholars of political institutions has demonstrated the value of characterizing governmental institutions as unitary actors with discrete corporate interests.[17] Certainly, state governments are not monolithic entities whose thousands of officials and employees personally subscribe to a single set of beliefs,[18] but institutional theory holds that, in their official professional roles, employees or officials within institutions generally act on the preferences of the institution rather than (solely) on their personal preferences. As Stephen Skowronek has explained, "Different institutions may give more or less play to individual interest, but the distinctive criteria of institutional action are official duty and legitimate authority. Called upon to account for their actions or to explain their decisions, incumbents have no recourse but to repair to their job descriptions. Thus, institutions do not simply constrain or channel the actions of self-interested individuals, they prescribe actions, construct motives, and assert legitimacy."[19] This view comports with Madison's well-known proposition that, over time, the interests of an officeholder come to be connected with the duties and authority associated with his or her job.[20] This institutional perspective is also consistent with theories of political ambition because ambitious officials within institutions generally recognize that the way to advance within the institution is to learn and internalize the interests of the institution and to promote them effectively. Obviously, one must be careful not to imply that officeholders' preferences are solely determined by the institutional contexts in which they serve, but it is similarly problematic to assert that institutions have no influence on the views of the individuals serving within them. As institutional scholars James March and Johan Olsen explain, "The values and preferences of political actors are not exogenous to political institutions, but develop within those institutions."[21]

The corporate interests of political institutions stem from their status as "collections of standard operating procedures and structures that define and defend values, norms, interests, identities, and beliefs. The argument that institutions can be treated as political actors is a claim of institutional coherence and autonomy."[22] Institutional features such as mission statements, unitary executives, public spokespersons, and press releases make organizations univocal and accountable with respect to other political entities, and governors and other state executives regardless of party are often quite united in their basic policy preferences vis-à-vis the federal government.

It is easier for the executive branches of federal and state governments to unify around a single message or agenda than it is for their legislative counterparts. As heads of executive branches, governors can more easily articulate and enforce fealty to their administration's message. Governors also use their high profiles and their state-of-the-state addresses to try to set their states' legislative agendas.[23] In terms of state–federal relations, "many governors require other state officials to receive approval from the governor's office before lobbying the federal government or endorsing a position of their [professional] association,"[24] such as the National Association of State Budget Officers. As the head of the Austin office of the Texas Office of State–Federal Relations, explained, that office

> keeps track of every state employee that goes to Washington. You
> have to notify [an employee of the office] whenever they're going
> up, the purpose of the meeting, the duration of the meeting, and I

think maybe even who they're meeting with. . . . [The employee] keeps a database of that. And at the end of the year, we turn that over to the lieutenant governor and the speaker and, I believe, the chairman of the Finance and Appropriations Committee, so that they can have a better handle on what agency people are going to Washington, why they are going to Washington, [and] can we as a state–fed office interact with them more?[25]

In these sorts of ways, the views that a particular state government articulates with regard to federal policy issues can be coordinated to some degree from the top down.

Any executive (in the public or private sector) faces challenges keeping his or her subordinates in line, but in terms of state–federal relations, the task is somewhat narrower for a governor than it might seem: he or she need only articulate the reasons why the state government will benefit more by presenting a united front to the federal government rather than a multitude of voices. In fact, although a governor and, say, the head of a state social services agency may not perceive the same interests on behalf of their state governments, these interests may simply be different rather than in conflict. Federalism scholars have developed the idea of "picket-fence federalism" to make this point, explaining it as follows:

The main sources of power in the federal system are the various functional bureaucracies, not the national, state, or local governments. Program specialists, such as educators, have more in common with their counterparts in other levels of government than they have with other people who work in the same level of government but not in their particular specialty. The bonds between agencies in a particular specialty but at different levels of government are the result of personnel who have had similar training, attend professional conferences together, move from one position to another in the profession (regardless of what level of government contains that position), and share the same set of goals and problems. Additional bonds result from grants that channel money to a specific program and cannot legally be spent for anything else.[26]

These vertical linkages between state and federal program specialists have been analyzed in detail by Denise Scheberle in the area of environmental protection and by Martha Derthick in the area of Social Security.[27] Although it is important to note the existence of these linkages to temper the "state-government-as-monolith" institutional approach, David Nice warns that the picket fence model "probably overrates the importance of the functional specialists . . . and probably underrates the importance of the national, state, and local governments."[28] In short, it matters what governors, as leaders of their states, say and do. Governors tend to set the policy agendas for their states, and they are institutionally well situated to perceive and act on the interests of their state governments vis-à-vis the federal government.

In sum, although there is some rhetorical shorthand involved in statements like "Iowa's interests are X, Y, and Z," they are well grounded in established theories of state autonomy and political institutions. Newspaper headlines such as "California Asks Justice Department to Investigate Energy Prices" and "U.S. Recommending Strict New Rules at Nursing Homes"[29] also capture the sense in which governments are thought of as discrete entities that develop, communicate, and act on identifiable collective interests.

The typology shown in figure 2 indicates that in policy disputes with their federal counterparts, state officials' concerns cluster around issues of legal authority, money, and administrative processes. On any particular policy issue, these interests may be perceived by all or most states, by a group of states, or by one state only. In the following sections, I elaborate on the nine types of interests state officials may perceive.

Scope of State-Governmental Interests

Universal State-Governmental Interests

Universal state-governmental interests are the institutional preferences that the officials of all (or nearly all) the states perceive vis-à-vis the federal government. It might strike observers of American politics as implausible that a broad collection of state officials (such as the nation's governors) could ever all agree on anything important. Indeed, years ago one commentator argued the following:

The values that individuals hold are so diverse that there is no "state" point of view in intergovernmental relations as a whole. Even if the forty-eight governors were considered to be spokesmen for their entire states, there does not emerge a single state approach to intergovernmental relations. Occasionally, all the governors will agree on a minor point or two but they have never agreed that a specific general reallocation of activities should take place between national and state governments. This is understandable since some of them are Democrats, some Republicans; some are liberals, others conservatives; some have national political ambitions, others do not; some come from poor states, others from well-to-do areas. These are only a few of the variables that affect the approach governors take on national–state relations. . . . If the governors as a group cannot produce a state point of view on intergovernmental relations, there is little likelihood that it will be found elsewhere.[30]

Even if such skepticism was warranted when this passage was written in 1955, one finds many examples today of substantial agreement on important state–federal policy matters among governors, state legislators, state attorneys general, state budget officers, and other state officials; hence, headlines like "50 Governors Unite Against Federal Cuts to Medicaid" or "51 Governors Resist Shifting Authority Over Guard" are not particularly surprising.[31] The stability over time of a state's interests vis-à-vis the federal government, regardless of the governor's political party, is evident by the example of John Katz, who remained the head of the Alaska governor's Washington, D.C., office for years.

Katz has kept his job from one administration to the next, be it Republican, Democratic or Alaskan Independence. . . . Governors, he said, differ in style and emphasis, but the issues haven't changed much in the two decades he's headed the office. Resource development. Extending federal programs to Alaska. Fending off federal encroachment on the state's sovereignty. "There's a basic core of federal issues that all the [Alaska] governors I've worked for seem to embrace, and that's made my life a lot easier," he said.[32]

In a similar manner, a staff member of a Republican governor explained as follows:

You have to remember [that] governors of states, whether they're Democrat or Republicans, are dealing with basically the same issues. Sometimes they have different philosophies on how to deal with those issues, but they're dealing with the same issues. So, oftentimes how an issue affects State A with their Democratic governor and State B with a Republican governor—the responses that those states have are going to be remarkably similar. . . . On a majority of [state–federal] issues, there isn't a Democrat or Republican way of doing things.[33]

An example of the limits of party ties linking state and federal officials was seen at the time of the passage of the 1996 welfare-reform law, the Personal Responsibility and Work Opportunity Reconciliation Act. In addition to the millions of Americans directly affected by the overhaul of the Aid to Families with Dependent Children program, state and local officials took great interest in the bill's provisions because of the key role subnational governments play in administering federal welfare policy. Just prior to congressional passage of the bill, the chairman of the House Budget Committee, Rep. John R. Kasich (R-Ohio), responded to the several prominent Republican governors (including George E. Pataki of New York and Pete Wilson of California) who had expressed reservations about parts of the Republican-sponsored welfare plan by telling them to "stop bellyaching."[34] Although such overt intraparty acrimony is not terribly common, it occurs frequently enough to conclude that there is something to the idea that state officials frequently view state–federal relations differently than even their fellow partisans in Washington.[35]

State officials develop their preferences toward the federal government in part through attempts to address problems in their states, which frequently require contending with federal regulations, mandates, or conditions attached to federal money and other assistance. A staff member for a Midwestern governor explained as follows:

I'd say there's a general evolution to governors in their approach to Washington in that governors don't come into office focused on what's happening in Washington. They have their own initiatives, their own things that they have to fix in their state. As they innovate and as they try to initiate more reforms, they realize over time—year one, year two, year three—how much of an impact Washington has on their ability to change things in their own states, and then they become more and more intensely interested in what's happening in Washington.[36]

Depending on their backgrounds, some officials may have a better sense of this than others, and some officials may have limited aspirations for reforming their state programs, thus avoiding the need to work with (or around) the federal government. Even so, this statement describes the wellspring of many of the specific state interests described in this book.

Institutionally, universal state interests are promoted by some of the main organizations that make up the "intergovernmental lobby," a collection of professional associations for state officials. Most of these associations meet periodically to discuss matters of common professional concern both within and among their states and with respect to the federal government. Many of the groups develop policy positions each year that indicate their collective institutional positions on policies being developed or considered by Congress or the executive branch. Association staff members as well as the public officials themselves often use these positions as the basis of lobbying efforts in Washington. (The content of these policy positions will be discussed below.)

Seven major associations comprise the core of the intergovernmental lobby: the National Governors' Association (NGA), the National Conference of State Legislatures (NCSL), the National League of Cities, the National Association of Counties, the International City-County Management Association, the U.S. Conference of Mayors, and the Council of State Governments. In the present work, I focus on state rather than local officials, although the groups sometimes find themselves unified in favor of or in opposition to certain federal policies.[37] In addition to these seven associations, there are scores of additional organizations of state officials, such as the American Association of State Highway and Transportation Officials, the National Association of State Budget Officers, the Association of State and Territorial Solid Waste Management Officials, the National Association of State Boating Law Administrators, the National Conference of State Historic Preservation Officers, and the

National Alliance of State and Territorial AIDS Directors. A 1991 estimate placed the number of such associations at 259,[38] and even a casual Internet search for "national association of" and "officials" indicates that the number today is much higher.

In the analysis below, I examine more closely the features of the policy positions adopted by these sorts of associations, and in chapter 4 I deal with the activities of the intergovernmental lobby in much greater detail. For now, it is enough to note that such groups exist because of their common interests in relation to the federal government's activities: if there were no universal state-governmental interests, bipartisan organizations like the NGA and the NCSL would have very little to do.

Categorical State-Governmental Interests

Categorical state interests are perceived by all or most officials of states that share a certain category of interest—a characteristic such as geographic location, benefits received under various federal programs or grants-in-aid, demographic characteristics, or large tracts of federally owned land. The categorical state-governmental interest most familiar to students of American history is perhaps population size, given the typical textbook portrayal of the 1787 Constitutional Convention as a contest between the large states and the small states (implying that states with large populations share a set of interests different from and contrary to their smaller counterparts).[39] Although the size of a state still has important implications for its interstate and intergovernmental relations,[40] Madison realized that coalitions of states would form around a larger variety of additional shared interests, noting "nor could it have been the large and small states only which would marshal themselves in opposition to each other on various points."[41] For example, sectional conflicts have also been a constant fixture of American politics,[42] and many scholars have noted the distinctive set of relationships the states of the American West, for example, have had with the federal government, given that "many westerners experience the federal government not only as taxpayers and beneficiaries of federal programs but also as landlords and business partners."[43]

Although many categorical state-governmental interests reflect sectional cleavages, others do not, instead implicating groups of states that are similarly affected by federal policies that direct federal funding to state governments or require state governments to take action (or forebear from it) in some way. For example, "several states have or are developing viable commercial space launch and recovery facilities or programs, including Alaska, California, Florida, Hawaii, New Mexico, and Virginia."[44] As such, federal regulations and licensing requirements of such facilities (under the aegis of the federal Commercial Space Launch Act of 1984 and federal environmental statutes) will collectively affect this group of states and their common interests.[45] Many other categorical state interests are perceived by groups of states with a common characteristic, such as large numbers of illegal aliens or refugees (who are subject to federal immigration laws), the presence of fishing industries (which are subject to the federal Magnuson–Stevens Fishery Conservation and Management Act), large tracts of federally owned lands (which are subject to Department of the Interior and Bureau of Land Management regulations), coastlines (which are subject to the federal Coastal Zone Management Act), federally recognized Indian tribes (whose federal recognition agreements may empower tribes to engage in activities—such as the operation of tribal casinos—opposed by state and local officials), international ports of entry (which are subject to international compacts, such as the North American Free Trade Agreement [NAFTA]), facilities that are part of the federal Department of Energy's nuclear weapons complex (whose contamination requires clean-up efforts that the states wish the federal government to fully fund), borders with Mexico and Canada (giving states an interest in NAFTA implementation), large yields of corn (for which federal laws requiring the addition of ethanol to gasoline in some regions currently create a sizable market), and proximity to the Great Lakes,[46] to name just some examples. Each of these categorical state interests prompts the formation of state coalitions that are based on their officials' perceptions of the benefits and drawbacks of certain federal policies in those areas.

Many categorical state interests are pursued through specialized institutions that are organized regionally, such as the Western Governors' Association and the Council of Great Lakes Governors, or around particular policy areas, such as the Northeastern Dairy Compact, the Northeast Association of State Transportation Officials, the Interstate Oil and Gas Compact Commission, the Northeast States for Coordinated Air Use Management, the seven-state compact governing the use of water from the Colorado River, and the Governors' Ethanol Coalition.[47] Like the NGA and other national public official organizations, most of these regional associations also draw up policy positions that guide their advocacy efforts throughout the year. The policy resolutions of the Southern Governors' Association and the Western Governors' Association, for example, may be found on their respective websites,[48] and these are clear statements of categorical state interests.

PARTICULARISTIC STATE-GOVERNMENTAL INTERESTS

Federal legislation may affect a single state only, or the same piece of legislation may have differential effects on states. A particularistic state interest is one perceived either by officials of a single state or by officials of different states in different ways. Although it is rare that a single state government perceives an interest vis-à-vis the federal government that it shares with no other state government, there are some instances in which this is clearly the case. One example involves the U.S. Department of Energy's efforts to locate an underground repository for spent nuclear fuel and high-level radioactive waste at Yucca Mountain in Nye County, Nevada. The Department of Energy had studied that site along with two others since the early 1980s; in its 1987 amendments to the Nuclear Waste Policy Act of 1982, Congress directed the Department of Energy to study and develop the Yucca Mountain site exclusively.[49] (Disgruntled Nevada officials, feeling they had been ganged up on, thereafter referred to the 1987 amendments as the "Screw Nevada bill."[50]) As a result, the State of Nevada (whose congressional delegation, U.S. senators, and governor typically all oppose the site) perceives this issue in a way that no other state does and has had deep concerns about whether the federal government can impose a storage site on the state over the objections of state officials. Another example of a particularistic state interest involves the complex legal relationships established by the Alaska Native Claims Settlement Act of 1971 among the federal government, the State of Alaska, and the native peoples of that state.

Many other particularistic state-governmental interests are related to federal budgetary politics. State (and local) officials, interested as they are in maintaining or creating healthy state economies, all generally seek to bring federal money and jobs into their states.[51] In this sense, they share an interest in congressional appropriations with the U.S. senators and representatives of their states. However, state officials view these interests somewhat differently, because their preferences may differ from those of the state's citizens or the state's major interest groups. State governments typically focus not only on maximizing the flow of federal funds into their state, but also on whether such money accords with the priorities of state officials and what sorts of strings Congress has attached to the expenditures of those funds. A member of Congress may attempt to earmark federal funds or projects for his or her district without considering how that money fits into state officials' list of priorities or their overall long-term strategy for meeting state budgetary require-ments. Likewise, the citizens of a state are unlikely to think much about whether such federal funds fit in with state officials' budgetary plans.

As with universal and categorical interests, there are institutional manifestations of particularistic state interests as well. About two-thirds of U.S. governors maintain individual offices in Washington, D.C., a fact that is overlooked in most accounts of the intergovernmental lobby. From these Washington offices, governors' staffs lobby Congress and the execu-tive branch individually (as opposed to collectively, such as through the NGA or NCSL).[52] These offices pursue the state-governmental interests that differ from those perceived and articulated categorically or univer-sally by other state officials as well. Larger state offices in particular have the resources to gather and analyze information on their own, rather than relying on information and strategies developed by the national associations' staffs. And although there is often a good deal of coopera-tion among the individual state offices, under certain circumstances states officials and their staffs may guard their information, decline to join coalitions, or try to maximize the federal resources their state receives at the expense of other states.[53]

It is admittedly difficult to cleanly separate a state government's interests from the interests of certain constituencies within a state, such as businesses, industries, or other groups. In the realm of economic development, state officials are generally eager to attract new businesses to their states and to retain the ones already there. Businesses contemplating relocation in a state are frequently offered packages of tax credits or exemptions and promises of state investments in job training and infrastructure, such as roads leading to proposed industrial facilities.[54] Do such incentives promote state-governmental interests, the interests of the business in question, or the interests of the citizens of the state? Probably all three. The rationale behind such efforts by state governments is that they will ultimately yield tax revenue for the state from the business as well as its employees.

In terms of federalism, state officials' attempts to bring federal funds into their states in the form of pork-barrel projects (such as funding for a sewer treatment plant, a federal research facility, or a highway) might not appear to help the state government as much as they benefit particular localities and the reelection prospects of the members of Congress who can claim credit for getting the items inserted into the federal budget.[55] Obviously the sorts of state-governmental interests that are promoted by such projects vary greatly and will frequently be negligible. In a general sense, though, such projects probably ultimately help state (and local) governments by improving the business climate and the state economy by encouraging economic growth, attracting new residents, raising property values, and so forth. Thus, although the benefits to state governments may not seem immediate from such federal expenditures, the indirect, long-term benefits are real.

CONTENT OF STATE-GOVERNMENTAL INTERESTS

Legalistic State-Governmental Interests

Legalistic state-governmental interests involve state officials' desire to be recognized as the authoritative decisionmakers in a given area of public policy without the threat that their decisions will be preempted (i.e., overridden) by the federal government by congressional legislation or agency rulemaking. A great deal of frustration among state officials stems from shared perceptions that they have final decisionmaking authority in fewer and fewer policy areas because of federal preemption of state law, such as the federalization of certain crimes.[56] (As the case studies in subsequent chapters will demonstrate, however, the states' loss of authority to the federal government is frequently overstated.) More recently, governors felt their authority over their state National Guard units diminished by the Iraq war's heavy reliance on those troops and by a provision in the 2006 defense authorization bill that empowered the president to federalize National Guard troops in a domestic emergency without the consent of state authorities.[57] This provision was partially repealed in the National Defense Authorization Act for FY 2008.[58]

To be sure, state officials do not oppose federalization of crimes (or other areas of the law) in all cases. The NGA, for example, has long called for the passage of a federal product liability law, and thirty-six states submitted an amicus curiae brief in the case of *United States* v. *Morrison* supporting the federal Violence Against Women Act.[59] Examples like these underscore the value of a typology of state-governmental interests that provides terminology to describe the variety of those interests as well as to acknowledge the fact that coalitions of state officials vary from issue to issue.

The notion of legalistic state-governmental interests is used here as an alternative to widely used but less analytically powerful concepts such as "state sovereignty" and "states' rights." The decision to avoid such terms herein warrants some explanation given the long history of their use as the organizing principle of a great deal of thinking about constitutional federalism.[60]

Unlike the Articles of Confederation,[61] the U.S. Constitution makes no reference to the "sovereignty" of government at any level, even in the Tenth Amendment, which is usually taken to be the most explicit textual statement of the independent legal status of state governments.[62] Some of the essays in *The Federalist* describe the states as "sovereign,"[63] but proponents of both state primacy and federal primacy have been able to cite *The Federalist* selectively to support their views.[64] The concept of sovereignty has long been a part of important political and legal debates in this country (as well as a civil war), but those debates have been largely inconclusive on the question of the respective boundaries of state and federal authority.[65] A tremendous amount of analytical clarity is therefore gained by resituating the concept within a broader typology of state-governmental interests, as the present study does.

The greatest advantage in replacing the notion of sovereignty with that of legalistic state-governmental interests is that the latter encompasses statutory, constitutional, and judicial indications of the boundaries of state and federal authority. Justice Lewis Powell wrote in his dissenting opinion in *Garcia v. San Antonio Metropolitan Transit Authority* that "the States' role in our system of government is a matter of constitutional law, not of legislative grace,"[66] but in fact their role is determined by both the constitutional text and—more importantly and frequently— political action and state and national policymaking efforts. Because the Constitution does not say enough about state and federal authority to clarify the boundaries of state and federal authority, those boundaries must be continuously renegotiated in the context of specific policymaking episodes involving elected and unelected officials at all levels of government.

Some readers may wonder how the notion of state-governmental interests differs from the perceptions and interests of individual citizens and groups within states. In this book, I adopt the viewpoint that federalism involves legal, fiscal, and administrative relationships between state governments (individually and severally) and the federal government. This approach is not universally shared, however, and a small group of primarily conservative scholars views federalism as a means for protecting the liberties of individuals rather than the interests (or rights or sovereignty) of state governments.[67] This view is rooted in Madison's explanation in "No. 51" of *The Federalist* that the federal separation of power was intended to provide a "double security" to individual liberties. However, by focusing exclusively on the consequences of federalism for individuals, one risks ignoring the many ways that federal actions affect state governments as well.

Under the Articles of Confederation, only state governments had representation in the national government; state legislatures elected the delegates to the national Congress and had a variety of means of ensuring that the delegates voted in accordance with the views of the legislature. The Constitution gave individuals direct representation in the national legislature through members of the House of Representatives, and it appeared to provide representation in Congress for state governments in the form of U.S. senators, who, until 1913, were elected by state legislatures.[68] However, the Constitution by no means restricted federal legislation that acted on or through state governments; rather, representation of and legislation affecting individuals were *layered onto* the practices that had existed under the Articles instead of replacing them.[69] As such, a great deal of federal policy still affects state governments rather than citizens.[70]

Constitutional and judicial demarcations of state and federal authority are often grounded in notions of state sovereignty, but this approach ignores the many examples of Congress delegating statutory authority to the states. State sovereignty implies that subnational governments have a legally enforceable ability to resist federal compulsion and that state–federal relations are generally characterized by zero-sum contests for authority (where more authority for one level of government necessarily means less for another). Despite some notable Supreme Court cases in which the state governments *have* been handed such defeats, the development and implementation of public policy today tends to be much more messy, with a great deal of shared responsibility among federal, state, and local governments (as well as among various governmental, for-profit, and nonprofit entities). The federal government also offers states a variety of assistance and incentives to try to achieve its purposes more cooperatively than forcibly.

In short, although states may hold legal authority to make decisions in a given policy area, there are many cases in which it makes little sense to label the source of this authority as "state sovereignty" or "states' rights." Those terms imply that state governments may pull up the drawbridge to keep the federal government at bay, whereas state–federal relations have instead always been characterized by a great deal of mutual influence and shared responsibility for governance.[71] Attempts to draw fixed boundary lines around the spheres of state and federal authority or to sort out state and federal responsibilities will always fail because the text of the Constitution and the writings of its primary advocates during the founding era provide too little guidance for such an enterprise.[72]

The putative sovereignty of Native American tribes further clouds the notion of sovereignty under the U.S. Constitution,[73] and yet more ambiguity about the term in the American context stems from the notion of popular sovereignty—that "We the People" are the ultimate sources of governmental authority in this country. A great deal of ink has been spilled debating what really happened during the founding era: did 13 sovereign states enter into a compact from which they could withdraw at will, or did one sovereign People enter into a perpetual union which only they could subsequently alter through some act of higher lawmaking? More than two centuries of debate, numerous Supreme Court decisions, and a civil war have all failed to produce permanent consensus. The lack of consensus simply will not be overcome by digging deeper into historical sources such as *The Federalist* or by re-theorizing the legal relationship between state governments and the federal government; it is more productive to sidestep such debates by devising a new framework—state-governmental interests—that does not rely on such essentially contested and analytically imprecise notions as sovereignty. For all of these reasons, the framework presented in this book is intended to demonstrate that the political and constitutional aspects of state–federal relations are best understood by avoiding the term "sovereignty" altogether.[74]

As noted above, the policy positions developed by the NGA and the NCSL are a useful indicator of the various sorts of universal state interests. In terms of legalistic interests, we will see below that these associations almost never use the terms "states' rights" or "state sovereignty" today. Governors and state legislators are obviously interested in winning decisionmaking authority for themselves, but they nearly always make pragmatic, policy-based arguments rather than assertions of sovereignty.

Fiscal State-Governmental Interests

State officials rarely rest easily over their states' financial health. During economic upturns, state leaders must make difficult decisions between spending, saving for rainy days to come, or cutting taxes. During economic downturns, state governments are hit hard because "their tax systems are leveraged so highly on bases that are sensitive to economic changes. For example, the general sales tax base is riddled with exceptions and exclusions that tend to make revenue from the tax hyperventilate with changes in discretionary spending. . . . Similarly, state income tax systems tend to rely on the biggest earners when they are earning the big bucks. But those revenues wither when capital losses replace gains. Also, states over the years have turned to lesser charges that are cyclically sensitive, such as levies on deeds and property transfers."[75] Economic downturns also increase the numbers of state residents seeking welfare, Medicaid, and other benefits, further stressing state coffers. Aside from fluctuations in the business cycle, state officials are keenly interested in the levels of federal funding that their governments receive and the conditions placed on the receipt and expenditure of those funds.

On average, approximately one-quarter of the money state governments spend today comes from the federal government. Millions of Americans receive a variety of remunerative benefits directly from the federal government (in the form of Social Security checks, tax credits, reimbursements, and so forth), but a great deal of federal money goes first to state governments (in the form of block, categorical, or program grants), which then pass it on to individuals in the form of services or cash payments.[76] (Federal money is also directed to cities and other governmental units, nonprofit organizations, and for-profit firms.) In fiscal year 2003, for example, states received $324.7 billion from the federal government in the form of approximately 174 formula grant programs (so named because the amount of money each state receives is determined by a congressionally developed formula). [77] The largest of these grants for fiscal year 2003 were the Medicaid block grant ($159.7 billion), highway planning and construction ($23.9 billion), Family Assistance Grants under the Temporary Assistance to Needy Families (i.e., "welfare"; $16.6 billion), Title I education funding ($11.4 billion), and the special education grants ($8.5 billion).[78] Of these, Medicaid spending has been of the greatest fiscal concern to state officials in recent years, given the rapid growth of expenditures under the jointly funded program.[79] There are several hundred additional federal grant programs, many of them project grants awarded on a competitive basis.

State officials therefore have a strong interest in how much federal money flows into state-governmental coffers, how it gets there, and how states are allowed to spend it.[80] This money is different from the total amount of federal funds that flows to other entities within a state in the form of pork-barrel legislation or earmarks of all sorts: government contracts to private firms, grants to nonprofit organizations or federal research facilities, the construction of new courthouses and post offices, and so forth. As discussed here, fiscal state-governmental interests concern only federal funds that are transferred directly to the state government.

Fiscal state interests are affected by other sorts of federal legislation as well. For example, beginning in 1926, state governments received a portion of the taxes levied by the federal government on the estates of affluent Americans. When the estate tax was repealed in 2001 as part of a $1.35-trillion tax cut, state governments lost a significant source of revenue. State governments received $5.5 billion in 2000 from their share of the federal estate tax, with California receiving $937 million, Florida receiving $779 million, and New York receiving $450 million, for example.[81]

Another well-known fiscal concern of state governments vis-à-vis the federal government is the latter's imposition of unfunded mandates—state activities that the federal government requires but doesn't pay for. Examples include the federal requirement that states provide special education facilities and instruction to any child who needs it, the expensive testing requirements of the No Child Left Behind Act,[82] the 1993 National Voter Registration Act (the "motor voter" law) requiring that "each State . . . include a voter registration application form for elections for Federal office as part of an application for a State motor vehicle driver's license,"[83] and, more recently, the federal REAL ID law mandating that all state driver's licenses incorporate certain security features. Unfunded mandates such as these impose costs on state governments and have long been one of the biggest complaints of state officials.

From Congress's point of view, unfunded mandates are a cheap way to achieve federal policy goals without spending federal dollars. Even so, at the behest of a number of state and local officials' organizations, in 1995, Congress passed the Unfunded Mandates Reform Act (UMRA). The law created a legislative procedure designed to allow any member of Congress to challenge legislation during a floor debate that imposes an unfunded mandate greater than $50 million per year on state governments.[84] Five years after the law's enactment, the NGA's executive director testified that the law's provisions "have largely succeeded in ensuring

debate and accountability during the consideration of legislation con-
taining unfunded intergovernmental mandates."[85] However, state officials
tend to have a broader definition than members of Congress of what
constitutes an unfunded mandate, and the impact of UMRA has not
been as significant in protecting the fiscal interests of states as state
officials had hoped.

Another serious intergovernmental finance problem from the perspective of state officials is the widespread congressional practice of "conditional spending"—giving the states federal funds that must be spent in
accordance with certain conditions. Federal funding nearly always comes
with strings attached, and accepting federal funds thus often requires
state governments to take actions they otherwise would not. Failing to
fulfill the conditions typically means losing some or all of the federal
funds, and "federal agencies have available a number of mechanisms—
for example, financial audits, field inspections, reporting requirements,
and the cultivation of professional allegiances—to encourage state and
local governments to use federal grants appropriately."[86] From the state
perspective, the conditions attached to federal funds are often out of
proportion to the amount of money they accompany, resulting in an
underfunded mandate. For example, in a comment that exemplifies state
officials' viewpoint, the Michigan Superintendent of Education explained,
"The Federal government pays less than seven percent of the overall
education budget. If the tail wants to wag the dog, let's make sure the
tail has a lot more financial resources tied to it. Then the states will be
interested. But more mandates and calls for accountability without the
corresponding resources is not helpful."[87] Federal mandates in the form
of grants-in-aid conditions should thus be thought of as arrayed on a
continuum ranging between fully funded and unfunded.

Constitutionally, many scholars, judges, state officials, and others
view conditional spending as a means by which Congress circumvents
limits on its legislative powers by essentially blackmailing states to
implement policies that Congress itself lacks the constitutional authority
to legislate directly.[88] Some of the best-known examples of conditional
spending are the requirements attached to the receipt of federal highway funds. Congress has over time used such conditions to require states
to use the metric system on highway signs and to use recycled rubber

in their asphalt pavement; in addition, Congress has used such conditions to require states to pass legislation establishing a 55-mile-per-hour speed limit, helmet laws, a drinking age of 21, "zero-tolerance" laws for underage drinkers caught driving, and seatbelt laws. (Several of these requirements were eliminated in 1995.) Other conditions promote more significant public purposes, such as the civil rights and nondiscrimination requirements in section 2000d of the Civil Rights Act of 1964 that apply to any entity receiving federal funds.

The Supreme Court upheld the practice of conditional spending in *South Dakota v. Dole*,[89] essentially endorsing the old adage that "he who pays the piper calls the tune." Chief Justice William Rehnquist wrote for the majority that "objectives not thought to be within Article I's 'enumerated legislative fields' . . . may nonetheless be attained through the use of the spending power and the conditional grant of federal funds."[90] The justification for this view was that state governments always retain the option of declining the funds if they dislike the conditions.[91] Conservatives in particular have criticized this decision, arguing that state authority and the doctrine of enumerated power cannot be sustained as long as the courts uphold these sorts of congressional practices.[92]

In sum, state governments have ample reason to be concerned about federal funding and the ways they receive it. When the federal government enlists state governments to carry out federal policy, state officials attuned to their states' fiscal interests quickly turn to the fine print before deciding whether they support the federal policy.

Administrative State-Governmental Interests

State officials implement or help implement a great deal of federal policy. Because of the size of the country and the existence of 50 mature state bureaucracies, the federal government relies extensively on state officials to perform the day-to-day tasks involved in delivering governmental services. "Since the end of World War II, virtually every major domestic policy initiative in the United States has involved state and local governments. . . . From welfare to economic development, health reform to environmental policy, transportation to housing, the national government in the United States has almost no direct hand in administering the domestic policies it establishes."[93] This role in policy implementation means that state officials have a large stake in how the federal government asks or tells them to do the job. In general, state officials prefer being handed broad guidelines and goals rather than prescriptive, detailed instructions from Washington. A theme repeated by many governors over time is reflected in Utah Governor Michael Leavitt's message to the federal government following the 1994 congressional elections: "Give us the ball and then get out of the way. We can solve these problems."[94]

In a word, state officials want *flexibility* to carry out federal programs in ways that accord with their own states' circumstances. They complain about cookie-cutter and one-size-fits-all federal solutions to problems that manifest themselves differently in different states. Administrative state-governmental interests, then, concern the processes by which federal policies are implemented by state officials. States want to be given options rather than mandates, incentives rather than penalties, goals to achieve rather than procedures to follow, and reasonable time frames in which to achieve them rather than strict timetables and deadlines. The title of a seminal 1977 general statement of state governmental interests published by the National Governors' Conference (the forerunner of the NGA) is instructive: *Federal Roadblocks to Efficient State Government*. The document presents a number of recurring gubernatorial complaints regarding federal restrictions placed on state governments that make the work of the latter more difficult. These complaints alleged the following:

- Lack of coordination among federal departments or agencies limits the effectiveness of programs in solving problems and increases the administrative burden on states.
- Federal regulations are prescriptive in methodology rather than oriented toward results.
- Excessive reporting requirements must be met by states participating in federal programs.
- Funding and program implementation are delayed by lengthy approval procedures, absence of program guidelines, and other administrative practices, which cause serious dislocation and inequities at the state level.

- Lack of federal coordination and consistency in implementing indirect cost determination procedures create continuing administrative confusion for States.[95]

The report goes on to list numerous examples of ways that each roadblock hampers the activities of state governments. Although this document was written more than 30 years ago, its themes still figure prominently in state officials' complaints about the federal government.

Content Analysis of Policy Positions Adopted by Leading State Officials' Associations

The preceding sections have described the legalistic, fiscal, and administrative state-governmental interests that are perceived by the officials of all states, some states, or one state. However, state officials do not spend equal amounts of time worrying about these interests. They appear to spend little time today, for example, thinking "legalistically" about their state governments as sovereign entities entitled to engage in anti-federal maneuvers like interposition and nullification. Instead, state officials today mainly pursue the fiscal and administrative interests they perceive vis-à-vis the federal government.

To get a rough sense of the relative weights state officials attach to their universal legalistic, fiscal, and administrative interests, I analyzed the materials that appear to shed the brightest light on the collective state–federal priorities of leading state officials: the policy positions adopted by two leading associations of state officials, the NGA and the NCSL. A systematic examination of these positions reveals a number of interesting features about how these officials view state–federal relations.

Many public officials' associations adopt resolutions or policy positions in some form, but those adopted by the NGA and the NCSL cover the widest swath of contemporary federal policy issues. Speaking of the governors' association in particular, Deil Wright notes that "meetings of the NGA come closer than any other institutional arrangement for assessing the temperament as well as the power position of the states in state/national relations."[96] As such, the policy positions adopted at these meetings are a valuable data set for measuring how state leaders prioritize their concerns in federal policy matters.

The NCSL and NGA are associations of public officials that help their members (state legislators and governors) govern better in their own states. Both organizations also lobby in Washington, D.C., for the passage of state-friendly federal legislation and administrative rules and regulations. The legislators meet annually to vote on their policy positions, and the governors meet twice a year to adopt their positions. The legislators' positions are developed by nine NCSL committees, and the governors' positions are developed by the NGA's executive committee and its respective committees on economic development, human resources, and natural resources. In addition, the NGA has a permanent policy that outlines general principles for state–federal relations. NCSL positions must be approved by at least a three-fourths majority of the states and territories present and voting. NGA policies require a two-thirds majority of governors present at their plenary sessions.

Not all governors or state legislators are likely to agree with all of the positions their respective associations adopt. When it proves impossible for governors or state legislators to agree on a specific policy position, they may simply agree to disagree. In spite of the difficulties of reaching consensus on some issues, state officials do manage to articulate a surprisingly detailed set of policy positions across a broad range of policy areas, which indicates that their common location within the federal hierarchy frequently trumps the policy preferences they hold because of their partisanship or the geographical location of their states.

I analyzed the 1998 policy positions of the NGA and NCSL to get a rough sense of the relative importance of each type of state-governmental interest. (Because these are national associations, their positions articulate what I am calling universal state-governmental interests of various sorts; a regional body such as the Western Governors' Association would articulate categorical interests.) A full description of the methodology appears in the appendix, but in short I developed coding categories that would allow me to characterize the extent to which governors and legislators today view federal coercion of state governments as necessary (category A), constitutionally permissible but advisable only under certain circumstances

TABLE 1

Frequency of various assertions of state-governmental interests in NGA and NCSL policy positions

Rank	Percentage of all coded statements	Coding category	Description of Category
1	19.7	B1	Federal government should give sufficient, predictable funding and avoid cost shifts to states
2	15.7	C3	Preemption is unwise in general; feds should preserve state authority/primacy in specified policy areas
3	13.6	B2	State officials should be included in federal decisionmaking processes
4	7.7	B4d	Federal government should generally give states flexibility and determine ends rather than means
5	7.3	B6	Federal programs should be coordinated and should consolidate multiple programs into one
6	6.4	B3	Federal regulations should be clear and should "sort out" state and federal responsibilities
7	5.7	B4A	States should get to spend federal money as they wish
8	4.8	C4	Feds should help state governments to solve problems; not all national problems need a federal solution
9	4.1	B7	Federal government should have to meet a high burden of proof before preempting states
10	2.6	B5	Federal programs should be complementary to existing state laws
11	2.3	C6	Federal programs should be optional for states, not mandatory
12 (tie)	1.6	C7	Federal government should use incentives to encourage state action rather than penalties
12 (tie)	1.6	B4F	Deadlines imposed on states by federal law should be flexible; phase-in periods should be lengthy
13	1.3	B4E	Federal government should set only minimum national standards and allow states to exceed them
14	1.1	C1	Federal government should exercise forbearance because sufficient state programs exist now
15	1.1	C2	Feds should exercise forbearance because state programs are better, more efficient, adaptable
16	0.9	B4b	Federal government should use penalties and crossover sanctions sparingly, reasonably
17	0.8	A	Federal government can coerce state governments
18	0.7	C5	Traditional state-federal divisions of labor should be respected
19	0.5	B4c	Federal government should allow states to apply for waivers of federal regulations
20	0.4	D1	Federal government may not coerce states in a specified way because U.S. Constitution prohibits it
21	0.1	D2	Federal government may not coerce states in a specified way because federal statutes prohibit it

Note: NGA = National Governors' Association. NCSL = National Conference of State Legislatures. Items from these organizations' policy positions were coded into one of four general coding categories that reflect these officials' views of the appropriateness and constitutionality of federal authority in various policy areas. Category A = federal coercion of state governments is necessary to establish national standards; B = federal coercion of states in constitutionally permissible but advisable only under certain circumstances; C = federal coercion of states is constitutionally permissible but unadvisable; D = federal coercion of states is constitutionally impermissible. Numbers in each coding category name are arbitrary labels for the subdivisions of each, as indicated in the description of each category.

TABLE 2

Totals of items coded from policy positions of NGA and NCSL by
type of state-governmental interest

| | Number of items coded from policy positions of: | | | | | |
| | NGA | | NCSL | | NGA + NCSL | |
Type of state interest	n	%	n	%	n	%
Legalistic	269	27.5	384	25.9	653	26.5
Fiscal	221	22.6	405	27.3	626	25.4
Administrative	489	49.9	695	46.8	1,184	48.1
TOTALS	979	100.0	1,484	100.0	2,463	100.0

Note: NGA = National Governors' Association; NCSL = National Conference of State Legislatures.

(category B), constitutionally permissible but inadvisable (category C), or constitutionally impermissible (category D). By "coercion," I mean the types of intergovernmental regulation (such as federal preemption of state law, federal mandates, or conditional spending[97]) used by the federal government to get state officials to do something they otherwise might not do. Categories B, C, and D were divided into a number of subcategories to capture the full range of policy positions that fall into each category. Table 1 provides a description of the 22 categories and subcategories ranked by respective frequencies of related statements found in the NGA and NCSL policy positions.

Overall, 2,463 words or phrases in the policy positions of the NGA and the NCSL fell into one of the 22 coding categories. Of these, the NGA's positions accounted for 979 coded statements, and the NCSL's positions yielded 1,484. The difference in these numbers is an artifact of the length of each association's policy positions: the NGA's ran to a total of 178 pages compared with the NCSL's 221 pages, so the number of coded statements per page was roughly the same for each association.

To determine how the content of these associations' policy positions corresponds to the three types of state-governmental interests outlined above, I counted all the coded items related to states' constitutional authority as legalistic interests, all coded items related to money as fiscal interests, and all coded items related to implementation as administrative interests. Table 2 presents these totals sorted into the three types of state-governmental interest. The most striking findings of the content analysis are the primacy of administrative interests in the policy positions adopted by the national associations of governors and state legislators as well as the coherence and sophistication of these officials' view of intergovernmental relations. Table 2 indicates that when governors and state legislators collectively articulate state-governmental interests in their policy proposals, about half the time these are administrative interests. Moreover, such interests are articulated twice as often as either legalistic or fiscal interests. This finding runs contrary to the sorts of conventional wisdom about state officials described above. In contrast to the conception of state–federal relations articulated by state officials in previous eras, state officials today rarely challenge basic federal authority to act in most policy areas. Rather, they accept federal supremacy and seek instead to make their own jobs as intergovernmental administrators and subnational legislators as unburdened by federal restrictions as possible.

The relative infrequency with which legalistic state-governmental interests are articulated by the NGA and the NCSL is to some degree a reflection of the purpose of their policy documents: to influence congressional policymaking. Therefore, we perhaps should not expect to see the same kinds of arguments in those documents as would appear in materials generated by, for example, the State and Local Legal Center.[98] Even so, the overall tone of the NGA and NCSL documents is one of acquiescence to, rather than defiance of, federal authority, coupled with strong assertions that it matters greatly *how* the federal government enlists state governments to help implement federal policy.

CONTENT ANALYSIS OF GOVERNORS' 2002 STATE-OF-THE-STATE ADDRESSES

Like presidential state-of-the-union addresses, gubernatorial state-of-the-state addresses allow governors to speak univocally as the heads of their state governments and attempt to set the legislative agenda for the state in the year ahead.[99] Given the important role state governments play in the implementation of many federal programs, state-of-the-state addresses could conceivably provide a good indication of the governors' views of the federal government, federal officials, and state–federal relations. These views would presumably reflect the legalistic, fiscal, and administrative interests the governor perceived vis-à-vis the federal government at the time. To test this possibility, I performed a content analysis of all of the 2002 state-of-the-state addresses to gauge the extent to which governors talk about the federal government in these addresses. A full discussion of the methodology of this analysis appears in the appendix.

The goal of the analysis was not necessarily to count every single reference to any federal program but, rather, to get a reasonably complete quantitative sense of how often governors talk about state–federal relations in these addresses. The total number of references to the federal government in each governor's speech was counted. Overall, the mean number of federal references was 8.0, ranging from 0 references by the governors of New Hampshire and North Carolina to 33 references by the governor of Alaska.

On average, Republican governors made almost twice as many references to the federal government (10.2) than did their Democratic counterparts (5.2), and governors of both parties referred to the federal government more than did the two independent governors (3.5). There was almost no statistical correlation ($r^2 = .02$) between the population size of a state and the number of references to the federal government made by that state's governor.[100] There was also no correlation between the governor's degree of institutional power and the frequency of his or her references to the federal government ($r^2 = .03$).[101] On the other hand, the amount of federal program grant dollars per capita that the state received in 2000 was somewhat more strongly correlated with the governor's number of references to the federal government ($r^2 = .18$),[102] as was the percentage of a state's land owned by the federal government ($r^2 = .20$).[103] An additional (albeit crude) indicator of the regional effect is the difference in the average number of federal references by governors west of the Mississippi River (9.8) versus those east of it (6.5). It should be noted that the length of a governor's speech was also correlated with the number of references to the federal government ($r^2 = .23$), so it may simply be the case that some governors choose to make concise speeches focused solely with state issues rather than delving into federal matters as well. Those who choose to speak longer have more time to broaden their discussions to include federal issues.

Overall, this analysis reveals a lot of variation in the content of governors' state-of-the-state addresses. Despite the important role of governors and state legislatures in helping to devise and implement many federal programs, many governors make few or no references to the federal government in their annual addresses, although there are important exceptions to this generalization. There are several possible explanations for this finding. First, when speaking to their state legislatures and to the people of their states, governors appear to want to talk about programs and policy initiatives they can claim as their own for credit-taking purposes during the next election cycle. Federal programs implemented by states are, for the most part, inherited by governors and are poor vehicles for governors to make names for themselves politically. (An important exception was welfare reform in the one to two years following passage of the federal welfare-reform law in August 1996.)

Second, as Alan Rosenthal has noted, governors focus their energies on a small number of issues that are related to the particular needs of a state and its government.[104] As such, governors devote most of their addresses to state-specific aspects of issues like education, state universities, economic development, reorganization of state agencies, and alteration of the selection process for state judges.

Finally, these results imply that there is a discrete arena in which governors talk about state–federal issues. This is an important finding for researchers trying to locate the most comprehensive and coherent version of the governors' (and other state officials') views of the federal government, federal programs, and state–federal relations. These results illustrate that although a handful of governors use their annual addresses to highlight state-governmental interests vis-à-vis the federal government, a better statement of those views can be found elsewhere. The analysis of state-of-the-state addresses appears to confirm the value of looking instead at the policy positions of the major state officials' associations.

State-Governmental Interests and the
Political Safeguards of Federalism

The typology of state-governmental interests outlined in this chapter provides a needed terminology for describing and explaining the political safeguards of federalism today. Instead of relying on imprecise formulations of how states are affected by federal policymaking efforts, we can instead specify how broad or narrow groupings of state officials perceive and act on legalistic, fiscal, and administrative interests of their governments. With such a typology, we can evaluate a policy like the 1996 welfare-reform law in terms of the decisionmaking authority it gives state governments in devising state welfare programs and setting eligibility standards and time limits (legalistic interests). We can assess the law in terms of whether the Temporary Assistance to Needy Families block grant gives states sufficient funds to run their programs and why state officials were so insistent that the law establish a $2-billion rainy day fund so that state welfare budgets would not be overwhelmed in the event of a serious economic downturn (fiscal interests). And we can assess the many provisions of the law that require or allow state governments to implement their respective welfare programs in certain ways (administrative interests). Specifying the interests of state governments in such policymaking episodes allows us to say which of these interests are promoted by the resulting law and which are not. Generally speaking, when a federal action or law promotes state-governmental interests rather than ignoring or overriding them, federalism is politically safeguarded. By examining whether the state governments' interests tend to be promoted today across a variety of policy areas, we can begin to formulate some conclusions about the health of American federalism today.

Having outlined *what* state officials are fighting for when they try to influence the federal policymaking process, we now turn to a general account of *how* those officials try to affect decisionmakers in Washington.

CHAPTER 2

THE POLITICAL SAFEGUARDS
OF FEDERALISM TODAY

*The remaining points on which I propose to compare the federal
and State governments are the disposition and the faculty they
may respectively possess to resist and frustrate the measures of
each other.*

—James Madison, "No. 46," *The Federalist*

State officials today use a variety of means to safeguard the legalistic,
fiscal, and administrative state-governmental interests described in the
previous chapter. Some of these safeguards have been assessed individually by scholars, but in this chapter I frame them as a coherent set of
interrelated practices that, in combination, constitutes a substantial
counterweight to federal authority today. Despite the focus by scholars
like Herbert Wechsler on the formal safeguards of federalism found in
the U.S. Constitution, the most useful today are the wide range of
informal, extraconstitutional practices that state officials have developed
in recent decades. Case studies in subsequent chapters will highlight three
of these safeguards in detail, but it is important to indicate their full
variety to make clear state officials' multiple opportunities to influence
federal decisionmaking at every stage of the policymaking process.

Formal versus Informal
Political Safeguards of Federalism

Although James Madison and other leading advocates of the Constitution apparently thought that the separation of powers between the states and the national government—like those between the legislative and executive branches—would be maintained through the Constitution's "internal provisions" like those Wechsler identified, the external, informal means have proven to be more important.[1] Wechsler believed that state interests would be protected because of the local orientation of members of the U.S. House of Representatives and Senate. He believed that the state-based electoral college would tend to reward presidential candidates who showed concern for the interests of a wide range of states.[2] And he believed that state legislatures' authority to set voter qualifications and draw the boundary lines of congressional districts would further preserve the "intrinsic localism"[3] of Congress and thus preserve state authority. Other constitutional features that might be said to safeguard federalism include the requirement that constitutional amendments be ratified by a supermajority (three-quarters) of the states and the stipulation that no state be denied equal suffrage in the Senate.

Madison did not completely ignore the external, informal safeguards of federalism, however, and a careful reading of *The Federalist* indicates that he had a broader conception of the political safeguards of federalism than did subsequent commentators. In "No. 46" of *The Federalist*, Madison inventories the means available to state governments in the event that, despite the internal safeguards of federalism, the federal government nonetheless attempted "to extend its power beyond the due limits."[4] The first of these stemmed from the administrative authority of state executive-branch officials. If state officials attempted to carry out a state-governmental act that the federal government opposed, federal officers would be largely powerless to resist, because "the evil could not be prevented or repaired, if at all, without the employment of means which must always be resorted to with reluctance and difficulty."[5] However, if state officials wished to resist an "unwarrantable measure" of the federal government, "the means of opposition to it are powerful and at hand."[6] Madison lists four of these means: the "disquietude of the people; their repugnance and, perhaps, refusal to co-operate with the officers of the Union; the frowns of the executive magistracy of the State; [and] the embarrassments created by legislative devices which would often be added on such occasions."[7] These would create "very serious impediments" to the enforcement of the federal act and, "where the sentiments of several adjoining States happened to be in unison, would present obstructions which the federal government would hardly be willing to encounter."[8] Federal encroachments on state authority would "be signals of general alarm. Every [state] government would espouse the common cause. A correspondence would be opened. Plans of resistance would be concerted. One spirit would animate and conduct the whole. . . . Unless the projected innovations should be voluntarily renounced, the . . . appeal to a trial of force would be made."[9] In short, Madison expected that the federal government would have a great deal of difficulty implementing federal policies in states where those policies were unpopular with the people, the state officials, or both.

The modern reader of this passage may think of the many cases in which state resistance to federal action came to naught or was eventually overcome. The Virginia and Kentucky Resolutions of 1798 and 1799 protesting the Alien and Sedition Acts failed to win the support of other state legislatures, as did the Hartford Convention's call for state interposition to block federal military recruitment for the War of 1812.[10] The seceding Southern states were forcibly compelled to renounce their efforts to leave the Union. Southern resistance to federal desegregation efforts was eventually overcome. And, as described in the previous chapter, state governments have nearly always complied with or helped implement a great many federal programs and regulations in return for federal funding to do so. In light of this sort of evidence, the state-governmental glass looks decidedly half empty.

Despite the apparent repeated failures of states' overt resistance to federal authority throughout U.S. history, Madison's emphasis on the administrative aspects of state–federal relations was prescient, and state governments have indeed succeeded tremendously in resisting, delaying, or altering the implementation and enforcement of federal policies at the state level. Madison's famous prediction that "violence of faction" (i.e., the influence of special interest groups) at the national level could be controlled rested on the observation that the size of the country would make it very difficult for potential members of factions to recognize their mutual interests.[11] Although the power of this argument has been diminished considerably by a host of new information and communications technologies,[12] the challenges to federal administrative efforts posed by the size of the "extended republic" remain daunting.[13] In contrast to the widespread view of the federal government as an efficient agent of nationalization, noted public administration scholars John DiIulio and Donald Kettl argue that "Washington has had, and continues to have, tremendous difficulty in executing even relatively straightforward policies precisely because state and local governments enjoy such wide latitude in deciding how best to translate federal policies into action, or whether, in fact, to follow federal policies at all."[14] (These authors also point out that a great deal of federal policy is carried out by the private sector.[15]) In a similar manner, Donald Haider, an early scholar of the intergovernmental lobby, contends that "in practice, the federal government's powers to impose definite and enforceable choices on states, their subdivisions, and other executors of public policy are severely limited."[16]

Although it is contrary to much of the conventional wisdom concerning state–federal relations, this viewpoint implies that a closer look at the role state officials play at all stages of the federal policymaking process will reveal a wide array of means states have for influencing federal efforts to develop and carry out policies and regulations. It must be emphasized that many of these efforts are less adversarial and conflictual than is implied by the terms Madison used: "resist," "frustrate," and "trial of force." Louis Fisher has characterized relations among the elected branches of the national government as "an intersection where congressional and presidential interests converge," and he notes that "despite the heavy traffic, head-on collisions are rare. Instead, individual drivers merge safely at high speeds."[17] In a similar manner, state–federal relations today rarely involve one level of government attempting to stop the other in its tracks; rather, these relations are typically marked by various forms of negotiation, bargaining, and compromise.

Between the extremes of armed rebellion and acquiescence, then, state officials have a great many options as they promote their states' interests in dealings with the federal government. In the remainder of this chapter, I inventory the forms that those interactions take in the federal policymaking process today and note four basic state strategies for influencing the federal government's policy processes in ways that promote state interests. From strongest to weakest, I refer to these strategies as "state resistance," "coordinate governance," "participation," and "exhortation." State officials choosing the first strategy in effect say to the federal government, "We won't comply with this federal law, whatever the consequences." States choosing the second strategy use their status as independent political entities to pass effective legislation that makes preemptive federal laws unnecessary for solving public problems. The participation strategy leads state officials to work with members of Congress or federal agencies (or both) while they are writing laws and regulations so that state interests are reflected in the final product. Finally, state officials adopt public relations campaigns to draw attention to their disagreements with proposed or existing federal policies, exhorting federal policymakers to act in more state-friendly ways. Taken as a whole, these general strategies and their many manifestations constitute the full range of political safeguards of federalism available to state officials today.

STATE OFFICIALS' MULTIPLE POINTS OF ACCESS TO THE FEDERAL POLICYMAKING PROCESS

Scholars of public policy have offered several general characterizations of the American policymaking process, indicating the steps between the point when someone says, "There ought to be a law to fix this problem!" and the implementation and assessment of that law. At the early stages of the process, policy scholars look at how social, economic, and cultural phenomena come to be viewed as political problems and how they make it onto the policymaking agenda for consideration by Congress or other legislatures.[18] Once bills become law, scholars of public administration examine how federal legislation gets translated into rules by executive branch agencies[19] and how those rules are (or are not) implemented and enforced by street-level bureaucrats.[20]

Political scientists John W. Kingdon and James E. Anderson have developed two prominent ways of characterizing the steps in the policymaking process. Kingdon's framework breaks the policymaking process into a problem stream, a policy stream, and a political stream.[21] The problem stream contains the various activities involved in defining some social phenomenon as a problem that ought to be addressed by government. The policy stream consists of efforts by scholars, researchers in think tanks, and others to develop policy solutions and alternatives. The political stream consists of features of the national political environment, such as "public mood, pressure group campaigns, election results, partisan or ideological distributions in Congress, and changes of administration."[22] In Kingdon's view, events in these three steams proceed largely independently of one another, coming together only through the efforts of policy entrepreneurs during the short-lived moments when the policy window is open.

Although Kingdon's framework usefully indicates the complexity and nonlinearity of the policymaking process, there is also value in viewing the various steps of the process as a sequence of successive activities. Viewed retrospectively, policymaking efforts do move through a series of discrete stages, as many narrative histories of particular policymaking battles have shown.[23] James Anderson divides the policy process into five stages: problem identification and agenda setting, policy formulation, policy adoption (by the legislature), policy implementation (by the executive branch), and policy evaluation.[24] As shown in figure 3, in this book, I simplify somewhat and refer to the first of these stages as the prelegislative phase, the second and third together as the legislative phase, and the last two together as the postlegislative phase. The case studies in chapters 3 through 5 will detail how states affect policymaking at each of these three phases. Despite the linear layout of Anderson's framework, Anderson views it as a policymaking *cycle*, because policy assessment may yield revised views of the nature of a problem or the best solution, which can then lead to revisions of an existing law.

Both of these frameworks are analytically useful: Kingdon's captures the messiness and frequent serendipity of the policymaking process, whereas Anderson's allows us to specify after the fact the various steps that were taken to bring a policy into being, even if the process in the real world is never as analytically neat as his five-step framework implies. Kingdon's focus on the process leading up to the passage of a

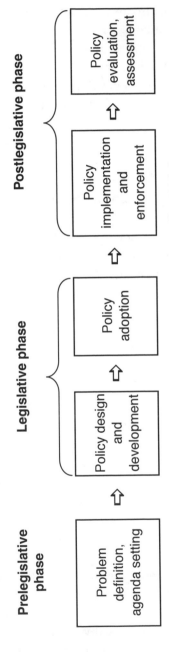

FIGURE 3

A model of the policymaking process

Prelegislative phase

Problem definition, agenda setting

Legislative phase

Policy design and development

Policy adoption

Postlegislative phase

Policy implementation and enforcement

Policy evaluation, assessment

Adapted from James E. Anderson, *Public Policymaking*, 6th ed. (Boston: Houghton Mifflin, 2006), 4.

law means that he does not discuss what happens after the law is passed, and Anderson's scheme fills this gap nicely. Anderson acknowledges that "the various segments or stages of the framework are interrelated and sometimes smudged together. What happens at one stage of the policy process has consequences for action at later stages. And stages, such as policy adoption and implementation, may blend together."[25] Still, his framework is analytically useful because it allows a more formal explication of what happens at each step along the policymaking path.

The informal political safeguards of federalism described in this book can be seen as attempts to influence one or more of the five stages of the federal policymaking process. As Kingdon's analysis implies, state officials are constantly engaged in a variety of advocacy efforts at all stages of the federal policymaking process. By the time a bill reaches the floor of the House or Senate for debate, it is much too late to begin efforts to influence its content. However, even when legislation is enacted that state officials have opposed, state officials still have a variety of means by which to influence both the rulemaking process and how the policy is implemented. Anderson's framework indicates that there are at least five stages of the federal policymaking process that present opportunities for state officials' involvement.

MODES OF STATE INFLUENCE ON FEDERAL POLICYMAKING

State officials can attempt to influence federal policymaking efforts in several basic ways. Officials (such as governors and state legislators) may be reactive, meaning that they take actions following the passage of federal legislation to alter or minimize its negative effects on state-governmental interests. State officials may also be proactive in their attempts to influence the nature of federal policy while it is still in the developmental stages (such as when a bill is being considered by a congressional committee). Table 3 indicates four general modes of influence available to state officials, and table 4 summarizes the strategies and modes of influence available to state officials at each stage of the federal policymaking process.[26]

TABLE 3
Modes of state-governmental influence in the national policymaking process
(from strongest to weakest)

State refusal to comply; informal veto: Stems from the states' informal "veto power" over congressional legislation, federal regulations, and executive orders they dislike

- States officials can work to scuttle federal initiatives that do not command the support of subnational officials
- States can work to kill minor provisions of bills as they are being considered by Congress
- States can try to compel the inclusion of provisions in bills being considered by Congress

Examples: States' 1982 rejection of Reagan's "big swap" proposal; states' "push back" on Clinton executive order 13083 leading to its replacement by EO 13132; Montana's and Washington State's 2007 legislation repudiating the federal REAL ID Act of 2005.

Coordinate governance: Stems from the states' ability as autonomous governmental entities to make high-quality public policy in their states and to implement federal policy in ways consistent with their own interests

- States can pass quality legislation to stave off interest group pressures for a uniform federal law
- States can thwart or influence the implementation of federal programs in states

Examples: Uniform state laws process; states' strategic use of administrative discretion to thwart perceived federal encroachment

Participation: Stems from the states' ability to compel or encourage federal officials to include state officials in deliberations

- States can gain access to decision-making processes and institutions such as Congress's legislative process, the rulemaking process, and federal advisory commissions.

Examples: Negotiations between governors and the Bush Administration officials regarding the future of Medicaid; inclusion of state officials on federal advisory commissions; participation of Republican governors in lawmaking during 104th Congress; inclusion of a "rainy-day fund" in the 1996 welfare reform law at states' behest; governors' and state legislators' testimony to Congressional committees

Exhortation: Stems from the ability of high-profile state officials to gain publicity and media exposure for their opposition to federal initiatives

- States can balk, gripe, complain, exhort, present information, offer alternative interpretations of federal actions

Examples: Intergovernmental lobby's 1993 National Unfunded Mandates Day to raise awareness of unfunded mandates; National Conference of Commissioners on Uniform State Laws' communications with Congress; memorials to Congress from state legislatures

---

TABLE 4

Summary of state officials' modes of influence on the three phases of the federal policymaking process

Strategy	Prelegislative phase		Legislative phase	Postlegislative phase	
	Agenda Setting	Policy Formulation	Policy Enactment	Policy Implementation	Policy Evaluation
State's refusal to comply with federal law	States' objections can put an issue on the federal agenda or keep it off	Expectations of states' refusal can influence federal policymakers' choices	Knowledge of states' objections can delay or prevent a bill's passage by Congress	States can refuse to fully implement or enforce federal law	State refusal to signal to Congress, president that policy is not working
Coordinate governance	State successes or failures in a policy area can keep items off federal agenda or put them on	State policies can serve as models for federal efforts or convince Congress to allow state discretion, flexibility	State officials can encourage members of Congress to vote against laws that preempt existing state efforts	States can implement federal laws in ways that conflict least with states' exosting policies	States can assert failure of federal policy relative to states' own policies
State officials' participation in federal policymaking	State officials' contact with federal officials can put additional items on federal agenda	State officials can participate directly in committee hearings, markups	State officials can individually or collectively lobby members of Congress for bill passage	State officials can participate in agency rulemaking; play key roles in in implementation, enforcement of federal policy	State officials can be in the best position gauge successes, failures of federal policy; committee testimony can reflect this
Exhortation, persuasion	Frequent complaints by state officials can alert federal officials to the need for action	State officials can indirectly appeal to Congress to design policy in particular ways	State officials can indirectly appeal to members of Congress to vote for or against specific legislation	States can call for certain modes of federal implementation, discourage others	States can appeal to federal government to study the negative effects of a federal law

State Refusal to Comply with Federal Law

Different political safeguards of federalism give state officials varying degrees of influence over federal policymaking and implementation. None gives state officials a formal veto power over federal policy decisions (although a few observers have proposed creating such a power[27]). Moreover, these safeguards today rarely involve the sorts of extreme anti-federal actions—interposition, nullification, or secession—that were used or advocated in the past.[28] This still leaves a great deal of room for state officials to "resist and frustrate" federal efforts they oppose, and it is a mistake to conclude that states are at the mercy of the federal government simply because they lack a trump card for use against their federal counterparts. Indeed, as noted above, federal officials themselves possess few trump cards for use against determined state officials, despite constitutional provisions indicating federal supremacy. Modern readers, accustomed to thinking about federal authority as unchallenged and unable to be challenged, have trouble taking seriously Hamilton's assertion that "it will always be far more easy for the State governments to encroach upon the national authorities than for the national government to encroach upon the State authorities."[29] However, an examination of recent examples indicates the ways that this prediction is not so far off the mark.

The strongest political safeguards of federalism today involve state officials telling or signaling to their federal counterparts that they will not implement federal laws or policies in their existing form. These objections arise because of perceived negative impacts on one or more of the state-governmental interests described in the last chapter. Donald Haider has argued that, because of their expertise and responsibility for implementing programs at the street level, state and local officials possess something like an informal veto power over federal policies: "Federalism builds into our political system veto politics: a certain conservative bias which tends to expand geometrically as access points on all government levels increase and new constituencies are created. The government interest groups constitute such a veto instrumentality, but also one which has proved to have a significant capacity for joint action as well."[30] An example of state officials exercising this sort of de facto veto power over federal actions was the Reagan administration's abandonment of its

1982 "big swap" federalism proposal to give states full responsibility over food stamps and Aid to Families with Dependent Children (i.e., welfare) in return for the federal government assuming full responsibility for Medicaid. The major intergovernmental lobby groups had not been consulted during the formulation of the initiative, and their subsequent alarmed opposition forced the Reagan administration to abandon the effort.[31] In a similar manner, President Bill Clinton suspended his Executive Order (EO) 13083 (titled "Federalism") after it was opposed by all of the major intergovernmental lobby groups, "in order to enable full and adequate consultation with State and local elected officials, their representative organizations, and other interested parties."[32] Following extensive consultations with the state and local groups, Clinton issued the new, state-friendly EO 13132.[33] State officials again forced the federal government to reverse course in early 2002 when the NGA and the American Public Human Services Association concluded that the Bush administration's proposals for the reauthorization of the 1996 welfare-reform law were unrealistic and unworkable.[34] A week later, media reports indicated that, "bowing to criticism from state welfare officials, House Republicans said today that they would adopt work requirements more flexible and less stringent than those proposed by President Bush when they extend the 1996 welfare law later this year."[35] A final example involves the U.S. Department of Education's steps in 2005 to relax some provisions of the No Child Left Behind (NCLB) law because of complaints from states about its unworkability or undesirability.[36]

States may simply refuse or neglect to comply with the requirements or mandates of federal law and take their chances in terms of consequences.[37] An example of outright refusal was California's "decision to defy a federal mandate to provide special education services to youth inmates in adult prisons."[38] In this case, the defiance was overt: a California official wrote a letter to the U.S. Secretary of Education "notifying him that the [California] Corrections Department does not plan to provide the services."[39] In response, the federal government nonetheless chose not to withhold the state's Individuals with Disabilities Education Act (IDEA) Part B grant money in order to avoid hurting other disabled children funded by the money.[40] In another example, states reacted strongly against the federal REAL ID Act of 2005, which requires state-issued driver's licenses to contain a prescribed set of security features. One seasoned observer of state legislatures characterized the states' strong backlash against the law as "without precedent in the last 20 years."[41]

In March 2008, as states were supposed to be changing their driver's licenses to comply with the federal law, Montana's Democratic governor, Bryan Schweitzer, summed up his opposition to the law as follows:

> We are putting up with the federal government on so many fronts, and nearly every month they come out with another harebrained scheme, an unfunded mandate to tell us that our life is going to be better if we'll just buckle under on some other kind of rule or regulation. And we usually just play along for a while, we ignore them for as long as we can, and we try not to bring it to a head. But if it comes to a head, we found that it's best to just tell them to go to hell and run the state the way you want to run your state.[42]

There are countless other examples of more or less overt state-governmental resistance to federal laws and regulations.[43] These episodes are tricky to assess as safeguards of federalism because one does not wish to celebrate instances in which state shirking or inaction results in socially undesirable outcomes (pollution, substandard education or health care, and so forth). On the other hand, states often act responsibly and progressively on the basis of their independent assessments of public problems and the best solutions to them, particularly when Washington is deadlocked or unwilling to act.[44] Education experts critical of the testing requirements contained in the NCLB law have been cheered by some states' resistance to the law,[45] noting that that NCLB "undermined school improvement efforts already under way in many states."[46] States have also resisted attempts by the federal government to weaken or not enforce federal environmental protections and in some cases have pushed for stronger environmental regulations than federal law allows.[47] Finally, states have challenged federal Medicaid rule changes that might limit states' ability to provide health care to low-income families.[48]

Depending on one's view, states' resistance to federal policymaking efforts can be viewed as irresponsible shirking or as the responsible actions of governments who simply see the world differently. In chapter 6,

I sort through these issues in more detail; for present purposes, I am interested mainly in presenting some of the forms that policy-based state resistance takes today.

Coordinate Governance

As coordinate political communities in a federal system of government, states frequently possess the authority to enact laws and policies independent of or parallel to those promulgated by the federal government. This authority can be used strategically by states to thwart encroaching federal policies before they are passed or, alternatively, to affect the implementation of federal policies at the state level. One way that states act collectively to proactively stave off federal entry into a state-dominated policy area is the uniform-state-laws process. In its most common form, this process (which has received almost no attention from political scientists[49]) entails the drafting of model legislation by state-appointed commissioners to the National Conference of Commissioners on Uniform State Laws (NCCUSL), which was formed in 1891. These model laws are recommended for adoption by all the state legislatures without amendment, and where this succeeds, the result is a law that is national in scope without being federal. Adoptions of model laws by all 50 legislatures are rare, although the NCCUSL succeeded in the 1950s and 1960s in drafting a Uniform Commercial Code and having it adopted in every state, as will be discussed in chapter 3.

Even if state officials cannot thwart the development and passage of federal legislation that they view as harmful to their governments' interests, those officials can still strategically use their authority as implementers of federal policy to lessen the negative impacts. The inherent fluidity in the principal-agent relations between federal policymakers and state administrators give the latter opportunities to implement federal legislation in ways that comport with state priorities. State officials can obviously exercise their administrative discretion in either good or bad faith, although interpretations of a state's motives will likely depend on who the interpreter is.

As defined by Anderson (and others), at the problem-definition and agenda-setting stages of the policy process, certain social conditions or phenomena come to be viewed as social problems deserving of governmental action whereas others do not. As Deborah Stone notes, problems are not simply "out there" waiting to be identified; rather, "problem definition is strategic because groups, individuals, and government agencies deliberately and consciously fashion portrayals so as to promote their favored course of action."[50] Thus, "there is no such thing as an apolitical problem definition. In confronting any definition of a policy problem, the astute analyst needs to ask how that definition also defines interested parties and stakes, how it allocates the role of bully and underdog, and how a different definition would change power relations."[51]

Agenda setting follows close on the heels of problem definition and involves focusing the attention of the public and of authoritative decisionmakers "on one problem rather than another."[52] Many policy scholars follow Roger Cobb and Charles Elder in differentiating the systemic agenda (the "issues that are commonly perceived by members of the political community as meriting public attention") and the institutional agenda (the "items explicitly up for active and serious consideration of authoritative decision-makers"),[53] although Kingdon notes that "quite often, items on a governmental agenda never were on a public agenda, or they were on a public agenda in a form so inchoate as to have only a minimal impact on governmental officials."[54] This caveat is particularly important in the context of intergovernmental agenda setting, because the sorts of interests state officials perceive vis-à-vis the federal government may be completely unknown to the average citizen or even to a state official's strongest electoral supporters. One commentator notes, "It is hard to imagine that even fairly well-educated Americans of today would be . . . confident in their knowledge of which courts have jurisdiction over a particular legal issue, or which level or agency of government should provide them with services they desire. In many Americans' mind, federalism seems an abstract concern at best: Who cares, they are likely to ask, what agency or level of government outlaws (for example) the possession of firearms in schools, so long as the right thing is done?"[55] State officials, on the other hand, have a keen perception of these sorts of distinctions, and their attempts to influence the federal policymaking agenda proceed even when the general public knows little about those efforts.

State officials' efforts at intergovernmental problem definition and agenda setting may be proactive or reactive, depending on whether they take place in advance of or as a result of signals that Congress or an executive branch agency is planning to act (or fail to act) on a particular policy. Proactively, state officials attempt to solve social problems at the state level so that federal officials do not have a pretense to address the problems themselves. There is a widespread view that the federal government tends to get involved in new policy areas only when a number of states have shown an inability to address the needs of their citizens. President Dwight Eisenhower articulated this view in his address to the 1957 Governors' Conference meeting: "Never, under our constitutional system, could the National Government have siphoned away state authority without the neglect, acquiescence, or unthinking cooperation of the States themselves. . . . Every State failure to meet a pressing public need has created the opportunity, developed the excuse and fed the temptation for the National Government to poach on the States' preserves. Year by year, responding to transient popular demands, the Congress has increased federal functions."[56] Pressures for federal policymaking also come from regulated entities like corporations and businesses, who find it easier to comply with a single national regulation or standard than with those developed by the different states.[57] (This situation is often characterized as a choice between one federal law or fifty different laws, but numerous "diffusion of innovation" studies of state policymaking demonstrate that the states tend to borrow one another's ideas, typically resulting in something like three to five versions of a particular policy in the states.[58]) The idea that states serve as laboratories for policy experimentation looks unappealing to a company that does business in multiple states, each with different laws. When citizens or businesses look to Washington rather than their own state capitals for policy solutions, they attempt to control the scope of political conflict, as E. E. Schattschneider described in his classic work *The Semi-Sovereign People*. Overlapping federal, state, and local jurisdiction in many policy areas means that "it is possible for contestants to move freely from one level of government to another in an attempt to find the level at which they might try most advantageously to get what they want."[59] Madison apparently anticipated this sort of "venue shopping," noting that "if . . . the people should in the future become more partial to the federal than to the State governments, the change can only result from such manifest and irresistible proofs of a better administration as will overcome all their antecedent propensities."[60]

Although expanding the scope of conflict may yield benefits for the constituents involved, state officials prefer to keep the policymaking responsibility at the state level in most cases. To stave off efforts to nationalize a policy conflict, state governments try to respond to the needs of citizens, groups, and businesses within their borders. Successes in this regard keep issues off the federal policy agenda by discouraging citizens, groups, and businesses from appealing to the federal government and by providing evidence to counter the arguments of potential policy entrepreneurs (in Washington and elsewhere) who may be trying to build a case for federal action.

Some scholars have argued that political parties safeguard federalism to the extent that they promote the recruitment of local and state officials for federal offices and to the extent that they facilitate communications between local, state, and national officeholders. Parties link "the fortunes of officeholders at state and federal levels, fostering a mutual dependency that protects state institutions by inducing federal lawmakers to take account of (at least some) desires of state officials."[61] The safeguarding role of parties in this regard seems to have been greatly diminished by judicial decisions limiting state discretion in setting voter eligibility and reapportioning congressional districts,[62] efforts by the national party organizations to exert control over state party activities,[63] and by the top-down efforts of presidents and their advisors (rather than state officials) to draft their party's strongest candidates into specific congressional and gubernatorial races.[64] Although it is difficult to find causal evidence that partisan ties that cut across the levels of government have specific effects on policymaking, interviews with staff members of state and national officials reveal that close personal ties between, for example, governors and members of Congress can certainly develop.[65]

Participation-based Safeguards

A third mode of influence for state officials is their actual participation in the federal policymaking process. This mode is listed third in terms of its potential effectiveness because it depends in large part on state officials being invited to participate in federal policymaking, whereas the coordinate governance safeguards are fully within the control of states.

State officials' participation may take a variety of forms. One of these is service on federal advisory commissions and advisory committees. Presidents and Congress frequently create advisory commissions to study particular events, conditions, or problems and to make policy recommendations.[66] Commissions allow the involvement of both the public and experts in the national policy process and may be temporary (such as the Commission on Intergovernmental Relations—the Kestnbaum Commission[67]—and the National Gambling Impact Study Commission[68]) or ongoing (such as the Clean Air Act Advisory Committee). Many federal advisory commissions deal with matters that do not have federalism implications, but there are important examples of those that do; the presence of state officials on these commissions gives them the opportunity to participate both in the fact-finding hearings and in writing the final report, which contains policy recommendations for the president, Congress, or both. The legislation or EO establishing a commission or committee typically specifies the size of the body and may require the selection of a certain number of members from state or local governments, certain professions or sectors of the economy, or certain political parties. The Advisory Commission on Electronic Commerce, for example, was created by Congress in 1998 to study federal, state, local, and international taxation on Internet commerce and Internet access. In legislation creating the Commission, Congress stipulated that it would have 19 members, as follows:

(A) 3 representatives from the Federal Government, comprised of the Secretary of Commerce, the Secretary of the Treasury, and the United States Trade Representative (or their respective delegates).

(B) 8 representatives from State and local governments (one such representative shall be from a State or local government that does not impose a sales tax and one representative shall be from a State that does not impose an income tax).

(C) 8 representatives of the electronic commerce industry (including small business), telecommunications carriers, local retail businesses, and consumer groups . . .[69]

To the extent that the recommendations of advisory commissions and committees become the basis for federal legislation or rulemaking, the presence of state officials on such bodies is a safeguard of federalism at this early stage of the policy process. To be sure, national politicians have sometimes used advisory commissions as a way to delay or prevent policymaking efforts, but there are important examples where the findings of a commission have clarified the dimensions of a problem and catalyzed the policy process. This phenomenon is consistent with Kingdon's account of how studies are used in the problem-definition and agenda-setting stages of the policymaking process.[70]

The intergovernmental lobbying organizations play an important role in the policy-formulation process by attempting to influence congressional lawmaking. Governors and state legislators testify frequently at congressional committee hearings, either on their own behalf or as representatives of organizations such as the NGA or the NCSL. State officials use these opportunities to indicate the sorts of provisions they would like to see in federal legislation. Occasionally, a state official may even have a direct role in writing federal legislation. During committee markups of the 1988 welfare-reform legislation (the Family Support Act), Governor Bill Clinton (D-Ark.), who chaired the NGA at the time, was present, and "they ran all the amendments by him, they discussed what the governors would and would not find acceptable in terms of the amendments that were being offered."[71] In a similar manner, several Republican governors were given a great deal of access to the political and policymaking meetings of the new Republican congressional leadership in 1995 and 1996. For example, "during key negotiations on a welfare reform bill in December [1995], key congressional leaders invited [Michigan Governor John] Engler into the room to participate in crafting the bill. . . . Mr. Engler and his welfare commissioner were practically in daily contact with key congressional leaders."[72] An observer at the time noted that "it is no longer surprising to see Republican governors entering a room in the Capitol where major bills are taking shape—not to testify but to take part in the actual writing of legislation."[73] More recently, in 2005, governors and Bush administration officials from the Department of Health and Human Services met for several days to try to work out an approach to controlling Medicaid costs.[74]

Several specific types of state-governmental "oversight" of the federal legislative process also deserve mention. State officials concerned about congressional imposition of unfunded mandates pay close attention to the Congressional Budget Office's (CBO's) mandate cost statements, which the UMRA of 1995 requires the CBO to prepare for authorization bills that would impose mandates greater than $50 million on state, local, and/or tribal governments. The CBO "has also given information to Members of Congress and Congressional staff about mandates at other stages in the legislative process—before bills are introduced, when amendments are considered on the floor of the House or Senate, and when conference committees develop their reports."[75] For intergovernmental lobbyists, these reports serve as early warnings of the legislation's fiscal impacts on their subnational governments; in turn, the intergovernmental lobbyists can use this information to influence congressional decisionmaking. From the perspective of some state officials, the UMRA was more successful than initially expected. Michael Bird, a Washington lobbyist for the NCSL, noted in 2000 that the mandate cost statement provision of UMRA

> has really worked. You can't point to research to that effect [but] you can certainly feel it and perceive it from our standpoint. I mean, it has really worked well. . . . [Ohio congressman] Rob Portman, who was one of the original co-sponsors of the bill, said to us point blank—he says, "This law is going to have no effect." Now, he has members who come to him, beforehand, saying, "Am I going to be in trouble? What if I do this? Is this going to create a— what kind of rain is going to be on my parade?" In fact, we tried to use it [UMRA's point-of-order provision] last week on what is going to be a gruesome fight over electronic commerce. We tried to mount a point of order on the floor. We lost, but using it on the floor of the House was a message to the Senate that, under your rules over here, we're going to make tremendous grief for you.[76]

The efforts of the intergovernmental lobby spill over into the policy adoption phase as well, in the form of their efforts to work for passage or defeat of particular legislation in committee and on the floor of the House and Senate. These efforts appear to be most successful when the various organizations of the intergovernmental lobby are in agreement and working together.[77]

Exhortation-based Safeguards

When all else fails, state officials can complain loudly about what they perceive to be encroaching or misguided federal law and policies. The prestige and visibility of high-ranking state officials, such as governors and attorneys general, give them a bully pulpit of sorts for communicating with their federal counterparts. Although exhortation is less preferable than the modes of influence mentioned above, over time it may serve to portray federal actions in a negative light and thereby promote state-governmental interests over the long term. Exhortations by a group of state officials may attract other such officials to their cause and ultimately create a critical mass of subnational officials needed to put an issue on the national policy agenda. An example of such an episode was the National Unfunded Mandates Day staged by state and local interest groups on October 23, 1994. In what Paul Posner has called a "catalytic event," state and local officials

> held news conferences, public forums, and other events in Washington, as well as in other locales around the country. It was here that the national studies of mandate costs were released to the press. A study by Conlan, Riggle, and Schwartz showed that this event succeeded in transforming the mandate issue from specialized intergovernmental discourse to the broader public agenda. Their research shows a significant increase in media coverage leading up to and following the National Unfunded Mandates Day. The number of newspaper articles on unfunded mandates rose from 22 in 1992 to 836 in 1994.[78]

Congress ultimately passed the legislation, which, as noted above, has been seen as a boon to state-governmental fiscal interests.

In addition to these proactive means of defining problems and attempting to put things on (or keep things off) the federal policy agenda, state officials engage in a great many reactive efforts in response to signals that Congress or an executive branch agency is contemplating policymaking action. Organizations such as the NGA and the National Association of State Budget Officers, for example, issue press releases, meet with members of Congress and executive branch officials, send letters to federal officials on the association's letterhead stationery, testify before congressional committees, hold press conferences, write op-ed pieces for national newspapers, commission studies and publish the findings, maintain websites and e-mail listservs, hold meetings, and develop positions on federal policy matters.

• • •

In these four general ways, governors, state legislators, and heads of state agencies attempt to influence the policymaking environment—perhaps even before specific federal legislation has been contemplated. The political safeguards of federalism vary in the degree to which they give state officials influence in the federal decisionmaking process. The safeguards available to state officials at the problem-definition and agenda-setting stages appear to be among the weakest, which may reflect the fact that state officials have greater leverage when there is a concrete policy for them to contest, which is not the case during these pre-policy-formulation stages.

The next stage in the national policymaking process is that in which the specific provisions of a piece of legislation or an agency rule are deliberated and settled on. State officials have a variety of ways to influence decisionmaking in Washington—ways that give them varying degrees of influence over the final legislative product.

Uniform-laws organizations, such as NCCUSL, also participate in policy formulation by drafting legislation for state legislatures. The enactment of such legislation by states may help keep particular policy items off the federal policy agenda; thus, the state role in this form of policy formulation influences activities in the problem-definition stream as well as the reverse.

The political safeguards of federalism available to state officials today thus amount to much more than the meager assortment of constitutional provisions that Herbert Wechsler identified in his early work.

Indeed, their variety more closely reflects Madison's wide-ranging account in *The Federalist* of how state officials would respond to perceived federal encroachments on their prerogatives, and it goes well beyond it as well.

I have indicated how state officials conceive of and act on a coherent theory of federalism and intergovernmental relations. These officials persistently assert an understanding of the respective constitutional roles played by the federal and state governments in ways that frequently yield large and small resolutions and settled understandings in their favor that may persist for quite some time. The rich set of intergovernmental checks and balances that exist today indicates that the balance of state–federal authority is determined through a congeries of activities more complex than many scholarly accounts imply. The case studies in the following chapters provide additional details of three of the main political safeguards of federalism available to state officials today.

CHAPTER 3

PREEMPTING FEDERAL PREEMPTION

The Uniform-State-Laws Process

It's not that the states hadn't done anything, it's that they had done completely different things.
　　　　　—Michael Kerr, deputy director of the NCCUSL (2002)[1]

From the very beginning . . . it has been a theme that uniformity of law by voluntary state action was a means of removing any excuse for the federal government to absorb powers thought to belong rightfully to the states.
　　　　　—Uniform-laws commissioner Allison Dunham (1965)[2]

In a federal system, the initial phase of the policymaking process involves two questions: whether government should take action at all to address a problem (rather than leaving it to the private sector) and, if so, which level of government ought to have primary responsibility for acting.[3] Debates over the latter question often imply a binary choice between a single, uniform national policy determined by the federal government or relying instead on a "crazy quilt" or "confusing patchwork" of "50 different state laws."[4]

For well over a century, however, state governments have used a third way of addressing public problems in the United States—the model legislation or uniform-state-laws process (the latter term will be used in this book). In this process, some individual or organization drafts a piece of model legislation and then recommends it to all the state legislatures for adoption—preferably without amendment. In the best-case scenario, every state legislature adopts the act as drafted and the result is a single policy that is national but not federal. In such cases, the benefits of uniform national policy are achieved without federal overrides or preemptions of states' decisionmaking authority. States have long borrowed and adapted one another's policy ideas in a phenomenon political scientists call the "diffusion of innovation," [5] and the uniform-laws process is a more formal and complete version of this sort of interstate sharing of policy ideas. Although such diffusion may yield similar policies in often-small clusters of adjoining states, the uniform-laws process aims for much wider adoptions of identical laws as a way of reducing state-to-state variations in law and the accompanying problems. As the first quote at the beginning of this chapter indicates, state governments legislate widely but not always in ways consistent with one another. Often, state-to-state differences result from random variations in the legislative process rather than from differences in opinion about the nature of public problems and how to solve them. In fact, all or most states may be willing to enact the same version of a well-written law once they agree on its goals and an approach to achieving those goals.

As Allison Dunham's statement at the beginning of the chapter indicates, uniform-laws advocates believe this rather roundabout approach to nationwide (but not federal) policymaking safeguards federalism at the prelegislative phase of policymaking by answering calls for workable legislation at the state level and making additional federal action unnecessary. Reducing interstate policy variation by collectively developing uniform laws can forestall federal preemption of state laws by encouraging forbearance among federal policymakers (on the grounds that a federal policy would be redundant or counterproductive). "To the extent the uniform laws process is effective, it can delay the development of national legislation in areas that have become areas of interstate concern for significant periods of time." [6] Even if the uniform-laws process works imperfectly and some state-to-state variation remains in a given policy area, those state laws may still be sufficient to "occupy the field" in that area and dissuade federal efforts to legislate in it. "Uniformity" of state law should thus be viewed as a range rather than an all-or-nothing matter, and the uniform-state-laws process can effectively safeguard state prerogatives even if it promotes *greater* (but still incomplete) uniformity in a policy area.

In this chapter, I chart the development of the uniform-laws process in the United States and demonstrate through case studies of the Uniform Commercial Code (UCC) and the Streamlined Sales Tax Project (SSTP) how state-governmental interests—particularly legalistic interests—have been protected. The UCC is a massive collection of uniform state laws that constitutes the bulk of commercial law in the United States, and it exemplifies the sorts of long-established uniform laws that have addressed public needs well enough to forestall the development of a comprehensive body of federal commercial law by Congress. The SSTP is an effort by states to simplify and coordinate state sales tax rates on various goods so that states can prepare the way for collecting taxes on purchases made on the Internet. It exemplifies a recent, somewhat different use of the uniform-laws process to try to convince Congress to "un-preempt" states' collection of sales taxes on online sales by removing the federal moratorium on their collection.

Origins of the Uniform-State-Laws Process

The uniform-state-laws process originated in the late nineteenth century when continuing advances in transportation and communications spurred interstate commerce to a degree not previously seen in the United States. The need for greater uniformity of the commercial law in the states had been recognized since the founding era,[7] but the problems had not yet grown acute enough to prompt a concerted effort to reduce variations among the states' diverse laws. By the 1870s and 1880s, attempts to transact business across state lines were increasingly frustrated and impeded by differences in the commercial laws of different states. An American Bar Association committee appointed to investigate the uniform-laws process concluded in its 1891 report that "the annoyance arising from variant and conflicting laws seemed common to all the states, viz: perplexity, uncertainty, confusion, with consequent waste; a tendency to hinder freedom of trade, and to occasion unnecessary insecurity in contracts, resulting in needless litigation and miscarriage of justice."[8] Commercial developments had outpaced the legal developments needed to cope with them, and uncertainty existed over such basic issues as whether commercial paper (such as warehouse receipts or bills of lading) would be recognized as having negotiable value under the laws of another state (for use as collateral for a loan, for example).

In addition to these problems with the commercial law, nonuniform state laws on social matters, such as marriage and divorce, were of great concern to many politicians, clergy, and other observers and were the focus of a great deal of early efforts to develop uniform state laws and have them adopted by the states.[9] Uniform child labor acts were also proposed,[10] particularly after the Supreme Court struck down the federal Keating–Owen Child Labor Act in 1918 in its *Hammer v. Dagenhart* decision,[11] leaving state legislative action as the only viable alternative.

WHY *Not* HAVE A SINGLE FEDERAL LAW?

Despite increasing nationwide concern over these and other issues, most observers around the turn of the twentieth century believed that the federal government had no authority under the U.S. Constitution to legislate on matters of banking, commercial transactions, and the range of social policies falling under the broad banner of the police powers (which give state governments the authority to legislate to protect the health, safety, and morals of their citizens). Many voiced concerns about "centralization" and looked for alternatives to federal action;[12] thus, "the chief motive for suggesting the necessarily cumbrous method of separate state action was that many of the evils arising from the conflict of laws could not be reached by Congress. The states had subsequently to be appealed to where Congress could not act."[13] Resolving the ambiguities of diverse state commercial laws through lawsuits was, in theory, a possibility but was too uncertain and slow to be a practical option.[14] Moreover, during the pre–New Deal era, the federal courts typically held narrow interpretations of federal powers under the Commerce Clause of the U.S. Constitution, maintaining that Congress's reach did not extend to manufacturing or other elements of commercial activity that did not actually involve goods physically moving across state lines.[15] Other means of remedying the negative effects of nonuniform state laws were available (such as interstate compacts),[16] but none of these had as much institutionalized support during this era as the uniform-laws process.

In this context, getting each state to enact an identical law, although laborious, was nonetheless conceivable as a "practical and workable alternative to further centralization in many fields."[17] President Calvin Coolidge endorsed the uniform-laws process in 1924, noting that "each State must shape its course to conform to the generally accepted sanctions of society and to the needs of the Nation. It must protect the health and provide for the education of its own citizens. The policy is already well recognized in the association of the States for the promotion and adoption of uniform laws. Unless this policy be adopted by the States, interference by the Nation cannot be resisted."[18] The process thus made sense as a solution that encouraged legislatures to address pressing social and economic issues of the day while remaining faithful to the "dual sovereignty" conception of American federalism that was being enforced by the courts, and as a practical matter there were few other alternatives to the uniform-laws process once the possibility of federal legislation was taken off the table.[19]

Perhaps it was predictable that actually getting more than a handful of state legislatures to pass an act without amending it often proved quite difficult. State legislatures had particularly bad reputations in the early twentieth century and faced seemingly contradictory criticisms of meeting too infrequently[20] and passing too much legislation.[21] The initiative and referenda processes emerged during this period to bypass state legislatures perceived as being corrupt, ineffective, and undemocratic.[22] Despite these inherent liabilities, the uniform-laws process did enjoy some notable successes in the pre–New Deal era: by 1933, nine proposed uniform acts had been adopted by 20 or more states, and two of these (the Negotiable Instruments Act and the Warehouse Receipts Act) were adopted by all states.[23]

After the judicial revolution of 1937, which left in its wake a much broader conception of Congress's constitutional authority to regulate interstate commerce,[24] pressures for uniform legislation eased somewhat. However, there still remain many areas of public policy in which state governments have wholly or partly retained legislative responsibility (examples include regulation of the insurance industry; domestic relations law; most criminal law; commercial law; the law of torts, wills, and trusts; consumer protection law; and corporate law). Although Congress today certainly *could* find justifications for legislating in at least some of these areas, the fact that it chooses not to creates opportunities for the development of uniform laws that will diminish interstate policy variations, and it implies that those efforts have succeeded in at least some cases in forestalling federal policymaking in areas where states have legislated successfully.

Sources of Uniform-Laws Proposals

National Conference of Commissioners on Uniform State Laws

The primary source of uniform acts since about 1890 has been the NCCUSL, whose members are appointed by the governors of their states. According to its current mission statement, the NCCUSL "provides states with non-partisan, well-conceived and well-drafted legislation that brings clarity and stability to critical areas of the law. NCCUSL's work supports the federal system and facilitates the movement of individuals and the business of organizations with rules that are consistent from state to state."[25]

Commissioners must be members of the bar association of their states and are typically practicing attorneys, judges, or law professors. Commissioners tend to be self-selected, asking for and generally receiving appointment or reappointment by the governors of their states without regard to partisan affiliation.[26] The exact means by which uniform-laws commissioners are appointed differ from state to state (ironically), and the number of commissioners per state currently ranges from three to fourteen and averages about seven. Commissioners generally serve three-year terms, with the opportunity for renewal; at this writing, the NCCUSL website listed about 365 active commissioners from the 50 states, the District of Columbia, Puerto Rico, and the U.S. Virgin Islands. Notable NCCUSL commissioners have included Woodrow Wilson; legal scholars Roscoe Pound, Ernst Freund, and Karl Llewelyn; and future Supreme Court justices Louis Brandeis, William H. Rehnquist, Sandra Day O'Connor, and David H. Souter.[27]

The NCCUSL has its origins in a bill passed by the New York legislature in 1888 calling on the governor to appoint three commissioners to explore the possibilities of developing and then working for the enactment of uniform state laws "upon the topics of common and public concern with reference to which the interests of the people in every state are identical, to wit: marriage and divorce law, insolvency, the form of notarial certificates, and other subjects."[28] As suggested by the passage's reference to the "identical" interests of people in all states, the uniform-laws process is premised on the idea that variations among the laws of different states are essentially random and do not reflect substantive differences in opinion of the people or lawmakers of the different states. Thus, the remedy for states laws' nonuniformity is for some organization to examine existing state laws, identify the best practices contained in them, and codify these in a uniform act that can then be sent to the state legislatures for debate and adoption. From the earliest days of the NCCUSL, uniform-laws commissioners have contended that they do not write *new* law but, rather, use their specialized skills as attorneys to draft legislation that incorporates the best features of existing state legislation and eliminates the worst.[29] As such, the uniform-laws process is one means for realizing the promise of the states as "laboratories of democracy" developing varying public policies and allowing the determination of which ones work best and might be fit for export to other states or to the federal government.

As a political safeguard of federalism, the uniform-laws movement differs from the other case studies in this book because the individuals involved in effectuating the safeguard are not state-governmental officials per se. Although appointed by the governors of their states, uniform-laws commissioners are volunteers who serve without compensation (except for the reimbursement of their expenses) and retain their day jobs as attorneys, judges, or law professors. Commissioners over the years have expressed differing views on the question of whether they represent their states or state governments. One commissioner noted that "members of the NCCUSL are, by virtue of their appointments, government officials,"[30] but went on to say that "the states have no official control over [the NCCUSL's] procedures or over the subject matter of the laws it promulgates, and its members do not view themselves as official representatives of their states' interests in the process. Indeed, the primary defining characteristic of the National Conference of Commissioners on Uniform State Laws is that it is neither a democratically elected representative body, nor one owing allegiance, or having any accountability, to any political body."[31] Echoing this dual set of roles, NCCUSL's chief counsel and legislative director John McCabe described commissioners as follows: "They are all lawyers by the rules of the organization and by the tradition governing their appointment. They are also state officials—though unpaid state officials—and regard state government as a kind of client for their wares, the uniform and model acts. So, the Uniform Law Commissioners have a double identity, a double obligation—part of the spectrum of organizations of the legal profession and part of the spectrum of organizations representing state governmental interests."[32] Therefore, not only is the uniform-laws process *not* a constitutionally created institution, office, or process, but it is effectuated by individuals for whom the protection of state-governmental authority may only be one of several goals. The inclusion of the uniform-state-laws process in this study illustrates both the variety of the informal safeguards of federalism that exist today and the importance of casting a broad net when trying to discover all of the factors that affect the balance of state–federal authority today.

What, then, motivates commissioners to volunteer their time and effort to the NCCUSL, donating "hundreds of otherwise billable hours"?[33] McCabe explains as follows:

> They're all lawyers. They like to play with the law. . . . The average commissioner is a private practitioner with a middle-level practice. Their practice skills and specialties are extremely various. . . . It's a way to do public service, to do good work on the law, and to do so as a counterpoint to what they do practice-wise. There are people who pass through this organization quickly— they do a term and they don't stay—they go on to do other things. They don't participate actively. But the organization has always had the ability to attract a core group of people always—I mean, I've been with this organization for 30 years—a core group of people who are extraordinarily loyal to it and who thrive on

participation in what the Conference does. Most commissioners—
the commissioners out there who are not in the leadership—thrive
on the committees that exist. They love the committees. They want
to be a drafting participant in drafting committees. They want to
draft statutes, because that's where, from their perspective, the
bang for the buck is, the contribution is, and it's what they love. . . .
So, it becomes a life love for a lot of the members and they are the
people who keep it going over the years. They keep going back to
their states and asking to be reappointed.[34]

This sort of sentiment has apparently been present since the early days
of the conference, and the published proceedings of the conference's
annual meetings contain many similar statements.[35] Commissioners are
also motivated by the opportunities for professional and personal net-
working with attorneys from their own state and other states and by
the opportunity to improve the law that they deal with in the course of
their daily work. A more ideological assessment of the commissioners'
motives would note the class bias of the commissioners (given the requirement that they be members of the bar), the caution and conservatism
that characterize the legal mind,[36] and the fact that "the expertise and
training that provides [commissioners with] the expertise necessary to
work on a Drafting Committee probably shades one's perspective toward
the views of the clients who provided the experience to gain the expertise."[37]
Currently, about 80% of the commissioners are men. Although these
factors may be part of a complete explanation of commissioners' motives,
the best explanation seems to involve taking at face value the statements
of the commissioners, sentimental though they may sometimes be, that
they simply enjoy taking part in the activities of what amounts to a national
association of a profession into which they have been socialized.

Other Sources of Uniform Acts and Model Legislation

Other organizations involved in or supportive of the uniform-laws
process in the pre–New Deal era included the American Bankers Association, the American Boiler Manufacturer's Association, the American
Law Institute, the American Legislators' Association, the American Title

Association, the American Warehousemen's Association, the Commercial Law League of America, the League of Women Voters, the National Association of Credit Men, the National Association of Real Estate Boards, the National Civic Federation, the National Consumers' League, the National Tax Association, and the Russell Sage Foundation.[38] As this list implies, progressive reformers and businessmen alike looked to the process as a way of obtaining greater certainty, uniformity, and clarity in those laws that they were most concerned with. Despite the cumbersome nature of the uniform-state-laws process, it is instructive about the tenor of that era that such a diverse group of organizations—conservative and progressive—would be convinced that it was worthwhile to invest time and effort in such an unwieldy means of responding to the problems of a nation that was becoming truly "national" for the first time.

Model legislation today is drafted by a wide variety of professional and industry associations, interest groups, think tanks, legal scholars, and federal agencies. (Moreover, at the international level, various United Nations agencies have drafted model legislation for adoption by nation-states.[39]) Obviously, state legislatures themselves draft legislation that may be borrowed by other states for passage. Since 1940, this process has been facilitated by the publication of the Council of State Governments' *Suggested State Legislation*, a compilation of laws developed by state legislatures and other sources and recommended to the legislatures of other states.[40] The introduction to one of these volumes explains that the council's Suggested State Legislation Committee "has chosen to include this legislation because it concerns topics that states are actively considering or beginning to discuss, and the approaches outlined in this legislation are thought by veteran legislators, legislative staff accustomed to dealing with these items on a daily basis, and executive branch officials charged with implementing and enforcing these policies to be effective means of solving the problem the legislation addresses."[41] The American Legislative Exchange Council (ALEC), a nonpartisan group founded in 1973 and composed of conservative state legislators, also drafts model legislation for passage by state legislatures. ALEC describes its mission as "promot[ing] the principles of federalism by developing and promoting policies that reflect the Jeffersonian principles that the powers of government are derived from, and assigned to, first the people, then the states, and finally the national government."[42] At the other end of the ideological spectrum, the Center for Policy Alternatives has emerged as a leading source of progressive and liberal model legislation, "disseminating more model legislation than any state group besides ALEC."[43] The American Law Institute is another important source of model legislation today, and its Model Penal Code, which was published in 1962 (and whose chief reporter was, incidentally, Herbert Wechsler), has influenced the penal codes in many states.

The various organizations that draft model legislation vary in the importance they attach to having each state adopt the legislation without amendment. The U.S. Consumer Product Safety Commission, for example, *encourages* alterations of its model child product safety legislation:

> The model legislation can easily be adapted to meet the specific concerns of particular states. For example, a state could narrow its legislation by excluding antique products that are not intended for use by children. (It could do so by revising the definition of "children's product.") A state could broaden its legislation by requiring the listing of consumer products intended for adult use. (It could do so by substituting a broad definition of "consumer product" for the existing definition of "children's product.")[44]

At the other extreme, the NCCUSL distinguishes between "uniform acts" and "Uniform Laws Commissioners' Model acts" and takes the position that its uniform acts "should be proposed and supported for adoption as promulgated to achieve necessary and desirable uniformity." Its model acts "should be proposed and supported to minimize diversity and improve the law, but without the same emphasis on adhering to the verbatim text."[45]

The focus in this chapter will be on the development of model or uniform legislation by organizations that are affiliated in some way with state governments, although the basic safeguard-of-federalism mechanism is the same regardless of a model law's source. Obviously, model laws are not necessarily drafted for altruistic reasons or simply to promote good government; the organization that does the drafting may have a policy agenda it is trying to promote. Thus, model legislation drafted by industry groups or associations might be viewed with suspicion as an effort by an industry to write the regulations to which it will be subject. On the other hand, assuming that the legislative process in each state will produce amendments to the original version of the model law, the end result might be a compromise policy that nonetheless looks favorable enough to the industry that it is dissuaded from widening the scope of conflict by seeking a federal alternative. In such a scenario, the primacy of the state government to act in that policy area would be preserved even if some interstate nonuniformity remained.

HOW THE UNIFORM-LAWS PROCESS SAFEGUARDS FEDERALISM

The uniform-laws process primarily protects state governments' legalistic interests by preserving state-governmental primacy to legislate in particular policy areas. If states in their role as coordinate systems of government enact policies that respond to the needs of affected and interested parties (citizens, interest groups, and so forth.) within their borders, they reduce the chances that those parties will appeal to the federal government for preemptive federal legislation that will do so. "The existence of a comprehensive state law dealing with a subject matter area is also likely to delay any federal enactment in the area,"[46] and when all or many states act in concert toward this end, the incentives for groups to appeal to Congress for a single federal law diminish further, because the efficiencies that may result from having a single policy have already been realized.

The success of this safeguard of federalism does not require members of Congress to closely monitor the development and status of NCCUSL's uniform laws or even to know of the organization's existence. Instead, advocacy groups attentive to both the state and federal laws affecting their interests monitor the latest legislative developments at both levels and, if satisfied, implicitly signal their satisfaction to Congress by *not* pressing for federal legislation.[47] Thus, even though NCCUSL is not exactly a household name in the United States, as long as the effects of its work are known to attentive publics in this country, pressures for preemptive federal laws may be dampened.

It should also be noted that states need not fully "occupy the field" in a particular area of public policy to keep the federal government from legislating in that area.[48] Although it is ideal to have all or most states ratify a proposed uniform act with few or no changes, there are many areas where states either partially occupy a policy area or do so with varying laws, which may still be enough to dampen federal enthusiasm for entering that area. One should think of the difference between complete uniformity of state law in a policy area and complete nonuniformity as a continuum with lots of variation between the extremes. There is no magic point on this continuum at which state nonuniformity triggers federal action; rather, the states' ability to preempt preemption depends a great deal on context.[49]

To the extent that the uniform-laws process diminishes pressures for federal preemption of a policy area, then, it serves as an informal safeguard of federalism. Although this hypothesis has been the underlying premise of the uniform-laws process from its inception, almost no scholarship has investigated the process as a political safeguard of federalism or even identified it as such.[50]

Federal preemption of state decisionmaking authority is a complex phenomenon.[51] Although it would seem an easy matter to determine when the U.S. government has passed a law that, per the Constitution's supremacy clause (article 6, clause 2), displaces any conflicting state laws, in fact it is not always clear when Congress or a federal agency has done so. To identify when preemption has occurred, one must know what state laws do in a particular policy area and how a particular federal law or regulation would partially or totally remove state authority to make or enforce law in that area.[52] There are at least six varieties of federal preemption of state authority. According to a long line of Supreme Court decisions, preemption occurs (1) when Congress, in enacting a federal statute, expresses a clear intent to preempt state law; (2) when there is outright or actual conflict between federal and state law; (3) where compliance with both federal and state law is in effect impossible; (4) where there is implicit in federal law a barrier to state regulation; (5) where Congress has legislated comprehensively, thus occupying an entire field of regulation and leaving no room for states to supplement federal law; and (6) where the state law stands as an obstacle to the accomplishment and execution of the full objectives of Congress.[53]

Despite the difficulties sometimes involved in identifying individual cases of preemption, it is clear that federal preemption increased greatly

during the 1980s and 1990s.[54] The Supreme Court has long indicated
that if Congress wishes to preempt state authority, it must make its
intention to do so "unmistakably clear in the language of the statute."[55]
Although the Constitution's supremacy clause dictates that federal law
supersedes state laws with which it conflicts, the Supreme Court
"start[s] with the assumption that the historic police powers of the
States were not to be superseded by the Federal Act unless that was the
clear and manifest purpose of Congress."[56] However, the Court's record
of enforcing this requirement has been mixed because of the aforementioned difficulties in identifying preemptions as well as the judicial
discretion afforded by these difficulties.[57] Thus, the judicial safeguards
against undue federal preemption have been, at best, incomplete.

This description of how the uniform-laws process can safeguard
federalism suggests that success hinges on the ability of NCCUSL and
other organizations to craft high-quality law and to get it enacted in a
significant portion of the states. The following sections indicate the
features of the process that permit the creation of such legislation. One
difficulty in evaluating the work of NCCUSL in particular is that, since its
beginnings, much of the scholarly literature concerning the conference
has been written by commissioners themselves, and a good deal of it
has been rather enthusiastically supportive of the NCCUSL and its legislative products. Thus, relatively few independent scholarly assessments
of the conference's work have been published, although there are some
thoughtful and strident critiques that will be discussed below—some
from scholars or attorneys who have become disillusioned with the
process after participating in it.

The uniform-laws process is largely removed from the glare of the
national political spotlight. The word "largely" is important here, because
political pressure and media coverage may penetrate almost any institution or process involved in making decisions that may have important
consequences. But when it is possible to step out of the klieg lights of
Washington to draft a uniform or model law, more coherent laws may
result, particularly when the subject matter is highly technical or comprehensive in its coverage of a policy area (like commercial law). As described
by a commissioner, a uniform act is generally drafted as follows:

Each uniform act in the making has a drafting committee. The chair and members of the committee must be commissioners. Non-commissioners can be involved as advisors, consultants, liaisons, or reporters, but only the commissioners have a vote. It normally takes at least two years to produce a uniform act. Drafting committees often meet twice or even three times a year. Committee meetings are intense, mentally and physically exhausting affairs. They typically start early Friday morning, go all day Friday, resume early Saturday morning and go all day, and then resume again early Sunday morning and go until noon, when the members scramble to make airplane flights to take them back home.[58]

The NCCUSL has long prided itself on the high quality of its acts,[59] which the commissioners believe stems from the relative seclusion of the drafting committees' meetings as well as the annual meetings of the conference as a whole, at which the final versions of all conference uniform acts must be read and approved. In the view of John McCabe, legal counsel of the NCCUSL, the technical superiority of its acts is a consequence of Congress's comparatively poor institutional capacity for drafting quality legislation: "We don't regard Congress as being particularly good at these things—particularly proficient—and not good at all at distinguishing things and not good at all at drafting. They're terrible drafters. Their processes for drafting legislation—accurate legislation—is, even as it compares to the states, atrocious. They have never given themselves the institutional framework to appropriately draft legislation."[60] Others have noted that the processes by which Congress drafts legislation are not particularly transparent or open, that interest groups have disproportionate access to decisionmakers, and that staff members rather than the elected representatives themselves seem to make many of the important decisions.[61]

Not everyone agrees that the NCCUSL's acts are of consistently high quality, and even some commissioners believe that the quality of the acts of themselves has little to do with the number of states that adopt the acts.[62] More important, there is a long line of criticism of the NCCUSL that alleges that its drafting process is overly responsive to

and subject to "capture" by business interests (such as the banking industry), resulting in the promulgation of uniform acts that do little to protect
the interests of consumers or other noncorporate interests. This view is
exemplified by law professor Edward Rubin's following statement:

> The drafting process has been dominated by exactly the same orga-
> nized, powerful interest groups that are accused of dominating
> Congress or state legislatures. Moreover, this defect has severely
> undermined the expected benefit of [commissioners'] expertise, as
> the judgments reached by the Reporters have been systematically
> diluted or reversed by business interests. . . . Few defenders of the
> uniform state law process have had the temerity to assert that this
> interest group domination has not occurred; their point, rather, is
> that the process remains better than its alternatives.[63]

The conference's drafting sessions are open to all who wish to attend,
although the obscurity of the uniform-laws process means that an interest
group has to be paying close attention to follow and participate in the
drafting process, and it obviously costs money to send representatives
to drafting meetings around the country. One biting assessment of the
drafting process notes the following:

> Most of the people in the room at any meeting are there for a
> reason. It may be that a few persons wandered into the meeting
> because it is raining or cold outside and they prefer to be dry and
> warm. A few may be consumed by a platonic interest in the subject
> or suffer from a rare mental illness that leads them to prefer attending
> a drafting committee meeting rather than joining their family by
> the seashore or the mountains. Nevertheless, most of the practi-
> tioners and academics at such meetings are there because they are
> being paid directly or indirectly for their attendance by someone
> who wants their views represented.[64]

Other critics have argued that the interests of consumers and other
groups get short shrift by the conference, and specifically that many of
the conference's uniform acts have identifiable substantive shortcomings.
The "noncommissioners" who sometimes participate in NCCUSL drafting

sessions, for example, are likely to be attorneys sent by corporations or business interest groups to monitor the drafting of a uniform act and offer their input. The allegations of business interests exerting undue influence on the conference's drafting processes are not new; a commentator in 1927, for example, wrote that "I have not failed to observe the presence at these Conferences of representatives of the most powerful interests in the country."[65] A proposed act may be technically sound and elegantly crafted but still do a poor job of addressing the concerns and interests of all of the various stakeholders in a policy area. One's views of the technical soundness of a uniform act is likely to depend on one's political views and interests, and "the 'public interest' means different things to different people."[66] If a proposed uniform act hurts one's political interests, it will be little consolation that it is well crafted.

Setting aside the merits of any particular piece of draft legislation, the participation of interest groups enhances the uniform-law process's ability to safeguard federalism by limiting the need for interest groups to appeal to Congress for legislative relief since they can get it at the state level via a uniform law they've had a hand in developing.

The foregoing criticism of the NCCUSL does not apply equally to all of its uniform-law endeavors. Many of its proposals do not involve economic matters that may pit the private interests of firms against the public interest but, rather, involve a wide spectrum of political interests and public and private activities. For example, in the mid-1990s, the National Collegiate Athletics Association asked the NCCUSL to develop a uniform act regarding the sometimes-unscrupulous practices of sports agents, which were governed by specific legislation in only about half the states.[67] The resulting uniform legislation, the Uniform Athlete Agents Act (which had been adopted by 32 states as of the end of 2004[68] and 36 by mid-2007[69]), was designed to protect the interests of colleges and college athletes as well as those of honest and legitimate sports agents. This and other NCCUSL-promulgated uniform acts—concerning the rights of the terminally ill, anatomical gifts, the status of children of assisted conception, and drug dependency and treatment, for example— indicate that the conference's acts now go beyond the areas of commercial law and finance.

Two Case Studies

Uniform Commercial Code

The UCC is by all accounts the greatest success story of the uniform-laws process, embodying "the major corpus of American commercial law."[70] The law governing commercial transactions (i.e., the law of contracts, payment, warranties, and the shipping and storing of goods) has been and remains primarily state law. This is true despite the fact that the Supreme Court's decisions regarding the Commerce Clause since 1937 make eminently clear and uncontroversial the idea that Congress *could* preempt state law in this field with federal legislation if it chose. The legalistic interests of state governments are strongly affected by the UCC, given the scope of the activities it covers. Why, then, has this vast area of state law *not* been preempted by a federal commercial code, particularly in light of the nationalization (and, indeed, globalization) of the American economy?[71]

Since the early days of the NCCUSL, commissioners discussed the possibility of attempting "a universal codification" of the commercial law, with one commissioner noting in 1895 that "Judge Brewster, of Connecticut, for instance, is of opinion that an exhaustive commercial code should be recommended by the commissioners and adopted by all the States."[72] The UCC was developed by the NCCUSL and the American Law Institute in a long process that began with an agreement between the two organizations in 1935, followed by the adoption of a plan in 1940 to revise the conference's Uniform Sales Act. In 1945, the conference voted to expand the project significantly by codifying all of the commercial law in one code.[73] The UCC was not created out of whole cloth; rather, it combined, updated, and ultimately supplanted a number of uniform acts the conference had promulgated between 1896 and 1933, including the Negotiable Instruments Act, the Uniform Sales Act, the Uniform Warehouse Receipts Act, the Uniform Stock Transfer Act, the Uniform Bills of Lading Act, the Uniform Conditional Sales Act, and the Uniform Trust Receipts Act.[74] Because each of these uniform acts "had become a segment of the statutory law relating to commercial transactions, there was a need to integrate each of the acts with the others."[75]

The final official draft of the code was voted on by the NCCUSL and the American Law Institute in 1952, after which the task shifted from drafting to winning enactments in state legislatures. Ultimately, only Pennsylvania adopted the 1952 version of the UCC. The New York Law Review Commission studied the act from 1953 to 1955 and ultimately recommended against its enactment in that state. Given the importance of having New York—the nation's commercial capital—adopt any commercial code that aspired to be uniform, the editorial board of the UCC revised its 1952 draft to reflect the recommendations of the New York commission. This draft was completed in 1958, and this time, New York's commission recommended that its state legislature adopt the code. The legislature did so but also made a number of changes to the code's official text that had been promulgated by the conference.[76] Several other states had adopted the 1958 text with changes, and the UCC editorial board made another round of revisions in the code's official text, resulting finally in a 1962 version of the text that became the standard act adopted by all states except Louisiana by 1967.[77]

The history of the UCC illustrates the importance of winning the approval of the major commercial states and also shows that, despite its unwieldiness, the uniform-laws process can work, even in the case of a massive codification of commercial law. Since 1967, the nine articles of the UCC have been subject to additional revisions, and articles 2 through 9 have each been revised and readopted by the states at least once since the late 1980s.[78] As can be anticipated, throughout this process various states have made changes to the code when enacting it, and the result is that today the UCC is not perfectly uniform nationwide. Scholars disagree on whether the resulting uniformity is "good enough"[79] or whether it demonstrates the nonviability of the uniform-laws process in an age of globalized commerce.[80] For the purposes of the present discussion of the uniform-laws process as a political safeguard of federalism, the key question is not whether certain states have enacted variations on the official text of the UCC—they have—but whether the actions of the states overall have been sufficient to deter extensive federal preemptions of state commercial law. [81]

During the first 150 years of U.S. history, contract and commercial law was primarily judge-made, common law rather than statutory or codified law enacted by legislatures. Furthermore, the Supreme Court's 1842 ruling in *Swift v. Tyson*[82] made it clear that the federal and state commercial law cases would be decided separately by state courts and federal courts rather than amalgamating them into a single national body of common law.[83] During the late nineteenth and early twentieth centuries, Congress was periodically pressured to enact various federal commercial laws that would displace those of the states. As noted above, the Commerce Clause of the U.S. Constitution gave Congress clear authority to enact such laws, even prior to the judicial revolution of 1937.

A federal sales bill was drafted by the American Bar Association in 1922 by Samuel Williston, who had also drafted the NCCUSL's Uniform Sales Act. To stave off pressures for congressional passage of this bill, the NCCUSL amended its Uniform Sales Act, and support for the federal bill waned.[84] Another federal sales bill was introduced in Congress in 1937, and by 1940, strong pressures were developing for a federal sales bill that would preempt the conference's Uniform Sales Act, which had been promulgated in 1906 and adopted by 36 states.[85] These pressures stemmed in part from the Supreme Court's overruling of its *Swift* decision in *Erie Railroad v. Tompkins*[86] in 1938. Supporters of federalizing this area of the commercial law included the New York Merchant Association, the American Bar Association, and the commercial law expert Karl Llewellyn (who later reversed his view on federalization and led the drafting process of the UCC for the conference). In response to these pressures, the executive committee of the NCCUSL convened an emergency meeting and "got in touch with the people who were handling and backing the proposed federal bill and induced them to hold off until such action as this Conference might take at this [1940 annual] meeting."[87] At the Conference's 1940 meeting, as noted above, the commissioners voted to begin work on revising the Uniform Sales Act in such a way that it could be incorporated into a more general commercial code. "In light of this independent committee, congressional consideration of the Federal Sales Act was delayed, and work began on the second stage of the effort to obtain uniformity of commercial law without federal legislation."[88] As a result, "although the federal sales bill was reintroduced in 1939, it was never enacted; the momentum for revision of the sales law passed to the Conference after 1939."[89]

As noted previously, the articles of the UCC have each been revised at least once in the last 20 years, and these revisions contribute to the ongoing viability of the code. The deterrent effect of the code has not been complete; Congress has enacted a number of measures that have federalized portions of commercial law, particularly with regard to consumer protection, bills of lading, and warehousing. One commissioner pointed out the following:

> Although it is often said that commercial law in America is primarily state, not federal, law, such an assertion is an overstatement. For example, as soon as bankruptcy is considered, we are in the realm of federal law. Much of banking law and consumer rights legislation and regulations are federal. In addition, much of this federal law preempts the state law—a prime example of this is Article 7 of the UCC which is greatly restricted by the preemption of federal law governing bills of lading and warehouse receipts.[90]

Still, even critics of the code concede that "despite the presumed benefits of such a federalized UCC, Congress has not made any serious movement towards enacting a national commercial code. Where the interest in national uniformity has been particularly compelling, however, there have been specific 'federalizations' of commercial law issues."[91]

Although the code may have held the line thus far against greater federal preemption of commercial law, what does the future hold? In this regard, the central question is, Under what circumstances might Congress act to federalize all or substantial parts of the UCC? Several scenarios of federalization can be imagined. In one, regulated entities (such as banks) would perceive at least several of the following circumstances: that the existing code is inadequate because it is technically flawed, incomplete, or otherwise unworkable; that it is burdensome to interstate commerce because of state-by-state variations; or that it fails to promote their interests as profit-seeking businesses. These perceptions would lead some businesses to appeal to Congress to pass a federal commercial code "that would essentially consist of the current UCC, minus conflict-of-law provisions currently needed to resolve conflicts between different state versions."[92] The result would be a commercial code that was by definition uniform nationwide (although Congress, like the drafters of the UCC, would probably allow states to develop or choose from certain variations).

Despite the attractions of such a code and its potential benefits in terms of eliminating state-by-state variation, the federalization of the commercial law might have several drawbacks. First, as noted above, Congress probably lacks the institutional capacity to draft a commercial code as large and complex as the UCC. Assuming that Congress simply adopted the UCC as it currently exists, Congress would still face great challenges when it came to making future revisions of the code, as would inevitably be needed. The fragmentation of congressional committees and the interest group feeding frenzy that would attend such a revision could be avoided by appointing a commission of lawyers to do the drafting, but such a move would then differ little from the current system. In short, Congress simply may not want the job. Although there would undoubtedly be great political payoffs for members of Congress who were in charge of drafting a new version of a federal commercial code, it is not clear that they cannot receive these benefits by other means today without facing the challenges of writing or revising a commercial code. For all the criticisms of the UCC and the uniform-state-laws process more generally, it is not clear that there is sufficient political pressure to federalize the code. The leading critics of the UCC have been groups and individuals who believe it should do more in terms of consumer protection. However, the NCCUSL's latest revision project, article 9, received a "neutral" rating from the Consumer's Union, which, although not a ringing endorsement, reflects the Consumer Union's view that "On balance, we find the revised Article 9 no better or worse for consumers than current UCC Article 9. There are some provisions, however, that should remain unchanged to ensure that the pro-consumer aspects of the revision are not lost in the state legislative process."[93]

Certainly, if the NCCUSL did not exist, or if it failed to undertake periodic revisions of the code, pressure might build for Congress to take over the job. As it stands now, however, the conference's efforts to keep the code up to date seem to be succeeding in safeguarding state-governmental authority to enact the bulk of American commercial law. Furthermore, under the current system of imperfect uniformity of the code, state legislatures that wish to make minor amendments to the

UCC have done so without seriously disrupting the overall roughly uniform nature of the code; thus, it is not the case that state discretion has been completely eliminated under the uniform-laws process in this case. Rather, it appears that the best initial hopes for the uniform-laws process have been realized: most of the state-by-state variations in commercial law (which are largely accidental rather than the result of substantive differences of opinion among state legislatures) have been ironed out, but room has been left for state-by-state variations when there is strong support for them in particular states.

Taxing E-Commerce: The Streamlined Sales Tax Project

Overview. The Internet's rapid growth since the 1990s has changed the ways that Americans communicate, access digital audio and video entertainment, learn about the world, and shop. Savvy online shoppers know that they can often save money by buying online because sales taxes are rarely collected by the retailer. Online retailers are not obligated by law to calculate and collect sales taxes from customers if that retailer does not have a physical "bricks and mortar" retail store or other presence in the customer's state.[94] (This is known legally as a "nexus" requirement.)

Although good for consumers, untaxed Internet purchases substantially hurt the fiscal interests of state and local governments, who lose out on revenue they could potentially be receiving. As such, the 46 states that collect both sales and use taxes on retail sales share a major, near-universal fiscal state interest that affects their ability to pay for state services and programs.[95] According to one estimate, "states and local governments lost $15.5 billion in taxes in 2004" from their inability to collect taxes on all the various forms of Internet access and commerce, and those losses "will escalate to $21.5 billion in 2008."[96] Other estimates have run much higher, and one observer has written that "the rise of electronic commerce is something like the global warming of state finance."[97]

A major cause of this problem for states is their widely varying sales tax rates for different products, and this is the sort of situation that a uniform law can remedy. This case study illustrates the states' use of a version of the uniform-laws process to develop uniform sales tax rates and thus demonstrate to Congress the feasibility and wisdom of "unpreempting" states from collecting those taxes on online sales.

Legal background. The Supreme Court has twice ruled on the issue of taxation of remote sales (those done by mail or online rather than in a store). In 1967, in *National Bellas Hess, Inc. v. Department of Revenue of Illinois*,[98] the Court held that allowing states to compel the calculation and collection of such taxes would impose too great a burden on businesses because of the complexities stemming from the wide variations regarding which goods and services in various jurisdictions are taxed and what the tax rates are. Requiring businesses to negotiate these complexities would amount to an unconstitutional barrier to interstate commerce, the Court held. In 1992, in *Quill Corporation v. North Dakota*,[99] the Court upheld its 1967 ruling even though it acknowledged that the Commerce Clause and Due Process Clause underpinnings of the earlier decision were now obsolete in light of the Court's rulings in other cases related to taxation and interstate commerce.[100] Technology now existed that would ease the burdens of calculating and collecting the taxes. Moreover, the requirement that states could only compel collection of sales and use taxes if a "remote" retailer had a physical presence (a nexus) in the customer's state had softened. In spite of these developments, the Court upheld the *Bellas Hess* ruling because it saw practical value in a bright line nexus rule that had created a stable and predictable business environment for remote retailers.[101] In the end, the Court stated clearly that "Congress is now free to decide whether, when, and to what extent the States may burden interstate mail-order concerns with a duty to collect use taxes."[102] This statement opened the door for states and localities to begin asking Congress to allow them to collect sales taxes and safeguard their fiscal state interests. As will be seen below, Congress has not yet done so, although such legislation has been introduced numerous times since 2000.

The collection of sales and use taxes on online purchases was traditionally viewed as burdensome because of the wide variations among taxing jurisdictions, and states largely brought the problem on themselves by having such widely varying tax rates. If the differences could be ironed out, presumably the burden would be reduced to an acceptable level and Congress might be open to the idea of allowing such taxation. Moreover, the Supreme Court has held that businesses need to collect state sales taxes from customers only if the business has a physical presence in that state. Under existing law, an Alaska consumer's Amazon.com purchase is not taxable because there is not an Amazon.com retail outlet in that state. This requirement of a physical nexus led some large national retailers to create somewhat artificial distinctions between their online and retail businesses. Borders bookstore, for example, operated separate business entities known as "Borders Books and Music" and "Borders Online" in an effort to retain a competitive market advantage by not collecting sales taxes. The parent company, Borders Group, "presumably structured its brick-and-mortar and online divisions in this way to avoid the imposition of sales taxes on most of its Internet sales since an online retailer that lacks a physical presence, including warehouses and the like, in one state would generally be free from that state's taxation."[103] Although this is good news for online retailers and consumers, it poses a problem for state governments facing growing losses of sales tax revenues as people increasingly shop online.

In May 2005, the California Court of Appeals held that the distinction between the online and bricks-and-mortar elements of Borders was artificial and that the firm was obliged to collect taxes on its online sales in California because of the physical nexus of the firm's retail outlets and its California customers.[104] The decision applies only to California and still leaves many questions unanswered, but it points to the need for greater clarification of Internet commerce taxation law by either the Supreme Court or Congress.

Any organization attempting to standardize the taxation rates of the 7,600 taxing jurisdictions in the United States obviously faces a great challenge. W. Brooke Graves, a scholar of the uniform-laws process, wrote in 1934 that "it is frankly to be recognized and admitted that there are matters, such as taxation, with regard to some phases of which uniformity is probably neither possible nor feasible."[105] A great deal of the variation among jurisdictions appears to be without rhyme or reason. Nine states exempt clothing from sales tax. In eight of these states, shoelaces are considered clothing; in Texas they are not.[106] Some jurisdictions classify orange juice as a fruit and some as a beverage, products which are taxed differently. Some jurisdictions tax large marsh-mallows as taxable food but classify miniature marshmallows as a nontaxable ingredient.[107]

Some of the differences in tax rates stem from state and local politicians' manipulation of the tax code to reward certain constituencies or industries; hence, unifying these rates nationwide would remove their ability to use the tax code for political purposes. However, it appears that the choice facing state and local officials today is between retaining their authority over sales tax rates and having Congress rescind their authority to collect any taxes on online purchases.

In its first effort to address the complex issues arising from online commerce, Congress's Internet Tax Freedom Act of 1998 (ITFA)[108] placed a moratorium on states' imposition of two forms of Internet-related taxes: "taxes on Internet access, unless such tax was generally imposed and actually enforced prior to October 1, 1998," and "multiple or discriminatory taxes on electronic commerce."[109] (Multiple taxation exists when two states attempt to tax the same sale or transaction, and discriminatory taxation exists when a jurisdiction taxes an online transaction at a higher rate in order to encourage a local, nononline purchase.) The ITFA did not ban states from collecting sales taxes on Internet commerce in general—given that such taxes are already against the law of the land because of the Supreme Court's *Bellas Hess* and *Quill* rulings—but it signaled that Congress's general position, at least for the time being, was to call a time out on all taxation of Internet access and commerce.

The moratorium on new state taxation of Internet access was extended in 2003 and later, with the Internet Tax Nondiscrimination Act passed by the 108th Congress (Public Law 108-435), through November 1, 2007. In November 2007, Public Law 110-108 extended the moratorium to 2014 but still did not make it permanent, as some had called for.[110] The ITFA moratorium will not be addressed further in this chapter because it concerns only state taxation of Internet access (i.e., taxation of Internet service providers like Yahoo) and multiple and discriminatory taxation rather than taxation of Internet commerce. State officials' efforts to convince Congress to permit state taxation of online commerce have proceeded under a different set of federal legislation, which is described below.

The ITFA also established an Advisory Commission on Electronic Commerce (ACEC), which began work in 1999 to develop recommendations for Congress on a variety of issues.[111] At the behest of the NGA and other state and local groups, for example, the commission was tasked with studying ways to tax electronic commerce and "to recommend legislation requiring companies to collect sales taxes from customers who live in states where a company does not have a physical presence."[112] The commission ultimately ended in deadlock, unable to win the required two-thirds (13 of 19) of votes required to make *any* of its findings or recommendations official under the terms of its charter.

Given ACEC's inability to agree on any official recommendations, Congress received no clear mandate from the commission regarding the taxation of online commerce. Beginning in 2000, senators and House members introduced legislation each session to formally overturn the Supreme Court's *Quill* decision and thereby allow states to require companies to collect sales taxes on online sales and remit the money to states. At this writing, the most recent iterations of these bills are S 34 (introduced on May 22, 2007) and HR 3396 (introduced on August 3, 2007), both titled the Sales Tax Fairness and Simplification Act. A House subcommittee hearing on the bill was held on December 6, 2007, but as of June 2008, no action toward passage had been taken.

The central question, then, for states concerned about threats to their fiscal interests from untaxed online commerce is whether state officials can convince Congress to pass legislation authorizing states to begin collecting sales taxes on online purchases. To convince Congress to pass such legislation, a variety of state officials looked to the uniform-laws process to make their sales tax rates uniform so that taxes could easily be collected by online retailers. In light of the Supreme Court's *Quill* decision, the states' strategy was to make the taxes easy to calculate and collect in order to allay the Court's concerns that that collection would be overly burdensome on interstate commerce.

Uniform-laws process as a means of developing a simplified tax system. Given the enormous fiscal stakes facing state governments, circumstances were ripe for the development of a model or uniform state law that would facilitate the collection of sales and use taxes. There are two basic ways to reduce the burdens on businesses in calculating and collecting sales and use taxes during online transactions. The first is to have states tax the same goods at the same rates, so that a business engaged in e-commerce need only perform one calculation to determine what a buyer from anywhere in the country owes in sales tax. Such a system might tax all clothing, books, and compact discs at 6 percent, for example, regardless of where the buyer and seller are located. The adoption of this method would require all jurisdictions to agree that 6 percent is a proper level of taxation for those goods, and historically the sales tax rates among jurisdictions have not been marked by such consensus.

The second means of reducing the burden of tax calculation and collection is to leave current sales tax rates intact but to create a quick and easy means of calculating and collecting the proper sum during the course of an online transaction. Although the time, effort, and cost of performing such a calculation for each customer may have been substantial ten or twenty years ago, today it can be performed easily by computer software. Furthermore, the use of third-party vendors might be encouraged as a way for online retailers to subcontract the responsibility for tax calculation and collection.

States have chosen a combination of these two options. Fearing the loss of an increasing percentage of their revenue, state and local officials began a coordinated effort in 1999 to draft a uniform law that would facilitate the collection of taxes on online commerce. The initial effort in this regard was the National Tax Association's (NTA's) Communications and Electronic Commerce Tax Project. The NTA has a long history as a forum for the discussion and evaluation of tax policy, and it is composed of members from business, government, and academia. As early as November 1996, NTA members had contemplated the possibility of a uniform state law as a solution to the difficulties of collecting sales taxes on e-commerce.[113]

The NTA project overlapped with the establishment by the ITFA of the ACEC, and ITFA explicitly encouraged the members of ACEC to take into consideration the findings of the NTA project. The history of the NTA project will not be described in detail here, but in the end, its business and government members were unable to reach a consensus on the future of e-commerce taxation.

The major effort toward creating a uniform system of sales taxes for the nation's 7,600 taxing jurisdictions is the SSTP. In early 2000, state officials initiated the SSTP, and it was sponsored by the NGA, the NCSL, the Federation of Tax Administrators, and the Multistate Tax Commission.

> The SSTP issued its initial report (the Streamlined Sales and Use Tax Agreement) (SSUTA) to both the NGA and the NCSL in 2001. The NGA adopted the proposed legislation, while the NCSL modified the initial report and issued a unique version. Despite this perceived disagreement, the NGA issued a statement that "there is only one state and local sales and use tax simplification effort underway among the states, and there should continue to be only a single simplification effort." To further emphasize the cohesive nature of the SSTP, membership was extended to all states that enacted legislation based on either the SSTP or NCSL version of the tax simplification acts or a hybrid of the two proposals.[114]

The terms of the SSUTA declared that it would take effect when adopted by at least 10 states whose combined populations totaled at least 20% of the population of all states with sales and use taxes. On November 12, 2002, representatives from 33 states voted to approve the SSUTA,[115] and the NCSL Task Force began an outreach effort to encourage state consideration of the agreement in their 2003 legislative terms. The aim of the 70-page SSUTA was to "significantly simplify and modernize the existing sales and use tax rules and administrative systems by reducing the number of applicable tax rates, making the definitions of items in the tax base more uniform from state to state, and reducing the overall compliance burden on sellers."[116] The SSUTA is a uniform law in the sense that it

> obliges would-be member states to enact a variety of amendments to their own statutes or constitutions. Perhaps most significantly, the Agreement sets out a "library" of putatively uniform definitions for the myriad of items that could be subject to sales tax. States must then establish a tax "matrix" in which they check off which of the library items they will tax. A state cannot impose a tax on

any item that would also be covered by a library definition unless it defines that item in the same terms as the library's definition. States can have only a select number of tax rates, including rates imposed by sub-state entities such as cities or counties. Furthermore, the states must adopt uniform administrative procedures, set out in the Agreement.[117]

By May 2006, 44 states and the District of Columbia were participating in the SSTP as either participants or observers,[118] although only 13 were "full-member" participants that had enacted the SSUTA. By June 2008, 18 states were full members,[119] and a number of other states were considering legislation to become full members.[120] By December 2007, the president of the Streamlined Sales Tax Executive Committee noted in congressional testimony that "Over 28 percent of the country's population now lives in a Streamlined state. . . . I believe there are another 10 states that are likely to join in the next two years if we can continue the progress we have made so far. Some states are waiting to see if there is movement in Congress, so this hearing is particularly encouraging for them."[121]

As a case study in the political safeguards of federalism, the SSTP tests the hypothesis that concerted policymaking action by states can convince Congress to overturn a preemption of state authority. It also demonstrates both the power of universal fiscal state-governmental interests to induce state-level action as well as the role of intergovernmental lobbying groups in facilitating such efforts.[122]

From a political standpoint, states' efforts to collect sales taxes on online sales pits them against consumers (who like paying lower prices) and online retailers (who fear losing business if they lose their pricing advantage relative to bricks-and-mortar retailers who must collect sales taxes).[123] Traditional bricks-and-mortar retailers, however, have supported the SSUTA because the taxation of online commerce would eliminate its pricing advantage, which currently averages 6 percent—the average state sales tax rate. As one retail business owner explained in congressional testimony on behalf of the National Retail Federation, "Considering that most retail profit margins are on the scale of 3 or 4 percent, a non-negotiable price disadvantage of 6 percent on top of the cost of the goods being sold is clearly a significant discrimination against Main

Street sellers."[124] Aligned against the SSUTA are numerous groups that support tax cuts and oppose the imposition of new taxes. "Every major free-market and pro-growth association opposes the SSTP. These groups include Americans for Tax Reform, the National Taxpayers Union, Citizens for a Sound Economy, Club for Growth, Citizens Against Government Waste, the Cato Institute, the Heritage Foundation, the American Enterprise Institute and dozens of state-based think tanks across the nation."[125] Americans for Tax Reform, for example, characterizes the SSTP as a "stealth tax hike," and in a statement aimed at legislators, notes that "all pro-taxpayer lawmakers should oppose the creation of this tax-and-spend cartel. As a legislator, you should oppose this tax harmonization scheme for the reasons cited below, and also because SSTP is not providing an honest analysis of the plan's impact on taxpayers."[126] Supporters of the SSTP respond that it does not represent any new taxes, only the collection of taxes that are already legally due to states.[127]

It is not outside the realm of possibility that Congress would vote to "unpreempt" the states and allow them to tax online commerce. Discussing Herbert Wechsler's theory of the political safeguards of federalism, leading preemption scholar Joseph Zimmerman wrote that "This theory has a degree of validity as evidenced by Congress' failure to enact numerous preemption bills and clearly explains congressional responsiveness to state complaints and requests in a number of instances." He goes on to note that in recent years, "Congress enacted five preemption relief acts in response to state complaints."[128]

As noted above, since 2000, members of Congress have introduced numerous bills to require online retailers to collect sales taxes and remit them to states. The most explicit congressional proposal to unpreempt states by endorsing the SSTP was a Senate bill introduced by Sen. Byron Dorgan (D-N.Dak.) in December 2005, the Streamlined Sales Tax Simplification Act (S 2153). The bill gave the states Congress's blessing to collect sales taxes on online commerce once at least 10 states whose population equaled at least 20 percent of the total U.S. population in states imposing sales taxes had joined the SSUTA.[129] This bill was sent to committee after its introduction, and no further action was taken. In May and August 2007, respectively, bills similar to the Dorgan bill described above were introduced in the U.S. Senate (S 34) and House of

Representatives (HR 3396). The key section of each bill reads simply "The Congress consents to the Streamlined Sales and Use Tax Agreement."[130]

In addition to Senator Dorgan's approach—allowing the state signatories to the SSUTA to collect online sales taxes—Congress could also resolve the entire matter quickly by passing a law *requiring* all states to adopt the SSTP framework. Although it is rare for Congress to mandate state adoption of a uniform law, it would not be unprecedented. Section 321 of the 1996 welfare-reform law required states to adopt NCCUSL's Uniform Interstate Family Support Act, which limits child and family support orders to a single state, eliminating interstate jurisdictional disputes. (This was an important element of the welfare-reform law because it requires states to make sure that applicants for welfare benefits are receiving any child support payments due to them.) In another example, the Gramm–Leach–Bliley Act of 1999 directed the National Association of Insurance Commissioners to draft uniform standards for insurance sales and licensure. Specifically, section 321 of the law stated that federal licensure provisions would take effect "unless, not later than 3 years after the date of the enactment of this Act, at least a majority of the States have enacted uniform laws and regulations governing the licensure of individuals and entities authorized to sell and solicit the purchase of insurance within the States, or have enacted reciprocity laws and regulations governing the licensure of nonresident individuals and entities authorized to sell and solicit insurance within those States."[131] In other words, if a majority of states adopted a uniform law, Congress would let those state laws stand; if not, it would create federal standards. "Faced with this pressure, 39 states adopted the standards."[132]

There is no indication that Congress is considering this approach, but it would conclude the issue in a way favorable to states (although forcing the states to adopt a uniform law is somewhat paradoxical, in essence preserving states' legalistic interests by overriding them). The debate over Internet sales taxation has been framed as an anti-tax measure rather than as a preserve-state-services measure. If the SSTP effort could reframe the debate and make it clear that the collection of sales taxes by online vendors is not overly burdensome, states may yet protect the important fiscal interests at stake here. At this writing (in early 2008), worsening state finances held some possibility of strengthening the states' case to Congress to give them the ability to collect desperately needed sales tax revenue from online commerce.[133] Until Congress takes positive action to endorse state collection of sales taxes on online commerce, states can singly and collectively take steps to help reduce the amount of uncollected sales and use taxes, including using consumer education campaigns, promoting interstate cooperation and information sharing, attempting to collect sales taxes on income tax forms, and advocating for a federal income tax form deduction for payments of state sales and use taxes.[134]

STRENGTHS AND WEAKNESSES OF THE UNIFORM-LAWS PROCESS AS A SAFEGUARD OF FEDERALISM

Nonadoption of Uniform Acts by Jurisdictions

Although I use the term "uniform state law" here, historically, very few model acts have actually been adopted by all 50 states. The major—and very important—success story of the NCCUSL is the UCC it developed in conjunction with the American Law Institute, which since 1968 has—with numerous individual state amendments—been the basic law governing commercial transactions in 49 states and the District of Columbia (Louisiana's Napoleonic Civil Code has made it difficult for that state to adopt the UCC, although since 1974 it has adopted—with amendments—each of the nine articles of the UCC[135]). Even when a proposed act is adopted by fewer than 50 states, the resulting imperfect uniformity may still be enough to stave off federal preemption in that policy area. Indeed, the conference's criteria for preparing a uniform act requires that the drafting of the act "will be a practical step toward uniformity of state law or at least toward minimizing its diversity" and there "must be a reasonable probability that the Act . . . either will be accepted and enacted into law by a substantial number of jurisdictions or, if not, will promote uniformity indirectly."[136] Certainly, it matters a great deal *which* of the states adopt the act, and an act adopted by major commercial states, such as California, New York, and Texas, will be harder for federal policymakers to ignore.[137]

The NCCUSL has always been very good at keeping track of the number of adoptions of its acts each year, and in recent years, the number of enactments has declined somewhat. In 2004, NCCUSL President Fred Miller reported, "In 1991, the first year of the Conference's centennial year, we had 112 enactments—the first time in our long history we had ever posted more than 100 enactments in a legislative year. Just two years later, we had 103 enactments. In 1997 we had 130 enactments, our best year ever. But since then, our enactment totals have been steadily falling. In 2002, we posted only 53 enactments; last year, we finished with 78 enactments."[138] He offered a number of explanations for the decline—the complexity of many of the acts, opposition from industry groups, and the difficulty of relying on volunteer commissioners to help shepherd the acts through state legislatures. Noting that "the credibility of the Conference depends in no small measure on how successful we are in the state legislatures," Miller put his finger on a challenge that has dogged NCCUSL since its creation—getting uniform laws, however admirable and well crafted, passed by dozens of state legislatures, each with a different agenda, tradition, culture, political composition, and set of institutions and process.

In NCCUSL's 2004–2005 annual report, Miller reported that "nationwide, during the 2004–2005 legislative year, there were 201 introductions of uniform acts and 86 enactments. The Uniform Environmental Covenants Act topped the list of legislative enactments with 10 adoptions in 2005. The Uniform Child Custody Jurisdiction and Enforcement Act moved closer to total uniformity, with four new adoptions in 2005, bringing its total number of enactments to 44."[139] The conference's success rates ebb and flow over the years and decades, and it seems unwise to worry too much about year-to-year fluctuations in the absence of firmer evidence that something is permanently amiss with the uniform-laws process.

Postadoption Amendments

Even when a state adopts a uniform act without amendment, it may subsequently decide to change the law, creating nonuniformity with other states' version of the enacted uniform law. Although these amendments may reflect the good-faith attempts of state lawmakers to tailor the law to the needs and circumstances of their states, from the uniform-state-laws perspective, they diminish uniformity among states. As such, it is not enough simply to get a uniform act enacted; vigilance must be exercised to maintain rough uniformity over time. For example, scholars of the Model Penal Code note, "Even the best of codes will slowly deteriorate without active oversight, as later generations of legislators unfamiliar (or unconcerned) with the original code's scheme add, delete, and revise provisions, oblivious to the effects of these changes on the code as a whole. History indicates that the quality of the American criminal codes enacted in the wake of the Model Penal Code's promulgation has been eroded by subsequent modifications that disrupt the codes' initial clarity and coherence."[140] It is obviously quite difficult to identify the precise tipping point at which postadoption amendments strike the fatal blow to an act's cross-state uniformity. Perhaps the best that can be done to minimize such "damage" is for the organization promulgating a uniform or model act to encourage few amendments and to specify the acceptable bounds of such future amendments.

It should be strongly emphasized that most *federal* laws are not uniform across states either, and the implication that we are comparing 100-percent-uniform federal laws with only partially uniform state laws is wildly incorrect. As will be discussed in chapter 5, federal laws tend to be nonuniform because of the exemptions, waivers, exceptions, loopholes, and options for state flexibility typically written into federal law and because of differences in the ways that state agencies administer federal laws when enforcement duties are delegated to them. Examples include the wide state-to-state variations in benefit levels under the federal Temporary Assistance to Needy Families (welfare) and Medicaid programs. As such, some state-to-state nonuniformity ought not make these efforts look substandard in comparison with federal policies, because the latter generally contain substantial nonuniformity as well.

Diverse Interpretations by State Courts

Once a uniform act has been adopted in a number of states, it is subject to litigation in the courts of those states. Although this fact has the advantage of reducing the caseload on the federal courts and preserving the role of state courts in interpreting state law,[141] it also opens the possibility of a uniform law being interpreted differently by judges in different states. When this situation occurs, nonuniformity results. To combat this problem, "starting in 1906, the [NCCUSL] resorted to the insertion of a clause: 'This act shall be so interpreted and construed . . . as to effectuate its general purpose to make uniform the laws of those states which enact it.'"[142] As judicial experience in interpreting uniform laws increased, the conference's clause apparently had its intended effect, and by 1928 one observer could note that "the binding effect of decisions of other jurisdictions, in the case of uniform laws, must now be regarded as a firmly established principle of jurisprudence."[143] The conference's uniform and model acts also contain an annotation "which supplies an index to the decisions of all the jurisdictions in which any model or uniform law has been enacted and construed."[144] In the case of the UCC, the *Uniform Commercial Code Law Journal* was founded in 1968, providing an additional source of information about judicial interpretation of the UCC. Moreover, "the UCC adopts the useful strategy of stating its rules on two levels: a formal rule that is intended to have binding force and a more chatty commentary that serves as an interpretive guide."[145] Finally, since 1987, the Permanent Editorial Board of the UCC has issued supplemental commentaries that state "a preferred resolution of a UCC issue on which judicial or scholarly opinion has differed."[146] In sum, a number of measures have been taken to minimize the nonuniformity that could result from diverse interpretations of uniform laws.

Does the Uniform-Laws Process Really Safeguard Federalism Per Se?

Some argue that healthy federalism requires states' autonomy not only from the federal government, but also from one another. The uniform-laws process, when successful, preserves state decisionmaking autonomy vis-à-vis the federal government, but it reduces each state's ability to freely pass laws that differ from other states'. To that extent, some argue that very little is gained by avoiding federalization of a particular policy area, because true state autonomy is lost in either case. One early observer of the uniform-laws process made this point vividly, noting that "Mr. Madison's ideas of the rights of the States are still worth fighting for; it is not yet futile to contend against federal larceny by constitutional amendment, and it is still worth while to give battle against the half-brother of federal larceny, the pressure for uniformity."[147]

There is some truth to this charge, which resonates with the idea that the American states function as "laboratories of democracy," running 50 simultaneous experiments to determine which policies work best. However, although the laboratories metaphor seems compelling, state governments rarely come up with 50 different versions of policies in a given issue area. Even without something as formal as the uniform-laws process, state policymakers continuously borrow policy ideas from one another, adopting best practices from other states that they learn about from conferences, symposia, public officials' associations, and publications like *State Legislatures*, *State Government News*, *Governing*, and others. Indeed, policy scholars' study of the diffusion of innovation across states is premised on the idea that sound policy created in one state is likely to spread to others. As such, it seems misguided to argue that the uniform-laws process preserves only a substandard form of state autonomy. State officials properly worry much more about federal threats to their policymaking autonomy than they do about having policies that resemble those of neighboring states.

• • •

The case studies in this chapter indicate one way that state governments have maintained their legalistic decisionmaking authority, particularly in the vast area of commercial law, for over a century. The uniform-laws process is unwieldy as a means of making policy that is (at least somewhat) national but not federal. The reasons for the not infrequent failures of the process are quite clear, but so are the successes it has achieved in varying degrees since 1891. These successes have been due to the reluctance of federal policymakers to enter fields of private law with which they have little experience or expertise; the ability of the uniform-laws process to address the interests of regulated business entities well enough to prevent those entities from appealing to the federal government for different or better policies; and the imperfect uniformity that the process yields, which actually serves as an escape valve for state legislators' desire to put their own imprint on legislation while still achieving rough uniformity. The UCC case study supports the general proposition that the uniform-laws process deters Congress from preempting state authority in policy areas where quality legislation is being passed. The SSTP case study shows a uniform law work in progress that has done much in a short span of years.

It has been written that if the NCCUSL did not exist, something like it would have to be invented.[148] Politics and policymaking in this country have always been characterized by the tensions implied in its name: it is "United," but it is also "States." The uniform-laws process is a reflection of and a response to those tensions. Rather than resolving those tensions, it aims to soften or eliminate their negative consequences. One observer argues that policy "experimentation and competition are best served by a refereed federalism. . . . To make the most of our federal system, we need to develop the institutional expertise to evaluate parallel programs, and the institutional will to implement best practices that may run contrary to purely local interests. Achieving those goals will often mean that the market, or the market as intermittently regulated by a fairly limited federal court system, must be supplemented by other actors working in coordination with courts, with one another, and with private stakeholders."[149] The uniform-laws process provides the "other actors" needed for high-quality state policy making. As a viable alternative to the federalization of a variety of public policy areas, the process has safeguarded federalism by demonstrating that state legislatures can pass legislation on important policy matters that often meets the needs and satisfies the interests of the various attentive individuals, groups, and business sectors. The safeguarding of federalism is only one goal of the uniform-laws commissioners (in addition to drafting good law and facilitating interstate commerce and other transactions), and the commissioners are not strictly officials of state governments. Nonetheless, the salutary effects in promoting state-governmental interests seem clear: by developing and passing high-quality legislation in various policy areas, the uniform-laws process generates practical—if not formal, legal—limits on the federal government's reach.

CHAPTER 4

STATE PARTICIPATION IN FEDERAL POLICYMAKING

The Intergovernmental Lobby

Do we [governors] draw together simply as friends, or has there arisen in our minds the thought that we have some quasi-constitutional function?

— Governor-elect Woodrow Wilson, addressing
the second meeting of the Governors' Conference, 1910[1]

When the governors get determined about something, there is no limit to their authority in Washington, once they determine that that's something they want. . . . I think when two-thirds of the governors say that something ought to be done, that that becomes the law eventually. I have no doubt about that.

—James L. Martin, Director of State–Federal Relations, NGA[2]

In a true Madisonian sense, the government interest groups and their members provide another form of political representation at the national level, one founded not on functional lines or shifting congressional boundaries but on representation of interests based essentially on geopolitical units—states, counties, municipalities. These groups constitute a kind of "third house" of elected representatives at the national level as well as an institutional interface between the President and Congress. . . . They have indeed become

a significant counterbalance in the federal system to the rising influence of national government, which pervades all of American life.
—Donald Haider, *When Governments Come to Washington*[3]

Does the governor of your state have an office and staff in Washington, DC? Your first response is probably, "Why in the world *would* she?" In fact, 35 of the nation's 50 governors (70%) currently have offices in the nation's capital, and the populations of these governors' states comprise over 85% of the population of the United States. So, chances are quite good that your governor does have a Washington office, which prompts the next question: what do the staff in these offices *do*?

Governors' Washington staff work alone and in conjunction with staff of other governors and associations like the NGA to track federal policymaking efforts and to try to convince members of Congress to legislate in ways that preserve state-governmental interests. In this chapter, I examine these efforts—and those of the intergovernmental lobby more generally—to assess their effectiveness as a political safeguard of federalism.

The Constitution's framers thought that the U.S. Senate would safeguard state-governmental interests, but as early as the 1820s it was clear that senators were doing so inconsistently at best.[4] Nonetheless, Congress's power to legislate on a multitude of issues affecting state-governmental interests gives state governments strong incentives to find other ways to influence the federal legislative process. The primary response of state (and local) officials in this regard has been to create organizations capable of monitoring Congress on an ongoing basis and lobbying its members on issues of state concern. Although the activities of these organizations—known collectively as the intergovernmental lobby—have been analyzed elsewhere,[5] most of the existing work has focused on their strategic behavior as interest groups rather than on the implications of their activities for the constitutional theory and practice of federalism, the direction in which Woodrow Wilson's quote above points.[6] In the spirit of Donald Haider's quotation above, I document in this chapter the intergovernmental lobby's development into an effective means of safeguarding state-governmental interests through its participation in the federal policymaking process. If members of Congress today do not reflexively perceive and promote state-governmental interests, they nonetheless may be persuaded to do so if lobbied by state officials. The intergovernmental lobby's wide-ranging advocacy efforts on federal policy promote a wide range of states' legalistic, fiscal, and administrative interests, and the lobby's various institutional manifestations ensure that universal, categorical, and particularistic interests are voiced. As such, intergovernmental lobbying provides a particularly rich illustration of an informal political safeguard of federalism today.

• • •

State governments have always lobbied the federal government in one form or another.[7] Because the national government has always relied on the cooperation of state governments to administer a wide variety of federal programs,[8] state governments' legalistic, fiscal, and administrative interests are substantially affected by the forms those federal programs take. Accordingly, states have regularly sought to clarify their roles vis-à-vis the federal government and to increase their autonomy and flexibility in carrying out federal programs.

As noted in the previous chapter, joint state–federal policy interactions became more widespread as the pressures for expanded governmental activity at all levels increased around the turn of the twentieth century and particularly during the New Deal era. If state governments and the national government were previously less implicated in one another's activities than they were after 1932, it was not because states had no interests vis-à-vis the national government, or because it was strictly an era of "dual federalism"—one in which spheres of federal and state authority were clearly demarcated—but, rather, because government *at all levels* did comparatively little by today's standards. The national government's activities were limited largely to internal improvements (building roads and canals and so forth), subsidies, tariffs, public lands disposal, patents and copyrights, and currency, whereas the bulk of governmental functions and services were performed by state and local governments.[9]

As that situation changed, elected officials at the state and local levels created formal organizations under whose auspices they could meet regularly to exchange ideas about best practices, to commiserate about common problems, and to devise and execute strategies for promoting their common interests. These public officials' associations closely resembled similar professional organizations, such as the American Medical Association, the American Bar Association, and many, many others.

INTERGOVERNMENTAL LOBBY

Although there are hundreds of nonpartisan associations of American public officials, seven are of particular note, because they represent the major elected officials at each level of subnational government.[10] As seen in table 5, the "Big Seven" associations represent governors (the NGA), state legislators (the NCSL), local officials (the National League of Cities), mayors of cities with populations over 30,000 (the U.S. Conference of Mayors), city managers (the International City–County Management Association), and counties (the National Association of Counties). More generally, the Council of Governments (founded in 1933) serves the legislative, executive, and judicial branches of state governments in a variety of capacities and facilitates interstate cooperation on policy implementation. In addition to these organizations, a multitude of regional and local associations of public officials articulate more specific sets of governmental interests.

These organizations serve many of the same functions as other professional associations: offering opportunities for professional development, socializing newcomers into the field, providing information and assistance in meeting professional goals, and providing regular opportunities to meet and network with others similarly situated. These organizations also offer opportunities for subnational officials both to develop clear statements of their institutional interests vis-à-vis the federal government and to engage in coordinated efforts to advocate those interests at various stages of the national policymaking process.

In this chapter, I focus mainly on the Washington lobbying activities of governors because they appear to articulate and advocate for state-governmental interests most clearly and directly today. As noted in chapter 1, it has been said that that "meetings of the NGA come closer than any other institutional arrangement for assessing the temperament

TABLE 5

The "Big Seven" organizations of the intergovernmental lobby

Organization	Founded	Membership[a]	Location(s)	Website
National Governors' Association	1908	50 state and 5 territorial governors	Washington, D.C.	http://www.nga.org/
National Conference of State Legislatures	1975	State legislators	Denver, Colo.; Washington, D.C.	http://www.ncsl.org/
National League of Cities	1924	1,600 member cities, villages and towns (of the 18,000 in the United States)	Washington, D.C.	http://www.nlc.org/
U.S. Conference of Mayors	1932	Mayors of cities over 30,000 (there are 1,139 currently)	Washington, D.C.	http://usmayors.org/uscm/home.asp
International City–County Management Association	1914	City and county managers (8,200 members)	Washington, D.C.	http://icma.org/main/sc.asp
National Association of Counties	1955	Two-thirds of all U.S. counties are members (more than 2,000 of the 3,066)	Washington, D.C.	http://www.naco.org/
Council of State Governments	1933	No members per se; some affiliated organizations	Lexington, Ky.	http://www.csg.org/

[a] Members' staff are also de facto members and use the services of these associations.

as well as the power position of the states in state/national relations,"[11] so they merit close examination in the context of this study. Four types of gubernatorial lobbying will be examined: lobbying by the NGA, lobbying by regional governors' associations, lobbying by single-issue governors' associations, and lobbying by individual governors' offices in Washington. Each tier of governors' associations promotes a different variety of state-governmental interest, ranging from the universal state-governmental interests perceived by all or most governors to the categorical and particularistic interests perceived by groups of governors or single governors on behalf of their state governments. Although the focus here will be mainly on governors, most of the insights apply to other state official associations' Washington lobbying efforts as well.

National Governors' Association

Origins of the NGA

The Governors' Conference (which became the National Governors' Conference in 1965 and the NGA in 1977) has its roots in a May 13, 1908, meeting held at the White House, at the behest of President Theodore Roosevelt, who wanted to discuss conservation, a pet issue of his. Thirty-four governors attended that session, during which Roosevelt tried to enlist the support of the governors for natural resources legislation he favored that was bogged down in Congress. The governors met again in 1910—this time of their own accord—and have met every year since, with the exception of 1917.[12] "In 1912, the governors established the Governors' Conference as a permanent organization and called on each governor to seek an appropriation from his legislature."[13]

In contrast to its current standing as an important player in the federal policymaking process when state-related legislation is developed, the conference initially decided that it would not attempt to influence Congress: "The dominant faction within the Governors' Conference firmly opposed the creation of a strong, activist group of governors. Most of all they were opposed to the suggestion that the governors should strive to influence national policy, either as a formal instrument of government or as an *ad hoc* pressure group."[14] Nonetheless, the seeds of the organization's future advocacy role were planted, as "some governors, such as Colorado Governor John F. Shafroth, disagreed with the strong state bias and urged the governors to act collectively to influence national policies."[15]

The New Deal and World War II ended speculation over whether governors would ever play a role in forming or administering national policies: governors were called on to cooperate with various national efforts to address economic problems and prosecute the war.

> The overriding fact of the period was not that certain governors favored the New Deal while others opposed it, but rather that governors on both sides of the fence had accepted the clear necessity of being involved in national politics. The Governors' Conference in the thirties talked about national issues with gusto. They passed public resolutions on national questions with no regard for the moribund conference tradition against resolutions. And they began to look around for more workable means of putting their opinions into action.[16]

Following the war, as the federal government maintained many of the programs that had been created under President Franklin Roosevelt, governors realized that the activities of state governments would henceforth be increasingly intertwined with those of the federal government. At its 1945 and 1946 meetings, the conference passed resolutions calling both for cooperative and coordinated efforts between state government and the national government in solving national problems and for federal forbearance in policy areas traditionally reserved to states.

Other scholars have provided more detailed accounts of the history of the Governors' Conference and its development into the NGA of today,[17] and readers are referred to those works for more details. For this book's purposes, we are most interested in how the NGA today safeguards federalism through its Washington-based lobbying efforts.

Structures and Processes of the NGA Today

Like Congress, much of the NGA's work is done in committees. The NGA currently has four standing committees[18] plus an executive committee that is authorized to adopt interim policies with a two-thirds vote between meetings in order to guide the lobbying efforts of the NGA. Each governor belongs to one of the four permanent committees, and the policy positions adopted in plenary sessions originate in these committees. Each committee has several NGA staff members devoted to researching and lobbying on legislation falling within its purview. It is the practice of the NGA to appoint lead governors on issues (such as welfare reform or safe drinking water reform) in order to have a small number of governors (with at least one from each party) who specialize in a single issue area and to whom other governors can look for guidance. Reducing the number of governors who speak for the association on a given issue also helps the NGA present Congress with a unified, bipartisan message. When governors testify at congressional hearings, it is often the lead governors on a particular issue who do so. In addition to this committee structure, task forces may be formed to respond to particularly complex or fast-moving policymaking efforts by Congress.

Each year, the NGA develops or updates positions on leading matters of state–federal relations. As a whole, these positions constitute one of the best articulations of universal legalistic, fiscal, and administrative state-governmental interests. NGA policy positions emerge from the standing committees and are voted on by the governors at the NGA's semiannual meetings. An NGA committee staff member described the process as it works today:

> After the policy is developed by staff representing the governors—and the staff's job is really to massage the policy and to get the clearest possible statement that has a broad consensus among governors. The first step is at committee; it takes an absolute majority of members at the committee. The Natural Resources Committee has 16 governors on it, so it takes nine affirmative votes to pass a statement through the Natural Resources Commit-tee. When it goes through the committee, it then goes to all 50 governors in plenary session and there it's two-thirds of those present and voting. But an absentee or an abstention or a gover-nor who gets up and walks away from the table to go to the

restroom or answer the telephone or something [does not affect the decision]—when a committee vote is taken, that's the same as a "no" vote. It's fairly difficult to get an absolute majority sometimes.[19]

Once out of committee, nearly all of the policy positions in recent years have been adopted by unanimous or near-unanimous votes in the plenary sessions. The governors adopt policy positions on a wide variety of topics, and the positions then become the basis of lobbying efforts either by NGA staff or by the governors themselves. Today, the NGA's policy positions run to several hundred pages each year and can be found on the association's website.[20]

REGIONAL GOVERNORS' ASSOCIATIONS

The second tier of the governors' lobby consists of the several regional governors' associations that exist to help promote the categorical interests of clusters of state governments. Six major regional associations currently exist, but the number has fluctuated during the twentieth century as regional groupings have variously formed, disbanded, or reorganized. From oldest to newest, these are the Western Governors' Association, the Southern Governors' Association, the Midwest Governors' Conference, the New England Governors' Conference, the Coalition of Northeastern Governors, and the Council of Great Lakes Governors. The activities of these associations vary widely, but—like the NGA—their missions all include discussing policy issues and proposals of interest to the member governors, tracking federal legislation of interest to their respective regions, exchanging information among member governments, and communicating their respective collective concerns to the federal executive and legislative branches. Each of the regional associations meets at least once annually and, like the NGA, adopts policy positions on issues relevant to its region.

Although the regional associations' activities regarding the federal government mirror the NGA's efforts in many ways, the strongest function of the regional associations appears to be the sharing of information of interest to the governors of a particular region. Although the NGA can provide general information regarding policy innovations that have been tried around the country, regional associations can facilitate more intensive cooperation on issues of unanimous concern to their members.

The regional associations lobby as well, and the positions they develop are likely to be stronger than those of larger associations because it is easier to reach a consensus among a smaller number of governors who share regional concerns. On issues like transportation funding, for example, the NGA can stake out a general position, but the major cleavages on this issue are regional. Therefore, the Southern governors, for example, are more likely to agree with their regional colleagues on federal policy options, and the regional associations provide an institutional means for developing and advocating stronger positions on such issues than can the NGA.

Although governors may sometimes offer the strongest representation for their respective state governments through regional associations, those associations also periodically develop positions on issues and then hand off the issues to the NGA for further, higher profile lobbying efforts. A staff member for one of the regional associations explained as follows:

> As an association, we work pretty closely with the National Governors' Association. In fact, when they're out on the lead on an issue, we try not to overlap, because it's just kind of a waste of resources. And a lot of times, what's happened in the past is we'll take an issue and get out in front and then the National Governors' Association will adopt it and carry it further from there. That's not uncommon. They will also defer to us on issues that are primarily [regional] in nature, where we obviously have a number of governors that are out in front.[21]

The regional associations perform other functions that, although often mundane, make governance in a particular region easier for governors. For example, a staff member of the Southern Governors' Association reported that that organization had recently reached an agreement on the particulars of transferring and sharing emergency equipment and personnel during natural disasters. By working out these details ahead of time, officials in, for example, Georgia will be able to come to the assistance of people in Florida without engaging in time-consuming negotiations regarding such transfers during the crisis itself. Similarly, the members of the Western Governors' Association have reached an agreement to notify one another when toxic waste is transferred across state lines. These sorts of communications among governors of a region are not the stuff of newspaper headlines, but they may benefit the citizens of those states in tangible ways.

From the standpoint of political theory, then, the regional governors associations are important because they provide the means for a slightly different form of representation of categorical state-governmental interests on a regional level. In addition, they demonstrate that regions, in addition to states, function as somewhat larger laboratories of democracy and can transmit regionally developed ideas into the federal policymaking arena. By helping coordinate public policies at the regional level, these organizations contribute to the overall maintenance of quality coordinated state governance in ways that help safeguard their interests vis-à-vis Washington.

SINGLE-ISSUE GOVERNORS' ASSOCIATIONS

Although it is difficult to determine their exact numbers today, there are or have been many single-issue associations that foster cooperation on categorical state-governmental interests. As we saw in the previous section, many of the regional governors' associations initially were formed to discuss one or a few policy questions facing those regions. Some, like the Council of Great Lakes Governors, even today still cooperate on a fairly limited set of policy questions. Other single-issue groups deserve some mention, however.

Several of the organizations that were later consolidated into the Western Governors' Association were formed around single issues. These included the Western Governors' Regional Energy Policy Office and the Federation of Rocky Mountain States, created in 1965 to examine issues related to public lands.[22] Another long-time single-issue governors' group still in existence today is the Interstate Oil and Gas Compact Commission (IOGCC). Based in Oklahoma City, the IOGCC represents the governors of the 36 states—29 members and 7 associate states—that produce virtually all the oil and natural gas in the United States. The commission was created in 1935 and serves as "the collective voice of member governors on oil and gas issues and advocates states' rights to govern petroleum resources within their borders." Through interstate cooperation and coordination of lobbying efforts in Washington, the commission attempts to influence national oil and gas policy to the benefit of member state governments.[23]

There are many other examples of interstate cooperation that are not intended to influence national decisionmaking.[24] Interstate compacts regarding matters like pollution control, electricity regulation, extradition, mutual aid in emergency services, the administration of cross-border school districts, and so forth are important to the governance of states but do not directly relate to the topic of this study.

INDIVIDUAL GOVERNORS' WASHINGTON OFFICES

Scholars of the intergovernmental lobby have written much about the activities of the associations within the intergovernmental lobby, but the individual Washington offices maintained by governors or state governments, counties, cities, and townships have received almost no scholarly attention,[25] and their existence is almost never noted in media coverage of state-federal issues.[26] This lack of attention is a major oversight, given that 35 governors currently maintain offices in the nation's capital, as do literally hundreds of individual counties, cities, townships, and other special districts.[27] Listed below are the states or governors with Washington offices as of February 2008:

Alaska	Kentucky	Ohio
Arizona	Louisiana	Oregon
Arkansas	Maryland	Pennsylvania
California	Massachusetts	Rhode Island
Connecticut	Michigan	South Carolina
Delaware	Minnesota	Texas
Florida	Nevada	Utah
Georgia	New Jersey	Vermont
Illinois	New Mexico	Virginia
Indiana	New York	Washington
Iowa	North Carolina	Wisconsin
Kansas	North Dakota	

(*Sources*: State Services Organization list of affiliates, http://www.sso.org/affiliates.htm; and list of Washington representatives found on NGA's website, http://www.nga.org.)

The relationships between the activities of the individual state offices, the national and regional associations, and state congressional delegations have received very little attention from political scientists, although they are the primary vehicle for the pursuit of particularistic state-governmental interests today.

Generalizations about state offices in Washington are difficult to make, and one's initial assumptions about the activities of these offices may be incorrect. For example, at the outset of this research, I assumed that the governors of states with large populations would be more likely to have Washington offices, but Alaska, Rhode Island, Delaware, Nevada, and several other states with small populations have maintained Washington offices for many years. I assumed that the larger states' offices would rely less on NGA for information and lobbying expertise, whereas smaller offices would rely more on NGA information for lack of information-gathering capacities of their own. This was true in some cases, but there was always more to the story than that. To be sure, the states with the largest Washington offices—California, New York, Texas, and Florida—often have their own sources of information and influence and therefore need not rely on NGA materials or staff. Indeed, news reports in 2004 indicated that the Republican governors of California, Florida, New York, and Texas had been "pooling their considerable influence to advance the interests of their states. . . . The alliance represents the first time in recent memory that the governors of the nation's four most populous states have entered into a formal agreement to jointly lobby members of Congress." [28] However, a number of states with small Washington staffs were also identified as being just as independent as some larger states. South Carolina's office was pointed out as an example by one informant. The director of that office "has a one- or two-person office, and she is as up to speed as—it's amazing. She's up to speed on all of these issues and is totally engaged and works with NGA, works with RGA [the Republican Governors' Association], but also works very closely with her agencies on specific stuff. . . . I think a lot of it is how much value your state capital places on the work that we do here. I mean, there are some offices that struggle for recognition back in the state." [29]

None of the state offices rely *solely* on NGA materials and staff support for reasons outlined above—the sometimes-debilitating generality of NGA policy positions—although states without offices in Washington are perhaps somewhat more reliant on them. A state government that has a good idea of its particular interests in a given piece of legislation has little to learn from general, bipartisan briefing materials that are directed at all the states. Most state offices reported receiving a good deal of their specific and detailed information from state agency employees back home. A staff member from a state office in Washington with nine staff members reported the following:

> NGA—frankly, we don't use them a whole lot. They do have staff that track [bills] and they do summaries, things like that. We always find that helpful. But we do not use NGA extensively. A lot of that has to do with the size of our staff . . . we have a big enough staff [that] we can track things ourselves, for the most part. And the policy side—because they have a research side of NGA as well as a policy side—the research side we've never really used at all. I've never requested information or things like that. Again, we usually just do it ourselves in this office.[30]

Even so, the director of another state office with a comparatively large Washington staff (six people) noted that "the NGA provides a lot of good analytic material on different issues, and I think that's helpful. We could produce it if we had to, probably, or our state agencies could help us produce it, but I'm glad they do it because it takes a big burden off us."[31] Thus, reliance on NGA materials and staff support does not seem to be a function simply of how large a staff a state office has.

A state with a large or well-placed (or both) congressional delegation has a greater opportunity to pursue its interests through direct appeals to those members and thus may not need to rely on lobbying through an association to pursue particularistic interests. For instance, in 1995, "Sen. Mark Hatfield's (R-Ore.) decision not to seek reelection put Alaska's two senators and one representative in line to take over key committee chairmanships, assuring the 'huge but sparsely populated state' will wield 'unprecedented clout' on Capitol Hill in many areas, including natural resources protection . . ."[32] On the other side of the coin, in 1992 a Florida newspaper reported that "the announced retirement of Florida's most senior member in Congress—the sixth of 19

House members to call it quits so far this year—has stirred a debate over how much political muscle the state can expect to flex on Capitol Hill after Election Day."[33]

Particularistic interests may also be advanced by killing or damping provisions of a bill in order to lessen its impact on the state. A former head of the State of Delaware's office recalled "an interstate-branch banking bill that passed Congress about a year ago, which he said 'was not the best bill for Delaware,' with its large banking community. The most [the state office] could do was get provisions added to lessen the possible impact on the state."[34] A staff member in another state office said that a common strategy is to "play a lot of defense, that's for sure. Probably some of the best things we've done have been the things that we've killed. . . . I think it's a little bit easier to kill something than to get it through [laughs]."[35]

DYNAMICS AMONG THE ELEMENTS OF THE GOVERNORS' LOBBY

The various associations and individual offices of the governors' lobby in Washington are organizationally distinct; however, in practice the lines between them are often blurred. Most staff members of governors' Washington offices (particularly directors) perform multiple roles in the organizations of the governors' lobby, a fact that both improves their prospects for successful lobbying and makes it difficult for the outside observer to determine exactly which interests are being pursued by a staff member at any given time.

For a governor who maintains a Washington office, the director of that office is the governor's primary contact with the NGA. States without Washington offices also have such a person back in their state capitals, but such a person is linked to the NGA primarily through phone calls, faxes, and conference calls rather than through the face-to-face daily interactions that characterize contact in the Hall of the States. Moreover, the director of a governor's Washington office is likely also to be the governor's contact person with the regional association(s) to which the governor belongs, particularly if those associations maintain Washington offices (as is the case with the Southern Governors' Association, the Western Governors' Association, and the Council of Northeastern Governors).

This role overlap leads to a great deal of interaction among staff members of governors' Washington offices as they represent their governors in various organizational contexts. One area in which this interaction is particularly apparent is the sharing of information among governors' Washington staffers. Anyone tracking and evaluating legislation with an eye toward influencing its final form needs to stay apprised of changes in the legislation as they occur in committee markups and floor amendments. Information about such changes is often difficult to get quickly. A staff member of one governor's office explained the resources her office uses to stay abreast of congressional activity, using the 1996 welfare-reform bill as an example:

> The welfare bill was kind of a real pain because it was this thick. Every version of it is this thick [holding her fingers about five inches apart]. So, the way the thing goes, you can't get the bill from the normal sources. You can't go to the [congressional] document room and say I'd like a copy of the welfare bill. They just— you can't get them. They're lucky to get them to the members. So, we rely on the National Governors' Association. They pull it off the computer normally, so we get a printout copy, and they make them available. We go get the printout copy, bring it back to our machine, and make two copies of it: one for us and one to ship to the state. And then we overnight it, and this goes on constantly. Sometimes we feel like we're just here to churn paper! It's just constant. So, you've got a bill like the welfare bill introduced. We go to the hearings. If we can't go we send an intern. We get the testimony. We stay on top of it from the very beginning. Again, NGA is an invaluable resource for this kind of thing. Something as big as welfare and Medicaid reform where it affects the state in the pocketbook, then you know you're going to have a weekly meeting on it [sponsored by NGA]. They have the health reps meeting. They have the welfare reps meeting. And they keep you on top of where things are going—who's trying to do what to whom. We always knew who the players were. And then you get summaries. We subscribe to just about everything here. We get CQ [*the Congressional Quarterly Weekly Report*], we get BNA [the Bureau of

National Affairs' daily publication], we get the [*Congressional*] *Monitor* every morning, we get [National Journal's] *CongressDaily*'s afternoon fax and morning fax. I mean, you know, we get just about everything they get on the Hill. It costs us a great deal of money to do this, but we have to have it. We now get House Action Reports, because it's the only place we can get a decent copy of the amendments on the House side. So, all of these pieces of paper help us track the legislation. We usually know where it's going.[36]

It should be clear by now that during the development of public policy, a given member of a governor's Washington staff may perceive "the opposition" to be Congress or the executive branch, governors and state governments of other regions, governors of the opposite party, or any governor or state government that, by increasing its share of federal money or other benefits, decreases the amount available to the staff member's state government. These perceptions, of course, correspond with the three sorts of state interest outlined in chapter 1. When one of these interests is being pursued, it will quickly become clear which groups of states have common interests at stake, and these common interests are the basis for interoffice cooperation.

When a universal state interest is at stake, chances for cooperation among all the offices are greatest, because potentially divisive matters of region, party, or a state's self-interest are not present. Thus, many staff members of governors' Washington offices told me that bipartisan cooperation among offices is frequent. Certain individuals in state offices located in the Hall of the States have built reputations for expertise in particular issue areas and are frequently consulted by staffers from other state offices. As the head of Mississippi's (now defunct) Washington office explained, "Rather than having to run all over the city to find out about a particular situation, if you just come up here and ask, 'Which one of the states has been working on this issue?' and go to that state's office, you can save yourself a month of research in 15 minutes."[37] Also within the Hall of the States, informal groups of staffers meet periodically to discuss particular policy areas. Another staffer explained, "There's an immigration policy group in the building so when I need to know information on immigration, I don't necessarily go to NGA; I go to the immigration policy [group]."[38] Even less formally, the director of one of the offices joked that "You can learn *a lot* just by walking around the building [the Hall of the States]. I sometimes call it management by walking around. [*Laughs.*] If you're out there in the hall and you see the people who are the Community Development Agencies, and their—one big concern of theirs has been LIHEAP [Low Income Home Energy Assistance Program] funding for low-income energy assistance. I mean, I can be out in the hall and you can find out a lot about what's going on in certain areas just from sort of hanging out."[39] On policy questions involving regional or partisan interests, cooperation may occur along these lines, with staffers from Republican offices working with other Republicans (and likewise for Democrats) or working with other staffers from one's region.

When particularistic interests are concerned, the offices are most likely to work alone. With much at stake for individual state governments, the director of a southeastern state's Washington office explained the relations among governors' staff in the Hall of the States as follows:

> You've pretty much got your colleagues in the building, so, we've got issues that we differ greatly and we're in major turf battles with Virginia. We've got some issues where we work very cooperatively with Virginia on [*sic*], so it just depends—it's issue by issue.
> . . . The camaraderie is that there are very few people that understand what we do, and that understand the pressures and balancing act of dealing with your state capital and dealing with the White House and your congressional delegation—the intricacies of the federal government. So, from colleague to colleague there is a tremendous amount of support, but we are all competitors. There is no doubt about it. Sometimes we're on a big Democratic team versus a big Republican team, and sometimes it's small states versus large states, and sometimes it's everybody else versus California, you know. It depends on the issues. But, by and large, the easiest way to describe it is that we are all professional, we are all colleagues, and we are all incredibly competitive. When the National Governors' Association meets twice a year, your job is to maximize your boss's attendance, and that may mean working

very cooperatively with the staffer whose chair—whose boss is chairing the committee, in order to get your boss recognized on C-SPAN to ask questions or to make a presentation or whatever. So, you've got to have a very friendly atmosphere, but there is no doubt in anybody's mind that we are all very competitive.[40]

Thus, there is a great deal of interaction—both cooperative and competitive—among the state offices themselves, which provides a good deal of "lubrication" to all levels of the governors' lobby.

Modes of Gubernatorial Lobbying in Washington

How does one measure the influence of a given lobbying effort on a piece of legislation? To assess gubernatorial influence in this research, I have relied on the judgments of regular participants and observers of the legislative process—members of Congress and their staffs, governors and their Washington staffs, and journalists and other chroniclers of the legislative process—as they discuss several policymaking episodes. Such assessments, whether gathered through research or personal interviews, are one of the few ways to determine the influence of groups and individuals on the legislative process. By liberally quoting a large number of informants, I have tried to provide enough of what Donald Haider has called "the nuances that accompany any study of influence attribution."[41] Although self-reported accounts of influence can sometimes be impressionistic and self-serving, if a variety of participants or observers agree that a particular person or group was influential, that assessment is likely valid. Moreover, self-reports of influence may not be biased in the manner one assumes. For example, interest groups often downplay their influence in front of certain audiences while exaggerating it for others. Washington staff members of governors' offices often argue that their concerns are frequently ignored by members of Congress but also that when governors talk loudly enough, Congress listens. In a similar manner, members of Congress and their staffs may deny or readily admit to acting at the behest of an organized interest, depending on their audience. Context therefore is important for understanding a claim of influence, and the case studies that follow provide as much context as possible to aid the reader in evaluating the evidence of state officials' influence in the federal lawmaking process.

The conditions under which gubernatorial lobbying can be successful have changed over the past decade. For governors to be effective in Washington today, they must help members of Congress and the executive branch understand how federal programs will affect state governments and try to encourage federal decisionmakers that national problems can best be addressed by giving state governments money and leeway in carrying out federal programs. Although governors are still quite occupied with maintaining or increasing the levels of federal funding their states receive, they take a broader approach. One statement of this new approach was offered by then-Governor Bill Clinton (D-Ark.) following the passage of welfare reform in 1988. In describing the conditions under which governors are likely to be able to work with and influence members of Congress, Governor Clinton stated, "Whenever you've got a problem where there's a core American value that Republicans and Democrats can agree on, and which you know will have to be addressed at the federal level, and where the federal government cannot solve the problem without heavy involvement from the states, I think there is this opportunity."[42] Clinton's statement usefully identifies both the limits of and the potential for gubernatorial involvement in national policy-making, and it indicates the contribution governors are best situated to make: insight into the sorts of policies state governments are administratively capable of carrying out and the sorts of policies that are already working in one or more states.

In rare instances, governors have actually attended congressional mark-up sessions, giving them direct participation in writing legislation. Prior to the passage of the 1988 welfare-reform law (the Family Support Act of 1988), Clinton, as Arkansas governor and NGA chairman, "sat with the [House] Ways and Means staff during subcommittee mark-up and answered questions about how specific provisions would affect the states. According to a respondent, 'Bill Clinton sat at the table with the committee. They ran all the amendments by him, they discussed what the governors would and would not find acceptable in terms of the amendments that were being offered . . . [and] the bill that was produced had tremendous gubernatorial support.'"[43] As discussed in chapter 2, such involvement may also occur with governors acting on their own behalf rather than as representatives of an association. A staff member for the House subcommittee in which the 1996 welfare-reform bill was written confirmed this notion regarding the role of governors in that piece of legislation:

> Don't discount the role of individual governors. Thompson [R-Wisc.]. Engler [R-Mich.]. Bush [R-Tex.]. Wilson [R-Cal.], certainly. Even Chiles [D-Fla.] on some issues, and Carper [D-Del.]. Carper had a pretty big role in this, especially since he was a Democrat. He has a close relationship with [Rep. Clayton] Shaw [R-Fla., chairman of the House subcommittee that wrote the welfare reform bill]. [Rep. Michael] Castle [R-Del.], who was a former governor, had a big role to play. I mean, individual governors had a lot of clout. So, that's distinct from sort of the larger Governors' Association.[44]

The day-to-day lobbying activities of the NGA and the individual state offices are given direction by the weekly Monday morning meeting at the Hall of the States in Washington. In general, the NGA's director of state–federal relations begins the meeting by outlining the coming week's legislative activity on matters of concern to state governments—hearings, mark-ups, floor votes, and so forth. The NGA also invites officials and staff members from Congress and executive agencies to speak at the meeting in order to explain their positions on pending policy decisions and answer questions from gubernatorial staff members. As the NGA's director of state–federal relations explains, "These are not feely-touchy meetings. They're pretty nasty questions."[45] Staff members of governors who do not have Washington offices can participate in such meetings via conference call; it was surprising to find that several staff members of governors' Washington offices believe that states without Washington offices were not necessarily at a disadvantage as long as they were vigilant in keeping up with events in Washington from their state capitals. As a past state–federal relations officer for Rhode Island noted, "The fact that we don't have a Washington office doesn't mean that we ignore Washington. With faxes and telecommunications and one-hour plane rides we have good access to our congressional delegation as well as involvement with the National Governors' Association."[46]

Although NGA has about a dozen lobbyists of its own, James Martin, longtime director of state–federal relations, believed that the governors themselves are the best lobbyists: "I consider all of them my lobbyists for NGA. . . . 85% of my lobbying is back to governors,"[47] who then contact members of their state congressional delegations, personally or through staff. "Just sending a resolution to Congress is like mailing a dead letter. . . . I'm constantly lobbying the governors to follow through. . . . After all, the members of Congress aren't going to pay attention to me, but they'll pay attention to their governors."[48] Lobbying "by governors" is most often lobbying by their staffs, although governors themselves may send letters and make phone calls to members of Congress or the executive branch at important junctures to indicate the importance of the state-governmental interests involved. In a similar manner, governors may testify before congressional committees. NGA staff also testify occasionally, and an interesting and humorous exchange between a member of Congress and the NGA's Martin at one hearing shed light on the nature of governors' testimony on behalf of the NGA:

> Mr. Martin: Rarely does NGA staff testify. It is the governors that are the lobbyists and the testifiers. . . . We have 48 [governors] signed up to be at our annual meeting in Vermont in a week and a half, and hardly any of them are leaving their States right now because they are going to be gone for a week. But I will just summarize the things that I have heard. I have been with NGA for 29 years as their legislative counsel and director of State–Federal Relations. And my job is to lobby Governors to come here and testify and do what they say they care about. I am, this morning, failing because I couldn't catch a couple.

> Mr. [Christopher] Shays [R-Conn.]: When the Governors come, are they just saying what you give them to say?

> Mr. Martin: They say what they believe in and then I remind them what they believe in.[49]

When governors testify on the positions of the NGA, they generally make it clear that they are speaking on behalf of that organization to avoid misunderstandings about whose position is being articulated. Governors may act on their own behalf or on behalf of some larger group or association of governors, and these various configurations may cause confusion. As an NGA staffer explained,

> Just recently there was this hearing on Superfund, and I got a call from congressional staff and they said "We have invited Governor So-and-So, and that governor has accepted and is going to be here testifying on Superfund. Will that be an NGA statement?" And I said, no, that will be an individual governor's statement. If you want an NGA statement, you come to NGA and we will get you the best witness on that subject. We have lead governors on certain subjects. We have a committee structure set up. There are obvious spokesmen, or women, from NGA on various subjects. . . . If it's going to be an NGA statement, it's one that we would write, first of all, and make sure the governor delivering the statement was comfortable with it, so that he or she could honestly represent the consensus view.[50]

Governors state their affiliations at the outset when testifying on Capitol Hill in order to minimize confusion.

CASE STUDIES OF GUBERNATORIAL INFLUENCE IN WASHINGTON

Donald Haider's 1974 book *When Governments Come to Washington* presents case studies of intergovernmental lobbying between 1964 and 1973 during an era of expanding federal grant money to states. Anne Marie Cammisa's 1995 *Governments as Interest Groups* extended Haider's inquiry into an era of shrinking federal grants, assessing how state officials' influence had changed under these new budgetary circumstances. The case studies below further extend the analysis into an era where devolution of major federal policy became a reality (with the 1996 welfare-reform law), although developments since then have certainly not been in a consistently pro-state direction.

My purpose here is not to present comprehensive original narratives detailing the passage of every piece of legislation important to state governments during this period but, rather, to indicate the ways that gubernatorial involvement in their passage continues to function as a political safeguard of federalism. Because the number of *major* legislative episodes the governors' lobby has been involved in since 1995 is relatively small, the case studies below also call attention to the more typical form gubernatorial influence in Washington takes—there are many *minor* alterations of legislation for which governors lobby that individually make few headlines but that collectively represent ongoing, highly focused, and often-successful representation of state-governmental interests.

It is important to keep in mind that these examples are successes for the intergovernmental lobby in the sense that the state officials saw their key policy preferences embodied in measures passed by Congress and signed by the president. These policies are not singled out here because they have achieved all of their goals and produced salutary social outcomes but because they exemplify ways that state officials used the processes involved in this safeguard of federalism to influence legislation as it wended its way through Congress.

Reauthorization of the Safe Drinking Water Act, 1995–1996

Subnational governments bear a large responsibility for carrying out various sorts of environmental protection in the United States,[51] and, as such, state governments' interests are affected by decisions made at the national level regarding clean air, clean water, toxic waste, and so forth. Because states implement most federal environmental policy, their administrative state interests are heavily affected by decisions made in Washington, and their legalistic interests are affected by the constraints federal law imposes on states' authority to regulate, for example, nitrogen oxide emissions. Because environmental protection is often expensive to carry out, the fiscal interests of state and local administrators may also be affected.

The 1996 reauthorization of the Safe Drinking Water Act of 1974 was a policymaking episode in which state and local governments cooperated to win for themselves increased flexibility and authority to monitor the quality of drinking water within their jurisdictions. The episode is instructive because of the clarity with which the states' legalistic and administrative interests were adversely affected by the existing federal law, which state and local officials convinced Congress to change. It is

also instructive as an example of governors' success in seeing their preferences reflected in national policy as a result of their lobbying efforts.

The original Safe Drinking Water Act was passed "in the salad days
of environmentalism by a Congress willing to use federal muscle to stop
all exposure to pollution. Through the drinking water law, Congress
sought to close the gap it left when it passed the Clean Water Act,
which targeted pollution in rivers and oceans but didn't address the
safety of the tap water used in homes and businesses."[52] The law prescribed specific technologies local water treatment plants had to use
and standards of safety they had to meet.

The 1974 act was amended in 1986 by congressional Democrats upset
with the lack of attention the Environmental Protection Agency (EPA)
under the Reagan administration had given to drinking water quality.
According to an NGA lobbyist on environmental issues, the 1986 amendments to the act were "written at a time when Anne Gorsuch was
running EPA and the Congress didn't trust her and they said 'We're
going to make sure that she does it, by God.'"[53] The 1986 changes to the
act were designed to force the EPA to take action by setting strict
requirements for controlling a host of chemical and biological contaminants. The EPA was thereafter required to add 25 new contaminants
every three years to the list of substances local water systems were
required to test for, and by 1995, the list included 111 substances. Moreover, the law required water systems to monitor and regulate these
contaminants at the level of the most affordable technology for a large
regional water system, which was defined as one serving 500,000 people
or more. However, only about 10 systems that size existed; hence, the
vast majority of water systems were left to find ways to adopt technologies deemed affordable for much larger systems and to monitor for a
growing list of substances, regardless of whether those substances were
likely to exist in a particular system's water supply. As a staff member
of the Senate Environment and Public Works Committee explained,
"The Drinking Water Act wasn't working the way they'd revamped
it in the '80s. . . . People weren't able to comply. The cost of the
technology was too expensive, the monitoring—they just couldn't do it,
and people weren't getting healthy water, and the public health wasn't

being protected. As soon as someone whose responsibility it is to protect public health can't comply, something's wrong."[54] From the standpoint of state and local groups, the old "command and control" form of federal environmental regulations had outlived its usefulness. In the words of the NGA lobbyist quoted above:

> What we believe is that the nation has made enormous progress in the last 25 years in the 1970s model for environmental legislation, where EPA sets a standard or a technology requirement, and a prescriptive process on what has to be done by pollution sources. . . . And frankly we came a long way with that. Twenty-five years ago when states were unsophisticated and lacked resources, that model made some sense, I would think. Today it doesn't. At least in the environmental area, states have ten times more personnel engaged in natural resources and environmental protection than the federal government does. We're far closer to the problem, and perhaps more importantly, the problems that remain to be addressed are very site-specific, so you need solutions devised close to home.[55]

State (and local) governments' fiscal and administrative interests were clearly harmed by the law. The federal government mandated compliance with national drinking water standards by requiring the use of expensive monitoring technologies without providing funding that would make the technologies affordable to water systems. Local water systems were required to test for all substances identified by the EPA, regardless of whether they were likely to exist in that area, which limited the flexibility those administrators had to focus on local needs. The state interests perceived by the governors were outlined in the NGA's policy position on safe drinking water legislation adopted at its winter meeting in 1995:

> The Governors . . . are troubled by obstacles to state compliance with federal environmental requirements. First, the Governors note a rapidly increasing disparity between demands placed on states and localities and the resources provided to meet those demands. Governors lack the flexibility to implement them in accordance with state and local public health priorities. In addition, federal programs must provide adequate resources for state program

management and the water supply community's capital needs to comply with new requirements. Second, the values of risk-based rulemaking and risk assessment principles have not been adequately incorporated into the law. This had led to costs that outweigh benefits and to requirements that are not justified by the risks to public health or the environment. The Safe Drinking Water Act program is an unfortunate illustration of these two obstacles to state compliance. The challenge is particularly difficult now because implementation of the Safe Drinking Water Act must compete not only with other environmental programs required under, for example, the Clean Air Act, the Clean Water Act, and the Resource Conservation and Recovery Act, but also with increasing demands for health care, education, correctional facilities, and other social programs at a time when most state budgets are shrinking or growing only modestly.[56]

The final sentence of this passage is particularly interesting as an example of the difference in congressional and gubernatorial perceptions of state-governmental interests. Given their electoral incentives and the piecemeal nature of the committee-based congressional policymaking process, members of Congress are unlikely to evaluate potential policies on the basis of their aggregate effects on the fiscal health of state governments. Governors and their state administrators, on the other hand, must look for ways to meet a multitude of federal requirements while attempting to avoid resorting to budgetary triage for allocating scarce state resources.

In light of these state interests, the governors recommended the following revisions to the Safe Drinking Water Act:

- A revised process for selecting contaminants for regulation based on their occurrence in drinking water and health effects data, as opposed to existing requirements for EPA to regulate specific contaminants on a schedule mandated in the statute
- A revised process for setting standards to ensure that EPA considers risk reduction benefits and costs when setting federal drinking water standards
- Enhanced state authority to provide monitoring relief to systems for contaminants that do not actually occur in water at levels of public health concern

- A new drinking water state revolving loan fund for states to provide loans to communities for drinking water infrastructure projects
  (this type of loan program had been successful under the Clean
  Water Act)
- Gubernatorial authority to transfer funds between the drinking
  water revolving loan fund and the clean water revolving loan
  fund depending upon state and local priorities.
- Funding authorization for state management of drinking water
  programs, beginning at $100 million.[57]

This statement's references to state authority, cost, and flexibility to act
in accordance with state priorities underscore the state-governmental
interests that governors perceived during this policymaking episode.

In lobbying for changes to the act, an effort that began in 1992, the
governors coordinated their efforts with a group of ten state and local
groups, known as the State and Local Drinking Water Coalition. These
groups were the National League of Cities, the U.S. Conference of Mayors,
the National Association of Counties, the NCSL, the Association of State
Drinking Water Administrators, the Association of Metropolitan Water
Agencies, the American Water Works Association, the National Water
Resources Association, and the National Rural Water Association. The
Safe Drinking Water Act reauthorization is thus a notable example of
the governors' lobby working with other state and local groups to see
its policy preferences embodied in law.

The bill's central features mirrored those in the NGA's proposal. The
Senate bill required the EPA to certify that the costs of any new water
contaminant standards did not exceed their health benefits, replacing
the requirement under the existing law that contaminants be removed
to the extent possible using the best available technology, regardless of
cost. It repealed the requirement that the EPA establish standards for 25
new contaminants every three years, allowing states to set less stringent
monitoring requirements than those outlined in federal law as long as
those water supplies met federal health standards. Small water systems—
those serving fewer than 10,000 people—would be eligible for exemptions from federal requirements. The Senate bill also required EPA
drinking water standards to take into account the potential health risks

of contaminants on vulnerable populations, such as children, the elderly, and people with immune deficiency disorders. And in a provision favored by state and local groups, the bill established and funded a $7-billion state revolving loan fund from which states could draw.

Following House and Senate passage of similar bills and a week of conference negotiations, an agreement was reached that passed overwhelmingly in the House and unanimously in the Senate. Largely overshadowed at the time by the landmark welfare-reform bill President Clinton had three days earlier agreed to sign, the reauthorization of the Safe Drinking Water Act became law on August 6, 1996. The final bill included the right-to-know provisions favored by Democrats, the Clinton administration, and environmentalists. Large water systems were required to mail plainly worded information to customers annually, whereas systems serving fewer than 10,000 customers could be exempted from the requirement by governors, so long as they notified the public they would not be mailing the reports, made them available on request, and printed the information in local newspapers.[58] Water systems were also required to inform their customers if they failed to comply with safe levels of exposure to contaminants or failed to follow the proper treatment or testing techniques called for by law.

The consumer information provision had been opposed by the state and local coalition over concerns that the requirement "would cost millions of dollars to administer and might cause suppliers of water to make misguided decisions about controlling pollution based more on adverse publicity than on demonstrable risks to public health."[59] Because consumers might misperceive the risks of low levels of contaminants in their drinking water, the coalition's position was that the right-to-know provision might do more harm than good. In the end, the coalition did not get what it wanted, and a National League of Cities tally of the positive and negative aspects of the bill counted the right-to-know requirement among "what cities lost."[60]

In general, the reauthorized drinking water law contained the basic framework of the Senate bill. The law established new EPA procedures that would require more detailed findings regarding a contaminant before issuing a regulation, including the requirement to determine that the contaminant affects public health, that it is present or is likely to be present in drinking water, and that the regulation would meaningfully reduce health risks. From state and local groups' standpoint, these changes would prevent the EPA from requiring water suppliers to monitor their water for substances that might not be present and to remove substances from water even if there was no proof that doing so would reduce public health risks. The law also eliminated the requirement that the EPA add 25 new contaminants to the list water suppliers were compelled to monitor.

In determining the costs and benefits of drinking water regulations, the EPA was directed to use the best available science and the most up-to-date data. The law requires the EPA to publish a cost–benefit analysis of most of the regulations it proposes. This analysis must include the health benefits of the regulation, an examination of the uncertainties associated with the regulation, and studies that examine the public health threat of the contaminant in question. Under the law, the EPA is permitted to set a standard below the highest feasible level of purity if it determines through cost–benefit analysis that the benefits of the higher standard do not justify the costs.

The law also imposed a number of requirements on states to ensure the quality of water suppliers in their states. States were required to have in place legal requirements to ensure that all new community water systems beginning operations after October 1, 1999, demonstrate technical expertise, managerial competence, and financial resources to comply with all drinking water regulations when they begin operations. Under the law, each state must also prepare and submit to the EPA a list of existing water systems that have a history of failing to meet such standards.

Finally, the law authorized $7.6 billion for a state-administered revolving loan fund. States are generally required to make a 20 percent match of their federal allotments under the program. As proposed by the NGA, governors were given the authority to consolidate administration of the drinking water loan fund with other similar state loan funds. States were also allowed to reserve up to one-third of their annual allotment and to combine this money with funds provided under the Clean Water Act. This provision gave governors the flexibility to spend federal funds as they saw fit, promoting states' universal fiscal state interests (as defined in chapter 1). The law delegated the development of guidelines and regulations necessary to implement the loan fund, and lobbyists for the governors were involved at that stage as well. In March 1997, a staff member for the Senate Environment and Public Works Committee reported that the EPA "just put out the guidance on how states should run their state revolving loan fund, and in putting that guidance together, they had states in the room and helping to put it together, so they're invested in it as well. And also, having the people in the room, they can't come back and say they're not responding to us, when they helped put it together. I think that the states are realizing—I mean, they've got a good deal of clout."[61]

In the end, all of the interested parties got some of what they wanted from the bill. But in particular, the state and local groups set the tone for the legislation and were able to change the provisions of the old law that caused them the most problems. The onerous monitoring requirements placed on water systems were replaced by procedures designed to allow water systems to monitor and regulate for contaminants that are actually present in their water supply and to do so in a manner that allows systems to use scarce resources where they are needed most to protect public health. As such, the governors got nearly all of what they wanted from the new safe drinking water law, taking advantage of the political context of 1996 to hit the fiscal trifecta vis-à-vis the federal government: federal money, flexibility in determining how to spend it, and freedom from costly and restrictive federal mandates. Political scientist Joseph Zimmerman has called the 1996 Safe Drinking Water Act amendments the most important example of Congress reversing federal preemption of states because of its effect of "reducing significantly expenditures to improve drinking water quality."[62]

Although the politics surrounding the passage of the new drinking water law did not test the limits of gubernatorial influence against a recalcitrant Congress—in part because of the eagerness of members of Congress to avoid having to explain to voters that fall why they had opposed safe drinking water—the law could have been reauthorized in a number of different ways, but it was done according to the blueprint drawn up by the NGA and other state and local groups. The most superficial test of influence—comparing the NGA's policy before the passage of the law with the law itself—reveals remarkable similarity between the two. More subtle indications have also been presented here that governors participated in the national policymaking process and designed a new law that attracted the votes of all but 30 members of Congress.

Welfare Reform, 1995–1996

In the policymaking effort that culminated with the signing of the Personal Responsibility and Work Opportunity Reconciliation Act of 1996, the nation's governors acted in various combinations to put a welfare-reform proposal on the congressional agenda in response to a president's general call for reform. The governors recommended policy provisions to lawmakers, worked closely with members of Congress, and negotiated the political shoals of a presidential election year to keep attention focused on the bill. As was true during Congress's more limited welfare-reform efforts in the 1988 Family Support Act, substantial gubernatorial participation was once again invited by members of Congress, although this time Republican governors participated disproportionately in negotiations with Congress, at least initially. Moreover, the 1995–96 welfare-reform effort was only part of a larger reform agenda pursued by congressional Republicans following their capture of both houses of Congress in the November 1994 elections.

After the 1994 elections, an intimate relationship was forged between a group of Republican governors and the Republican congressional leadership. Although *all* governors ultimately joined together to endorse a detailed welfare-reform proposal in early 1996, the initial outlines of the reform effort were drawn by Republican governors like Tommy Thompson and John Engler, who had made a name for themselves as welfare reformers in their respective states, and by Republican leaders of Congress eager to replicate the results of these state reforms on a national level. The welfare-reform effort of 1995–96 thus took place against a backdrop of complex and shifting relationships between President Bill Clinton, congressional leaders, and governors of both parties. The substantial participation of various subsets of governors in the writing of the law cannot be understood without recourse to the typology of state-governmental interests presented in chapter 1, as the initial versions of the welfare-reform bill appeared driven by partisan interests of governors participating in its formulation and later by universal state interests reflected in an NGA policy position on welfare adopted at the governors' 1996 midwinter meeting.

The 1995–96 round of welfare reform stemmed from Bill Clinton's 1992 campaign promise to "end welfare as we know it." Because the domestic agenda of the first two years of Clinton's presidency was devoted largely to an attempt to get a health care bill through Congress, there was little time for other major legislative efforts. The Clinton administration released a detailed welfare-reform proposal on June 14, 1994, but Democratic congressional leaders showed little enthusiasm for the measure, which proposed a two-year limit on the receipt of benefits under the Aid to Families with Dependent Children (AFDC) program and sought to improve on the modest successes that the 1988 welfare-reform effort had in putting welfare recipients to work.[63] Several committees held hearings on the measure, but no other action was taken in 1994.

In the summer of 1994, congressional Republicans embraced welfare reform as the third plank of the Contract with America, which constituted the electoral platform of most of the Republican candidates for the House of Representatives in 1994. The contract, devised by Rep. Newt Gingrich (R-Ga.) and other prominent House Republicans, pledged that if Republicans gained control of the House in 1994, a vote would be held on each contract item within the first 100 days of the 104th Congress.[64] Republicans did indeed take back the House (and the Senate) and, intent on keeping their word, began hearings on welfare reform during the week of January 9, 1995. Gubernatorial involvement in welfare reform began that week as well, although in a different form than was seen in the Safe Drinking Water Act case study. Instead of action by all governors acting through the NGA, "it was a series of closed door meetings among influential governors that changed the face of the welfare plan. Eventually, a deal was struck between the House GOP leadership and GOP Govs. John Engler of Michigan, Tommy G. Thompson of Wisconsin and William F. Weld of Massachusetts. The three governors, representing the Republican Governors' Association, essentially offered to accept limited federal funding for welfare and related social services over the next five years in return for unprecedented state control over the programs."[65]

• • •

The initial House Republican bill proposed ending the federal guarantee of cash assistance to low-income individuals and giving states broad discretion to determine eligibility for new state-run social services programs, which would be paid for in part by a federal block grant. Most recipients would be required to work for their benefits and would be eligible to receive them for only five years. No federal funds could be used to provide welfare benefits for children born within 10 months of the date a family received welfare benefits. No federal funds could be used to provide benefits for children born out of wedlock to a mother under the age of 18. Finally, most legal immigrants who were noncitizens would be ineligible for Supplemental Security Income (SSI), cash welfare, funds provided by the new block grant, Medicaid, and food stamps. Overall, the House bill would have saved an estimated $62.1 billion over five years.[68] The bill, HR 4, passed on March 24, 1995, by a vote of 234–199, almost entirely along party lines.[67]

The Senate version of the bill moderated these provisions somewhat, in some cases giving states the *option* to curtail benefits for particular populations rather than mandating it. It retained the general form of the House bill, a social services block grant for state governments to spend with some discretion in place of the existing system of direct federal payments to individuals. Whereas the House bill had cleared that chamber in short measure, the Senate version of HR 4 bogged down because of objections from both Republicans and Democrats, particularly over the precise nature of the block grant funding formula, on the questions of whether to allow states to provide benefits for children born out of wedlock or for children born while the mother was receiving welfare benefits (the so-called "family cap"), over child care provisions, and over so-called maintenance-of-effort requirements that state governments continue to spend a specified amount of their own funds on social services annually.

Gubernatorial involvement in welfare reform continued along partisan lines, with Democratic governors largely looking on from the sidelines while GOP governors traveled frequently to Washington to meet with congressional leaders. As the Senate prepared to debate its bill on the floor, the outgoing chair of the NGA, Gov. Howard Dean (D-Vt.), warned, "We need to see the details. I am very nervous about what is going on in Congress."[68] In contrast, incoming NGA chair Tommy Thompson was privy to the details of the plan than Dean apparently knew little about. At the opening news conference of the NGA's summer meeting, Thompson reported that Senator Dole "had assured him that the revised welfare bill Dole will bring up next week will have enough funding to guarantee every state at least as much money as it has now and to provide additional funds for fast-growing states."[69] Despite the reservations of many Democratic governors, a week before the Senate voted on their welfare plan, Governor Michael Leavitt of Utah, chairman of the RGA (and future Secretary of Health and Human Services during President George W. Bush's second term), pledged that organization's strong support for the bill: "This welfare package needs to pass. . . . This is a formula that the vast majority of states will feel good about."[70]

Following floor debate, the Senate bill passed on September 19 by a vote of 87–12, a vote whose lopsidedness belied the remaining differences of opinion on the measure—differences that would complicate the conference negotiations with the House. Further complicating matters were the resignation of Senate Finance Committee Chairman Robert Packwood (R-Ore.) on ethics charges and the simultaneous inclusion of welfare-reform measures in the budget reconciliation packages in the works in each house. Congressional Republicans hoped to include the savings from welfare reform in their budget packages and were including the financing elements of welfare overhaul in their reconciliation bills as well, creating a two-track welfare-reform effort. GOP leaders saw the reconciliation bill as a potential fallback for welfare reform in the event that the free-standing bill failed.

GOP governors' access to congressional leaders continued, and in late September, Governor Engler, chairman of the RGA's welfare task force, "presented GOP senators with the governors' final wish list before the negotiators convened to fashion a welfare legislation conference report."[71] The two houses needed to resolve key disagreements over what sorts of social services the block grant to states should fund; what maintenance-of-effort requirement to impose on states, if any; whether to prohibit states from giving benefits to children born to mothers who are unwed or receiving welfare benefits, or to give states the option of doing so; and whether to deny benefits to legal immigrants permanently or for the first five years they were in the United States. These disagreements were generally resolved in a manner consistent with the more moderate Senate bill.

On October 27, Democrats in the Senate successfully used the Senate's "Byrd Rule" (named for Sen. Robert C. Byrd) to strike down the key welfare-reform provisions of the reconciliation bill.[72] Democrats used the rule to remove what they felt were the harshest items in the welfare bill, although Republicans countered that in doing so Democrats had gutted the bill. The question turned out to be academic when later, on December 6, President Clinton vetoed the budget reconciliation bill of which welfare reform was a part, in effect vetoing one of the two tracks of welfare-reform legislation (and also leading to a shutdown of the federal government for want of operating funds).

Republican governors had been involved in these budget talks as well, by invitation of Speaker of the House Newt Gingrich. Governor Engler and three other GOP governors were invited to sit in on budget negotiations "to make sure the final agreement gives governors enough flexibility and freedom to efficiently run welfare and other programs. 'If we fail to get this deficit disaster under control now, we will never do so,' Gingrich said in an address to the [RGA]. 'We're going to need the help of the governors. It's impossible to balance the budget if you keep all the red tape and power in Washington.'"[73] Again, Democratic governors were nowhere in sight.

Although the conference committee had agreed on a free-standing version of welfare reform as well, Clinton had threatened to veto it as well and did so on January 9, 1996, describing the bill as "burdened with deep budget cuts and structural changes that fall short of real reform."[76]

• • •

Despite the flurry of Republican gubernatorial involvement in developing the welfare-reform proposal in early 1995, the governors as a whole, working through NGA, were unable to agree among themselves on a welfare-reform proposal to present to Congress. As one governor recalled later, "Throughout the course of 1995, as you wrestled here in

Washington with what should be an appropriate welfare reform policy for our Nation, we, as Governors, were wrestling with what we should recommend to you; and we struggled unsuccessfully throughout the course of the last year."[75] The bipartisan spirit that had marked NGA proceedings in the past seemed to have disappeared, and "it didn't take long for spurned Democrats to diagnose an institutional crisis at NGA and to suggest the venerable organization might not survive."[76]

When Republican Tommy Thompson took over the chairmanship of the NGA in the summer of 1995, he pledged to restore the bipartisan nature of NGA proceedings, but no immediate attempts to mend the partisan rifts among governors were made and the institutional presence of the NGA continued to be obscured in Washington by that of the RGA. The situation changed in February 1996 at the winter meeting of the NGA, when Chairman Thompson convinced the governors that if there were to be any reform of welfare and Medicaid, two of the governors' top priorities, governors would have to present a united front to Congress and the president in the form of specific proposals. At the meeting, the governors agreed unanimously to policy proposals on welfare reform and Medicaid reform. The governors hoped to link the two reform plans and enact them in tandem as part of a comprehensive reworking of existing state-federal programs for the poor. Although congressional Republicans initially supported this idea, growing criticism of the contentious Medicaid reforms led the leadership to separate the two reform measures in July, and as a result, Medicaid reform went no further that year.

The NGA's welfare-reform proposal began by listing several general principles of welfare reform endorsed by the governors:

> Welfare must be temporary and linked to work; both parents must support their children; and child care must be available to enable low-income families with children to work. Additionally, we believe that block grants should be entitlements to states and enable states broad discretion in the design of their own programs based upon mutually agreed upon goals. We also believe that states should have access to supplementary matching funds for their cash assistance programs during periods of economic downturn.[77]

The governors supported the broad outlines of Congress's free-standing welfare-reform bill that had been vetoed by President Clinton in January, but they noted a number of changes that would need to be made to win their support. The NGA policy proposal continued as follows: "The conference agreement on HR 4, the Personal Responsibility and Work Opportunity Act, incorporated many of these elements, but we also believe further changes must be made to create a sound and workable welfare-reform bill. The National Governors' Association would support the HR 4 conference agreement with the changes listed below." The policy proposal went on to list about 25 changes to the HR 4 conference agreement that would render the plan acceptable to the governors. The most important of these provisions were as follows:

- An additional $4 billion for states for child care services, raising the $11 billion proposed in the conference agreement to $15 billion over seven years
- Flexibility for state governments in meeting the work requirements imposed by the bill; the conference bill decreased a state's block grant funds if it failed to move people into work activities, and the governors wanted a broader range of activities to count as "work" than did the congressional proposal
- The addition of $1 billion to the existing $1 billion contingency fund in the conference bill that would provide extra funds for state welfare programs during recessions
- Giving cash "performance bonuses" to state governments that exceeded specified targets for moving people into jobs and for reducing out-of-wedlock births.
- Giving states the *option* to restrict benefits for additional children born while a family is on welfare (the family cap), rather than prohibiting them from giving such benefits
- Allowing states to exempt 20 percent of their welfare caseload from the five-year time limit on welfare benefits, rather than the 10 percent allowed by the conference bill
- Giving states the option of receiving foster care, adoption assistance, and independent living federal funding as a capped entitlement and putting other child welfare programs and child abuse prevention

programs into a block grant; under a capped entitlement, the
states would get a fixed amount of money but would have to
cover all eligible recipients; under a block grant, states could spend
the money as they see fit; requirement that states maintain effort at
100 percent based on state spending in the year prior to accepting
the capped entitlement (i.e., states could not reduce the amount
they contributed to their programs); requirement that states maintain
protections and standards under then-current law

- Retention of food stamps and school lunch programs as uncapped
entitlements but acceptance of the provision in the Senate bill to
fund food stamps through a block grant.[78]

The NGA proposal took no position on the politically divisive matter of
whether to deny benefits to legal immigrants. In general, the proposal
endorsed some of the more moderate provisions of the Senate reform
bill that were not included in the conference bill and added several
others that served a number of universal state-governmental interests,
such as flexibility, predictability in the receipt of federal funds, and
assurances that state governments would not bear the full weight of
increased demands for social services during economic recessions. The
governors' proposal clearly reflected the universal state interest of budgetary predictability sought by governors. One observer noted that,
"The governors' success in reaching a tentative bipartisan agreement on
such a package, after earlier efforts at bipartisanship had failed, stems
largely from their own governance dilemmas, notably their need to be
able to plan budgets that meet state balanced budget requirements."[79]
And as Governor Thompson explained shortly after the NGA policy
was approved, "We are asking [Congress] to give us the flexibility to
design our own programs and the guaranteed funding we need at appropriate levels, and we will transform the welfare system into a program
of transitional assistance that will enable recipients to become productive,
working members of society."[80]

Although the NGA policy was written with great difficulty and was
nearly scuttled at several points, it reflected the concerns of Democratic
as well as Republican governors. The concerns of the Republican governors
had been well known, given their involvement in the development of

the House and Senate bills vetoed by President Clinton. However, Democratic governors were also reassured by the funding for child care, and according to one observer, "the additional money for child care was widely considered to be the key to getting an agreement."[81] Democrats were also reassured by the maintenance-of-effort requirements contained in the proposal, as these would prevent states from simply cutting programs to save money. Under the original House bill there was no maintenance-of-effort requirement, and states would have been allowed to contribute whatever they chose to their own welfare programs.

As with the Family Support Act of 1988,[82] governors were again credited with jump starting this round of welfare reform. President Clinton had twice vetoed congressional proposals, and there were few indications that common ground could be reached between Congress and the administration. In his 1996 State of the Union address, Clinton had once again called on Congress to send him a bipartisan welfare-reform plan and stated that he would "sign it immediately." However, "it was the nation's governors who revitalized Congress' quest to overhaul welfare programs and related social services. Meeting in Washington on February 6, the National Governors' Association did what Congress and the president had been unable to do in weeks of budget talks: They reached bipartisan agreement on controversial plans to overhaul welfare and Medicaid."[83]

The governors' proposals were met with caution as well as curiosity about how the sometimes wishy-washy NGA had managed to reach bipartisan agreement on a far-reaching and detailed welfare proposal. Conservative and liberal critics alike wasted little time before condemning the governors' proposal, but in the week following its passage, "Republican aides were transforming the governors' sketchy six-page outline into legislative language, seeking cost estimates from the Congressional Budget Office, and preparing for speedy action if the congressional leadership decide[d] to move."[84] Conservatives charged that the governors' plan would save $16 billion less than the conference agreement, that it did little to prevent out-of-wedlock births, and that it made the family cap optional for states. Liberals contended that the plan would hurt the poor—particularly children—and they opposed any efforts to end the federal entitlement to welfare benefits. Criticisms were multiplied because the governors considered the welfare and Medicaid plans to be one package, and their combined reforms were extremely far reaching. Speaking on behalf of the Clinton administration, Secretary of Health and Human Services Donna E. Shalala outlined a series of objections to the NGA proposals and said that the administration would not support the NGA welfare proposal as passed by the governors.[85]

Following February congressional hearings on welfare reform, the hubbub surrounding the reform effort subsided somewhat because of the presidential bid of Senate Majority Leader Dole, who was hesitant to take a stand on welfare reform. Congressional Democrats and some Republicans voiced objections to the linking of the welfare and Medicaid reform plans. Clinton himself labeled the Medicaid provisions of a combined bill a "'poison pill' that would prompt him to veto the welfare legislation if the two matters were linked. Although Clinton had signaled his willingness to end the federal guarantee of welfare checks, as the GOP proposed, he wanted to retain the Medicaid entitlement."[86] Clinton continued to send mixed signals on welfare reform, refusing to state explicitly what provisions a welfare bill would have to contain to avoid his veto.[87]

On May 22, House and Senate Republicans introduced their new welfare-reform bills (HR 3507 and S 1795), which combined original features of 1995's HR 4 with new provisions from the governors' proposal. In addition, the bills contained Medicaid reform provisions as well, which would weaken support for the whole package in the months ahead. The welfare provisions of the bills predictably ended the federal entitlement of welfare aid, replacing it with a block grant. States were required to spend at least 75 percent of the state funds that they had spent on AFDC and related programs in order to receive the full amount of their block grant allotment. States were given the option of instituting a family cap on benefits or denying them to unwed mothers under 18. Adult recipients would be required to work within two years of receiving aid. The new bill also included much of the additional child care funding—$13.9 billion—and all of the contingency funding—$2 billion—that the governors requested.[88]

However, the bills also contained stricter requirements for moving welfare recipients into work activities than the governors had proposed and embraced a narrower definition of what constituted work than the governors' proposal contained. The governors had asked that 25 hours per week of employment be counted as work and that job search and job readiness training be allowed to count as a work activity for up to 12 weeks. The House and Senate bills allowed 25 hours per week of employment to be counted as work for single parents but required 35 hours per week of two-parent families. Lawmakers accepted the governors' proposal that only 20 hours of employment a week count as work for parents with a child below age six. The standards for calculating participation rates in work activities were of such interest to governors because states falling below required participation rates would not receive the full amount of their block grant allotment. Although the welfare-reform bill was generally thought of as a devolutionary measure, these sorts of requirements amounted to conditions on the receipt of federal aid to state governments. From Congress' standpoint, they were included to ensure that the goals of national lawmakers were met as well.

As committees in both houses considered the various aspects of the combined Medicaid–welfare-reform bill, congressional leaders continued to insist that they had no intention of separating the two. Even so, "congressional Republicans increasingly" felt that they needed "significant legislative accomplishments to solidify their own re-election campaigns. A welfare overhaul would fit the bill. And some Republicans" were "reluctant to lose a historic opportunity to remake the nation's welfare system."[89] Governors had generally favored consideration of Medicaid and welfare reform together, viewing a combined bill as an unprecedented opportunity to overhaul the two largest state–federal programs in a comprehensive bill. However, "the Republican governors most involved in the legislative effort told GOP congressional leaders in a July 9 telephone conversation that they were unhappy with the changes made by the Finance Committee in the Medicaid portion of the combined bill," changes that gave states "less authority to define the amount, duration, and scope of Medicaid benefits."[90]

During the week of July 8, the Republican leadership decided to sever the Medicaid provisions and to move a stand-alone welfare-reform bill through both houses. Republican members of the House Ways and Means Committee had shortly before sent a letter to Speaker Gingrich and Senate Majority Leader Trent Lott (R-Miss.) urging them to consider the Medicaid and welfare provisions separately. The chairman of the House Commerce Committee, Thomas J. Bliley, Jr. (R-Va.), whose committee had jurisdiction over Medicaid matters, demurred, stating "I promised the governors we'd keep it together. If you really want to do something about welfare, you really ought to do both."[91] Even so, the political environment favored separating the two bills; with elections approaching, GOP leaders grew increasingly concerned with perceptions that, for all its initial fanfare, the 104th was a "do-nothing Congress."

Following the decision to consider welfare as a free-standing bill, the budget committees of the House and Senate reported new bills that omitted the Medicaid provisions. As the House bill was being debated, Clinton still had not sent a clear signal regarding his position on the new welfare-only bills Congress was considering. Debate in the House centered on food stamp provisions, the question of benefits for legal immigrants, and consideration of a bipartisan substitute bill sponsored by Delaware Republican Rep. Michael N. Castle (a former governor of that state who had been involved in the NGA's 1988 welfare-reform effort) and Rep. John Tanner (D-Tenn.). The substitute measure also ended welfare as a federal entitlement but provided more money to states for children, job training, and economic downturns. The measure was defeated but attracted the votes of 159 Democrats, signaling that many in that party were in fact willing to consider ending the federal guarantee of welfare benefits. Just before the vote on the main House bill, "the administration stepped up demands for further changes in the bill, then urged House Democrats to oppose the bill in order to increase White House leverage in the forthcoming House–Senate conference."[92] All but 30 Democrats did so, making the vote track party lines more closely than it might otherwise have. On July 18, the welfare bill passed the House on a 256–170 vote.

In the Senate, it remained to be seen how many Democrats would support welfare reform. A group of senators led by Sen. Daniel Patrick Moynihan (D-N.Y.) had decided earlier to oppose any bill that ended the federal welfare entitlement. As in the House, a Democratic substitute bill was voted on and defeated. On the issue of food stamps, an amendment was approved to strike language in the bill that would have allowed some states to gain control over their food stamp programs by receiving the federal money in a block grant. Democrats had feared that this would lead to cutbacks of the benefit.

Another amendment to the bill that made it more acceptable to Senate Democrats was one introduced by moderate Rhode Island Republican Sen. John Chafee extending Medicaid eligibility beyond the limits in the Senate bill as introduced. Under existing law, recipients of cash welfare benefits were eligible for Medicaid but might lose it if state-run welfare programs adopted stricter eligibility standards for welfare. Under the Senate bill, Medicaid coverage would have been guaranteed only to pregnant women and to children under the age of 13. Under Chafee's amendment, the guarantee was extended to cover nonpregnant women as well as children ages 13–18. Democrats also secured a provision that extended the time food stamp recipients would be allowed to engage in job search activities from one month to two. The Byrd Rule was invoked to strike down several sections of the bill, most notably the family cap provision.

The bill passed the Senate on July 23 by a vote of 74–24. In conference, House and Senate negotiators agreed to time limits on the receipt of food stamps and dropped a House proposal for a food stamps block grant. States were given the options of instituting a family cap on benefits, denying Medicaid benefits to adults dropped from the welfare rolls because they did not meet work requirements, and denying Medicaid benefits to legal immigrants. A proposal in the House bill to combine eleven child protection programs in a single block grant was removed, and a provision was added to deny benefits to legal immigrants. The conferees agreed to deny cash assistance and food stamps to most individuals convicted of a drug felony, although other family members could continue to receive benefits. Finally, to receive their full allotment of funding under the block grant, states were required to spend at least 75 percent of the amount they had spent the previous year on AFDC and related programs. States failing to meet work participation requirements included in the bill had to spend 80 percent of what they had spent before; thus, states had an incentive to move individuals into work activities. The conference report on the bill was filed on the night of July 30, 1996.

On July 31, President Clinton announced that he would support the conference bill. The decision was reached after a tense meeting with his closest advisors, who debated the merits of the bill and the impact of a Clinton veto on his reelection chances in the elections three months hence. An administration official who spoke on the condition of anonymity reported that "War is going on in the White House."[93] Although Clinton indicated his support for many aspects of the bill, his demeanor was less than celebratory given his concerns that the bill would make overly deep cuts in the food stamps program and hurt legal immigrants and children. Advocates for children and the poor offered dire predictions of the bill's impact, whereas many conservatives viewed the bill as an overdue reformulation of the incentives to work facing welfare recipients.[94] Not overlooked were the budgetary savings that would result from the measure, estimated at about $54 billion over six years. The House approved the conference agreement that day, and the Senate did so the following day. Clinton signed the bill with somewhat more fanfare on August 22, 1996, noting, "This is not the end of welfare reform; this is the beginning. And we have to all assume responsibility."[95]

It was the first instance in American history of a federal entitlement being converted to a block grant for allocation to state governments.

● ● ●

The governors' response to the new welfare law was rather muted at first. Publicly, governors reported themselves pleased, although some noted that the law still did not go as far as their own state reforms, carried out under waivers of federal requirements, had gone.[96] The official NGA statement regarding the bill portrayed it as embodying "many of the principles and recommendations put forward by the governors in their welfare reform policy."[97] Specifically, the NGA noted that the bill "sets time limits for welfare recipients; emphasizes placing recipients into unsubsidized employment; enables states to do a better job of collecting child support; and encourages the formation of two-parent families, while providing financial incentives to discourage teen pregnancy. In the area of food stamps, Congress agreed to the governors' recommendations to maintain the food stamp program in its current form as an open-ended entitlement."[98] However, some governors had complained about various provisions in the bill, which earned them the scorn of House Budget Committee Chairman John Kasich. In my initial round of interviews with governors' staff members in Washington about two weeks after President Clinton announced that he would sign the bill, many staff members of governors of both parties were somewhat disappointed with the final bill. Some worried about the sharp focus of congressional Republicans on strict work provisions and felt that members of Congress had been more concerned with scoring political points (with those who viewed welfare reform as an opportunity to force allegedly lazy welfare recipients to work) than with making it workable at the state level.

When I returned to Washington for more interviews five months later, members of the governors' lobby were much happier with the law, and so far it had not turned out to be the disaster for state governments many had predicted.[99] A strong economy had sharply reduced demand for welfare services from states, the Department of Health and Human Services had issued long-awaited clarifications of many provisions of the bill, and Congress was in the process of considering a technical-corrections bill to fix some of the problems with the administrative features of the bill.[100] Responding to a question regarding the apparent change of heart, an NGA staffer noted, "You're right, immediately [after the bill's passage] certain states disagreed with this part or that part, but I think overall, there's a much greater sense of supporting welfare reform now that they're in charge of making it successful."[101]

A number of observers have made some version of the statement that "if the governors had not reached their bipartisan agreement, there would be no welfare reform enacted."[102] This assessment seems accurate, although it must be noted that governors did not get everything they wanted out of the bill, nor were all governors collectively involved in its design from the beginning of the process. As an NGA lobbyist who worked on the welfare bill noted, "By the time we were able to be involved fully as an organization with a policy statement, the basic structure had already been done. It was going to be a block grant. So, the fundamental philosophical issues were basically over last year [1995]."[103] In other words, by using HR 4 as the basis of its welfare policy proposal, the NGA inherited rather than created the basic form of the welfare-reform law.

Even so, several prominent governors were *heavily* involved in the crafting of HR 4 as representatives of the RGA, so that legislation bore the gubernatorial imprimatur as well by promoting universal state-governmental interests. These governors pressed for important changes in the welfare-reform proposal that was part of the Contract with America, and HR 4 was thus much more state-friendly than it otherwise would have been.

> Although the Contract's welfare provisions did eliminate many existing strings, in other ways it was close to being the states' worst nightmare: It capped funding for AFDC and a number of other programs . . . and reduced state discretion with a number of new mandates, including very tough (and costly) work requirements. It had the potential to transfer obligations to support legal immigrants from the federal government to the states. Thus the governors' incentive to try to push welfare reform in a different direction than the Personal Responsibility Act [called for in the Contract] was very high.[104]

Although it is true, as mentioned above, that the close cooperation between the new Congressional leadership and the RGA shut out bipartisan involvement through the NGA for most of 1995, the Republican governors and congressional Republicans were not of one mind on welfare reform, and the governors working on behalf of the RGA shaped many provisions of HR 4 in a way that would later benefit governors of both parties. When NGA was able to agree unanimously on a bipartisan welfare proposal in early 1996, they used HR 4 as their starting point, indicating broad support for the principles Republican governors had worked to get included in HR 4. One should thus not be too quick to assume that the interests represented by Republican governors in their negotiations with congressional leaders were necessarily partisan interests. The fact that all the governors subsequently ratified (with specified changes) the bipartisan welfare proposal indicates that RGA involvement had promoted universal state interests as well.

Although one would not want to argue that RGA involvement in welfare-reform deliberations with members of Congress was tantamount to NGA participation, a lobbyist for NGA noted that "there were Republican governors in the room during private committee members' meetings and that was unusual, and . . . they were Republican governors but I think they were representing broadly—more broadly, than the RGA concerns. I mean, basically, they adopted our list and put it in Republican jargon."[105] If so, Republican governors' participation in welfare-reform deliberations cannot be written off as mere partisan shoulder rubbing but, rather, must be considered an important, if rather unique, example of state-governmental representation at the national level.

Although the governors certainly borrowed from congressional Republicans when devising their policy proposal, President Clinton's influence was felt as well. As a lobbyist for NGA explains:

> I don't think there would have been a bill after the [January 1996] veto if the governors hadn't come together and come up with a policy statement, and that also wouldn't have happened—in other words, the [governors who are] Democrats wouldn't have gone on board if they, I think, hadn't gotten at least some signal from the White House. And all you have to do really is to look at the veto message, which did not criticize the conversion of the individual entitlement to the block grant. I mean, that was sort of the fundamental issue, and that was not an issue that the president raised.[106]

Thus, a congeries of forces involving governors, Congress, and the president was involved in the development and passage of the February 1996 NGA welfare proposal, which helps locate the governors as fixtures in the national policymaking process, in particular when state interests are implicated as directly as they were in the welfare-reform debate.

As in the 1988 round of welfare reform, governors in 1995–96 were tapped for their intimate knowledge of welfare implementation at the state level. Although the RGA's institutional framework was used for policy development purposes in a way not seen before, the NGA can also claim to have restarted a stalled attempt at policymaking, demonstrating that bipartisan agreement was possible—and indeed necessary—for progress to be made on the contentious matter of welfare reform. It is of course possible to overstate the importance of the governors' unanimous agreement on a welfare-reform policy proposal, but it is possible to understate it as well, and there can be little doubt that the governors acting as a whole placed welfare reform back on the congressional agenda and moderated the earlier congressional proposal in a way that made it more amenable to state governments as well as Democrats and moderate Republicans in Congress.

Smaller Victories Won by Gubernatorial Lobbyists

An accurate portrayal of the activities of the governors' lobby in Washington also requires giving some attention to the numerous minor victories it achieves. The governors' efforts should not be judged solely on their ability to place major legislation on the congressional agenda and win its passage; it is important to understand the many smaller ways that the governors' lobby effectively promotes state-governmental interests in Washington, even if these efforts rarely make headlines.

There are methodological difficulties in identifying minor legislative victories. In particular, many of these victories take the form of legislative provisions that governors and their staffs persuade members of Congress to change or eliminate from bills early on in the process—at the committee and subcommittee level. Tracking these actions is difficult because there may never be anything on paper to document the change or elision. As such, interview data are often the only source of information regarding the small, behind-the-scenes efforts of staff members working for governors in Washington. Describing such efforts, one such staff member explained as follows:

> We go and make personal visits on appropriations matters but we go way ahead of time when they're having their hearings and before the markup of the bill. And we'll take 'em a list, and they'll say, "That list is 40 items long, and there's no way you're going to get $52 million out of this committee." And we'll say, "Well, we understand that; we'd like you to do your best and we've prioritized them in order of importance to the state," and they will say, "thank you." Our job—we see our job as making it easier for them to make decisions, [to] serve as the facilitator.[107]

Another governor's staffer gave this account:

> I do energy issues, so the electricity deregulation is a big issue. It's probably going to be a big issue in the next Congress. It's starting to percolate right now. There have been bills introduced on the House and Senate side[s] that probably are not going to move this year, but I was right there for those early meetings to see what they were saying about it, what the committee chairs were saying, and as soon as those [committee hearings] were dropped [printed and released] I mailed a copy up to our policy office to have our public utilities commissioner and attorneys in the policy office start reviewing them. . . . That issue is probably not going to be voted on until next year or the following year even, but you want to make sure early on you know what's going on, and you're prepared, and we might bring some folks down from our public utilities commission to meet with the committee counsels early next year.[108]

Members of Congress who are considering introducing legislation may also solicit information from governors' Washington offices, which gets the state's point of view in the mind of the legislator at an early stage. A governor's staff member in one Washington office explained it this way:

> They [the state's congressional delegation] come to us a lot. Even when they're doing letters—they're doing letters to constituents and it's on a state–federal matter and they don't know much about it, we do have a lot of people here who are very expert on both the federal and the state side of very difficult issues. If you want to talk about an environmental Superfund issue, talk to our guy here. He knows both the federal and the state side, knows all the issues in and out—which it's hard to find on the House side. The Senate, you can find some that way, they work on the committee staff. On the House side, that's hard to find. So we get used more and more as an informational tool, which is then nice because we do get in on the ground level of the bill that way.[109]

Many respondents noted in one way or another that a major part of their work in the individual governors' offices is "to try to educate the delegation as to what the impact of their actions are."[110] Many governors' staffs do not limit these activities to their own delegations. The director of one governor's Washington office characterized her office as "the eyes and ears and voice of the Governor's Office and of the state to our delegation, to the rest of the leadership of Congress, whether it's the political leadership or the committee structure. [And] with the federal agencies like FEMA [the Federal Emergency Management Administration] and with the administration and specifically the White House."[111]

Following natural disasters, the effects of which tend to be limited to one or several states, governors' staffs may work with FEMA to secure federal funds for cleanup and rebuilding. The director of Iowa's state office in Washington reported that "during the floods of '93, we spend a lot of time on that. By the time that was over we had $1.3 billion in federal aid."[112] According to a news account at the time, "six state representatives [i.e., governors' Washington staffers], all of whom have offices in the Hall of the States Building near the Capitol, first gathered together within days after the rain started and have been meeting regularly ever since to plot strategy and trade information. They've also been coordinating with NGA staffers, who've been looking out for Kansas and the Dakotas," states without Washington offices.[113] In the end, a supplemental disaster appropriations bill was signed that provided $5.7 billion in federal money for the states. In addition to helping to secure the money, the states' Washington staffers helped their states negotiate the bureaucratic procedures for actually getting the money and assistance back home. The news report continued, "The six state lobbyists have been meeting with the executive branch officials who actually dole out the money. The same week the disaster bill was signed, the six met with staff from the Commerce Department's Economic Development Administration, which hands out money for planning and technical assistance; the Department of Transportation, which provides money for highway and local rail freight assistance; and the Army Corps of Engineers, which is in charge of restoring washed-out levees and rebuilding ravaged dams."[114] This example demonstrates the sorts of particularistic benefits governors' staffs in Washington can secure for their states by working with Congress, the executive branch, the NGA, and other governors' Washington staffs. Even a small staff in Washington gives a governor significant advantages in the ways outlined here.

Strengths and Weaknesses of Intergovernmental Lobbying as a Safeguard of Federalism

These case studies show that the nation's governors, acting through a variety of institutions, can negotiate the shoals of the national policymaking process and convince members of Congress and the executive branch to adopt policies that will allow them to govern their states in ways consistent with the legalistic, fiscal, and managerial interests they perceive. Although the governors' lobby resembles other interest groups in many ways, the status of governors as elected chief executives gives their efforts particular importance in the realm of state–federal relations, as reflected in the quotes at the beginning of this chapter. By resisting and frustrating—but also *participating constructively in*—congressional legislative efforts, the governors can present Congress with policy proposals that have already secured bipartisan support among the officials they will most directly affect. Governors thus can effect political safeguards of federalism by representing the interests of their state governments in the national policymaking process.

The main weakness of intergovernmental lobbying as a safeguard of federalism is simply that Congress's legislative process is extremely slow and complex, and it offers multiple access points for all sorts of organized interests to make their views known. When Congress writes legislation that affects the interests of state governments, it typically affects the interests of other organized entities as well. As such, governors and other state officials may be part of a crowded field of advocates attempting to get Congress's ear. Their status as elected officials helps them gain access and get their phone calls returned, but at the end of the day a bill needs 218 votes in the House, 51 in the Senate, and the signature of a president to become law. Members of Congress who in principle support local control and shifting authority to the states may get different ideas when faced with concrete legislative proposals. Shifting partisan control of state and federal governmental institutions and offices further complicates matters, as do the internal politics of public official associations like the NGA and the NCSL. All of this is to say that the legislative process is filled with uncertainty, and although governors and state legislators lobby from a somewhat privileged position relative to other organized interests, nothing is certain. Their privileged position stems from power, professional and personal respect, and perhaps partisan alliances, rather than from money, which obviously speaks loudly in Washington.

To say that the governors did not get everything they wanted from, for example, the Personal Responsibility and Work Opportunity Reconciliation Act of 1996 is simply to say that the system of checks and balances worked. But one can also say that they got a lot of what they wanted and that they promoted a variety of state-governmental interests in a manner that commanded the attention of Congress and the president. As the NGA lobbyist involved throughout the welfare-reform debate explained, "Notwithstanding when tempers flare and [Rep.] Kasich says 'Tell those governors to stop whining,' or whatever—I think there is very real respect for the governors. I mean, we are so clearly the legitimate players here—the partners, the ones who are going to be doing it—and if it's not all the governors maybe it's the Republicans, who'd be appealing to the Republican governors. You know, I think we are very influential. We're very important, and I think that's recognized."[115]

In this chapter, I have noted that state officials come to understand the strengths and weaknesses of particular federal policies through their work implementing them. The local knowledge they possess makes their claims harder for members of Congress and federal agencies to ignore, and it is a potential source of power in state–federal relations. In the next chapter, I delve more deeply into the states' role as implementers of federal policy and the ways that the strategic uses of these roles allows states to protect their interests vis-à-vis the federal government.

CHAPTER 5

STATE IMPLEMENTATION OF
FEDERAL POLICY AS A
SAFEGUARD OF FEDERALISM

*As administrators of federal programs under grants-in-aid, the
state governments have acquired something in the nature of an
added check upon the national administration. Political power, like
electricity, does not run all in one direction.*
>—William Anderson, *The Nation and the States,
Rivals or Partners?* (1955)[1]

As the previous two chapters have demonstrated, state officials have a
variety of means to defuse pressures for new, preemptive federal policy
and to influence and shape federal policy as Congress develops it. If state
officials' attempts to promote their interests at these stages fall short of
their hopes, their involvement in the third, postlegislative, stage affords
them additional opportunities to shape the direction of federal policy.
The postlegislative phase involves turning federal law into rules and
regulations that are often carried out and enforced by state officials. In
this chapter, I explain how state officials use their roles as implementers
and enforcers of federal policy in strategic but also principled ways to
promote the state-governmental interests described in chapter 1.

Although state governments are not formally administrative departments of the federal government, they have long served in that capacity,

and the leading framers of the Constitution apparently expected that this would be the case.[2] Madison, for example, thought it "extremely probable" that "the officers of the States will be clothed with the correspondent authority of the Union."[3] Hamilton similarly noted that "the plan reported by the [constitutional] convention, by extending the authority of the federal head to the individual citizens of the several States, will enable the government to employ the ordinary magistracy of each in the execution of its laws. . . . Thus the legislatures, courts, and magistrates, of the respective members will be incorporated into the operations of the national government *as far as its just and constitutional authority extends*; and will be rendered auxiliary to the enforcement of its laws."[4] Today, states have been "rendered auxiliary" to the federal government's implementation efforts in ways that probably exceed any framer's expectations. Thomas Anton notes that despite the size of the federal bureaucracy and the existence of a few purely federal programs, "delivery of virtually all domestic services is otherwise left in the hands of local and state governments."[5] Subnational government officials are thus regular, key implementers of federal policies, and this gives them an important role in determining *how* those policies get implemented. Robert Stoker put it as follows: "Participation implies representation of interest and, if state or local interests are not compatible with federal program goals, states and localities may use their autonomy to develop and pursue strategic responses to the federal initiative, undermining or circumventing the intentions of federal policy."[6] Many scholars treat any such state-governmental deviations from federal intentions and prescriptions as irresponsible shirking or principal-agent problems, but in Stoker's account of state–federal implementation arrangements, such deviations may promote American federalism by preserving state authority; they may also yield better policy outcomes for program beneficiaries. Moreover, it may be the case that federal intentions are either unclear or contradictory, leaving state implementers no choice but to improvise. In any case, later in this chapter I consider the potentially negative consequences of states exercising administrative discretion. First, though, I present and evaluate the case for viewing states' administrative discretion as a salutary political safeguard of federalism. Case studies of states' implementation of the No Child Left Behind (NCLB) law and the Clean Air Act document state officials' recent use of this safeguard.

BRIEF HISTORY OF THE STATES' ROLES IN IMPLEMENTING FEDERAL POLICY

Although state governments have played a role in implementing federal policies since the country's founding, these relationships grew sharply during the first half of the twentieth century. Contrary to the conventional wisdom that New Deal programs were all centralized—European-style national programs carried out by a large federal bureaucracy—many in fact delegated implementation and enforcement to the states. State governments played a major role in implementing the Federal Emergency Relief Act, unemployment insurance, many elements of the Social Security Act, and the network of public employment offices.[7] Since the 1930s, this basic pattern of cooperative federalism—characterized by a state–federal partnership in carrying out federal policy—has continued, although the precise balance of authority has fluctuated significantly over the decades.[8]

State governments were not all up to the task of implementing federal programs, however, and states were frequently criticized during the first half of the twentieth century for their outmoded state constitutions, weak governorships, malapportioned legislatures, and meager fiscal capacities.[9] Beginning in the early 1960s, most states began to reform and invigorate their governments. In accordance with the U.S. Supreme Court's "one man, one vote" decisions,[10] state legislative districts were reapportioned— some for the first time in over half a century—helping to end the dominance of rural interests in those legislatures and strengthening the representation of residents of urban areas. Legislatures were also given new resources and powers with which to do their jobs (such as bigger staffs and additional support agencies), and governorships were strengthened by lengthening their terms and shifting elections to nonpresidential years to focus elections on state rather than national issues.[11] Many governors and legislatures also worked to increase the fiscal capacities of their states by enacting personal income taxes or broad-based sales taxes.

In the wake of the initial wave of state-governmental reforms, national policymakers increasingly looked to subnational governments to implement a wide variety of new federal programs. Most notably, the Great Society programs of President Lyndon Johnson were instrumental in bringing state and local governments into greater contact with the federal government, as a web of contacts formed among administrators at all three levels of government as subnational governments were given the responsibility for carrying out federal programs. Samuel Beer has noted that, in contrast to the many regulatory programs of the New Deal, "only one major program of the Great Society was a direct act of federal regulation: the Voting Rights Act of 1964. Otherwise, it built on the spending foundations laid by the New Deal in the form of the Social Security system and especially of cooperative federalism. Within this tradition, however, the Great Society acquired a special character by its emphasis upon spending for services provided largely by state and local governments."[12] Although these sorts of programs undeniably centralized decisionmaking and revenue-raising efforts in Washington, they strengthened the hand of subnational governments as well. Beer continues as follows:

> A paradoxical and quite unanticipated consequence of this new phase of centralizing federalism was to create powerful counter-vailing forces. The Great Society programs did impose federal policies upon subnational governments. By the same token they greatly heightened the concern and increased the contacts of sub-national governments with federal policy-making and administration. . . . Moreover, even though subnational governments were given ever greater reason and opportunity to concern themselves with federal action, they were also endowed with new means of influence on the federal government. As the federal government in the Great Society period extended its responsibilities by means of state and local governments, it also became dependent upon them for the successful discharge of those responsibilities. . . . The lesser jurisdictions acquired an ability to negotiate and bargain with the federal government.[13]

Consequently, governors and state governments have been revitalized such that they are now "arguably the most responsive, innovative, and effective level of government in the American federal system. State governments have reformed and strengthened their political and economic houses. Taxes have been increased and made more progressive. . . . The states' governors, legislators, judges, and bureaucrats are setting national agendas."[14]

Despite this progress, not all states today are equally committed to or capable of addressing problems facing their citizens. As political scientist Donald Kettl argues, "In terms of administrative capacity, the states are all over the lot. Some are on the level with the Federal Government. Some are innovative and exciting. But some are a long way from that kind of competence."[15] Many state legislatures remain relatively unprofessionalized and unduly susceptible to the influence of interest groups. Sixteen states limit the number of terms their state legislators can serve, and the evidence on term limits' effects has revealed some serious negative consequences, including inexperienced leadership, the loss of institutional memory, and the general weakening of state legislatures as independent branches of government.[16] State fiscal conditions have fluctuated wildly during the economic booms and subsequent recessions of recent decades, and state finances remain highly susceptible to business-cycle fluctuations. Moreover, although little research has focused on the policy effects of state-governmental reforms, some fear that the institutional development of state governments has reproduced many of the pathologies of national government at the state level. "Students of state legislatures, for instance, contend that a number of developments, most notably an increase in careerism and partisanship, have produced fragmentation, increased conflict, promoted parochialism, undercut the ability of legislative leaders to lead, and, ultimately, produced policy incoherence and stalemate."[17]

How Implementing Federal Policy Gives States Opportunities to Promote Their Own Interests

States' strategic uses of their implementation roles take a variety of forms and can be thought of as a continuum running from outright refusal to follow federal dictates to the renegotiation of more state-friendly terms of a state–federal implementation arrangement.[18] For analytical purposes, we might think of this continuum as shown in figure 4. This continuum reflects variation in the degree to which state governments "flout" the intentions or provisions of federal law as they are implementing it. On the left-hand side, states charged with implementing federal law simply balk at the task and do nothing or continue with their current activities.

I have called this approach "noncompliance." In the middle of the continuum, states fill in the ambiguities and silences of federal laws and regulations in ways consistent with their interests, which I call the strategic use of "discretion." On the right-hand side, states implement and enforce the federal policy as written but seek to change its provisions through the rulemaking process, when the law is reauthorized, or in some other way. I have called this approach "renegotiation." States' abilities and inclinations to exercise each of these basic (and simplified) options depends on the nature of the authority that the federal government has delegated to them and the potential sanctions they face for demonstrably diverging from the federal government's intentions.[19]

The Federal Government Needs State Officials in Order to Carry out Its Policies

In a very basic sense, the executive branch of the federal government simply cannot carry out all the tasks that Congress and voters ask of it without help from subnational and private entities.

> It is impossible to imagine the federal government being able to fulfill its mission without encumbering the state and local workforce. The Environmental Protection Agency is just as dependent on state and local employees and contractors to do its job as it is on its own full-time-equivalent civil service. To pretend that its total workforce is a mere 17,000 civil servants is to deny the realities of how that agency is organized to operate and to ignore the potential dependencies created when government pushes responsibilities downward and outward.[20]

The federal government also needs state officials' assistance in implementing a great deal of federal policy because of the expertise and local knowledge of state officials. The ever-increasing complexity of policy in some areas means that the federal government simply cannot hope for effective development, implementation, and enforcement of its policies without heavy state involvement.[21]

Donald Kettl has noted that subnational governments (as well as private entities) do enough of the federal government's work that we can view

FIGURE 4

Varieties of state administrative discretion when implementing federal policy

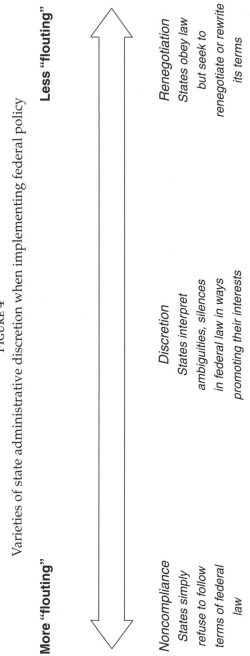

More "flouting"

Less "flouting"

Noncompliance
States simply
refuse to follow
terms of federal
law

Discretion
States interpret
ambiguities, silences
in federal law in ways
promoting their interests

Renegotiation
States obey law
but seek to
renegotiate or rewrite
its terms

"government by proxy" as a discrete form of policy implementation with unique advantages and drawbacks.[22] Although the extent of the federal government is often measured in terms of the number of full-time federal civil servants (about 1.9 million currently), another estimate that takes into account the pervasiveness of government by proxy places the number at close to 17 million.[23] Census data indicate that about 5.1 million of these are state employees, and another 13.3 million are local employees;[24] between 1962 and 1995, the size of state governmental workforce grew at ten times the rate of federal civilian workforce.[25] Not all of these state and local employees implement federal policies, but few remain wholly untouched by them.

State Officials Develop Valuable Expertise in Federal Policy while Implementing It

The decisionmaking authority state governments have gained as a result of their growing roles in administering federal programs is an important source of state influence in Washington—the ability of governors, for example, to advise members of Congress whether and how federal policies are actually working. Thus, although the central administrative mechanism of many federal programs since the Great Society era—intergovernmental grants—has undeniably been a source of confusion, consternation, and fragmented national policy,[26] it has also been the means by which state government officials have inserted themselves into the national policymaking process and have honed their skills as administrators, innovators, and constructive critics of federal programs. Today, "as the prime recipients of Federal grant funds and as channelers of Federal aid to their localities, states are pivotal intermediaries. They plan, supervise, partially fund, and sometimes directly execute large, costly, and socially significant intergovernmental programs."[27] As a result, state officials develop expertise regarding federal policy that is difficult to ignore. This expertise is a source of state officials' power in the intergovernmental lobbying process described chapter 4, and it also gives those officials power in various forms as they implement federal policies.

Complex Relations between Federal and State Officials
Inevitably Create State Discretion

John DiIulio and Donald Kettl have noted that any governmental action
has three components: designing the policy, financing the policy, and
administering the policy.[28] (These components correspond to the three
types of content of state-governmental interests—legalistic, fiscal, and
administrative—outlined in chapter 1.) Although state officials may therefore potentially object to a federal policy on as many as three levels,
they also have up to three avenues of influence on the policy as it
affects their state. State governments may be given discretion to "fill in
the blanks" of certain portions of a federal policy to tailor it to local
circumstances, they may be allowed to determine the level of funding
they will commit to it, and they may be allowed to determine various
managerial aspects of the policy—eligibility standards, implementation
timelines, procedures for attaining the policy's goals, modes of program
evaluation, and so forth.

The delegation of authority to another entity to define, fund, or
implement a federal policy creates the possibility of principal-agent
problems, in which the entity to which authority has been delegated
(the agent) uses it in ways not intended by the delegator (the principal).
Federal policies "exist to serve some national purpose, as shaped by a
complex policymaking system composed of the legislative branch, the
executive branch, courts, program administrators and staff members,
and interest groups."[29] When state governments are invited, induced, or
compelled to participate in the implementation of federal policies, their
own interests may clash with those embodied in the federal policy.

When state officials act as agents of the federal government, the extent
to which state activities can be overseen by federal officials is limited.
Many researchers have analyzed the theory and practice of principal-
agent relationships and the accountability problems inherent in these
relationships.[30] In many policy areas, such as environmental protection
and Social Security, the federal government has attempted to remedy
this problem by establishing regional offices that serve as intermediaries
between the headquarters in Washington and the state agencies. In practice, however, this apparent solution in fact exacerbates the problem by

adding yet another set of actors between the principal (Congress) and the agents (state officials).[31] As will be seen below, we need not characterize states' use of discretion in these principal-agent relationships as problems; rather, they might be thought of as principal-agent *opportunities* for harmonizing state and federal goals and interests related to public policy.

Severe Federal Sanctions against Noncompliant State Implementers Are Rare

As is commonly understood, federal grant money and program requirements for state implementation efforts come with the understanding that noncompliance will result in a reduction or cessation of federal grant money for the state. In practice, however, such sanctions appear to be rare, for several reasons. The most basic is the fact that cutting funding for a state-run federal program would hurt the recipients the program is intended to help, which conflicts with professional commitments to program goals that both state and federal administrators presumably share. Consequently, as Deborah Stone has pointed out, "sometimes inducements are designed so that by imposing a penalty, one hurts the very thing one is trying to protect. . . . The incentive (federal funds) contains an implicit penalty (withdrawal), but the penalty is virtually unusable. Unusable penalties convert an incentive into a guarantee."[32] In the realm of environmental policy, for example, the major pieces of federal legislation allow states to assume primacy for implementing and enforcing federal laws, with the understanding that if they do not, the federal government can step in and reassume control.[33] These "partial preemption" arrangements create an incentive for states to comply with the terms of their agreements with the federal government. For example,

> Under the Clean Air Act, EPA sets limits on certain air pollutants, including setting limits on how much can be in the air anywhere in the United States. . . . Individual states or tribes may have stronger air pollution laws, but they may not have weaker pollution limits than those set by EPA. EPA must approve state, tribal, and local agency plans for reducing air pollution. If a plan does

not meet the necessary requirements, EPA can issue sanctions against the state and, if necessary, take over enforcing the Clean Air Act in that area.[34]

In practice, however, the federal government rarely reassumes program control in this way, and sanctions such as withdrawing federal funds are also rare, because "this would leave the federal government with no program in those states or with the total responsibility for assuming enforcement."[35]

Because federal and state officials tend to be committed to the same general program goals, however, the most common federal response to laggard state implementation efforts may be to offer compliance assistance and technical information in order to help the state comply, rather than sanctioning the state. A regional official of the EPA, for example, noted that states "are our customers, and we try to provide technical support wherever we can."[36] The threat of litigation gives the federal government an added incentive to bring states into compliance. If a state environmental protection agency fails to enforce federal environmental standards, for example, citizen-suit provisions of the federal statute allow citizens or interest groups to sue the federal government, rather than the state agency, to bring polluters into compliance.[37] Such lawsuits generally ask for compliance enforcement rather than monetary damages, so the federal government has an incentive to make sure that state enforcement efforts are sufficient rather than waiting for problems to crop up.

Forms of State Influence in the Postlegislative (Implementation) Phase of Federal Policymaking

Political observers accustomed to viewing the federal government as a powerful entity that regularly issues nonnegotiable commands to lower levels of government may be surprised at the many opportunities for states to promote their own legalistic, fiscal, and particularly administrative interests while implementing federal policy. Congress typically has the option of passing "strong statutes" that limit the discretion of those implementing the policy, but it often instead passes legislation that sets a clear goal but gives wide latitude to "implementing agencies on other matters including selection of subsequent agents in the policy chain along with the tools, rules, and rationales" for the policy.[38]

Despite how frequently such discretion is granted by Congress, many scholars and other observers have been quick to accept the idea that state governments are largely or wholly at the mercy of the federal government under these principal-agent arrangements. To be sure, there are certain ideological advantages to believing that this is the case. As Ira Sharkansky noted several decades ago, "It is easy to exaggerate the role of the national government. One of the great ironies in federal–state relations is that both ultraliberal critics of the state governments and ultraconservative advocates of states rights argue that Washington has more control over the states than is actually the case."[39] Liberals have traditionally advocated uniform national standards and policies and have thus wanted to believe that when the federal government speaks, the states listen and do what they are told. Conservatives, particularly over the past 30 to 40 years, have—at least rhetorically[40]—supported the augmentation of states' policymaking autonomy and have similarly promoted the idea of an overweening national government in order to highlight its abuses and inefficiency. Despite the pervasiveness of these beliefs, however, "an entire generation of empirical research on intergovernmental affairs reveals that . . . Washington has had, and continues to have, tremendous difficulty in executing even relatively straightforward policies precisely because state and local governments enjoy such wide latitude in deciding how best to translate federal policies into action, or whether, in fact, to follow federal policies at all. The empirical evidence on this point is simply overwhelming."[41]

As such, we need to know what forms of discretion states enjoy and how they exercise that discretion. The following sections indicate the modes of influence available to state officials in the period following the passage of federal legislation. Obviously, not all federal legislation directly affects state-governmental interests, but when it does, state officials can try to influence the rulemaking process that often follows congressional action, they can negotiate the state implementation plans that many federal laws require, they can exercise discretion explicitly given to them by federal statute, they can ask for additional discretion by applying for waivers of federal requirements, and they can simply delay the implementation of federal policies they oppose.

Participation in Agency Rulemaking

The implementation of most major federal legislation begins with agency rulemaking. After receiving the president's signature, new laws are often sent to one of the federal executive branch agencies for additional codification and clarification of the precise means by which they will be implemented and enforced.[42] This process is done when Congress decides it does not have the expertise, inclination, or political will to spell out all of the technical details of a policy. The fine print—in the form of rules and regulations—that a federal agency develops has the force of law and tells affected parties what they must and must not do, when they must do it, and how they must do it. As such, states officials pay a great deal of attention to rulemaking processes stemming from congressional legislation affecting their interests.

The basic structure of the "notice and comment" rulemaking process is as follows:[43]

1. Congress passes a law authorizing a particular executive branch agency or department to engage in rule making and specifying the timeline, number of rules, degree of discretion the agency has in determining the rule's content, and so forth.
2. The executive agency develops a draft rule that incorporates and reflects relevant research, consultation, and analysis of the policy area in question.
3. After internal agency review, the draft rule is published along with an explanatory notice in the *Federal Register*, and public comment is solicited.[44]
4. Public comment on the rule is received in written form and through public hearings.
5. On the basis of the public comments received, the agency determines which of the following actions to take:

a. Prepare the final rule with no changes
b. Prepare the final rule with minor changes
c. Hold another round of public participation
d. Prepare the final rule with major changes
e. Abandon rulemaking and start over
f. Abandon rulemaking altogether.

Public comment periods provide state officials (and any other interested parties) with additional opportunities to influence policy development. Although an executive branch agency is not compelled to alter the rule in response to public comments it receives, it generally takes note of major concerns and may alter the rule to accommodate them.

Because Congress often passes broadly worded legislation, the rulemaking process may be the first time that interested parties begin to see all of the details of a federal policy—allowing them to determine exactly how the policy will affect their interests. When state officials see something they dislike in a rule, they may take individual or collective actions similar to those described in the previous chapter. For example, in early 2004, the Department of Health and Human Services (HHS) published a draft rule that "would give federal officials sweeping new power to review state decisions on Medicaid spending and the sources of revenue used by states to pay their share of Medicaid costs."[45] The rule was a response to HHS suspicions that states "have used creative bookkeeping and other ploys to obtain large amounts of federal Medicaid money without paying their share" for the jointly funded state–federal program.[46] The proposed rule "touched off an uproar among state officials,"[47] and after loud protests by both Democratic and Republican governors, the agency said it would reconsider the rules. Secretary of Health and Human Services Tommy Thompson (the former governor of Wisconsin) wrote a letter to the governors stating that "I intend to enter into consultations on the proposal with the states through the National Governors' Association (NGA) and the National Association of State Medicaid Directors. Once those consultations are complete, I intend to republish the notice in the *Federal Register* and provide for a 60-day formal comment period."[48] In the end, according to an NGA staffer, the HHS scuttled the rulemaking effort, "mostly because we made a big stink about it."[49]

In 2007, the federal government renewed its rulemaking efforts to curb what it viewed as excessive state Medicaid spending. The Centers for Medicare & Medicaid Services, a branch of the Department of Health and Human Services, issued seven regulations in May 2007 that would "reduce federal payments for public hospitals, teaching hospitals, and services for the disabled, among others."[50] The NGA said the regulations amounted to "a shift of billions of dollars in federal costs to states. According to states' own estimates, the impact of these regulations could reach up to four times the Administration's original five year $13 billion estimate."[51] In May 2007, Congress imposed a one-year moratorium on implementing the rules,[52] and in May 2008, the Centers for Medicare & Medicaid Services announced its intention to reissue the regulations. As this book went to press, the NGA and other interested parties were pressing Congress to extend the moratorium.[53] The House of Representatives and the Senate had approved different versions of the moratorium in appropriation bills that would have to be reconciled, but President Bush was threatening to veto the appropriation for what he viewed as excessive spending.[54] The secretary of health and human services deferred implementation of two of the most controversial of the rules until August 1, 2008, in hopes of reaching some compromise with Congress before that time.[55] Although it was not entirely clear how this episode would play out, other examples described in this book suggest that the federal government would end up negotiating a more moderate set of Medicaid rules that better reflects states' concerns and interests.

Influencing Presidential Executive Orders

As heads of the federal executive branch, presidents frequently issue executive orders (EOs) indicating how federal agencies will implement federal policy and operate during the course of their daily routines. Although presidents cannot unilaterally write legislation, they *can* issue directives to federal agencies that have important implications for how the latter issue rules and regulations and how they implement and enforce federal standards. Thus, in the postlegislative phase of federal policymaking, presidential EOs give state officials two ways to advance the interests of their governments: First, several recent EOs have required that federal agencies consult with state and local officials during the administrative rulemaking process under particular circumstances. Second, state and local officials play a more general role in the development of EOs themselves.

Recognizing the importance of state governments in implementing federal policy, several presidents have issued federalism-related EOs specifying what sort of consultation with state or local (or both) officials must occur before a federal agency develops and issues regulations. Ronald Reagan issued EO 12372, which required agency consultation with the states when an agency proposed actions that would impact inter-governmental fiscal affairs, and EO 12612, which presented a very narrow view of the national government's enumerated powers and required a federalism impact statement for rules under consideration by an agency.

More recently, EO 13132 (signed by Bill Clinton on Aug. 4, 1999) requires that "To the extent possible, State and local officials shall be consulted before any [action which would limit the policymaking discretion of the States] is implemented." The order defines "State and local officials" as elected officials of state and local governments or their representative national organizations (such as those public officials' associations des-cribed in the previous chapter).

This EO thus formalizes the role of state and local officials in the rulemaking process. Such a role existed prior to the EO, given that the normal course of *any* executive rulemaking includes a public comment period lasting between 30 and 90 days, during which time the agency drafting the rules solicits comments from affected or interested members of the public,[56] which could obviously include representatives of state and local public officials' associations. Even so, when an impending regulation will have particularly significant effects on state or local governments, federal agencies have sometimes made additional arrange-ments to solicit comments from state and local officials (among others) during a "pre-Notice of Proposed Rulemaking" process (i.e., prior to the agency's publication of its required *Federal Register* notice that it is going to begin the rulemaking process). For example, before the 1997 rulemaking for the prior year's landmark welfare reform law (the Personal Responsibility and Work Opportunity Reconciliation Act), the U.S. HHS implemented a broad and far-reaching consultation strategy prior to the drafting of the Notice of Proposed Rulemaking (NPRM). In Washington, we set up numerous meetings with outside parties to gain information on the major issues underlying the work, penalty, and data collection provisions of the new law. In our ten regional offices, we used a variety of mechanisms—including meetings, conference calls, and written solicitations—to garner views from "beyond the Beltway." The purpose of these discussions was to gain a variety of informational perspectives about the potential benefits and pitfalls of alternative regulatory approaches. We spoke with a number of different audiences, including: representatives of State, Tribal, and local governments; nonprofit and community organizations; business and labor groups; and experts from the academic, foundation, and advocacy communities.[57]

The formalization of this process is a boon to states in the sense that EO 13132 clarifies *every* agency's responsibility to do so, not just those agencies that make it part of their rulemaking process.

The development of EO 13132 is also instructive in terms of the role subnational officials play in the development of EOs by presidents and the susceptibility of the process to state and local officials' influence. EO 13132 revoked Clinton's earlier federalism-related EO 13083 (May 14, 1998), which was developed without consulting state and local public officials' associations and which outlined new criteria for executive branch rulemaking that was described as "establish[ing] broad but ambiguous and unconstitutional tests to justify intervention by the federal government in matters that typically are left to states and local communities."[58] The order generated "vehement attacks"[59] from state and local officials and was suspended on Aug. 5, 1998 by EO 13095. Fourteen months later, EO 13083 was revoked and replaced by the state-friendly EO 13132, which was the result of extensive consultations with state and local officials' associations.[60]

Presidential directives concerning the treatment of state and local officials during the rulemaking process have thus created institutionalized channels for state officials to apprise national policymakers of state-governmental interests. Although there is no guarantee that state officials' concerns will result in changes in proposed federal regulations, the comment periods prior to rulemaking afford the opportunity for face-to-face contact between regulators and state officials' representatives. Moreover, regulators are obliged to provide written responses to the concerns raised by commenters, indicating how the final rule has and has not incorporated state concerns.

Negotiation of State Implementation Plans

Federal statutes often require state governments to devise a state implementation plan specifying how the state will exercise its responsibilities for implementing a federal policy or spending federal grant money. For example, the 1996 welfare-reform law requires that in order to be eligible for a federal social services block grant, states must submit a plan to the Secretary of Health and Human Services certifying that the state will run a welfare program with the elements spelled out in section 402 of the statute. (Incidentally, many of the same requirements existed in the original Aid to Dependent Children legislation from the New Deal era.[61]) Under the Personal Responsibility and Work Opportunity Reconciliation Act (PRWORA), states have a number of options with regard to how their program will operate, and the state plan is mostly concerned with setting out a clear statement of what the state intends to do. As such, many state plans simply repeat the original language of the statute. Details of state plans are sometimes "negotiated" with federal officials, giving state officials more direct opportunities to resist or soften federal requirements. More will be said about this below in a case study of the states' role in enforcing the federal Clean Air Act.

Martha Derthick's classic account of Social Security implementation in Massachusetts contains useful detail about how state plans are written. She begins by noting that "federal goals are harder to realize in some states than in others. The conduct of state governments departs from the intended goals in varying degrees, and thus the extent to which the federal government seeks to exercise influence varies (as does the extent to which it succeeds)."[62] Concerning state plans in particular, she notes the following:

> In the approval of state plan material, federal administrators exercise a large amount of judgment. . . . It is through the process of reviewing plans that the federal officials decide precisely what it is they will require. Even if they begin the process with requirements fairly well defined, the question they must answer is not whether the state plan conforms to the requirements (the question is rarely so simple or clear-cut) but how close it comes. The presumption has to be in favor of the state or else the federal program would fail to function. . . . Even in the face of plan material that falls short of their requirements, federal officials may grant formal approval but attach qualifications, or seek from state administrators quasi-formal statements that interpret and supplement the formal plan material so as to clarify the nature of the state's promise to conform.[63]

More recent work by Derthick (and many others) finds that this pattern still holds. She notes that "bargaining and negotiation, not command and obedience, appear to characterize the practice of intergovernmental programs now as in the past, even if the past was far more mindful of a tradition called states' rights."[64] In general, the key point here is that state officials often bargain with their federal counterparts rather than simply accepting their marching orders.

To be sure, there are intergovernmental programs in which the states have little or no room to maneuver, and we should therefore think of state administrative discretion as a continuum ranging from essentially no discretion to substantial discretion.[65] For example, state agencies administer Social Security disabilities claims, but pains are taken to eliminate differences between offices and between states, so that a disabled individual in one state is compensated at the same rate as a similar individual in another state. As such, according to one state administrator, "the guidelines are pretty well set"[66] by federal law and by regulations promulgated by the Social Security Administration and its regional offices, and state and federal administrators alike try to ensure as much uniformity as possible.[67] In other policy areas, states may be given wide latitude to design and run federal programs as long as they comply with the basic requirements of the federal statute and its associated regulations and guidances.

State Authority to Define or Interpret Terms in Federal Legislation

Congress must often write legislation in vague or general terms to win the votes of a majority of its members and the president's signature. Even when Congress attempts to state clearly its meaning and intentions, federal law may still contain language that requires state implementers to define or interpret provisions of the law. Federal executive branch agencies may clarify the law through the rulemaking process or by issuing guidances or other memoranda for state agency officials.

To capture the complexity of state implementation of federal law, Malcolm Goggin and his colleagues proposed a communications theory of implementation that reflects the fact that state implementers are "the targets of implementation-related messages transmitted from both federal- and local-level senders. As recipients, state-level implementers must interpret a barrage of messages. The potential for distortion exists. . . . Therein lies the key to implementation's variability. Interpretation is a function of context. Therefore, a single message, such as a federal statute, may be interpreted differently in different states."[68] An example of this phenomenon is the states' responsibility to define academic proficiency under the NCLB law. The central aim of the law is for children to be proficient in mathematics and reading by the end of the 2013–14 school year, but "the federal law gives the states the power to define proficiency, and there are 50 different definitions of the term."[69] By empowering states in this way, NCLB supporters avoided a fight over whether to have national standards and what they should be, but they also created a situation in which there is a lot of state-to-state variation in what each states' standardized tests measure and how rigorous those tests are (compared with, e.g., the longstanding National Assessment of Educational Progress—the "nation's report card"). Another example of states' power to define was the "good cause" exemption that allowed states to excuse AFDC (welfare) recipients from cooperating with child support enforcement officers if doing so would not be in the child's interest. Although the exemption was contained in the federal law, "state administrators actually define[d] the rules confronted by street-level bureaucrats."[70]

Allowing states to define terms contained in federal policy preserves their authority to craft programs consistent with their interests and with existing state policy. Although this flexibility comes at the cost of national uniformity, it may also promote better policy to the extent that it produces programs that better reflect local circumstances. States certainly may have political incentives to water down or change federal policy as they promote their own interests. In the case of academic proficiency, some states have set the bar low for their students rather than risking the parent and teacher backlash that might result from large numbers of students being deemed not proficient.[71]

State Authority to Determine Program Funding

As discussed in chapter 1, states' fiscal interests include the desire for flexibility in how they can spend federal dollars. Federal law may give states the ability to make broad decisions about how to spend federal money, such as when it is delivered to the state in the form of a block grant. "Generally, states prefer a federal program like the General Revenue Sharing (GRS) Act of 1971, which from 1972 to 1980 allocated funds for state governments to use as they pleased."[72] States also typically seek additional flexibility to move federal funds from one program to another in response to perceived needs, as was seen in state efforts to have a revolving loan fund included in the Safe Drinking Water Act reauthorization described in the last chapter. This sort of discretion may promote better policy outcomes by better aligning resources with a state's needs, but it may also make program outcomes harder to determine. Members of Congress are typically less enthusiastic than state officials about such arrangements, because states may spend federal money in ways that diverge from legislators' intent, making it more difficult for members of Congress to hold states accountable and to claim credit for program successes.

State Authority to Determine Program Eligibility

State governments may be given the authority to determine who is eligible to receive benefits under a federal or joint state–federal program. If the federal government sets basic eligibility guidelines, states may be able to make additional populations eligible, particularly if the states pay for the additional beneficiaries. As described in the following section, many states have sought waivers from the federal government to provide federally funded Medicaid benefits to a broader group of state residents than called for under federal law. In other contexts, states may have an incentive to increase the number of program beneficiaries if the federal government is funding the entire program,[73] or they may wish to limit program benefits in order to save money. The scholarly literature is also full of examples of how street-level bureaucrats and social workers have restricted access to government and other benefits for reasons other than saving money—particularly racism, paternalism, and the pursuit of social control of the poor.[74] Such motives may or may not be part of a state government's official or unofficial approach to a particular policy area, but they must be kept in mind when thinking about bureaucratic discretion.

State Applications for Waivers of Federal Requirements

When Congress legislates in policy areas where state law already exists, instead of preempting (overriding) those state laws, Congress frequently makes provision for exempting states from some or all of the federal law's requirements. Such exemptions are called "waivers," and the waiver process generally works as follows: First, the statute must contain an explicit authorization for states to apply to the appropriate federal agency for waiver authority. For example, section 415 of the 1996 welfare-reform law stipulated that state waivers received prior to the passage of the law would remain in effect until their expiration, as would those waivers applied for subsequent to the law's passage but before the date on which it took effect (July 1, 1997).[75] Section 1115 of the Social Security Act provides for Medicaid research and demonstration waivers, typically to allow states to expand coverage to people who would otherwise not be eligible for Medicaid, and section 1915 of the law permits states to apply for the flexibility to use Medicaid money to fund, for example, home- and community-based services rather than the nursing home care explicitly funded by the program.[76] Under President George W. Bush, the HHS continued to view waivers as a valuable means of state policy innovation, approving more than a thousand Medicaid state plan amendments and waiver requests in the administration's first year alone.[77]

Second, federal agencies may outline additional conditions under which they will grant state waiver requests. This may be done in response to pressure from state officials themselves, as was seen during Bill Clinton's presidency. Early in his first term, Clinton directed the U.S. HHS to simplify its waiver processes. In remarks at the February 1993 NGA meeting, Clinton explained as follows:

> For years the Nation's Governors have been arguing that the process through which waivers from the Medicaid mandates imposed on them by the Federal Government is Byzantine and counterproductive. They are right. I have today directed the Department of Health and Human Services and its Health Care Financing Agency to take immediately a series of actions designed to streamline the Medicaid waiver process to enable the States of our country to serve more people at lower costs. These include a requirement that from now on the Health Care Financing Agency and its regional centers will have only one opportunity to ask for additional information and clarifications on States' waiver requests. I also want the Health Care Financing Agency to examine the development of a list of standard initiatives for automatic approval for State action. In consultation with the National Governors' Association, I want a rapid review of the entire waiver request process that produces a list of additional streamlining recommendations within 60 days. And I am directing the Health Care Financing Agency to reopen negotiations with the National Governors' Association to issue new regulations related to how they can use provider taxes and disproportionate share reimbursement to meet the needs of the people in their State.[78]

Later that year, Clinton signed an EO directing *all* federal agencies to streamline their processes for considering state waiver requests, which encouraged and rewarded state innovation under programs like the Medicaid and AFDC programs.[79]

The third step a state takes to attain a waiver involves submitting a formal application, which typically involves a good deal of paperwork.

Next, the agency considers the request and determines whether to grant it in full or in part. Finally, if the request is granted, the federal agency monitors the state's activities under the waiver, which may involve additional data collection and reporting on the state's part so that the federal agency can monitor and assess the state's compliance with the waiver's terms.

There are various reasons why states apply for waivers. A state may have recently created or changed one of its programs and would like to give it time to work without having it preempted by a federal law. A state might believe its current program is superior to a proposed federal replacement, and state officials generally try to avoid the time and expense of reconfiguring established administrative structures and processes. States' legalistic, fiscal, and administrative interests thus underlie each of the reasons they seek waivers of federal requirements.[80] For example, prior to the adoption of the 1996 welfare-reform law, some states sought to impose time limits—such as five years—on the receipt of welfare benefits, which would save the state money and signal that welfare payments would be temporary. States also sought administrative flexibility that would allow recipient families to accumulate certain assets without having that counted as income or wealth, thereby rendering them ineligible for benefits. Hence, states could avoid penalizing families who bought automobiles (for driving to better jobs, for example), whereas under the federal law such a purchase would normally have raised recipients' levels of income and personal assets above the welfare eligibility threshold. To be sure, many governors and state legislators at the time had political reasons for seeking to change the welfare programs in their states. For example, many states sought waivers that would allow them to impose family caps—under which no additional money was provided for additional children born to welfare recipients—not only to save money, but also because of the belief that the existing welfare payment structure led poor families to have children that they could not afford to support on their own. These sorts of assertions about the "moral hazards" accompanying welfare dependency played well to the public, which tended to have little sympathy for welfare recipients or support for generous welfare benefits.[81]

When states are allowed to implement federal programs under various types of waiver authority, the result is ironically a patchwork of varying state-by-state programs that federal law is supposed to prevent.[82] (Incidentally, this fact means that a uniform state law—see chapter 3—that achieves less than full support of the state legislatures may not be much worse than a so-called federal policy.) When states administer federal programs under waiver authority, large-scale reforms of those programs often merely ratify the sorts of approaches already in place in the states. For example, prior to the adoption of welfare-reform legislation in 1996, 38 states had been granted a total of about 60 waivers, and overall, 40 states were "doing some kind of federally approved welfare experiment."[83] As such, many states did not actually win a great deal more flexibility under the law than they already had, although it was certainly a move toward greater national policy coherence to have all the forms of state flexibility spelled out in a single law.[84]

The waiver process is a logical middle ground between state law and federal law, allowing the federal government to manage the ways that state officials adapt and tailor federal policy to the circumstances of their populations. Commenting on the Clinton health care proposal, former Vermont Gov. Howard Dean noted that "there may be legitimate differences among reasonable people (including state officials) as to the precise configuration that would prove most suitable given wide variations in the characteristics of Americans and the existing health care delivery system."[85] In an extended federal republic, waivers allow for federal policy that sets national standards but is flexible enough to avoid common state complaints about one-size-fits-all policy that is inappropriate to the needs of some states. As a safeguard of federalism, the waiver process gives states a chance to tailor federal policies to their particular circumstances even after the policy itself has been enacted and implemented. It should also be noted that Clinton's streamlining of the waiver process itself came about as a result of pressure from state officials,[86] further indicating state officials' influence in Washington.

Street-level Bureaucrats' Discretion to Implement Federal Policy

The aforementioned avenues of state-governmental participation in the development and implementation of public policy occur primarily through structured interactions between state officials and federal officials at rulemaking hearings, during state implementation plan negotiations, and in written form as formal waiver requests. State and local administrators also exercise discretion when working with clients of state–federal programs, and such discretionary behavior can promote administrative state-governmental interests in terms of greater flexibility, less prescriptive practices and routines, and solutions better tailored to local circumstances. Policy scholars have long focused on street-level bureaucrats as critical final links in the chain of policymaking and implementation.[87] A state's speed limit laws are only as good as their enforcement by police officers literally at the street level, and the basic logic behind this simple example applies to much more complex federal programs administered by state or local officials. Lael Keiser and Joe Soss studied how states exercise bureaucratic discretion in implementing the "good cause" exemption in federal child support law, and they note that "while the good cause exemption is a federal statute, state administrators actually define the rules confronted by street-level bureaucrats. In addition to formal refinements of the statute, state agencies also develop informal norms that define the meanings of these rules and expectations for worker–client interactions."[88] Street-level implementers of federal policy may also exercise discretion because they are unaware of state or federal rules, because time constraints lead them to pick and choose among large numbers of rules and procedures, or because of conflicts or contradictions among the rules they are supposed to follow.[89]

Case Studies of State Administrative Discretion

As seen in figure 4 above, we can think of states' strategic exercises of administrative discretion as falling along a continuum ranging from intentional noncompliance with federal law to substantial compliance with it. The following sections provide empirical evidence of these basic state responses to their implementation roles.

The Noncompliance Strategy

Over the course of U.S. history, state governments have periodically simply refused to cooperate with the federal government or to do its bidding. Although rare, examples of nullification, interposition, and other forms of overt state noncompliance reflect the continual contests for authority between the states and the federal government. As noted in chapter 1's discussion of states' rights, in the modern era, state flouting of federal directives often takes more subtle forms, such as defiant words from state officials but no action, lawsuits against the federal government, or administrative stalling.[90] Journalists' occasional announcements of "open rebellion" by state governments must thus be considered in the present-day context rather than that of 1798 or 1861.

A recent example of outright flouting of federal law involves state opposition to the REAL ID Act of 2005, which requires states to incorporate a common set of security features in state drivers' licenses. States generally view the law as both an unfunded mandate and an encroachment on their authority to design and issue licenses, and they have called on Congress to repeal the law or fully fund it. Most strikingly, in April 2007, the states of Montana and Washington passed legislation rejecting the federal law. The Montana law forbade the state's department of motor vehicles from enforcing the federal law, and Washington's law required its department of motor vehicles to do likewise unless full federal funding was received.[91] Under the federal law, defiant states would lose no federal funds for noncompliance, but their citizens would be unable to use their licenses for federal purposes, such as boarding airplanes.

There are more numerous examples of less strident state noncompliance with federal law. For example, under the Low-Level Radioactive Waste Policy Act of 1980, the possibility of congressional intervention to alter the terms of the state–federal relationship made stalling a reasonable form of "strategic noncompliance" to encourage Congress to alter those terms.[92] In other cases where the federal government has used conditional spending to secure state cooperation—backed by the threat of withdrawing federal funds if states opt for program nonparticipation—states have turned down federal funds in order to remain free of federal conditions and constrains on its expenditure. In 2005, the Utah legislature debated a bill rejecting all federal NCLB funds and calling for opting out of the program entirely. In the end, the legislature passed a law that "prioritizes Utah resources above federal No Child Left Behind mandates, and directs state leaders to seek flexibility in putting the federal law into practice."[93] Since then, Utah has spent federal money on NCLB program components but has not spent any state money on NCLB compliance.

The Discretion Strategy: "Highly Qualified Teachers" under NCLB

NCLB background. On January 8, 2002, President George Bush signed into law a six-year reauthorization of the 1965 Elementary and Secondary Education Act, better known as No Child Left Behind. Although states were already required by federal law to undertake regular standardized testing of their students at certain intervals,[94] the central feature of the new law conditioned states' federal education funds on *annual* reading and math testing of students in grades three through eight by academic year 2005–06. By 2007–08, states would additionally have to test students in science at least once during grades three to five, six to nine, and ten to twelve. The law heavily leveraged the small percentage of federal public education funding states receive to change the way that states and localities deal with underperforming schools.[95] The law provided states with additional administrative flexibility and increased federal funding while also requiring them to identify and deal with underperforming schools in ways determined by Washington.[96]

The law contains a variety of provisions related to elementary and secondary education, only a couple of which will be discussed here.[97] Under the new law's testing provisions, states can devise their own tests for assessing student learning, but they must test students annually, make the results public, certify that students in each school are making adequate yearly progress (AYP), and show within twelve years that all of their students have achieved academic proficiency. Schools failing to make adequate progress toward these standards face a set of increasingly severe sanctions. Two years of failure means that schools are eligible for technical assistance, and the neediest children at such schools are allowed to transfer to a better-performing school. Three years of failure means that schools must offer students additional educational options, including free tutoring. Schools with four consecutive years of inadequate progress are subject to corrective actions by their school districts that could include replacing certain staff, extending the school year, appointing outside experts to advise the school, or changing the curriculum. Five years of inadequate progress makes schools subject to being closed, being converted to a charter school, or being operated under state control.

Under NCLB, states were required to employ only "highly qualified" teachers by the end of the 2005–06 school year. The states' responses to the AYP and highly-qualified-teacher provisions of NCLB illustrate how state governments can use their authority as implementers of federal policy strategically to promote state interests, even if the overall thrust of a federal law is generally contrary to states' legal, fiscal, or administrative interests. Many states had genuine concerns about whether the NCLB-mandated testing regime would really improve educational outcomes in their states, and many also felt that the law imposed unacceptable additional costs on states while limiting their flexibility to act as they felt best. Supporters of the law felt that it was precisely this sort of state flexibility that had resulted in many schools and students (particularly racial minorities) being left behind. States had to be forced to set goals for continuous improvement in student test scores from a defined starting point, the argument went, because they had failed to do so voluntarily.[98] Because the law's passage was viewed as at least a partial defeat by states and localities because of these prescriptions, it provides a useful case for examining the options states retain when their intergovernmental lobbying efforts have fallen short.

State definitions of highly qualified teachers. Section 1119 of the NCLB law required states to develop plans for employing only highly qualified teachers (HQTs) by the end of the 2005–06 school year, a deadline that was later extended to 2006–07. The law defined such teachers as those with a bachelor's degree, state teacher certification, and demonstrated competency in the subjects they teach. Teachers not meeting these criteria are more common in rural areas, where teachers are often asked to teach in multiple subject areas because of limited staffing; in special education classes; and in the sciences, where a teacher with a bachelor's degree in biology might also teach chemistry, for example. The law also required states to ensure that HQTs are equitably distributed across the state and not just clustered into certain school districts.

Meeting the HQT requirements is straightforward for certified teachers who teach subjects in which they completed college course work. In the real world, however, many teachers do not fit this description, and many questions arose about how states would certify the qualifications of substitute teachers, paraprofessionals, and veteran multisubject teachers. NCLB allows teachers to demonstrate their subject-area qualifications through the holding of a college degree (or its equivalent) or an advanced degree or other credential; in addition, there is a provision for "an alternate method for experienced teachers to demonstrate subject-matter competency that recognizes, among other things, the experience, expertise, and professional training garnered over time in the profession."[99] These alternative methods, known collectively as high, objective, uniform state standards of evaluation (HOUSSE), are developed by each state; thus, states have some discretion in how they implement the HQT provision of NCLB. States' use of this discretion exemplifies the middle ground on the continuum of strategic state administrative discretion shown in figure 4, demonstrating how states have used discretion to guard existing policymaking arrangements that they believe are working. States' administrative interests are also affected to the extent that states lost a degree of control over and flexibility in their teacher-hiring practices. The HQT provision also implicates states' legalistic interests by restricting their ability to set their own criteria for hiring teachers in their states. States' fiscal interests are affected because of the additional expense involved in recruiting and retaining teachers who meet the federal criteria.

States did not have unlimited discretion in developing alternate methods for assessing teachers' subject-area competency, and they had to meet a number of federal standards. Specifically, HOUSSE processes had to meet the following requirements:

- be set by the state for both grade-appropriate academic subject matter knowledge and teaching skills;
- be aligned with challenging state academic content and student academic achievement standards and developed in consultation with core content specialists, teachers, principals, and school administrators;
- provide objective, coherent information about the teacher's attainment of core content knowledge in the academic subjects in which a teacher teaches;

- be applied uniformly to all teachers in the same academic subject and the same grade level throughout the state;
- take into consideration but not be based primarily on the time the teacher has been teaching in the academic subject; and
- be made available to the public on request.[100]

In addition, state processes could also involve multiple, objective measures of teacher competency.

In May 2004, the U.S. Department of Education announced that it would grant additional flexibility to states working to certify that their teachers were all highly qualified.[101] First, the department gave teachers already highly qualified in at least one subject three more years to become highly qualified in the additional subjects they teach. Second, states were henceforth allowed to certify teachers broadly in "science" in addition to narrower fields like chemistry, biology, or physics, which would make it easier for multisubject science teachers to satisfy the HQT criteria. Third, states were allowed to develop teaching assessments that would permit multisubject teachers to demonstrate competency in a single process rather than going through the HOUSSE process anew for each additional subject. This flexibility reduced the administrative burdens on both states and the individual teachers concerned. Additional flexibility for states was granted when, in October 2005, the U.S. Department of Education announced that states that had not completely met the law's HQT requirements would not be penalized as long as they could demonstrate that they were making good-faith efforts to comply.[102]

Initial reports from the states regarding teacher quality indicated great variation in the quality of states' data and the percentages of teachers deemed highly qualified. One report noted that "some states appear to have taken the reporting provisions to heart, working hard to provide an honest accounting of where they are and where they need to improve. But others took a different track. Some states simply didn't report any data, citing an inability to gather even this most basic information. And some states seem to have used their discretion in interpreting the law to cross the line that separates fact from fiction, to paint a rosy picture that is simply at odds with reality."[103] The report went on to note, however, that responsibility for this void of worthwhile information rests largely with the U.S. Department of Education. The federal government has a critical responsibility to serve as more than just a conduit for state-reported data of dubious value. It needs to provide clear guidance on what is required. It also needs to insist that the data meet basic standards of validity and reliability, and show a good-faith compliance with the letter and clear intent of the law. If states are unwilling to comply, the Department must take action. So far, the Department has simply refused to do so.[104]

Because there was no uniform federal HOUSSE process by which existing teachers could demonstrate their qualifications, states calculated their HQT percentages in varying ways.[105]

Because of the states' varying circumstances, it is difficult to summarize which states' HOUSSE processes constituted good-faith efforts to work through the NCLB law's requirements in its initial years and which ones constituted attempts to do nothing and simply continue existing state practices. A May 2006 U.S. Department of Education study found that no state met all of the NCLB teacher qualification requirements within the original time frame of the law. "The report said that 29 states had made 'good faith' efforts to comply with the law, and nine states faced the possibility of compliance agreements or sanctions—including the loss of federal funds—for failure to meet the requirements. When the report was released, the remaining 12 states had yet to be assessed."[106] A subsequent peer review of state efforts concluded that nine states had developed particularly strong teacher quality plans, thirty-nine had partially met the law's requirements, and four states' efforts were unacceptable. Given the U.S. Department of Education's relatively late start on clarifying this section of NCLB and offering guidance to the states, it is perhaps not surprising that demonstrable successes have to date been relatively few. On the other hand, after a slow start, many states have apparently accelerated their efforts and embraced the basic goals of the law. In its final report, the Aspen Institute's bipartisan NCLB Commission recommended backing away from such a strict focus on credentials in favor of ensuring that all students are taught by *effective* teachers. The NCLB focus on credentials, the commission believed, was an imperfect way to identify effective teachers: "The qualifications teachers bring into the classroom—the courses they have taken, the tests they have passed, their level of subject matter expertise—might suggest that they are likely to be successful. Yet there are many teachers with such qualifications who cannot effectively teach, while many people who lack the proper paper credentials *can* teach effectively. Only with demonstrated classroom success—including evidence of student achievement gains—can we be sure that every classroom indeed has a truly effective teacher."[107] An April 2007 joint statement from the NGA, the Council of Chief State School Officers, and the National Association of State Boards of Education similarly supported the goals of the AYP provision while asking for more support for teacher quality programs developed at the state level rather than according to a uniform federal blueprint.[108]

The HOUSSE processes were largely temporary measures meant to allow states to assess the subject-area competency of existing teachers. Once those teachers were deemed highly qualified or not, or put on a clear path toward qualification, the need for these processes would presumably disappear as states' teacher certification processes were updated to reflect fully the NCLB requirements. In September 2006, the U.S. Department of Education formally stated its hope that states would phase out the use of their HOUSSE processes as soon as possible, noting that "many of the HOUSSE procedures were substantially less rigorous than the other measures authorized in the statute for determining subject-matter competency."[109] In the meantime, however, states protected their administrative prerogatives by using the discretion given to them by NCLB.

The Renegotiation Strategy: AYP under NCLB

To be in compliance with the AYP provision of NCLB, states must show that all students as well as each of several subgroups of students (students in various racial–ethnic groups, disadvantaged students, students with disabilities, and students with limited English proficiency) meet or exceed the statewide objective for that year and that 95% of students in each subgroup participated in the assessment sessions. On the basis of these results, states must verify whether each school district as well as each school has met the standards. Failure to achieve compliance triggers the sanctions described above.

From the beginning, many observers objected to the NCLB-prescribed methodology for determining AYP, noting that comparing cohorts of, say, fifth graders within a school or a school district did not reveal anything about changes in the performance of individual students. The American Federation of Teachers found this "akin to requiring that every track-and-field record be broken every two years. But as the testing continues, just like in track, there will be strong cohorts of students in some years, which will set levels that following classes cannot surpass despite their best efforts."[110] Others noted that schools that improved but still fell short of the state's AYP benchmark would be unfairly characterized as having failed, whereas schools where performance declined but still remained above the benchmark might be mischaracterized as succeeding.[111]

As a formal response to their unhappiness with the AYP provisions of NCLB, a number of states asked the U.S. Department of Education for permission to use alternate methods of determining AYP. Louisiana initially sought to retain its method of measuring progress over two-year periods.[112] Other states sought waivers from the federal requirements, more time to meet them, or more money for programs to raise achievement levels.[113] In 2003 and 2004, many state officials and education professionals began advocating the use of a growth model to track the progress of each student over time, rather than comparing, say, this year's fourth graders with last year's fourth graders. If individual students made progress comparable to that expected under the AYP standard, the argument goes, this should satisfy the law's requirement. This approach, they argued, would allow more meaningful measurement of student achievement, even though tracking students in this way would require more onerous data collection and analysis.

In response, on November 18, 2005, U.S. Secretary of Education Margaret Spellings announced a pilot program in which up to ten states would be allowed to use growth models to determine whether their schools had made AYP.[114] These states would still be required to meet the goals of the law—individual student improvements would have to be substantial enough to ensure proficiency by the law's target date of

2014—and the plans would have to be approved by the U.S. Department of Education. The results of the initial round of the use of a growth model would also be assessed by a panel of education experts.

Following the secretary's announcement, fourteen states applied to be part of the pilot program, with six more indicating an interest for the following year. North Carolina and Tennessee received approval first, followed by Delaware, Florida, and Arkansas.[115] Soon thereafter, however, the U.S. Department of Education's moves to offer greater flexibility stalled, perhaps because of uncertainties surrounding the reauthorization of the NCLB law by the newly Democratic Congress.[116]

The reauthorization process was the focus of strong political pressure from the states, localities, and education professionals to—among other things—permit *all* states to use growth models to track students' AYP without applying for waiver authority to do so. On February 13, 2007, the Aspen Institute's bipartisan NCLB commission issued 75 recommendations, also proposing legislative language that Congress could use in rewriting the law. Noting that the NCLB's system of measuring AYP "does not distinguish between schools that are moving significantly in the right direction but have not yet reached the bar and those that are seriously struggling and show little or no progress," the commission recommended "including growth as a factor in AYP [to] yield richer and more useful data on student performance—both for the classroom and for school accountability."[117]

Testimony at U.S. House of Representatives subcommittee hearings outlined ways that the current law was unworkable and ineffective in a number of states.[118] The NGA, the Council of Chief State School Officers, and the National Association of State Boards of Education jointly issued a set of recommendations that included "allow[ing] states to use growth models to complement existing status measures. All states should be able to utilize a state-determined valid, educationally meaningful accountability system—such as growth models—to measure individual student progress."[119]

The interplay between the states and the federal government around AYP demonstrates how states' experiences implementing federal law can become the basis for renegotiating the terms of the state–federal relationship in a more state-friendly direction. In the case of AYP, state and local experiences generated sufficient evidence of the problems with AYP calculations to put states in a powerful position to renegotiate that portion of the law with the U.S. Department of Education. Sam Dillon noted in the *New York Times* that "many state, suburban, and rural district superintendents dislike the law, and their views are influential with Congressional delegations," and he quoted Arizona's superintendent of public instruction as saying that "you cannot run a complex, continent-wide education system through micromanagement by people living in an ivory tower at the Department of Education in Washington."[120] Federal officials acknowledged the validity of the states' claims through their initiation of the ten-state growth-model pilot program and through other moves to relax the law's requirements and give states more flexibility or time.[121] Rather than relieving pressures to change the law, however, the pilot program led to more dissatisfaction among state officials, who were frustrated that all states were not included in the program.

Not all growth models are created equal, and states and the federal government must do their part to ensure that they are implemented well.[122] If it is properly done, the use of growth models may prove politically popular and could even reinforce the law's central aim by making states less likely to challenge the law's proficiency goals and timetable.[123]

The two NCLB case studies presented here indicate the degree to which states' implementation efforts and their resistance to NCLB elements that conflict with state-governmental interests have yielded additional federal flexibility. After quoting a number of strident remarks by U.S. Secretary of Education Margaret Spellings that took states to task for failing to comply fully with the law, one observer noted that "Spellings' angry comments belie her department's strategy of co-opting and accommodating NCLB critics through waivers and other inducements. . . . This means that state resistance may elicit greater federal flexibility, but not seriously jeopardize NCLB."[124] Some states used the law's existing opportunities for discretion, and others successfully pressed for new discretion; on the whole, they resisted strenuously (and with some success) threats to their legal, fiscal, and administrative interests during the law's initial years. Reauthorization of the law will presumably work out some of its widely acknowledged problems and make it better policy, but from the constitutional perspective under investigation in this book, states appear to have safeguarded federalism through their implementation of NCLB.

The Renegotiation Strategy: Clean Air Act State Implementation Plans

Like most other federal environmental policy, the federal Clean Air Act is a partial preemption statute that allows states to apply for primary enforcement authority as long as state standards are at least as stringent as federal law.[125] This primacy is granted when the EPA approves a state's state implementation plan (SIP), and it can be revoked if the state falls below the federal regulatory threshold.[126] Primacy can be granted in several areas of Clean Air Act enforcement, including new source performance standards, Title V operating permits, new source review, and national emission standards for hazardous air pollutants.[127] Currently, states must submit a SIP detailing how they will meet National Ambient Air Quality Standards (NAAQS) for the following pollutants: sulfur dioxide, nitrogen dioxide, ozone, lead, carbon monoxide, and particulate matter smaller than 2.5 microns in diameter ($PM_{2.5}$). A SIP is "a collection of the regulations, programs and policies that a state will use to clean up polluted areas. The states must involve the public and industries through hearings and opportunities to comment on the development of each state plan."[128]

States' strategic uses of their implementation authority under the Clean Air Act (and other federal statutes) constitute a safeguard of federalism that can be used to protect their various administrative interests. Although it is true that states' legal authority to legislate in this policy area is preempted (partially) by the federal Clean Air Act, Joseph Zimmerman has noted the paradox that a SIP "encourages states to activate dormant regulatory powers or to exercise more fully such powers. This preemption type forges a national–state partnership."[129] As such, laws like the Clean Air Act prompt states to regulate air quality in ways that perhaps they otherwise wouldn't.

The basic SIP process resembles the rulemaking process in many regards. The steps in the process indicate the back and forth between state environmental officials and officials of the appropriate regional office of the U.S. EPA.[130] The "SIP Timeline" on the EPA's Region 1 website lists the following stages:

1. A draft SIP or SIP revision is submitted by a state to the EPA for initial EPA comment;
2. The state modifies the SIP in accordance with the EPA's comments;
3. The state holds a public hearing on the SIP, at which the EPA may present testimony;
4. The EPA submits official comments during the state's public comment period;
5. The state responds to the public's and EPA's comments it has received and modifies the SIP;
6. The state officially submits its SIP to the EPA regional office;
7. The EPA prepares a notice of proposed rulemaking; and
8. The EPA prepares a final rulemaking action to respond to public comment and modifies its administrative actions accordingly.[131]

The SIP process largely involves environmental professionals talking to professionals, and one EPA Region 1 official stated that "more often than not agreement can be reached" between state and EPA regional officials. "We try to resolve any issues as early in the process as possible by providing comments to the states on draft and proposed versions of the SIP, prior to the state formally submitting the SIP revision to EPA."[132] Even so, state environmental officials and EPA officials do not always see eye to eye, and the process by which SIPs are submitted by states and approved by the EPA presents opportunities for states to assert their interests vis-à-vis the federal government.

In developing a Clean Air Act SIP, a state's officials want to convince the EPA that they are making sufficient efforts toward meeting the air quality standard in question. A great many administrative state-governmental interests are implicated in these plans, as states explain their choice of air quality modeling methodologies, the adequacy of technologies that state regulations require polluters to adopt, the ways that the state or parts of it will be covered under the law, and so forth. The process is complicated by the fact that the Clean Air Act outlines fairly broad goals and processes and is supplemented both by additional federal regulations codifying the law as well as by EPA guidances offering clarification to states as they work to comply with federal regulations. Because guidances do not have the force of law and can be thought of advice rather than legal instructions, state and federal environmental officials may disagree over whether the state's SIP is, in fact, consistent with EPA guidances.

Examples of how state environmental officials "push back" against the federal government can be seen in a proposed revision to Connecticut's SIP regarding its efforts to control interstate air pollution. In this 2006 document, Connecticut Department of Environmental Protection (CTDEP) officials presented their case to the EPA that the state of Connecticut "has met its obligations under the transport provisions of CAA section 110(a)(2)(D)(i) to ensure that emissions from Connecticut do not contribute significantly to other states' nonattainment or interfere with maintenance of the 8-hour ozone or $PM_{2.5}$ NAAQS, or otherwise interfere with visibility protection or other states' efforts to prevent significant deterioration of air quality."[133] In plain English, because air pollution does not stop at state boundaries, under the Clean Air Act states must have a plan in place to ensure that their state meets federal air quality standards and does not contribute to nonattainment of those standards in downwind states. In Connecticut's proposed SIP revision, state officials raised several points of disagreement with the EPA's view of the state's efforts.

The excerpts that follow are designed to give a sense of the positions vis-à-vis the EPA that the state staked out in order to promote its administrative interests. These passages are good examples of a complicated and sometimes impenetrable language of "bureaucratese," but it is worth quoting them, I think, to demonstrate the ways that state administrators equal the EPA's uses of science and technical detail as they contest the federal agency's attempts to tell Connecticut what it must do. For the purposes of my argument about political safeguards, readers should focus on Connecticut officials' general tone of defiance and counterargument in these excerpts, rather than the technical details.

Connecticut officials' central claim in the document was that the state's efforts to control certain pollutants are substantial but cannot succeed because of pollutants (such as ozone) coming into the state from upwind states like New York and New Jersey.

Evidence is . . . provided in this SIP revision demonstrating that ozone levels in Connecticut are uniquely and overwhelmingly influenced by transport from upwind areas. EPA's remedy to the ozone transport problem, the Clean Air Interstate Rule (CAIR), provides inconsequential relief to Connecticut. EPA's CAIR modeling indicates that post-CAIR levels of transport in 2010, the required attainment date, continue to cause ozone violations in Connecticut regardless of the level of control assumed for Connecticut sources.[134]

Connecticut officials next suggested that the EPA review the SIPs of upwind states (like New York and Pennsylvania) and impose additional regulations on *them* so that Connecticut can attain compliance with federal standards: "EPA should ensure that all states significantly impacting ozone nonattainment in Connecticut include sufficient emission reductions in their SIPs to limit transport to a level where it is possible for Connecticut to attain the 8-hour ozone NAAQS, concurrent with the adoption of reasonable in-state controls. . . . To provide Connecticut citizens with the health protections required by the CAA, EPA must mandate additional upwind reductions."[135] Far from reflecting Connecticut's desire to shift the blame to other states and do nothing, the premise behind this request according to a CTDEP official was that "we now implement every program we're asking EPA to impose upwind of us."[136] Connecticut officials based their claim on the fact that the assumptions behind the federal regulations did not hold true for their state: "EPA's decision to limit upwind states' emission reduction obligations to what it defines as highly cost effective controls presumes that the downwind nonattainment state is able to achieve additional necessary reductions for attainment, without consideration of whether such additional reductions are available at any cost. This presumption does not hold true for Connecticut."[137] In terms of nitrogen oxide (NOx) standards, Connecticut recommended that the EPA broaden its regulation of this pollution's sources to include power-generating facilities.

Additional EGU (electrical generating units) reductions should be considered, especially those targeting peak summer demand periods when high emitting units are dispatched during ozone episodes. Controls from all other source categories should also be evaluated.

For example, in CAIR EPA elected not to pursue control of non-EGU boilers and turbines. EPA estimates that this group of sources contributes 16% of pre-CAIR NOx emissions in the region, versus 25% from the EGU sector. Both the on-road and non-road mobile source sectors, for which states have only a limited authority to regulate, also comprise a significant portion of NOx emissions and warrant further federal consideration for control.[138]

Connecticut officials also took exception to the way that the EPA calculated the attainment of federal standards.

For Suffolk County, New York, EPA's analysis indicated that emissions from Connecticut contributed at least 2 ppb of ozone during 28% (using zero-out modeling) to 36% (using source apportionment modeling) of the modeled exceedance grid-periods. On average, for the three simulated episodes, source apportionment modeling found that Connecticut contributed about 4% of the ozone during exceedance periods, the fourth highest contributing state after New Jersey, Pennsylvania, and Maryland. Since Connecticut is downwind of Suffolk County on high ozone days, CTDEP feels that EPA's conclusion may be an artifact of the modeling and grid specifications. Recent monitoring data indicate that measured ozone levels in Connecticut and elsewhere in the Northeast have improved dramatically over the last three years and may be improving at a greater rate than suggested by either EPA's CAIR modeling or OTC's preliminary modeling.[139]

The document ends by summarizing these and other points in a section titled "Recommendations to EPA." The fact that state officials use the SIP process to tell the EPA how it should implement federal law indicates that this is an important site of state–federal contestation. Although the above excerpts are highly technical and not framed in anything like the scholarly language used to discuss the political safeguards of federalism, they represent the contextualized sorts of ways that state and federal officials argue about the respective boundaries of state and federal authority in particular policy areas. Reading the proposed SIP revision, one gets the sense that the state is not trying to shirk its responsibility under federal law or "race to the bottom." Rather, Connecticut environmental officials are concerned that the EPA properly recognize the state's good-faith efforts to deal with pollutants coming into the state from elsewhere. By offering competing scientific evidence and recommendations for how the EPA could better use its authority under the Clean Air Act, Connecticut is attempting to preserve its legalistic and administrative interests in designing its environmental regulations in ways that comply with federal law but also embody state prerogatives.[140]

In November 2007, the EPA published a notice in the *Federal Register* proposing final approval of Connecticut's SIP revision and inviting any final comments. The notice stated that "CTDEP has adequately addressed the four distinct elements related to the impact of interstate transport of air pollutants."[141] According to a State of Connecticut environmental analyst, "The primary benefit of that submission, and EPA's approval, is to stop the 24-month sanction clock. It also provides a vehicle for us to once again point out that Connecticut's geography is responsible for its lack of attainment, and EPA must do more to require controls in upwind states."[142] In May 2008, the EPA gave final approval to Connecticut's SIP revision, giving it the force of law.[143]

As noted above, federal sanctions against noncompliant states are relatively rare in many policy areas, and the Clean Air Act is no exception. Under the law, states can be sanctioned for failing to submit a SIP or for failing to carry it out once approved by the EPA, but such sanctions have been imposed very infrequently.[144] The lack of imminent sanctions may not embolden states to disregard federal law as much as it leads them to present their cases to the EPA and work with EPA officials to reach common ground.

Strengths and Weaknesses of States' Use of Administrative Discretion as a Political Safeguard of Federalism

In focusing on how state and federal officials interact at various stages of the policy process, this book remains largely neutral on the wisdom of particular state policies in order to emphasize the constitutional implications of states' actions. That is, I have focused more on states' successes in protecting their interests vis-à-vis the federal government and less on whether they make and implement high-quality public policy.[145] The case studies presented above indicate how states have used administrative discretion to their advantage, but I have said less about whether doing so compromised the goals of the federal laws in question.

One must obviously take care to distinguish between responsible and irresponsible use of state administrative discretion. There is nothing to celebrate when states shirk their legal responsibilities by resisting federal laws and regulations intended to remedy pressing social, economic, environmental, and other problems. State officials may face powerful political incentives not to expend money or administrative effort in the service of federal policies, and they may simply drag their feet when it comes to meeting federal deadlines or performance standards. Without downplaying these troubling state administrative practices, they are sometimes simply examples of the "slippage" inherent in any principal-agent relationship. Some of the slippage is unproblematic, tolerated, and even intended, and it is important to recognize that not all of it can be blamed on the agents (i.e., the states). The federal government can also contribute to implementation problems by failing to issue regulations or guidances in a timely manner, by providing insufficient funding, or by issuing too many prescriptions and not enough flexibility.[146] Certainly the federal Department of Education's implementation of the NCLB (via the states) provides examples of implementation problems brought on by the federal government as well as by the states.

Theorists of intergovernmental policy implementation have confirmed that state governments often implement federal policies in ways that advance state-governmental interests but that this is not always at the expense of federal interests.[147] Although it is of course possible that states advance their interests by shirking their responsibilities, it is also possible for state interests and federal interests to be consistent with one another, or at least constructively inconsistent (i.e., state–federal disagreements may stem from good-faith differences of opinion). Thus, there is nothing inherently problematic about state efforts to implement federal policy in ways consistent with state interests, and in fact it is precisely this tension among interests that actuates this particular political safeguard of American federalism. Implementation scholars have traditionally viewed state–federal implementation arrangements as either "authority" relationships (in which the federal government tries to enforce top-down commands to lower levels of government) or "exchange" relationships (in which the federal government must bargain with state officials and offer side payments to win their cooperation). These approaches imply that federal policy goals can be achieved only if reluctant state implementers are coerced into carrying out federal programs or if the federal government waters down its expectations to the point where state officials will have no objections. As an alternative to these two views, Robert Stoker has proposed a "governance" approach to characterizing state–federal implementation efforts, holding that "the power to govern emerges from the creation of arrangements which allow those who control resources to cooperate in pursuit of collective goals. During the implementation process the power to govern may be created. . . . Reluctant partners do not disable national government, they generate the power to govern within a structure of constitutional representation of interest."[148] This view frames state administrative discretion as a positive feature of the American federal system's dispersed powers. It is consistent with the view that state officials represent the sovereign people in ways no less important than federal officials, as Samuel Beer has noted: "Like the federal government, state governments also express the national will. The nation can use both levels or either level of government to make itself more of a nation: that is, to make the United States a freer, wealthier, more powerful, and indeed more virtuous human community."[149]

Although it is important to distinguish between good-faith and bad-faith state actions when implementing federal policy, there is ample evidence that state governments frequently use their implementation powers in principled ways to resist perceived encroachments by the federal government and to carry out effective public policy in their states. (More will be said about this in the following chapter.) Such political safeguards of federalism at the implementation stage supplement those that are available to state official at the prelegislative and legislative phases of the policy process. This chapter and the two that precede it have presented the empirical evidence for this book's central claim: that state officials today have a variety of means of checking and balancing federal power. In the final chapter, I discuss the implications of this evidence for the health of American federalism today.

CHAPTER 6

SUMMING UP THE POLITICAL SAFEGUARDS OF FEDERALISM

Today, most state and local officials in both parties, and experts who care about the esoteric subject of federalism, worry that the relationship between Washington and lower-level governments has deteriorated badly. To an extent we've not seen in decades, Washington is trying to dictate what states, counties and cities must do and to disallow them from promoting policies of their own. . . . What's new is that the states are pushing back, and on many key issues federal officials have been backing down, largely because the political imperative rests with the states.

—Peter Harkness, *CQ Weekly*[1]

Charles Lindblom's classic article "The Market as Prison" argues that when governments attempt to regulate the business sector in this country, organized business interests either directly challenge those efforts or indirectly rebuff them through an "automatic punishing recoil" mechanism that yields negative social consequences, such as unemployment or economic slowdown.[2] Collectively, the political safeguards of federalism described in this book constitute a similar sort of mechanism with which state officials today respond individually and collectively to perceived federal encroachments on their interests, often rebuffing or softening federal efforts. One analyst of the Rehnquist Court's federalism jurisprudence concluded it was rooted in the idea that the state–federal relationship requires "judicial protection, not mere political self-help"[3] on the parts of states, but I hope the evidence offered in preceding chapters has demonstrated that there is nothing "mere" about states' manifold opportunities for protecting their various interests in the national policymaking process.

I began this book by asking how state-governmental officials today safeguard federalism by participating in federal policymaking. To answer this question, I first needed to clarify and operationalize the terms, and I began by stating the research question in terms that would be familiar to the Constitution's leading framers: What opportunities do the federal legislative and administrative processes provide for state officials to participate in the processes and advocate for their states' interests? Or, borrowing Madison's phrase, what opportunities do state officials today have to "resist and frustrate" measures proposed or taken by the federal government?

Instead of writing a normative treatise on the form I think American federalism *should* take, I outlined the various interests that state officials perceive in their interactions with their federal counterparts and indicated the ways that they pursue those interests today. Framing the issue in terms of state-governmental interests rather than sovereignty or states' rights, I presented a typology of those interests that allows us to characterize specifically what state officials think is at stake when the federal government legislates on matters involving state governments. "Safeguarding federalism" is thus operationalized herein as the protection and promotion of various identifiable state-governmental interests. Dividing the federal policymaking process into the prelegislative, legislative, and postlegislative stages allowed me to pinpoint when in that process state officials can try to protect their interests against perceived federal encroachments. In chapter 2, I described the full range of safeguards available to state officials today, followed in chapters 3, 4, and 5 by detailed case studies of three of them—the uniform-laws process, intergovernmental lobbying, and states' strategic use of administrative discretion when implementing federal policy. Within these three cases, I illustrated the workings of each safeguard in the context of specific public policies—the UCC, the SSTP, welfare reform, the Safe Drinking Water Act reauthorization, NCLB, and the Clean Air Act.

When the many details of these case studies are viewed as parts of a larger coherent system of state-governmental interest promotion, we can gauge the health of the American federal system as a whole. Since the founding era, political observers have worried about the states being swallowed up by an overweening federal leviathan. For example, the anti-federalist writer Brutus asked "whether the general government of the United States should be so framed, as to absorb and swallow up the state governments? or whether, on the contrary, the former ought not to be confined to certain defined national objects, while the latter should retain all the powers which concern the internal policy of the states?"[1]

There is apparently widespread scholarly and popular belief today that the federal government *has* swallowed up our state governments and that it is ever-growing, all powerful, and generally successful at running roughshod over those helpless governments. This book's contrary view—that state officials have numerous means at their disposal for resisting perceived federal encroachments on their interests—will seem implausible and incorrect to some. But I think the evidence provided herein demonstrates clearly that state officials work alone and together in various combinations to promote a coherent and stable set of interests vis-à-vis the federal government in the context of specific policymaking and implementation episodes. If states "lose" their fights with the federal government at one stage of the policymaking process, they almost always have opportunities during the next stage to affect a policy's content, interpretation, implementation, or reauthorization. Far from being caught unawares and swallowed up by the federal government, then, state governments today have multiple ongoing opportunities to learn the intentions of federal policymakers, to affect what makes it onto the federal policymaking agenda, to influence and participate in the making of federal policy, and to influence and participate in the implementation and enforcement of those policies.

This view of federalism is not widespread, for several reasons. First, media coverage of state-governmental policymaking and implementation tends to be inconsistent at best. The structure of local and national media outlets leads them to focus predominately on governance at those levels, with state news often falling through the cracks. The heroes and villains on the national political scene are often more interesting and better known than their state and local counterparts, and the media oblige our inclination to consume news as a form of entertainment by focusing on the national figures. Also, because few people care what is happening in states other than their own, political journalists have little incentive to present a broad comparative picture of how officials in a variety of states interact with their federal counterparts. Judging from media coverage of government, "Americans probably think Washington probably runs just about every program that affects them," and "for the press, 'national' is synonymous with 'important.' Few journalists have become nationally famous, not to mention rich, covering state or local governments."[5] In terms of media coverage of political safeguards of federalism, NGA meetings usually generate a few headlines twice a year, but otherwise the NGA and other such organizations receive little coverage. News of the uniform-laws process almost never appears in mainstream media coverage, and detailed information about states' implementation of federal policy is generally available only to those willing to wade through state and federal agency websites. State government is thus murky territory for both political scientists and the public, obscuring states' efforts to safeguard their interests vis-à-vis the federal government.[6]

The second reason that my view of federalism is not widespread is that national politicians of both major parties have little incentive to tout the power and capacity of state governments. Republicans interested in shrinking the federal government have political incentives to exaggerate its size and scope when proposing tax cuts, deregulation, and "less government in Washington." Democrats interested in initiating or maintaining federal programs have political incentives to emphasize and probably exaggerate the federal government's capacity to cure social and economic ills. Even state officials touting their states' accomplishments and capacity to solve problems often overstate the power of the federal government in order to promote the view that they are largely at its mercy. These inclinations, coupled with the earlier point about media coverage, mean that we are unaccustomed to hearing that state governments are *not* at the mercy of the federal government.

With all of this in mind, the following sections answer some concluding questions about the safeguards of federalism described in this book and indicate directions for future research.

Under What Conditions Are State Officials Most Likely to Protect and Promote Their States' Interests?

The case studies in earlier chapters illustrate how state officials have worked to protect state-governmental interests during policymaking and implementation episodes in the areas of commercial law, taxation, social policy, environmental policy, and education policy, among others. These cases prompt a number of conclusions about the possibilities and limitations of the safeguards of federalism described herein. These conclusions are, of course, preliminary and warrant further testing in a wider variety of policy areas. Moreover, the search for generalizations is complicated by the fact that each public policy generates its own constellation of supporters and opponents; takes place in a particular political, cultural, social, and economic context; and is driven by complex factors that may be difficult for the scholar to discern. Even so, the case studies allow us at least to say which broad factors appear to have been most critical in a particular policymaking episode.

The evidence in earlier chapters implies that states' successes in promoting their interests will depend on the following factors:

1. Are states defending existing authority against the federal government or trying to win it back (e.g., through the rolling back of a federal preemption or a devolution of federal power to states)? Because the American system of diffused authority makes lawmaking relatively difficult, the presumption is typically in favor of the status quo. In that sense, the uniform-laws process generally involves guarding states' existing legalistic authority against new federal incursions.[7] Absent compelling reasons or strong interest group pressures to change the status quo, states may have an easier time defending existing governing arrangements. Intergovernmental lobbying faces its toughest odds when state officials try to initiate "from scratch" congressional consideration of state-friendly legislation, but state officials' influence can be decisive when Congress has already committed itself to drafting legislation or if bills are already in the pipeline.

2. To what degree do state officials possess demonstrable competence or expertise in the policy area in question? The case studies on the UCC, Safe Drinking Water Act, welfare reform, NCLB, and Clean Air Act all demonstrate the power stemming from state officials' experiences and intimate understandings of state and federal policies. State officials' expertise may make them indispensable to Congress's work of drafting a workable bill. This expertise also serves state officials well during the implementation phase of the policy process, giving them strong grounds for resisting federal efforts to change existing state practices unless there are clear reasons to do so. State expertise is demonstrated through state policy innovations developed under waiver authority from the federal government, as was seen with many key elements of the 1996 welfare-reform law (family caps, work requirements, and so forth). States' expertise can also help win the good will of their federal counterparts by demonstrating that states are unlikely to race to the bottom if given more discretion.

3. To what degree is there a long history of the states (rather than the federal government) occupying the field in a particular policy area? The UCC illustrates how the states' long history as regulators of many aspects of commerce creates a presumption in favor of existing arrangements. Even if the states only partially occupy a policy area, this may be enough to safeguard state authority by forestalling new federal programs or regulations. For example, although the federal government's power to regulate interstate commerce is understood to be broad, states' regulatory efforts can occupy enough of the field to discourage Congress from exercising its dormant powers. Similarly, during the New Deal era, state social welfare programs forced the federal government to accommodate existing programs and forge state–federal partnerships in programs like Aid to Dependent Children and unemployment insurance.[8]

4. To what degree do state laws, regulations, and administrative practices exist in a policy area? Absent evidence of existing arrangements' failure, states will be more likely to hold off new federal legislation in a particular policy area. States' long experience with regulating commerce; monitoring drinking water quality; and certifying, hiring, and assessing teacher quality gives added weight to the states' claims of competence. If the SSTP ultimately succeeds and Congress permits states to collect sales taxes on Internet purchases, it will perhaps be because collection

of sales taxes is a settled state practice that can be adapted to modern technology and done in a minimally burdensome way.

5. To what degree does bipartisan consensus exist on a policy position among a critical mass of state and regional officials? Members of Congress and the executive branch are likely to be swayed by appeals from officials from a broad array of states or, when categorical interests are at stake, from officials of a particular region or other grouping of states.

6. To what degree are different sorts of state officials—governors, legislators, attorneys general, state school superintendents, and so forth—united behind a particular policy position? The example of Safe Drinking Water Act reauthorization indicated the power of a coalition of state and local officials, as does the states' implementation of various elements of the NCLB law.

7. To what degree are there strong interest groups aligned with or against the position taken by state officials in a policymaking or implementation episode? In the case of the SSTP, the states are aligned with traditional retailers seeking to eliminate online retailers' price advantage and are aligned against "pro-growth" groups opposing taxation. To date, those groups appear to have fought this issue to a standstill. In the case of NCLB, however, state officials' concerns have dovetailed with those of education professionals and their national associations and unions, increasing the power of state appeals for greater flexibility.

8. To what degree does a particular bill give Congress an opportunity to offload unpopular or expensive implementation duties on states or localities? The 1996 welfare law ended the federal government's guarantee of a cash welfare payment to any American falling below a particular income threshold. Given the general unpopularity of social welfare programs in the United States,[9] many members of Congress were eager to hand off this responsibility to state governments. The federal government attached many conditions to the federal block grant money it sent to the states to design and run their new welfare programs, but states gained a great deal of legalistic, fiscal, and administrative flexibility from the law.

9. To what degree are the putative advantages of federalizing a particular policy (e.g., reducing interstate policy variation, establishing

uniform national standards, unburdening interstate commerce, and so forth) outweighed by the benefits of allowing or encouraging interstate variations (e.g., having policy tailored to local conditions or having policy reflective of state public opinion or political culture)? States' appeals to federal agencies for the waiver of certain federal requirements appear more likely to succeed when there are demonstrable benefits to program recipients (such as expanding Medicaid coverage to additional populations). Ideologically speaking, states may have a better chance of being granted waivers when their requests are consistent with the political outlook of the president or the agency head, as in the case of Bill Clinton's calls for his executive agencies to streamline the waiver process.

Future research in a variety of policy areas is needed to determine whether these factors hold true generally or are limited to the policy contexts I have examined. Moreover, additional research should attempt to clarify whether these factors change over time or are relatively stable. Overall, though, I think the case studies span enough time and enough policy areas to serve as convincing evidence of state governments' ability to promote their interests in the national policymaking process.

Which State-Governmental Interests Are Easiest to Protect?

There is no simple answer to this question. Each of the safeguards of federalism highlighted herein protects state interests in different ways. The uniform-laws process most directly protects fundamental legalistic state interests by demonstrating that states are capable of making quality public policy without being preempted or mandated to do so by the federal government. By dampening pressures for preemptive federal legislation, states protect their fundamental abilities to make decisions for themselves without being overridden by Washington. The widespread use of federal preemption in recent decades shows the willingness of Congress and the president to override state decisionmaking prerogatives in pursuit of their own policy goals. Intergovernmental lobbyists are not always successful in blocking such preemptive legislation, but they may be able to soften its blow by winning additional federal funding or administrative flexibility. The policy-implementation literature surveyed in chapter 5 has noted repeatedly that administrative discretion often gives implementers an enormous degree of influence over policy processes and program outcomes, so states' successful defenses of their administrative interests ought not to be viewed as insignificant or second rate compared with legalistic interests.

Do States Race to the Bottom When Given the Chance?

Although I have tried in this study to characterize state–federal relations in a way that accurately portrays the less-well-known state perspective, we should also consider the potential problems that decentralized administration can create.

Just as the Vietnam War and Watergate cast a long shadow on presidential power, denials of civil rights to racial minorities throughout U.S. history have generated widespread suspicions about state governments' willingness or ability to protect the civil liberties and human rights of those populations within their borders.[10] In previous decades, these suspicions—which were justifiably directed at states in all regions of the United States—dovetailed with other shortcomings in the fiscal and administrative capacities of state governments to govern effectively, producing a phenomenon that has been called the "Alabama syndrome." This syndrome—the "tendency to lump all states with the worst"[11]—led federal policymakers to judge the motives and abilities of all state governments based on the qualities of those they trusted least. As one scholar explained, "In drafting the [1964] Economic Opportunity Act, the 'Alabama syndrome' developed. Any suggestion within the poverty task force that the state be given a role in the administration of the act was met with the question, 'Do you want to give that kind of power to [Ala. governor] George Wallace?' And so, in the bill submitted by President Johnson to Congress, not only George Wallace but Nelson Rockefeller and George Romney and Edmund Brown and all of the other governors were excluded from any assigned role."[12] Since the 1960s, doubts about the willingness or ability of states to do the right thing when given policymaking discretion have subsided somewhat, although less so among liberals and others who view the federal government as a necessary player in protecting the interests and rights of people who lack the political power to fend for themselves (children, racial and other minorities, the poor, the home-less, and so forth). There have been important recent examples of states granting greater legal protections and doing more to improve the lot of certain classes of people than the federal government. For example, "A growing number of state courts and legislatures have pioneered public-school finance reform, working to ensure that kids from poor neighbor-hoods are not stuck in inferior schools. Many states have civil rights guarantees that are stronger than those under federal law, especially with respect to sexual orientation discrimination, which federal law does not prohibit. . . . In many instances, what progressive states most want from the federal government is that it get out of their way."[13] There are numerous other examples of state governments taking action to address pressing public problems in the face of federal inaction.[14]

State exercises of discretion may be consistent with the authority granted to them by federal statute but still be reason for concern. Alternatively, those exercises of discretion may conflict with what federal decisionmakers had in mind. In the latter case, the states' discretion is problematic from the standpoint of democratic theory, because voters and interest groups that thought they were getting one sort of policy end up getting some-thing different. When this occurs, accountability for policy failures (or successes) is blurred, and voters' evaluations of incumbents are made more complicated. Such exercises of discretion are also problematic from an administrative standpoint, because they indicate that the principals are unable to monitor and correct agents' behavior when it violates the terms of the delegation of power.

Economists, public choice theorists, and policy scholars have long studied the conditions under which states engage in self-serving behavior at the expense of other states or targets of existing or potential state policies—passing costs on to other jurisdictions or loosening regulations in order to attract mobile firms.[15] Federal policy prevents these outcomes to the extent that it eliminates or constrains states' discretion. For example, in the realm of environmental policy, if there were not federal antipollution laws, states might impose the costs of their pollution on others by locating smokestack industries near the downwind borders with other states, and they might relax their environmental regulations in order to attract firms that generate pollution.[16] An example from the realm of social policy is the potential for states to provide welfare benefits at lower levels than adjoining states in order to avoid attracting benefit-seeking migrants from other states.[17] Policy scholars have also noted that policy designed to direct benefits toward politically weak or generally unpopular target populations tends to be characterized by decentralized administration, underfunding, undersubscription, and strict eligibility tests.[18]

If some or all of these fears are well founded, there is little to celebrate in state governments' use of the various political safeguards of federalism described in this book if, in safeguarding their legalistic, fiscal, and administrative interests, they consistently give comfort to the powerful and peanuts to the less fortunate. Although there will likely always be instances of this disparity, several factors constrain the inclinations states may have to race to the bottom in the realm of social policy. As one observer notes, "State governance is not devoid of compassion. Elected officials at the state level face the same level of responsiveness to the public that national politicians face. But they are also endowed with the information and incentives that make them more immediately responsive to the needs of their states and communities than the federal government could ever be."[17] In terms of state regulation of business, another observer similarly notes that "the states never had the incentive simply to race to the bottom. Regulation is too politically valuable to constituents, including in-state enterprises that benefit from state-legislated economic advantage."[20]

These sanguine assessments may not be warranted in all cases, however, given that politicians' responsiveness at all levels of government is typically directed more toward groups with political power and positive images in the public imagination. The targets of social policy, most notably the poor, have not traditionally received much sympathy from the public or politicians (at any level), leading to policy responses that have often been underfunded and even punitive.[21] The framework of this book suggests that such concerns should be considered on a case-by-case basis, examining the actual uses to which states have put their discretionary authority. In some cases, one would need to know more about the array of interest groups within a state to see which ones are capable of getting state officials to respond to and promote their interests.[22] One might also need to know about the partisan balance of the legislature and the governorship, the state's fiscal circumstances, the nature of the state's constitutional guarantees, the state's political culture, and the nature and size of its population in order to determine whether it has used its discretion well or poorly, defensibly or indefensibly. In addition, the level of policy activism by the federal government appears to strongly influence levels of state policy activism, and many states have passed a variety of legislation in recent years in response to federal inaction in those policy areas.[23]

In this study, I have gauged the degree to which state officials succeed in promoting their interests at various points in the federal policymaking process, and to some extent it is possible to remain agnostic on state motives in making this determination. Determining whether the state-governmental glass is half full or half empty when it comes to protecting the rights and interests of one's own favorite faction is probably ulti-mately a political exercise that cannot be resolved by the current study. There is compelling logic and evidence on all sides of the debate. However, it is important to note that this is a debate worth having, as it points toward elements of the policymaking process to which all should be attentive.

What Sort of "Federalism" do State Officials' Efforts Safeguard?

Some argue that American federalism today is not "real" federalism at all but, rather, a hollow shell of what the Constitution's framers had in mind. Unless state governments possess at least some decisionmaking authority that cannot be trumped by the federal government, they argue, there are no real limitations on federal authority. Law professor Edward Rubin, for example, contends that "real federalism is gone; America is a centralized administrative state. . . . Instead of a theory of federalism, we need a theory about what policies should be centralized, what policies should be decentralized, and, in both cases, the optimal way for a national government to supervise the regional subordinates that we continue to describe as states."[24]

Given the many examples in preceding chapters of the decisive roles played by state officials in implementing federal policy today, it is hard to agree that the American state is as centralized as Rubin says or that the states have been so fully stripped of their authority. Chapter 3's case study of the UCC implies that the federal government's broad authority to regulate interstate commerce faces definite practical limits because of the states' cooperative efforts to develop and update state-based commercial law. Chapter 4 provides examples of state officials' collective and individual successes in influencing the drafting and passage of federal laws. And the evidence in chapter 5 in particular indicates that the federal government has a very difficult time indeed "supervising" the states in the manner that Rubin implies. In this book, I have shown that today limits on federal authority are grounded not in some form of inviolable, enforceable state sovereignty but, rather, in state governments' individual and collective efforts at various stages of the policymaking process. States' ability to check and balance perceived federal encroachments on state-governmental interests stems from their capacity to generate effective public policy, the expertise they have as a result of implementing state and federal policy, the administrative capacity their large state workforce gives them, and the status of elected state officials as representatives of the popular will. In practice, these elements add up to meaningful limits on federal authority.

American federalism is certainly different today from what it was 50, 100, or 150 years ago, but it is not clear that states' defenses of their interests are markedly less vital or robust than in the past. Indeed, the evidence in this and other work suggests that states have greatly *increased* their capacity for democratic, professional, and effective self-governance and that they have developed a robust set of institutions to facilitate interstate cooperation and to strengthen their individual and collective hands in their dealings with federal officials. One observer has noted that "one of the strengths of the U.S. Constitution is that it draws up a fairly open floor plan for arranging the internal architecture of government. . . . With largely autonomous subnational governments, we get tremendous opportunities for experiments in the goals and design of government."[25] States have taken tremendous advantage of those opportunities and today find themselves well positioned vis-à-vis the federal government to safeguard their interests. Moreover, the institutions and processes states have developed are designed for the long term, so we ought not to interpret periodic "losses" for state governments (in the form of federal laws or Supreme Court decisions) as evidence of the "death of federalism" or the end of state authority.

How Do Political Safeguards Affect Constitutional Understandings of American Federalism?

My concluding claim is that the many daily interactions of state and federal officials generate relatively settled regime-level understandings of the respective boundaries of state and federal authority. This claim is important because it emphasizes that the state–federal relations described in earlier chapters do more than just resolve immediate questions of public policy, they add to and revise our understanding of the federal system created by the U.S. Constitution. To revisit the words of Arthur Schlesinger quoted in the introduction, the state–federal relations described in this book are the sorts of "daily experiences" that "explore the document's possibilities, reconcile its contradictions, and repair its omissions."[26] Although the text of the Constitution itself obviously does not change when, for example, the governors secure additional decisionmaking authority from Congress, the accumulated effect of such decisions is to create presumptions against similar future exercises of federal authority.

Arguing against the idea that policymaking processes generate constitutional meaning, Keith Whittington has noted the following:

> Policy may fulfill the promise of a constitution in governmental practice, yet it does not extend the meaning of the constitution itself. Policy initiatives may help solidify constitutional understandings and stability or help destabilize inherited constitutional arrangements by hastening fundamental crisis, but they elaborate on constitutional forms only indirectly. . . . Policy concerns are eminently contemporary, setting a particular course that will undoubtedly have implications for the future but without claiming any authority over it. Later policymakers have as much, and as

little, authority to determine the actions of government as their predecessors.[27]

This view relies on overly formal distinctions between the five levels of constitutional deliberation Whittington identifies—policymaking, interpretation, construction, creation, and revolution—and it treats elements of the Constitution as monolithic. As noted above, federalism is not a single relationship between states and the federal government but, rather, a heterogeneous set of relationships whose features and dimensions are not all agreed on or unidirectional. To say that the construction of constitutional meaning occurs only at the level of fundamental political principles at moments of unsettled understanding is to imply that those moments are rarer than they actually are and that the fundamental principles of federalism are clearer than they actually are. In the realm of American federalism, the fundamental principles depend a great deal on the particular circumstances, and neither Congress nor the courts have been able to outline fundamental principles that clarify once and for all where state authority ends and federal authority begins.

In theory, a constitution is supposed to allocate governmental powers definitively so that there is a level of legal certainty about who can do what. Without such definitive, settled allocations, the argument goes, the foundations of government are uncertain. However, the complexity of American federalism and intergovernmental relations makes it extremely difficult to say exactly where federal power ends and state power begins in any given policy area. Even an "authoritative settlement" of a federalism question by, say, the U.S. Supreme Court is unlikely to settle anything but the most general outlines of state and federal authority. Policy responsibilities are so frequently shared among governments that bright lines of demarcation can rarely be found. As a result, the multitude of negotiated settlements reached by state and federal officials in a host of policy areas move collectively to center stage as the clearest constructions at any given time of the governing authority held by each level of government. Although state-friendly observers of American federalism have long worried that the U.S. Constitution and judicial interpretations of it draw too few lines in the sand that the federal government simply may not cross, the political safeguards of federalism described in this book imply that there are very real limits to assertions of federal power even if they are not spelled out clearly or completely in the Constitution's text or in judicial decisions.

State officials have their own principled interpretations of the Constitution's vertical separation of powers, and state officials' pursuit of their states' interests should be viewed as a form of nonjudicial constitutional interpretation. In lieu of settled, fundamental principles that provide either states or the federal government with an authoritative warrant to make policy in a particular area, most state–federal relationships are continually open for renegotiation and contestation, with the result that the policymaking realm itself *is* the source of the most settled understandings at any given time of, say, the respective levels of state and federal authority in making social policy, economic policy, environmental policy, and so forth. This sentiment underlies John Ferejohn and Barry Weingast's conclusion that "statutory federalism, for all its political fragility, might be the only game in town, at least for now."[28] Federalism scholars like David Walker note this state of affairs with some dismay, describing the various elements of the federal system as ambiguous, paradoxical, and conflicted.[29] However, there is no reason not to revise our expectations away from clarity and toward complexity, and ongoing state–federal "conflict," if constructive in the ways suggested by Robert Stoker in chapter 5, may in fact promote the Constitution's separation of powers through the robust contest of countervailing powers.[30]

The construction of constitutional meaning with regard to federalism, then, is both something that—in Woodrow Wilson's famous phrasing— "cannot . . . be settled by the opinion of any one generation" and also cannot be settled in any comprehensive sense that ignores variations among policy areas and policymaking and policy-implementation arenas. In short, there is no single "American federalism" that we can say is either thriving or in trouble but, rather, a multitude of state–federal relations that need to be evaluated on their own terms. At any given time, state officials may be doing reasonably well at protecting their administrative state-governmental interests while doing less well regarding fiscal interests. Or, they may be succeeding at promoting their states' administrative interests in some areas of public policy but not others.

States do not win all of their battles with the federal government today, but they certainly do not lose them all either, and that is not by accident. Assessments of the health of the separation of powers between the three branches of the federal government should not rest on whether one branch consistently prevails over the others, and indeed such a condition would be the very definition of a *mis*functioning system of separated powers.[31] Moreover, federalism scholars and other observers should be careful to put judicial, legislative, and political developments into proper perspective when they occur. Legal scholarship on federalism has sometimes overstated the impact of new Supreme Court opinions by treating them either as death knells or phoenix-like renewals of American federalism as a whole.[32] In a similar manner, various annual assessments of the state of American federalism may lack the multiyear perspective needed to really tell how any particular aspect of state–federal relations is developing. Just as investors seeking to track the value of their portfolio might use, for example, a rolling 12-quarter average (to avoid overemphasizing temporary ups and downs), scholars and other observers should probably assess the health of various aspects of American federalism in five- or ten-year increments. Adopting this perspective, I have identified in this book numerous major and minor instances in which states have successfully protected their prerogatives against perceived federal incursions, and there is reason to believe that this general pattern will continue in the foreseeable future, even if the inevitable shifting of state–federal relations yields some variation at the margins.

RESEARCH METHODS
USED IN THIS STUDY

The central thesis of this book is that states today retain a significant reserve of authority in the American constitutional system because they successfully exercise a variety of political safeguards of federalism. This conclusion is rooted in an understanding of state-governmental interests that I developed as a result of two streams of original qualitative research in the forms of personal interviews and content analyses. The first stream consists of several dozen personal interviews with individuals whose work involves state–federal relations in some capacity. The second stream consists of content analyses of the 1998 policy positions adopted by the NGA and the NCSL and of the governors' 2002 state-of-the state addresses.

The empirical findings of the book are presented as a series of nested case studies of three particular political safeguards of federalism—the uniform-state-laws process (chapter 3), intergovernmental lobbying (chapter 4), and the states' role in implementing federal policy (chapter 5). These three safeguards operate at different stages of the federal policymaking process and were chosen as case studies from the larger universe of political safeguards of federalism described in chapter 2. Nested within the discussions of these three cases are public policy case studies that indicate how the safeguards have worked in the context of specific policymaking efforts. Figure 1 in the introduction provides a graphical representation of how the two levels of case studies relate to

James Anderson's five-stage model of the policymaking process I have
adopted for analytical purposes.

Here in the appendix, I describe in detail the research methods used
throughout the study, indicating the choices I made and the reasons for
them. In general, the interviews and the content analyses answered
some fundamental questions I had about the nature of the interests state
officials perceive vis-à-vis the federal government. For example, at the
outset of this research project, it was not clear to me how U.S. senators
conceptualize the interests of states they represent and how these were
different from the state-governmental interests perceived by governors,
state legislators, and others. The scholarly literature on senatorial representation offered some clarification but said rather little about whether
and how U.S. senators might—or might not—safeguard federalism through
their representational work in Washington, D.C.

When I learned that in recent decades about half of the nation's
governors at any given time have maintained offices in Washington, D.C.,
from which to lobby Congress and federal agencies,[1] I was intrigued
about what staffers in these offices did. Certainly the key essays in *The
Federalist* dealing with senatorial representation (especially nos. 62 and
63) implied that the mode of selecting senators would naturally lead
them to perceive and promote the interests of state governments. Talking
at length with several dozen staff members in governors' Washington
offices convinced me that state officials perceive interests that frequently
differ from those perceived by U.S. senators and other federal officials—
even when these latter individuals think of themselves as defenders of
decentralized government and states' prerogatives. I also learned that
governors' Washington staff also work a great deal with various governors' associations, such as the NGA and similar regional organizations.
The NGA and the NCSL develop policy positions each year on pending
federal legislation, and it seemed that these would be excellent indicators
of the nature and content of state-governmental interests at a particular
moment in time.

Ultimately, my goal is to show that state officials are periodically
successful in their use of various political safeguards. My aim is not to
show that they are *always* successful, because that is not the way that
the separation of powers in this country works. Branches and levels of

government win some and lose some. Echoing James Madison's famous dictum that constitutional powers were separated to avoid "a gradual concentration of the several powers in the same department,"[2] I am interested in explaining why, over time, all of the decisionmaking authority in our federal system has not come to be held by the federal government.

Personal Interviews

To get a sense of the interests that state governments perceive vis-à-vis the federal government, I interviewed a variety of governors' Washington staff members, state legislators, and congressional committee and federal agency staff. Nearly all of these interviews were conducted in person; a few were done by telephone. Interviews lasted between five and sixty-five minutes, and the average length was about thirty-five minutes. I conducted many of the interviews in Washington while Congress was not in session, which meant my informants could spare more time than might otherwise have been the case.

At the time of the interviews, most of my informants were told that they would not be quoted for attribution in any of my writings, so most are not identified by name when quoted herein. Nearly all of the interviews were tape recorded and transcribed, so all direct quotes in the text are verbatim rather than post-facto paraphrasings.

The interviews that influenced my theorizing the most were with staff members of governors in Washington, D.C. Very little has been written about these offices, so it was necessary to speak with them myself to learn about their work. Having acquired a list of the states and governors with Washington offices, I wrote to the directors of each office to inquire about their availability for an interview with me. I followed up the letters with phone calls and arranged times and dates within the constraints of the weeks I would be in Washington. These constraints meant that I generally spoke with anyone who could meet with me rather than with a random sample of all staff members of governors' Washington offices. In the end, I interviewed staff from 20 of the 32 states (about 63%) that had Washington offices at the time. These states varied greatly in population and physical size and were spread across regions of the United States. In terms of partisanship, at the time of the interviews, about two-thirds of the governorships were held by Republicans, and about two-thirds of the states with Washington offices were headed by Republicans. About 80% of my interviews were with staff members who worked for Republican governors, so there was a bit of an imbalance in that regard. However, because many of my questions related to the structures and processes of these Washington offices, I do not think that the information and insights I gained were so biased as to yield an incorrect or misleading view of these offices. My sense is that in the private setting of an interview with a graduate student, people working in a political town like Washington generally put their biases on the table rather than trying to bamboozle me. Indeed, one of the most striking aspects of the interviews was the frequency with which I heard the same sorts of comments and concerns about the federal government from all state-level staffers, regardless of party. Even though I have not identified most informants by name, in many cases I identify the party affiliation of the staffer's boss or the general region of his or her state (or both). As noted in chapters 1 and 4, partisan, home-state issues and politics recede into the background somewhat when governors engage in collective efforts to promote their interests in Washington. Individual state offices pursue somewhat different goals depending on the particular characteristics of their states and their governors, but they are generally united around the sorts of basic state-governmental interests described in chapter 1.

I chose interviews over other methods (such as surveys) because of the particularly rich information that interviews yield, particularly when the researcher is in the initial stages of a research project and may not yet know exactly which elements of the informants' work is most important to ask about. Talking with an individual in person allows clarification and detailed probing that is obviously not available through a survey instrument. As Richard Fenno noted, one learns a great deal by seeing the context in which one's informants work: the layout of their offices, the other staff in the office, the publications lying around on informants' desks, and so forth. (I was frequently offered documents or publications that provided additional information on the topics I discussed with informants.) Although I was not engaged in participant observation in the traditional sense, by keeping my eyes open throughout the interviews, my insights came to exemplify Fenno's point that "observation can be an aid to discovery, description, and theorizing."[3] In particular, because most of the governors' Washington offices are in a single building that also houses the NGA and other governors' and state-government associations, seeing the physical space in which these staff members worked turned out to be important in understanding their ability to work both together and separately, depending on the type of state-governmental interests affected by federal legislation at any given time.

The interviews were semistructured, and I used most of them to learn about what staff in governors' Washington offices do and why. In the initial interviews, I knew so little about these offices that the questions were very broad variations on "what do you do in an average day?" After a handful of interviews, I began asking questions aimed at validating and cross-checking information I had heard from other informants. Where there were differences of opinion, I have tried in the text to indicate whether a particular viewpoint was typical or not. In the concluding minutes of many of these later interviews, I would ask informants to comment on some of my inchoate hypotheses about the political and constitutional importance of governors' Washington offices. The basic set of questions that I asked most governors' Washington staff members (my largest group of informants) was as follows:

- How many people are on your staff?
- What is the legal status of your office (a state agency, part of the office of the governor, and so forth)? Whom do you answer to in your state's government?
- Why does your governor have an office in Washington, D.C.? Can you describe the work of this office and what it tries to accomplish? What sorts of disadvantages do states without Washington offices face?
- What have you learned about relations between the states and the federal government since you've worked here?
- Do you think actions affecting the states are given much thought by members of Congress? How do you get members of Congress to take the states' interests into account? What is their incentive to do so?

- Clearly you don't take positions on all of the hundreds of congressional votes each year. How do you decide which ones to focus on? How is your agenda set? Is your office guided by a formal policy priorities document?
- What do you think members of Congress and their staffs think of state offices? When you contact the offices of members of Congress, how are you received?
- How does coalition building with other state offices figure into your activities? Which states do you find yourselves building coalitions with frequently? I've read about regional differences in states' policy preferences, such as between the Northeast and the Southwest. How real are those differences?
- What issues among the states are unifying, and which are divisive? When do states go their own ways, and when do they work collectively through the NGA?
- What are things that you and your office consider noteworthy successes?
- How was the 104th Congress different from others? What has the 104th Congress meant for states?
- What has been the activity of your state in relation to the recent welfare-reform bill in Congress?
- What are your office's goals for the future? What would you like to see Congress do?

After many hours of listening to these informants describe their work, it became clear to me that the interests and priorities of governors are in most cases quite different than those of members of the U.S. Senate—even those members from the same state and of the same political party. Indeed, these offices are located in Washington precisely to lobby and educate members of Congress about the ways that existing and proposed federal legislation impacts state governments. I consolidated my informants' insights into the typology of state-governmental interests that appears in chapter 1. The interviews also underpin much of chapter 4's argument about how intergovernmental lobbying works as a political safeguard of federalism.

Listed below are the people I interviewed for this work as well as where and when I interviewed them. Interviews were conducted in person unless otherwise noted.

Congressional Staff

Wendy Audette, field director for U.S. Rep. Lloyd Doggett; Austin, Tex.; March 1996

Susan Combs, state director for U.S. Sen. Kay Bailey Hutchison; Austin, Tex.; March 1996

Bret Coulson, majority staff member, U.S. House of Representatives Budget Committee; Washington, D.C.; March 1997

JoEllen Darcy, minority staff member, U.S. Senate Environmental and Natural Resources Committee; Washington, D.C.; March 1997

Patti Everitt, district director for U.S. Rep. Lloyd Doggett; Austin, Tex.; March 1996

Herb Halvorson, aide to U.S. Rep. David Minge; Washington, D.C.; March 1997

Sarah Niemeyer, aide to U.S. Sen. Paul Wellstone; Washington, D.C.; March 1997

Matt Weidinger, majority staff member, Subcommittee on Human Resources, Committee on Ways and Means, U.S. House of Representatives; Washington, D.C.; Sept. 1997

State Legislative and Executive Agency Staff

Brenda Cook, assistant to Texas State Rep. John Hirschi; Austin, Tex.; April 1996

Merrily A. Gere, environmental analyst, Connecticut Department of Environmental Protection; telephone interview; May 2007

David A. Johnson, Virginia Department of Environmental Protection; Richmond, Va.; June 2000

Kirk Jonas, Joint Legislative Audit and Review Commission, Commonwealth of Virginia; telephone interview; June 2000

Edward Myers, Disabilities Section, Department of Rehabilitation Services, Commonwealth of Virginia; telephone interview; June 2000

Governors' Washington Office Staff

Debra Bryant, director, Washington Office of the Governor, State of North Carolina; Washington, D.C.; August 1996

Roy Coffee, Austin director, Texas Office of State–Federal Relations; Austin, Tex.; June 1996

Julie Davis, aide, Washington office, State of Mississippi; Washington, D.C.; August 1996

Carrie Doerr, aide, Office of State–Federal Relations, Commonwealth of Massachusetts; Washington, D.C.; August 1996

Joe Freeman, Special Assistant for State–Federal Relations, Virginia Liaison Office; Washington, D.C.; August 1996

Wade Griffin, policy director for economic development, Texas Office of State–Federal Relations; Washington, D.C.; August 1996

Jon Hinojosa, legislative liaison, Texas Office of State–Federal Relations; Austin, Tex.; March 1996

Ted Hollingsworth, director, Washington Office, State of Ohio; Washington, D.C.; August 1996

John Katz, director, Washington Office of the Governor, State of Alaska; Washington, D.C.; August 1996

Tina Kreisher, deputy director, New Jersey Washington Office; Washington, D.C.; August 1996

David McClung, legislative assistant, Washington office, State of Minnesota; Washington, D.C.; August 1996

Beth Meyer, director, Washington Office of the Governor, State of Rhode Island and Providence Plantations; Washington, D.C.; August 1996

Terri Moreland, director, Washington Office, State of Illinois; Washington, D.C.; August 1996

R. Leo Penne, director, Washington Office, State of Nevada; Washington, D.C.; August 1996

Andrew Peterson, acting director, Office of State–Federal Relations, State of Wisconsin; Washington, D.C.; August 1996

Laurie Rich, director, Texas Office of State–Federal Relations; Washington, D.C.; August 1996

Bryan Roosa, associate director, Office of the Governor, State of Michigan; Washington, D.C.; August 1996

Jan Shinpoch, director, Washington Office of the Governor, Washington State; Washington, D.C.; August 1996

Phillip Smith, director, Washington Office, State of Iowa; Washington, D.C.; August 1996

Susan Spencer, deputy director, Washington Office of the Governor, State of Pennsylvania; Washington, D.C.; August 1996

Bryan Webb, aide, Washington Office of the Governor, State of California; Washington, D.C.; August 1996

Holly Zimmerman, aide, Washington Office of the Governor, State of Connecticut; Washington, D.C.; August 1996

Staff of National and Regional Governors' and Legislators' Associations

Michael Bird, lobbyist, NCSL; Fredricksburg, Va.; May 2000

Tom Curtis, director, Natural Resources Committee, NGA; Washington, D.C.; March 1997

Kelly Donley French, Office of State Services, NGA; Washington, D.C.; March 1997

Garner Girthoffer, policy associate, NCSL; telephone interview; February 2008

Susan Golonka, policy analyst, NGA; Washington, D.C.; March 1997

Murray L. Johnston, III, policy analyst, Southern Governors' Association; Washington, D.C.; October 1997

James L. Martin, legislative director, Office of State–Federal Relations, NGA; Washington, D.C.; March 1997

Shaun McGrath, policy analyst, Western Governors' Association; Washington, D.C.; October 1997

Neal Osten, senior committee director, NCSL; telephone interview; February 2008

Anne Stubbs, executive director, Coalition of Northeastern Governors; Washington, D.C.; October 1997

Federal Agency Staff

Anne Arnold, manager, Air Quality Planning Unit, EPA Region 1 Office; telephone interview; May 2007

Lynne A. Hamjian, manager, Connecticut State Program Unit, Office of Ecosystem Protection, EPA Region 1 Office; New London, Conn.; April 2004

Other

Christy Heath, staff member, NCCUSL, Chicago, Ill.; telephone interview; June 2000

John McCabe, director, NCCUSL; Chicago, Ill.; January 2001

Francis J. Pavetti, uniform laws commissioner for Connecticut; New London, Conn.; March 2001

CONTENT ANALYSIS OF NGA AND NCSL 1998 POLICY POSITIONS

The NGA and the NCSL develop policy positions each year that guide their respective lobbying organizations. These positions are often quite detailed, and they cover a broad swath of existing and potential federal legislation and regulation. A brief look at these positions revealed that they were extremely rich statements of state-governmental interests vis-à-vis the federal government. Although many of the areas of interest were predictable and familiar (welfare, Medicaid, environmental protection, transportation), others were not (e.g., refugees and immigration, Indian gaming, ocean and coastal zone management, and asbestos litigation).

Because I was intrigued by the range of policy positions articulated by these state officials' organizations and wanted to generate a systematic portrait of what the positions contained, I performed a content analysis on the 1998 published policy positions of the NGA and the NCSL. At the time, 1998 was chosen simply because it was the most recent. However, many of these policy positions roll over from one year to the next and are revised rather than replaced, so there is a lot of continuity over time. For example, a 2007 NGA policy position on "education reform" covers the NCLB law in great detail but has a much longer lineage. The policy position's history is noted at the bottom as follows: "Adopted Annual Meeting 1993; revised Winter Meeting 1994; reaffirmed Winter Meeting 1996; revised Annual Meeting 1996, Annual Meeting 1998, Annual Meeting 1999, Winter Meeting 2001, Winter Meeting 2002, Winter Meeting 2003, and Annual Meeting 2004; reaffirmed Winter Meeting 2005 and Annual Meeting 2005; revised Winter Meeting 2006 (formerly Policy HR-4)."[4] Although ideally I would have analyzed several years' worth of policy positions, I believe the general findings would not differ much from those reported in chapter 1.

I developed coding categories that would allow me to characterize the extent to which governors and legislators today view federal coercion of state governments as necessary (category A), constitutionally permissible but advisable only under certain circumstances (category B), constitutionally permissible but inadvisable (category C), or constitutionally impermissible (category D). By coercion, I mean the types of intergovernmental regulation (such as preemption, mandates, crosscutting requirements, and crossover sanctions[5]) used by the federal government to lead state officials to do something they otherwise might not do. Categories B and C were divided into a number of subcategories to capture the full range of policy positions that fall into each category. (These subcategories appear in ranked order of frequency in table 1 in chapter 1.)

Overall, I coded 2,463 words or phrases from the policy positions of the NGA and the NCSL. Of these, the NGA's positions accounted for 979 coded statements, and the NCSL's positions yielded 1,484 coded statements. The difference in these numbers is an artifact of the length of each association's policy positions—the NGA's ran to a total of 178 pages compared with the NCSL's 221 pages—so the number of coded statements per page was roughly the same for each association.

Content Analysis of Governors' 2002 State-of-the-State Addresses

In addition to the NGA and NCSL policy positions, state-of-the-state addresses might provide a good indication of the governors' views of the federal government, federal officials, and state–federal relations. These views would presumably reflect the legalistic, fiscal, and administrative interests the governor perceived vis-à-vis the federal government at the time. These might include the particularistic interests of the governor's state only, or the analysis as a whole might indicate regional or other patterns of categorical or even universal state-governmental interests. To test these possibilities, I performed a content analysis of the 50 state-of-the-state addresses delivered in 2002 to gauge the extent to which governors talk about the federal government in these addresses. To measure the frequency of references to the federal government in general, federal officials and institutions, and federal programs, I searched by computer for the following 13 key words in the texts of the 50 state-of-the-state addresses delivered by governors in 2002: federal, feds, Washington, Congress, House, Senate, president, administration, department, Medicaid, welfare, Head Start, and public land. For the terms House, Senate, president, administration, and department, I examined the context surrounding each appearance of the word in the text to determine whether the term referred to, for example, the U.S. House of Representatives rather than a state legislature's lower house. Only those terms that clearly referred to a federal institution or program were counted. For easier reporting of the results of the content analysis, I condensed the results yielded by the thirteen search terms into three categories: (1) general, nonspecific references to the federal government or Washington; (2) references to federal institutions or officials; and (3) references to federal policies, programs, or features of them (e.g., "federal funding"). These results are reported in chapter 1.

Case Studies

To detail the workings of several political safeguards of federalism, I have used a nested case study approach. From the long list of safeguards outlined in chapter 2, I have focused on three: the uniform-state-laws process, intergovernmental lobbying, and the states' roles in implementing federal policy. These three safeguards constitute case studies in themselves, and I have further elaborated on them by additional case studies indicating their workings in the context of particular policymaking efforts. This structure is shown graphically in figure 1 in the introduction.

Case studies are used in this book as empirical underpinnings of my general argument that state officials have a variety of ways today to resist perceived federal encroachments on their legal, fiscal, and administrative interests. Because policymaking context is so important to the workings of each of the safeguards I emphasize, case studies are the best way to highlight all of the variables of interest to me: which state interests are at stake in a particular policymaking episode, which state officials are the key players at any given time, what sorts of leverage on the federal government a particular safeguard gives states, and so forth. There is no general correct number of case studies one must examine to yield valid findings, and even a small number of case studies may be representative if they are carefully chosen.[6] I chose my case studies from a range of policy areas and from a range of time periods across the late twentieth and early twenty-first centuries. Even so, the case studies I have examined are not intended to be representative of every other safeguard or policy that I might have selected. Rather, following Robert K. Yin, I have been interested both in presenting examples of the various types of state-governmental interests outlined in chapter 1 and in validating analytic generalizations about the theory of the political safeguards of federalism, indicating how each case illustrates some aspect of that theory.[7] To help readers evaluate the validity of my conclusions regarding the case studies—whether my explanations are better than any of the other "plausible rival hypotheses"[8] about whether or how state officials' efforts influenced several federal policymaking episodes—I have indicated the competing explanations that provide the strongest challenges to my conclusions. Certainly, many observers of state–federal relations today have concluded that the system is seriously misbalanced to the detriment of state governments, so the present book has its work cut out for it in trying to indicate why the states may be better positioned today than is immediately apparent. To present my conclusions as clearly as possible, I have taken pains in chapter 6 to specify the conditions under which political safeguards tend to succeed.

Safeguards of Federalism Case Studies

I selected the three safeguards of federalism described in chapters 3 to 5—the uniform-laws process, intergovernmental lobbying, and the states' implementation of federal policy—to demonstrate state involvement and influence at each stage of the federal policymaking process, referencing a five-stage model of that process developed by James Anderson. As I have noted in chapter 2, states have a wide variety of political safeguards at their disposal when attempting to influence the federal government, so I had choices to make in terms of which ones to focus on in chapter-length case studies. I chose cases of safeguards to highlight (1) a strategy available to states at each stage of the federal policymaking process, (2) the variety of state-governmental interests that these safeguards attempt to promote, (3) the wide variety of elected and appointed state officials (and others) involved in executing these safeguards, and (4) the ways that states' "losses" at one stage of the federal policymaking process can be recontested at a subsequent stage. Moreover, I wanted to show that none of these safeguards works 100% of the time; in contests with the federal government, the states sometimes win and sometimes lose. Most observers of American politics understand the states' losses, but it was important to choose cases that show state victories as well—where a victory is defined as having federal policy embody one or more identifiable state-governmental interests.

The uniform-laws process, when successful, can keep issues off the federal policymaking agenda and thereby forestall preemptive policymaking efforts by Congress and executive agencies. Intergovernmental lobbying by state officials gives them a voice in the development and passage of federal legislation. The states' many roles in implementing and enforcing federal policy give them additional opportunities to influence the ways that federal law is carried out. These examples thus indicate that state influence in federal policymaking spans all stages of that process. They also show the variety of individuals who are engaged in work that promotes the various interests of state governments relative to the federal government. Uniform-laws commissioners are not public officials per se, but their work can be seen as broadly promoting state decisionmaking authority by enhancing the quality of state legislation and by working to minimize the interstate variations in major policy areas that could lead influential interests to pressure Congress for a single federal law that would preempt nonuniform state laws. Governors, state legislators, state budget officers, state treasurers, and others who lobby Congress individually and through national associations are more typical of the sorts of state officials who are visible to the public and to scholars. Such individuals perceive and act on state governmental interests, particularly those related to decisionmaking authority and finances, as part of their everyday work. The various forms of intergovernmental lobbying also indicate clearly the various forms of state-governmental interests—those that are perceived by all state governments and those perceived by smaller subgroups of states or state officials. Finally, heads of state administrative agencies and lower-level employees of those agencies are perhaps best positioned to perceive and act on state interests related to administrative flexibility. They are directly affected by federal legislation and regulations that limit states' flexibility, impose strict deadlines, prescribe particular methodologies, and so forth.

Policy Case Studies

Nested within each of the three safeguards I have focused on are additional case studies of specific policymaking episodes. To illustrate how the uniform-laws process can safeguard state interests, I have focused on the NCCUSL, UCC, and the SSTP. The UCC is the most far-reaching product of the uniform-laws process to date, encompassing in its various articles an enormous swath of commercial law in the United States. This case study illustrates how states have protected their basic legal authority to legislate on commercial matters against attempts by the federal government to do so. Efforts since 1950 to develop, enact, and update the UCC make it a useful exemplar of the promise and limits of the uniform-laws process.

The SSTP illustrates the states' efforts to legislate collectively to forestall federal legislation that would hurt states' fiscal interests (in this case, their ability to tax Internet commerce). This case enriches the analysis in chapter 3 by looking at a uniform-laws process driven by an organization other than the NCCUSL. The states' generic fiscal interests are extremely clear in this instance, although the Republican Party's anti-tax stance in recent years has complicated the politics surrounding Congress's choice of whether to permit or preempt state taxation of online commerce in light of sometimes conflicting state views on the matter. This case study thus usefully exemplifies Paul Posner's point that "state and local groups are often disarmed by their lack of political cohesion on key policy issues; lacking agreement, they are often unable to articulate positions in national debates."[9] The SSTP shows, however, that the level of states' political cohesion is not static and can increase over time as momentum builds or political tides shift. As of this writing, the final outcome of the SSTP's efforts is not yet known, but it has gained a great deal more momentum than might have been predicted in its earliest days.

To illustrate the functioning of the intergovernmental lobby, I have presented case studies of the governors' lobbying efforts surrounding the 1996 welfare-reform law and the 1996 reauthorization of the Safe Drinking Water Act. The welfare-reform law—the PRWORA—is a far-reaching statute that affects nearly all of the state-governmental interests outlined in chapter 2. States had long called for the federal government to give them greater control over the payment of federal welfare funds as well as greater flexibility to tailor programs to the particular circumstances of their respective states. States also wanted to be the primary implementers of welfare programs in this country, free of as many federal strings as possible. The law Congress passed handed states an overall victory but one with numerous federal strings still attached. The law's passage clearly illustrates the role of the NGA and other associations of state officials. It shows the power and the limits of the NGA, particularly in terms of how governors' partisanship may affect the level of access they have to congressional leaders. Although this law is atypical because of its scope (major legislation like this does not happen every year), I felt it was important to include a social-services policy case in this book, particularly one where the state interests were so widespread and clear.

The Safe Drinking Water Act reauthorization implicated states' fiscal and administrative interests to the extent that under the pre-1996 version of the law it was very expensive for local water systems to implement the federal regulations aimed at keeping hazardous substances out of drinking water across the country. The federal regulations were highly prescriptive and required all water systems to test drinking water for a long list of substances regardless of the likelihood of their presence in a given area.

I have illustrated the states' strategic uses of their role as federal law implementers by describing the states' involvement in Clean Air Act enforcement and in their implementation of the 2001 NCLB law. The Clear Air Act case indicates very clearly the ways that states try to promote their administrative interests when negotiating SIPs with the federal government. NCLB is a preemptive piece of legislation that marked a major federal advance into a policy area traditionally reserved mainly to the states. Although this law may initially have seemed to override state-governmental policymaking authority so decisively as to call into serious question the ability of states to safeguard their interests today, I view the states' actions since the law was signed as a good example of the second and third chances states often have to protect their interests even if they "lose" at an earlier stage of the federal policy-making process. The case study in chapter 5 focuses mainly on how states have resisted the NCLB provision calling for all teachers to be "highly qualified" to teach in their areas, but states have also pushed back against the federal government in terms of who they have to test annually and how those results must be reported.

Taken together, the policy case studies presented in this book illustrate how various combinations of state-level officials exercise the available safeguards to promote and protect their legal, fiscal, and administrative interests today. The case studies reveal the complexity of the policy-making episodes that affect major state interests and also the rarity of unalloyed victories by either the federal government or the states in state–federal contests. The case studies of three political safeguards of federalism are not intended to reveal generalizable principles about the workings of all safeguards; rather, they are intended to show the variation among the safeguards and the ways that they work at different stages of the policymaking process. The policy case studies within each of the three safeguards are similarly not intended to be generalizable to all policymaking episodes but, rather, were chosen to show variation in how different types of legislation—social, environmental, fiscal, educational—implicate different state-governmental interests and provide different contexts in which states can work to promote those interests. Drawing on the case studies, I have identified in chapter 6 factors that appear to affect the success of state officials' attempts to influence federal policymaking. The diversity of the case studies seems to have captured the complexity of today's political safeguards of federalism and their chances of success, showing both the strengths and the weaknesses of these safeguards. Although additional research across policy areas is needed to further validate the central thesis of this book, in combination, the case studies, content analysis, and interviews give me confidence in my conclusions.

NOTES

INTRODUCTION

1. Caminker, "State Sovereignty and Subordinance," 1086.

2. As will be explained in greater detail below, essays 45 and 46 of *The Federalist* make clear the framers' expectation that the political and administrative processes would afford state officials numerous opportunities to "resist and frustrate" federal actions they view as encroachments on state authority. See Madison, "Nos. 45 and 46," in Rossiter, *Federalist Papers*, 288–300.

3. Madison, "No. 51," in Rossiter, *Federalist Papers*, 323 (emphasis added).

4. Here, I am purposely avoiding terms like "states' rights" and "state sovereignty" for reasons explained in Chapter 1.

5. For a good overview of this literature, see Peabody's "Congressional Constitutional Interpretation and the Courts" and "Book Review." See also Whittington, "Extrajudicial Constitutional Interpretation"; Whittington, *Constitutional Construction*; Tushnet, *Taking the Constitution Away from the Courts*; and Gant, "Judicial Supremacy," 359.

6. See, e.g., Ginsberg and Shefter, *Politics by Other Means*; Alfred Hill, "Opinion"; Manuel and Cammisa, *Checks and Balances?*; Whittington, *Constitutional Construction*; Lazare, *Frozen Republic*; Jones, *Presidency in a Separated System*; Fisher, *Politics of Shared Power*; Graber, "Nonmajoritarian Difficulty"; Crabb and Holt, *Invitation to Struggle*; Sundquist, *Constitutional Reform and Effective Government*; Burgess, *Contest for Constitutional Authority*; R. Douglas Arnold, *Logic of Congressional Action*; Knight, *Separation of Powers in the American Political System*; Tulis, *Rhetorical Presidency*; Goldwin and Kaufman, *Separation of Powers*; and Bessette and Tulis, *Presidency in the Constitutional Order*.

7. For evidence of this scholarly divide, see Whittington, "Crossing Over."

8. For excellent general surveys of the development of American federalism, see David B. Walker, *Rebirth of Federalism*; and Conlan, *From New Federalism to Devolution*.

9. This literature is too extensive to summarize, but it tends to react to the decisions of the Supreme Court, with each new federalism opinion generating a new body of research evaluating the merits of the decision. See, e.g., Cross, "Realism about Federalism"; and Rapaczynski, "From Sovereignty to Process."

10. Leonard D. White, *States and the Nation*, vii.

11. Wechsler, "Political Safeguards of Federalism"; Prakash and Yoo, "Puzzling Persistence"; Marci A. Hamilton, "Elusive Safeguards of Federalism"; Kramer, "Putting the Politics Back"; Cross, "Realism about Federalism"; Krotoszynski, "Listening to the 'Sounds of Sovereignty'"; Garrett, "States in a Federal System"; Dinan, "State Governmental Influence"; Yoo, "Judicial Safeguards of Federalism"; Kramer, "Understanding Federalism"; and Pittenger, "Garcia and the Political Safeguards of Federalism."

12. Madison, "No. 51," in Rossiter, *Federalist Papers*, 295.

13. Wechsler, "Political Safeguards of Federalism," 558.

14. *Garcia v. San Antonio Metropolitan Transit Authority*, 469 U.S. 528 (1985). (Wechsler and Choper are cited in footnote 11 of Justice Blackmun's opinion for the majority).

15. See, e.g., David B. Walker, *Rebirth of Federalism*, especially chap. 7; Greve, *Real Federalism*; Jackson, "Federalism and the Uses and Limits of the Law"; Yoo, "Judicial Safeguards of Federalism"; Gardbaum, "Rethinking Constitutional Federalism"; and DuPont, "Federalism in the Twenty-first Century."

16. See, e.g., Collins, "Towards an Integrated Model"; Sullivan, "From States' Rights Blues to Blue States' Rights"; Melnick, "Deregulating the States"; Noonan, *Narrowing the Nation's Power*; Nagel, *Implosion of American Federalism*; Baybeck and Lowry, "Federalism Outcomes and Ideological Preferences"; and Waltenberg and Swinford, *Litigating Federalism*.

17. The work of law professor Larry Kramer is most consistent with the present work in terms of its argument that there are important political safeguards of federalism other than those that Wechsler and Choper have identified. See Kramer's articles "Understanding Federalism," "Putting the Politics Back into the Political Safeguards of Federalism," and "But When Exactly Was Judicially Enforced Federalism 'Born' in the First Place?" In this book, I greatly extend his analysis by considering several political safeguards that he does not discuss and by rooting a book-length analysis in the public policy and public administration literatures in a way that Kramer's legal training does not lead him to do. Nonetheless, Kramer's work should be consulted for its excellent discussions of political parties as well as its extensive citations of founding-era writings and contemporary legal scholarship.

18. Prakash and Yoo, "Puzzling Persistence," 1460.

19. Corwin, "Constitution v. Constitutional Theory," 291.

20. Ibid. See also Elazar, *American Federalism*, 41–46.

21. Several scholars have attributed the tendency in the American system for this political development of constitutional meaning to the fact that it is so difficult to formally amend the text of the Constitution. In the face of such difficulties, other means are required to keep our understandings of the Constitution reasonably consistent with political realities. See, e.g., Donald S. Lutz, "Toward a Theory of Constitutional Amendment."

22. See generally Whittington, "Dismantling the Modern State?"

23. Anton, *American Federalism and Public Policy*, 208. This point has been made by many others over the years. See, e.g., Woodrow Wilson's well-known view that "the question of the relation of the States to the federal government . . . cannot, indeed, be settled by the opinion of any one generation, because it is a question of growth, and every successive stage of our political and economic development gives it a new aspect, makes it a new question" (*Constitutional Government in the United States*, 173–74). It should be noted that many scholars and judges, particularly conservatives, believe that the Constitution and other founding documents *do* contain reasonably clear principles concerning the limits on federal authority. See, e.g., Thierer, *Delicate Balance*; and Berger, *Federalism: The Founders' Design*.

24. Grodzins, *American System*; and Elazar, *American Partnership*. Deil S. Wright, one of the strongest proponents of using the concept of intergovernmental relations (IGR) in place of federalism, argues that "unlike federalism, IGR avoids an emphasis on national/state relations, goes far beyond legalism, does not presume hierarchical relationships, incorporates an extensive range of policy-connected interests, and is a more neutral concept than the often-politicized federalism" (*Understanding Intergovernmental Relations*, 2nd ed., 40). Taking a contrary view, Thomas R. Dye, a noted scholar of federalism and state government, has written that "the notion of federalism has fallen on such hard times that some leading scholars have urged its replacement with simple descriptions of 'intergovernmental relations.' Rather than search for a viable analytic or normative model of federalism, it seems easier to provide empirical descriptions of current relationships among national, state, and local governments" (*American Federalism*, 3–4).

25. See Wright, *Understanding Intergovernmental Relations*, 3rd ed.; and Reagan, *New Federalism*.

26. Reagan, *New Federalism*, 163.

27. Laski, "Obsolescence of Federalism." Gulick is the source of the oft-quoted remark that "The American state is finished. I do not predict that the states will go, but affirm that they are gone" ("Reorganization of the State," 420–421). For an assessment of post–New Deal views of the weaknesses of state governments, see Sanford, *Storm over the States*.

28. One of the earliest proclamations of an emerging "devolution revolution" in the mid-1990s was Richard P. Nathan's "Devolution Revolution: An Overview," in *Rockefeller Institute Bulletin*. For the view that Congress's actions have fallen far short of its rhetoric on devolving power to the states, even when controlled by Republicans, see Schmitt, "For Schiavo, Republicans Invite Federal Activism"; Stolberg, "Revolution that Wasn't"; Paul E. Peterson, "Changing Politics of Federalism"; Grunwald, "In Legislative Tide, State Power Ebbs"; and Conlan, *From New Federalism to Devolution*, chap. 13. For the view that the effects of the Rehnquist Court's alleged revolution in judicial federalism have also been overstated, see Sullivan, "From States' Rights Blues to Blue States' Rights."

29. The idea of clearly sorting out governmental functions and making one level of government primarily or solely responsible for each policy area has a long pedigree; the most sustained recent attempt to draw such lines is found in Alice M. Rivlin's *Reviving the American Dream: The Economy, the States, and the Federal Government*. Rivlin's book attracted attention in part because of her service as deputy director (1992–94) and director (1994–96) of the White House Office of Management and Budget.

30. For a concise summary, see Wise, "Supreme Court's New Constitutional Federalism." See also Waltenberg and Swinford, *Litigating Federalism*; Greve, *Real Federalism*; and Noonan, *Narrowing the Nation's Power*.

31. See David B. Walker's "Advent of an Ambiguous Federalism" and *Rebirth of Federalism*.

32. Melancton Smith, "Speech Delivered in the Course of Debate," 334.

33. See Cross, "Realism about Federalism."

34. See, e.g., Prakash and Yoo, "The Puzzling Persistence"; Yoo, "Judicial Safeguards of Federalism"; and David B. Walker, *Rebirth of Federalism*, especially chap. 11.

35. In a somewhat different context, Lawrence Sager notes, "If the judiciary is constrained by the durable features of its institutional role from fully enforcing the Constitution, it follows that we should encourage and welcome the assistance of other governmental actors in realizing more fully the Constitution's aims" (*Justice in Plainclothes*, 102).

36. Clark, "Putting the Safeguards Back," 341 (emphasis in original).

37. Schlesinger, *Imperial Presidency*, 13.

38. Here, I strongly concur with Clark's conclusion that "it is difficult to conclude that the political safeguards and judicial review are interchangeable features of the constitutional scheme. On at least some occasions, each mechanism provides distinct protection against unwarranted 'intrusions from the center on the domain of the states'" ("Putting the Safeguards Back," 340, quoting Wechsler).

39. Pickerill and Clayton, "Rehnquist Court and the Political Dynamics of Federalism"; and Clayton and Pickerill, "Guess What Happened on the Way to the Revolution."

CHAPTER 1

1. *Garcia v. San Antonio Metropolitan Transit Authority*, 469 U.S. 528 (1985), 546 (emphasis in original).

2. Throughout the book, I use the admittedly unwieldy phrase "state-governmental interests vis-à-vis the federal government." I use this phrase because I want to emphasize that federalism implicates *state-governmental* interests rather than the interests perceived by individuals or interest groups *within* a state. I also want to emphasize the interests that state governments perceive in their interactions with the federal government as the federal government develops, passes, and implements policies that affect state governments. Concise synonyms for the phrase "vis-à-vis" are unfortunately few, so I ask for the reader's indulgence for my repeated use of it.

3. Although this characterization seems to imply that members of Congress, presidents, and judges are nothing more than rational individuals intent on utility maximization of various sorts, there is room in such a view for concepts of institutional well-being, public service, and the common good. For example, while not denying that members of Congress calibrate their activities to promote their reelection chances, Joseph Bessette and Arthur Maass have demonstrated that these goals are consistent with views of Congress as a deliberative body and individual members as public-minded "serious lawmakers." See Bessette, *Mild Voice of Reason*, 135–36; and Maass, *Congress and the Common Good*, especially chap. 1.

4. See Fenno, *Congressmen in Committee*; Mayhew, *Congress: The Electoral Connection*; Bessette, *Mild Voice of Reason*; Kingdon, *Congressmens' Voting Decisions*; and Maass, *Congress and the Common Good*.

5. For recent evidence of such behavior—in the context of Senate debates over the future of the filibuster—see Toner, "Demands of Partisanship," who notes, "Some 'institutionalists'—those who think about the Senate they will leave behind—say that many senators are now putting short-term political interests above the constitutional prerogatives of the Senate"(A16).

6. For examples of presidents defending the use of executive privilege, see, e.g., Shenon, "House Votes to Issue Contempt Citations." For examples of attempts to resist inquiries of independent counsels, see, e.g., Ginsberg and Shefter, *Politics by Other Means*, 27–31. For examples of attempts to prevent public disclosure, see, e.g., Stout, "Appeals Court Backs Cheney"; Lardner, "Bush Seeks Secrecy"; Lardner, "Bill Aimed at Reversing Bush"; and Milbank, "Senate Panel Says Enron." For ability to challenge congressional assertions of war powers, see Ely, *War and Responsibility*; and Mike Allen and Eilperin, "Bush Aides Say Iraq War." For attempts to acquire "fast-track" authority, see, e.g., Rosenbaum, "Gephardt Says He Will Resist"; and Bumiller, "Bush Signs Trade Bill." Fast-track negotiating authority was granted to the president by the Trade Act of 2002, signed on August 6, 2002.

7. Regarding congressional challenges to presidential pocket vetoes, see, e.g., the remarks of Speaker of the House J. Dennis Hastert (R-Ill.) criticizing President Bill Clinton's use of the pocket veto during an intrasession adjournment in the 106th Congress (U.S. Congress, *Congressional Record*, E1523). For challenge to presidential exercise of the line-item veto, see, e.g., *Clinton v. City of New York*, 524 U.S. 417 (1998), which declared unconstitutional the line-item veto powers granted to the president by Public Law 104-130; and Farrier, *Passing the Buck*, chap. 6. For challenges to presidential recess appointments of judicial and executive branch officials, see, e.g., Wigfield, "Bush May Bypass Congress"; and Dewar, "President, Senate Reach Pact." Regarding executive branch rulemaking, Congress asserted its authority to overturn final agency regulations in the Congressional Review Act of 1996. This authority was first exercised in 2001, when Congress voted to overturn regulations requiring employers to make ergonomic modifications to the workplace to prevent repetitive stress injuries among employees. See Mike Allen, "Bush Signs Repeal of Ergonomics Rules." Regarding challenges to use of presidential signing statements to undercut Congress's legislative intent, see, e.g., Charlie Savage, "Hearing Set on Signing Statements." Finally, regarding the exercise of judicial review by the Supreme Court, see, e.g., Rehnquist, "2004 Year-End Report," criticizing proposals by some members of Congress to impeach or punish judges whose decisions they dislike; and Biskupic, "Hill Republicans Target 'Judicial Activism.'"

8. To be sure, American history provides many instances of one branch of government deferring to another, sometimes over a period of years. For a discussion of institutional deference in the realm of budgeting, see Farrier, *Passing the Buck*. More recently, many political commentators noted that the Republican-controlled 107th to 109th Congresses rarely challenged and exercised little oversight over the administration of George W. Bush, particularly after the September 11, 2001, terrorist attacks. See, e.g., Chapman, "Welcoming the Return of Divided Government"; and Carr, "Some in GOP Say Bush Abuses Powers." The passage of time will clarify whether the post–September 11 climate made this period an aberration or the norm. Although institutional deference appears to negate the Madisonian prediction of politicians steadfastly and ambitiously advancing their interests, such periods may be thought of as temporary abeyances that typically end with strenuous reassertions of institutional prerogative. See, e.g., the discussion of congressional attempts to reign in the "imperial presidency" following Richard Nixon's resignation in Peabody and Nugent's, "Toward a Unifying Theory of the Separation of Powers."

9. This terminology is used by, among others, Alexander Hamilton, who distinguished "STATES or GOVERNMENTS, in their CORPORATE or COLLECTIVE CAPACITIES, and as contradistinguished from the INDIVIDUALS of whom they consist" (Hamilton, "No. 15," in Rossiter, *Federalist Papers*, 108). This idea is also captured in the phrase "states as states," which has been used in a number of

Supreme Court opinions. See, e.g., Justice Sandra Day O'Connor's dissenting opinion in *Garcia v. San Antonio Metropolitan Authority*, 469 U.S. 528, 581 (1985), which appears as the epigraph to this chapter.

10. A similar view of state interests vis-à-vis the federal government is outlined in a remarkable but apparently little-noticed 1972 article by Richard Lehne called "Benefits in State–National Relations." While rereading Lehne's article as I was finalizing this book for publication, I was struck by the extent to which he had outlined a view of American federalism that I ultimately echoed to a larger degree than is reflected in the notes. I strongly commend this article to any interested reader. His view of state interests is informed by the typology outlined in Farkas, *Urban Lobbying*, chap. 8.

11. Interview with staff member for governor of New Jersey, Washington, D.C., August 1996. Most interviews were conducted in confidentiality; hence, the names of most interviewees are withheld by mutual agreement (see appendix for details).

12. Dinan, "State Governmental Influence."

13. Choper, *Judicial Review and the National Political Process*, 180–81.

14. Skocpol, "Bringing the State Back In," 9.

15. Skocpol, "Bringing the State Back In," 12.

16. See generally Robertson and Judd, *Development of American Public Policy*; and Stoker, *Reluctant Partners*.

17. March and Olsen, *Rediscovering Institutions*. This view is not limited to governmental organizations, as seen in the following exchange:

> "The bank isn't like a man."
>
> "Yes, but the bank is only made of men."
>
> "No, you're wrong there—quite wrong there. The bank is something else than men. It happens that every man in a bank hates what the bank does, and yet the bank does it. The bank is something more than men, I tell you" (Steinbeck, *Grapes of Wrath*, 35).

18. B. Guy Peters notes that government organizations are not monolithic, but that each of the many agencies and bureaus within a government "has its own goals, ideas, and concepts about how to attack the public problems it is charged with administering" (*American Public Policy*, 95).

19. Skowronek, "Order and Change," 94.

20. This is one of the best-known features of how the leading defenders of the Constitution thought. Madison believed that to allow officials in each branch of national government to resist the encroachments by those of the other branches, "ambition must be made to counteract ambition. The interests of the man must be connected with the institutional rights of the place" ("No. 51," in Rossiter, *Federalist Papers*, 322).

21. March and Olsen, *Rediscovering Institutions*, 40.

22. *Ibid.*, 17. See also Shepsle, "Studying Institutions."

23. Alan Rosenthal, *Governors and Legislatures*, 7. See the analysis below of the governors' state-of-the-state addresses.

24. Troy Smith, "What Safeguards of Federalism?" 12. On how New York State attempts to speak with one voice in Washington, see Liebschutz, *Bargaining under Federalism*, chap. 4.

25. Interview with head of the Austin office, Texas Office of State–Federal Relations, Austin, Tex., June 1996. The form ("Report of State Agency Travel to Washington, D.C.") that state employee must fill out is available on the office's website, http://www.osfr.state.tx.us/travelform.asp (accessed June 27, 2006).

26. Nice, *Federalism*, 10. More recently, commentators have used the terms "stovepiping" and "siloing" to refer to this sort of phenomenon.

27. Scheberle, *Federalism and Environmental Policy*; and Derthick, *Influence of Federal Grants*.

28. Nice, *Federalism*, 11.

29. "California Asks Justice Department"; and Pear, "U.S. Recommending Strict New Rules."

30. Weidner, "Decision-Making in a Federal System," 369. Alaska and Hawaii joined the Union in 1959, but at the time Weidner's work was written, there were 48 states.

31. Alonso-Zaldivar, "50 Governors United"; and Steinhauer, "51 Governors Resist Shifting." (The 51st governor mentioned in the headline was from Puerto Rico.)

32. Associated Press State and Local Wire, "Katz Resigns."

33. Interview with a governor's staff member, Washington, D.C., August 15, 1996.

34. Vobejda, "Welfare Bill Glides through Senate."

35. For other examples, see Dillon, "New U.S. Secretary Showing Flexibility" (noting the disagreements between Utah's overwhelmingly Republican state officials and the Bush administration's signature education law); Balz, "GOP Governors Want a Seat at the Table"; and Belluck, "Governors Unite in Medicaid Fight."

36. Interview with Midwestern governor's staff member, Washington, D.C., August 15, 1996.

37. Scholars of federalism disagree on the extent to which local governments are implicated in debates about the nature of American federalism. Scholars who focus on federalism tend to leave city and town governments out of their analyses, whereas scholars of intergovernmental relations include localities. Technically, local governments are creations of state governments and are autonomous only to the degree that a state government allows them to be. In practice, since the New Deal, the federal government has had increasing legal and fiscal relations with local governments, which explains the preference of some scholars to emphasize the intergovernmental relations between local,

state, and national governments. In the present work, I deal mostly with relations between state officials and national officials.

38. Donnay, "Politicians and Professionals," 84. For a general history of public officials' associations, see David S. Arnold and Plant, *Public Official Associations and State and Local Government.*

39. For a good general survey of how states' size differences affected the development of the 1787 Constitution's system of representation, see Zagarri, *Politics of Size.*

40. See generally Smylie, "Difficulties of a Small State"; and Lee and Oppenheimer, *Sizing Up the Senate,* especially chaps. 6 and 7.

41. Madison, "No. 37," in Rossiter, *Federalist Papers,* 230. See also Madison's comments at the Philadelphia convention regarding the dissimilarities among the three largest states—Massachusetts, Virginia, and Pennsylvania. ("Debate on State Equality in the Senate [June 28–July 2]," in Ketcham, *Anti-Federalist Papers and the Constitutional Convention Debates,* 93–94).

42. See generally Turner, *Significance of Sections in American History.* On the ways that regions are affected differentially by federal grant programs, see Havemann, Stanfield, and Pierce, "Federal Spending."

43. Glennon, "Federalism as a Regional Issue," 841. See also the description of the policy implications of the political culture of the modern West in Luton, *Politics of Garbage,* chap. 3; and Verhovek, "Drill, Say Alaskans."

44. NCSL, "Policy on Commercial Space Transportation," *Goals for State–Federal Action,* http://www.ncsl.org/statefed/energy.html. See also Kaufman, "If New Mexico Builds It"; Handberg and Johnson-Freese, "State Spaceport Initiatives"; and Chang, "States Rush to Build Spaceports."

45. For current information about the status of federal regulations on launch facilities, see the website of the U.S. Department of Transportation, Associate Administrator for Commercial Space Transportation, http://ast.faa.gov/lrra/ (accessed June 22, 2005).

46. See Mertens, "States Eye Stricter Curbs"; and Cauchon, "For Great Lakes."

47. On regional governors' associations and other councils, see Hall, *New Institutions of Federalism,* chap. 3.

48. See http://www.southerngovernors.org/resolutions/index.html and http://www.westgov.org/wga_resolutions.htm, respectively.

49. U.S. Department of Energy, *Yucca Mountain Science and Engineering Report,* p. 1-1; and Gerrard, *Whose Backyard, Whose Risk?,* 30.

50. See Greg Schneider and Pianin, "Nuclear Dump's Foes Hopeful"; and Scott Allen, "If We Can't Bury Nuclear Waste." The law was Public Law 100–203.

51. For an excellent detailed account of the federal-grant-seeking activities of a particular state, see Bullock, *Dollars We Deserve.*

52. Most of the governors' Washington offices are in a single building on Capitol Hill called the Hall of the States. For a current list of states and governors

with offices in the Hall of the States building, see http://www.sso.org/ affiliates.htm. As of April 2007, 35 states as well as three U.S. territories had offices in the building, as did the NGA and numerous other state public official associations. See also chapter 3's discussion and listing of states with Washington offices.

53. On this point, see Troy E. Smith, "What Safeguards of Federalism?"; Morrisroe, "State of 'State Offices' in Washington"; and Calmes, "444 North Capitol Street," 20.

54. Donahue, *Disunited States*, chaps. 5 and 6.

55. See, e.g., Morgan, "Hastert Directs Millions to Birthplace"; "Capitol Bloat"; and Morgan, "Funding Bill Contains Plenty of Goodies."

56. See, e.g., Ehrlich, "Increasing Federalization of Crime"; ABA Task Force on Federalization of Criminal Law, *Federalization of Criminal Law*; and Donn, "Making Federal Cases Out of Common Crimes."

57. Saulny and Rutenberg, "Kansas Tornado Renews Debate on Guard at War"; Kettl, "Senator Warner's Posse"; and Steinhauer, "51 Governors Resist Shifting Authority Over Guard." As the title of the latter article indicates, this issue concerns a universal state-governmental interest—one that all governors were able to agree on. On attempts by governors to roll back this provision, see Blumenthal, "National Guard Control Argued"; and Kavan Peterson, "Governors Lose in Power Struggle over National Guard."

58. See Donnelly, "House Reverses Course on Martial Law"; and Bruno, "Defense Policy Bill Outlines Major National Guard Changes."

59. *United States v. Morrison*, 120 S. Ct. 1740 (2000). See Martin, "*United States v. Morrison*," 322; and Biskupic, "States' Role at Issue in Rape Suit." The Supreme Court ultimately scaled back portions of the law on federalism grounds.

60. For general discussions of the uses of the concept as applied to the American states, see Drake and Nelson, *States' Rights and American Federalism*; Berger, *Federalism: The Founders' Design*; Virginia Commission on Constitutional Government, *We the States*; Bennett, *American Theories of Federalism*; and Kilpatrick, "Case for 'States' Rights.'"

61. Article II of the Articles of Confederation (promulgated on March 1, 1781) reads, "Each state retains its sovereignty, freedom, and independence, and every power, jurisdiction, and right, which is not by this Confederation expressly delegated to the United States, in Congress assembled" (in Ketcham, *Anti-Federalist Papers*, 357–364).

62. Amar, "Of Sovereignty and Federalism," 1456.

63. See, e.g., "No. 39," in which Madison notes that "each state, in ratifying the Constitution, is considered as a sovereign body independent of all others, and only to be bound by its own voluntary act" (in Rossiter, *Federalist Papers*, 244).

64. See Corley, Howard, and Nixon, "Supreme Court and Opinion Content"; and Ducayet, "Publius and Federalism."

65. Even the *militarily* conclusive American Civil War failed to eliminate political and cultural movements centered around state sovereignty and limits on federal authority. For a serious but entertaining account, see Horowitz, *Confederates in the Attic*.

66. *Garcia v. San Antonio Metropolitan Transit Authority,* 469 U.S. 528 (1985), 567.

67. The view that the federal structure was intended by the framers to preserve individual liberty and provide citizens with choices of different sets of state-governmental services is typically referred to as "competitive federalism" or "libertarian textualism." See, e.g., Greve, *Real Federalism,* 2–3; Thierer, *Delicate Balance,* 63–75; Dye, *American Federalism*; and Rockefeller, *Future of Federalism*.

68. A great deal has been written on the question of whether U.S. senators historically have represented state governments in any sense, or whether they have represented the interests of individuals and groups within their states. The effects of the Seventeenth Amendment, which called for the direct popular election of senators, have also been analyzed to determine whether it changed the nature of senatorial representation. In general, most scholars have found that long before the Seventeenth Amendment, U.S. senators already were acting as representatives of broad national interests rather than the interests of their state governments. See Swift, *Making of an American Senate,* especially chap. 6; Stewart, "Responsiveness in the Upper Chamber"; and Riker, "Senate and American Federalism." For the view that the Seventeenth Amendment *did* have important consequences, see Crook and Hibbing, "A Not-So-Distant Mirror"; Bybee, "Ulysses at the Mast"; and Hoebeke, *Road to Mass Democracy*.

69. For further explication of this point, see Donald S. Lutz, *Origins of American Constitutionalism,* chap. 10, noting that "from one-half and two-thirds of what was in the Articles showed up in the 1787 document" (p. 133), and that the Constitution "did not so much replace the Articles as evolve from it, a revision of an earlier experiment found to be flawed" (p. 135).

70. In the classic formulation of the modes of intergovernmental regulation, the federal government may act directly on the states in four ways: by direct orders, crosscutting requirements, crossover sanctions, and partial preemptions. See U.S. Advisory Commission on Intergovernmental Relations, *Regulatory Federalism*.

71. The classic statements of the cooperative federalism thesis come from Grodzins and Elazar. See Grodzins, "Federal System"; and Elazar, *American Partnership*.

72. See generally William Anderson, *Nation and the States,* 145–47; Cross, "Realism about Federalism"; and Ducayet, "Publius and Federalism." Ducayet concludes that over two hundred years of debate has "fail[ed] to provide any consensus as to the proper meaning of *The Federalist* with respect to the constitutional system of federalism" (p. 824).

73. Wilkins, "Tribal-State Affairs."

74. A view of federalism not centered on "sovereignty" need not imply a marginal status for state governments in the federal system. Indeed, as early as the 1810s and 1820s, thinkers such as John Taylor of Caroline had articulated a constitutional theory of federalism that emphasized the authoritative role of the states without recourse to notions of state sovereignty. See, e.g., C. William Hill, Jr., *Political Theory of John Taylor of Caroline*, 195–200. For example, in 1820 Taylor specifically renounced the "idea sometimes advanced, that the state governments ever were or continue to be, sovereign or unlimited."

The limits of the concept of sovereignty have also been noted by international relations scholars, who point to its limited utility in describing and explaining the inability of national governments to exercise control over their borders, their monetary policies, and their populations in the face of globalization, refugee crises, the international drug trade, and so forth. See generally Krasner, *Sovereignty*, especially chap. 1.

75. Petersen, "Check is in the Mail." See generally Barrett and Greene, "Staying Stable"; Prah, "Budget Picture Dominates Govs' Speeches"; and Mikesell, "Changing State Fiscal Capacity."

76. For an analysis of recent trends in light of the fiscal year 2009 proposed budget for federal grants to states, see Lav and Oliff, "Federal Grants to States."

77. U.S. Office of Management and Budget, *Budget Information for States*, 1. In February 2003, the U.S. Office of Management and Budget announced that it would no longer publish this useful document each year, although the data are still available from the Government Printing Office. See, e.g., GPO, "Budget of the United States Government, State-by-State Tables, Fiscal Year 2008," http://www.gpoaccess.gov/usbudget/fy08/bis.html.

78. U.S. Office of Management and Budget, *Budget Information for States*, 5–8.

79. See, e.g., Belluck, "Governors Unite in Medicaid Fight"; and Pear, "States Resist Bush's Appeal," which quotes Ohio Governor Robert Taft as follows: "We like ideas that save money for the federal government and the states through program efficiencies, but we do not support recommendations that would save the federal government money at the expense of the states."

80. For a discussion of state agency directors' preferences regarding federal grant programs, see Wright, *Understanding Intergovernmental Relations*, 2nd ed., chap. 9.

81. Weston, "Estate Tax Repeal to Hurt State Finances"; and Sack, "States Expecting to Lose Billions."

82. See, e.g., Dillon, "Some School Districts Challenging."

83. National Voter Registration Act of 1993, sec. 5(c)(1).

84. The best book-length treatment of the law is Posner, *Politics of Unfunded Mandates*.

85. U.S. House, Committee on Government Reform and Oversight, *Unfunded Mandates: A Five-Year Review and Recommendations for Change*, testimony of Raymond G. Sheppach, executive director of the NGA.

86. Chubb, "Political Economy of Federalism," 1004–05. See also Hills, "Federalism in Constitutional Context." Others have questioned the ability of federal administrators to adequately enforce grant conditions. See David B. Walker, *Rebirth of Federalism*, 324; DiIulio and Kettl, *Fine Print*, 16–19; and Wright, *Understanding Intergovernmental Relations*, 2nd ed., 35–36

87. Danitz, "State School Chiefs Concerned."

88. See "Federalism, Political Accountability"; Albert J. Rosenthal, "Conditional Federal Spending"; and McCoy and Friedman, "Conditional Spending," 85.

89. *South Dakota v. Dole*, 483 U.S. 203 (1987).

90. Ibid., p. 207.

91. Such instances are rare but not unheard of. Consider, for example, the case of former Gov. George Allen (R-Va.; later a U.S. senator), who repeatedly rejected Virginia's share of federal aid under the federal Goals 2000 education program and refused to let Virginia's localities participate in the program. See Matthew Bowers, "Virginia is the Last Holdout." More recent examples stem from the federal No Child Left Behind Act. One account noted that "in recent weeks . . . three Connecticut school districts have rejected federal money rather than comply with the red tape that accompanies the law" (Dillon, "Some School Districts Challenging"). However, such districts are the exception rather than the rule.

92. See, e.g., Greve, *Real Federalism*, 61; and McCoy and Friedman, "Conditional Spending," 90.

93. DiIulio and Kettl, *Fine Print*, 16–17. See also Stoker, *Reluctant Partners*.

94. Balz, "GOP Governors Seek Shift in Power."

95. National Governors' Conference, *Federal Roadblocks*, vii–viii.

96. Wright, *Understanding Intergovernmental Relations*, 2nd ed., 280.

97. See U.S. Advisory Commission on Intergovernmental Relations, *Regulatory Federalism*.

98. See Bragaw, "Federalism's Legal Defense Fund."

99. Alan Rosenthal, *Governors and Legislators*, 7; and Dye, *Politics in States and Communities*, 203–204, 212.

100. Data are from U.S. Census Bureau, *Compendium of Public Employment: 2002*, Table 2.

101. Thad Beyle, "Gubernatorial Institutional Power Index," 2001, University of North Carolina, http://www.unc.edu/~beyle/gubnewpwr.html (accessed March 5, 2005). The index is calculated by assigning a score ranging from 1 (lowest) to 5 (highest) to each governor's powers in terms of the degree to which executive branch officials are elected separately, the tenure potential of governors, the governor's appointment powers, the governor's budget powers, the governor's veto powers, and the strength of the governor's party in the legislature.

102. Data are from U.S. Office of Management and Budget, *Budget Information for States*, 3.

103. Data are from National Wilderness Institute website, http://www.nwi. org/Maps/LandChart.html (accessed March 5, 2005).

104. Alan Rosenthal, *Governors and Legislature*, 96.

CHAPTER 2

1. For a portrayal of interbranch and intergovernmental relations as a unified system of separation of powers, see Peabody and Nugent, "Toward a Unifying Theory."

2. Charles Fried, "How to Make the President Talk."

3. Wechsler, "Political Safeguards of Federalism." Wechsler's view echoes Madison's expectation that "a local spirit will infallibly prevail much more in the members of Congress than a national spirit will prevail in the legislatures of the particular states" ("No. 46," in Rossiter, *Federalist Papers*, 296).

4. Madison, "No. 46," in Rossiter, *Federalist Papers*, 297.

5. Ibid.

6. Ibid.

7. Ibid.

8. Ibid., 298. Note that this passage reflects the existence of categorical state-governmental interests—those shared by a group of states rather than by all states.

9. Ibid.

10. For an enumeration of many additional examples of antebellum state resistance of federal authority, see Goldstein, "State Resistance to Authority in Federal Unions."

11. Madison, "No. 10," in Rossiter, *Federalist Papers*.

12. See, e.g., Rauch, *Government's End*, chap. 3.

13. For additional predictions by a leading framer that this would be the case, see Alexander Hamilton, "Nos. 9, 16, and 17," in Rossiter, *Federalist Papers*.

14. DiIulio and Kettl, *Fine Print*, 18. See also Stoker, *Reluctant Partners*.

15. See generally Kettl, *Government by Proxy*.

16. Haider, *When Governments Come to Washington*, 308.

17. Fisher, *Politics of Shared Power*, ix.

18. Perhaps the best-known analysis of these stages of the policymaking process is Downs, "Up and Down with Ecology."

19. See Kerwin, *Rulemaking*.

20. The best-known work in this area is probably Pressman and Wildavsky, *Implementation*. The term "street-level bureaucrat" gained currency with the publication of Lipsky, *Street-Level Bureaucracy*.

21. Kingdon, *Agendas, Alternatives, and Public Policies*.

22. Ibid., 145.

23. For a thorough bibliography of such how-a-bill-becomes-a-law accounts, see the appendix of Bessette, *Mild Voice of Reason*.

24. James E. Anderson, *Public Policymaking*, 4.

25. Ibid., 309.

26. For a similar conception of the modes of influence over national policy that are available to states, see Lehne, "Benefits in State–National Relations."

27. See Thierer, *Delicate Balance*, 123, proposing a "supermajority veto power over federal legislation or regulation to force Congress to reconsider particularly egregious or potentially unconstitutional acts."

28. See Graves, *American Intergovernmental Relations*; Whittington, *Constitutional Construction*, chap. 3; and Goldstein, "State Resistance to Authority in Federal Unions."

29. Alexander Hamilton, "No. 17," in Rossiter, *Federalist Papers*, 119. Madison makes a similar point in "No. 45," noting that "the more I revolve the subject [of the federal government proving by degrees fatal to the State governments], the more fully I am persuaded that the balance is much more likely to be disturbed by the preponderancy of the last than of the first scale" (in Rossiter, *Federalist Papers*, 289).

30. Haider, *When Governments Come to Washington*, 307.

31. See David B. Walker, *Rebirth of Federalism*, 149–51; Conlan, *From New Federalism to Devolution*, 171–90; Williamson, *Reagan's Federalism*, 134–71; and Benton, "Economic Considerations and Reagan's New Federalism."

32. White House press release, August 5, 1998, quoted in Thierer, *Delicate Balance*, xii. See also David B. Walker, *Rebirth of Federalism*, 327.

33. Broder, "Federalism's New Framework."

34. Pear, "Study by Governors Calls Bush Welfare Plan Unworkable."

35. Pear, "House G.O.P. Softens Bush Welfare Plan."

36. See, e.g., Dillon, "Facing State Protests"; and Dobbs, "New Rules for 'No Child' Law Planned."

37. Alexander Hamilton anticipated this form of state resistance, noting "the essential difference between a mere NONCOMPLIANCE and a DIRECT and ACTIVE RESISTANCE. If the interposition of the State legislatures be necessary to give effect to a measure of the Union, they have only NOT TO ACT, or TO ACT EVASIVELY, and the measure is defeated. This neglect of duty may be disguised under affected but unsubstantial provisions so as not to appear, and of course not to excite any alarm in the people for the safety of the Constitution. The State leaders may even make a merit of their surreptitious invasions of it on the ground of some temporary convenience, exemption, or advantage" ("No. 16," in Rossiter, *Federalist Papers*, 117).

38. "Feds Give California Stern Warning."

39. Ibid.

40. Ibid.

41. Carl Tubbesing, "Is Anger over REAL ID Unprecedented?" *The Thicket* (a *State Legislatures* magazine blog), May 9, 2007, http://ncsl.typepad.com/the_thicket/2007/05/is_anger_over_r.html#more. See also "The REAL ID Revolt" and the discussion in chapter 5 of this law.

42. Schweitzer, interview by Melissa Block, "Montana Governor on 'REAL ID' Act."

43. See, e.g., Schemo, "States' End Run Dilutes Burden for Special Ed."; Schemo, "States Get Federal Warning on School Standards"; Watson, "EPA is Slammed on Dirty Water"; Steinhauer, "States Prove Unpredictable in Aiding Uninsured Children"; "The States Milk Medicaid"; Toppo, "States Warned about Medicaid Numbers"; Associated Press, "Study: States Ignore Special Ed Law"; Pear, "States Criticized on Lax Lead Tests for Poor Youths"; Meredith, "Tennessee Governor Talks of Revolt on E.P.A. Smog Rules"; and Cushman, "Virginia Seen as Undercutting U.S. Environmental Rules."

44. See generally Krane, "Middle Tier in American Federalism."

45. See Dillon, "Utah Delays a Challenge to Federal Law," who notes that the Utah legislature's threats to openly flout the NCLB law "had been useful in persuading federal officials to reverse course in disputes over some aspects of the federal law"; Dillon, "Report Faults Bush Initiative on Education"; "Let's Try 'No State Left Behind'"; Dillon, "New U.S. Secretary Showing Flexibility"; Schemo, "Effort by Bush on Education Hits Obstacles"; and Dillon, "Some School Districts Challenging Bush's Signature Education Law," who notes that "A Republican [state] legislator has introduced a bill that would prohibit Utah authorities from complying with the law or accepting the $100 million it would bring to the state. Half a dozen other state legislatures have voted to study similar action."

46. Dillon, "Report Faults Bush Initiative on Education."

47. Hakim, "10 States Sue E.P.A. on Emissions"; Hakim, "Battle Lines Set as New York Acts to Cut Emissions"; Bustillo, "States Sue EPA Over Mercury Emissions"; Lochhead, "Small Engine Smog Rules Snuffed"; and Murphy, "States Target Greenhouse Gases," who notes that "states are taking steps to reduce America's contributions to global warming in the face of federal inaction."

48. Pear, "Bush to Revisit Changes in Medicaid Rules."

49. The only modern work by political scientists appears to be Kim Quaile Hill and Hurley, "Uniform State Law Adoptions." The only book-length treatment by a political scientist is Graves, *Uniform State Action*. Legal scholars have written a great deal about the Uniform Commercial Code, and this literature is surveyed in chapter 3 for its insights into the contemporary functioning of the uniform-laws process.

50. Deborah Stone, *Policy Paradox*, 133.

51. Ibid., 251.

52. Kingdon, *Agendas, Alternatives, and Public Policies*, 115.

53. Cobb and Elder, *Participation in American Politics*, 85.

54. Kingdon, *Agendas, Alternatives, and Public Policies*, 67.

55. McClay, "Soul of Man Under Federalism," 21. See also Anton, *American Federalism and Public Policy*, 7. A staff member for a Texas state legislator explains that "a lot of folks, particularly in your more rural areas, don't really have a distinction between federal and state, and so we get a lot of Social Security calls. Well, that's a federal program, so we have to refer them to their congressman" (interview with the author, Austin, Tex., April 1996).

56. Eisenhower, "Address to the 1957 Governors' Conference," 191.

57. Walters, "'Save Us From the States!'"

58. Institutions such as the NGA's Center for Best Practices and the NCSL's Assembly on State Issues facilitate this sort of idea sharing between officials of different states.

59. Schattschneider, *Semi-Sovereign People*, 10.

60. Madison, "No. 46," in Rossiter, *Federalist Papers*, 295. More recently, Tom Stacy of the University of Kansas law school has said that "in a democracy, it's appropriate for the federal government to be most heavily involved in problems that the public views as most threatening," even if those problems have traditionally been areas of state-governmental concern (quoted in Donn, "Making Federal Cases Out of Common Crimes").

61. Kramer, "Understanding Federalism," 1523. See also Grodzins, *American System*, chap. 10; and Truman, "Federalism and the Party System."

62. Tushnet, "Constitution and the Nationalization of American Politics."

63. Elazar, *American Federalism*; and Tushnet, "Constitution and the Nationalization of American Politics."

64. Exemplifying the practices in which both parties engage, President Bill Clinton and Democratic members of Congress were known to make phone calls and personal visits to potential Democratic congressional candidates to encourage those they supported or discourage those with whom they disagreed. See, e.g., Cornell, "President Made Plea for Studds to Run Again." In a similar manner, news stories early in the presidency of George W. Bush reported that he, "Vice President Dick Cheney and the top White House political strategist, Karl Rove, are personally, even bluntly, injecting themselves into some [congressional] races, pressuring candidates they consider weak to get out and urging reluctant but promising runners (in the White House view) to get in" (Ayres, "Political Briefing").

65. For example, when asked how much contact her office had with then-Governor George W. Bush, the director of the state office of U.S. Senator Kay Bailey Hutchison (R-Tex.) replied, "Lots. Lots, lots, lots. I pick up the telephone—they call me because they know me. [The director had served in the Texas

Legislature.] I was there for two terms. Governor's office calls me, speaker's office calls me . . . Everyone calls me because they know I will call them back. And that's been very useful for [Sen. Hutchison] . . . Lots of communication" (interview with the author, Austin, Tex., Mar. 18, 1996). In a similar manner, a conversation with a majority staff member of the House Budget Committee, of which John Kasich (R-Ohio) was the chair, revealed close ties to George Voinovich, who was then the Republican governor of Ohio:

> Author: Has Kasich worked a lot with Governor Voinovich on [the Intermodal Surface Transportation Efficiency Act]?
> Staffer: Yeah. Quite a bit.
> Author: Because I know he's kind of one of the forefront governors who really pays attention to this.
> Staffer: We talk to them every day. (interview with the author, Washington, D.C., March 12, 1997)

66. See generally Flitner, *Politics of Presidential Advisory Commissions*; and Bledsoe, "Presidential Commissions."

67. The Commission on Intergovernmental Relations was created by Public Law 83-109 (1953). Its final report is *A Report to the President for Transmittal to the Congress*.

68. The National Gambling Impact Study Commission was created by Public Law 104-169 (1996). Its final report is available on its website, http://www.ngisc.gov/reports/fullrpt.html.

69. Section 1102 of The Internet Tax Freedom Act (formerly known as S. 442, now Title XI of Public Law 105-277, the Omnibus Appropriations Act of 1998). It is interesting that one of the eight state and local representatives was Gene Lebrun, a South Dakota attorney who at the time was the president of the NCCUSL. Lebrun is also a former member of the South Dakota legislature.

70. Kingdon, *Agendas, Alternatives, and Public Policies*, 91.

71. Cammisa, *Governments as Interest Groups*, 101. See also Rovner, "Welfare Reform," who notes that "Clinton seemed all but a member of Congress during a consideration of the measure, traveling to or phoning Washington repeatedly" (p. 21).

72. Conlan, *From New Federalism to Devolution*, 280–81; and Barton, "Voinovich Giving Governors a Voice." See also Hornbeck, "Engler Gets Front-Row Seat." Governor Engler made over two dozen trips to Washington in 1995 and 18 trips in 1996 as an NGA member and as chairman of the Republican Governors' Association. For a listing of these trips, see "Frequent Flier."

73. Shanahan, "Sudden Rise in Statehouse Status," 15.

74. Pear, "Governors and Officials Step Up Talks on Medicaid."

75. Congressional Budget Office, *CBO's Activities under the Unfunded Mandates Reform Act, 1996–2000*, 1.

76. Michael Bird, interview with the author, Fredericksburg, Va., May 19, 2000.

77. Haider, *When Governments Come to Washington*, 233–36.

78. Posner, *Politics of Unfunded Mandates*, 166.

CHAPTER 3

1. Quoted in Sostek, "Jock Trap," 42.

2. Dunham, "A History of the National Conference of Commissioners," 237.

3. For an example of how these questions get answered in a particular policy area, see Pickerill and Chen, "Medical Marijuana Policy and the Virtues of Federalism."

4. See, e.g., Barnes, "Supreme Court Strikes Down"; Eilperin, "EPA Chief Denies Calif. Limit"; Hampel, "Is Your Poker Game Legal?"; Lewin, "At Core of Adoption Dispute is Crazy Quilt of State Laws"; "A National Highway Priority," noting that a Senate vote to eliminate the national maximum speed limit requirements and other federal grant conditions will "let the states set 50 different laws for highway safety"; and Hendren, "50 States' Rules Regulating Pharmacists are a Confusing Patchwork."

5. A sizable scholarly literature examines this phenomenon. Notable discussions of the general phenomenon include Greenblatt, "Recipe for Respect"; Jack L. Walker, "Diffusion of Innovation among the American States"; Gray, "Innovation in the States"; Robert L. Savage, "Diffusion Research Traditions"; and Mooney, "Modeling Regional Effects on State Policy Diffusion." For specific policy examples, see Marks, "More States Try to Model."

6. Patchel, "Interest Group Politics," 154.

7. According to Daniel Webster, the "entire purpose" of the Annapolis Convention of 1786 was "to devise means for the uniform regulation of trade" (cited in Armstrong, *Century of Service*, 12). See also Wallace, "Want of Uniformity in the Commercial Law"; and Graves, *Uniform State Action*, 33. Some of the materials cited in this chapter—such as the Wallace work cited above—are obscure pamphlets and reprints of speeches that were located in the collections of the Library of Congress.

8. Cutcheon, "Uniform State Laws," 89. Another attorney during this period noted that "it is difficult to conceive of any subject more deserving of any American lawyer than the subject of uniformity of legislation between the States of our Union" (Eaton, "Uniformity of Legislation," n.p.).

9. James J. White, "Ex Proprio Vigore"; Cutcheon, "Uniform State Laws"; and Walter George Smith, "Uniform Marriage and Divorce Laws."

10. See Stovall, "Standards Proposed by United States Commission on Uniform Laws."

11. *Hammer v. Dagenhart*, 247 U.S. 251 (1918).

12. Cyphers, "Testing the Limits of Federalism," 6, 19; Graebner, "Federalism in the Progressive Era"; Baldwin, "Progressive Unfolding of the Powers of the United States"; Rogers, "Constitution and the New Federalism"; and Field, "Centralization in the Federal Government."

13. NCCUSL, *Proceedings of the Fourteenth Annual Conference*, 42.

14. Schofield, "Uniformity of Law in the Several States," 519.

15. See, e.g., *United States v. E.C. Knight Co.*, 156 U.S. 1 (1895) and *Hammer v. Dagenhart*, 247 U.S. 251 (1918). Although it is true that the Court's decisions during this era did not completely cabin federal authority to regulate commercial activity, the general pattern of the era is clear.

16. Graves, *Uniform State Action*, 16–27.

17. Ibid., 29.

18. Ibid., 28. The quotation is taken from the text of the address, available at http://www.presidency.ucsb.edu/ws/print.php?pid=24172.

19. Lapp, "Uniform State Legislation," 577; and Graebner, "Federalism in the Progressive Era."

20. James Bryce noted that "at one time every legislature met once a year. Now in all the States but five it is permitted to meet only once in two years. Within the last fourteen years, at least seven States have changed their annual sessions to biennial" (*American Commonwealth*, 560).

21. A leading legislative scholar at the time noted that the amount of legislation passed by state legislatures "is astounding in itself" and "indicates a crudeness of the legislative function, [and] a lack of careful consideration, which are alarming" (Reinsch, *American Legislatures and Legislative Methods*, 300).

22. See Reeves, *Question of State Government Capability*; and Magleby, "Governing by Initiative."

23. Graves, *Uniform State Action*, 42.

24. See generally Corwin, "Passing of Dual Federalism"; and McCloskey, *American Supreme Court*, chaps. 6 and 7.

25. From the NCCUSL's website: http://www.nccusl.org (accessed May 16, 2007). It is worth noting here, for lack of a better place, that Canada has a similar body—the Canadian Uniform Law Conference—that performs an analogous function in that country. Mexico, another federal system, has the Mexican Center on Uniform Laws, which plays a much less institutionalized role than either the Canadian or the American uniform-law organizations.

26. Francis J. Pavetti (uniform-laws commissioner for Conn.), interview with the author, New London, Conn., March 21, 2001; and Christy Heath (NCCUSL), telephone interview with the author, June 16, 2000.

27. See Armstrong, *Century of Service*, appendix F.

28. Text of the bill passed by the New York legislature is reprinted in NCCUSL, *Proceedings of the Annual Meeting*, 1915, p. 15. For a general history of

the Conference, see Armstrong, *Century of Service*; and Dunham, "History of the National Conference of Commissioners on Uniform State Laws."

29. One of the NCCUSL's criteria for developing a uniform act is that it "should avoid consideration of subjects that are entirely novel and with regard to which neither legislative nor administrative experience is available [or] controversial because of disparities in social, economic, or political policies or philosophies among the various States" (NCCUSL, "Statement of Policy Establishing Criteria," 112–13).

30. Gabriel, "Revisions of the Uniform Commercial Code: Process and Politics," 131, n. 22.

31. Ibid., 132, n. 23.

32. McCabe, "Foreword," 368.

33. Zekan, "Uniform State Laws," 264.

34. John C. McCabe (chief counsel for NCCUSL), interview with the author, NCCUSL headquarters, Chicago, Ill., January 10, 2001.

35. In 1938, for example, the president of the conference noted the following:

> I have been glad to witness here again an exhibition of what I have come to feel is the Conference spirit, a rather unique thing, which is composed of splendid loyalty and devotion to the interests of the organization, a willingness to serve at all times, and at any sacrifice, and more particularly, a mutual attachment of the Commissioners, the one for the other. . . . [This spirit] is something that takes possession of a man and causes him to feel that he would make any sacrifice rather than give up the opportunity of coming again year after year to meet his old associations and cooperate with them in the discharge of our common duties. (NCCUSL, *Handbook of the National Conference*, 1938, 217)

36. For an early explication of this point, see de Tocqueville, *Democracy in America*, 263–70.

37. Gabriel, "Revision of the Uniform Commercial Code—How Successful Has It Been?" 661.

38. See generally Graves, *Uniform State Action*, 68–73.

39. Examples include the U.N. Commission on Human Rights' proposed framework for model legislation on domestic violence and the U.N. Commission on International Trade Law's Model Law on International Commercial Arbitration and its Model Law on Electronic Commerce.

40. For the latest Council of State Governments' products, see their website at http://www.csg.org/programs/ssl/pubs.aspx (accessed April 7, 2007).

41. Feigenbaum, "Introduction," iv.

42. See ALEC, "Our Mission," http://www.alec.org (accessed June 17, 2005).

43. Vu, "Behind Scenes, Groups Shape State Policy."

44. U.S. Consumer Product Safety Commission, http://www.cpsc.gov/businfo/thrftmdl.html (accessed July 2001).

45. NCCUSL, "Statement of Policy Establishing Criteria." The NCCUSL has maintained this distinction since 1936, when it amended its bylaws to permit the development of "model acts" that states may amend and adapt to fit the particular circumstances of their states. As a commissioner explained the following year, "We cannot attempt in this Conference, to say to any individual legislature, for instance: 'You in Nebraska must take this [uniform] act as it is, or leave this subject alone.' We must say to them: 'If our draft is not adapted to your needs, of course it is your privilege—and perhaps your duty—to make such modifications as you think appropriate. We hope that you will follow its present form as closely as possible'" (*Handbook of the National Conference*, 1937, p. 151). Nonetheless, the bulk of the NCCUSL's drafting activity today remains in the area of uniform acts. An explanation of the NCCUSL's criteria for designating a proposed act as either a uniform act or a Uniform Law Commissioners' Model act can be found in NCCUSL's "Statement of Policy Establishing Criteria."

46. Patchel, "Interest Group Politics," 153–54.

47. "The interest groups that are most able to organize effectively are satisfied with current law, and thus there is no push by them for federal legislation." Ibid.

48. I am grateful to an anonymous reviewer for suggesting that I emphasize this point.

49. See Teske, "Checks, Balances, and Thresholds," which outlines the dynamics by which state regulatory efforts can trigger congressional attempts to preempt them. Teske concludes that the federal government rarely wins such contests outright; rather, "the result ends up being somewhere between the two extremes, but the states have had an important influence on national policy" (p. 367).

50. Two exceptions are Posner, "Politics of Preemption," 373–74; and Thierer, *Delicate Balance*, 130–32, who notes that "the uniform state policies suggested by these organizations [NCCUSL, ALEC, and the National Association of Regulatory Utility Commissioners] can help to alleviate many jurisdictional battles or federalism concerns *before* they develop."

51. For a good recent overview, see Zimmerman, *Congressional Preemption: Regulatory Federalism*, and the essays by Zimmerman and others in a symposium on preemption published in the July 2005 issue of *PS: Political Science & Politics*.

52. See generally Raeker-Jordan, "Pre-Emption Presumption that Never Was."

53. Julie Campbell, "Is There a Conflict between E-Sign and UETA?" (unpublished manuscript, Chicago Kent Law School, July 1, 2001). For an alternative typology of the forms of preemption, see Zimmerman, "Nature and Political Significance of Preemption."

54. Zimmerman, "Congressional Preemption"; Zimmerman, "Nature and Political Significance of Preemption"; Perlman, "Preemption Beast"; Zimmerman, "Preemption in the U.S. Federal System"; and U.S. Advisory Commission on Intergovernmental Relations, *Federal Statutory Preemption of State and Local Authority*.

55. *Atascadero State Hospital v. Scanlon*, 473 U.S. 234 (1984), quote at 242.

56. *Rice v. Santa Fe Elevator Corp.*, 331 U.S. 218 (1947), quote at 230.

57. Raeker–Jordan, "Pre-Emption Presumption that Never Was," 1468–69; and Grey, "Make Congress Speak Clearly."

58. Waggoner, "Symposium," 2080.

59. See generally Ring, "UCC Process"; and Overby, "Modeling UCC Drafting," 654.

60. John McCabe (legal counsel of the NCCUSL), interview with the author, Chicago, Ill., January 10, 2001.

61. Miller, "Is Karl's Kode Kaput?" 705–06.

62. James J. White, "Ex Proprio Vigore," 2132.

63. Rubin, "Uniform State Laws," 302–03.

64. UCLA law professor Arthur Rosett, as quoted in Gabriel, "Revision of the Uniform Commercial Code—How Successful Has it Been?" 661.

65. Ailshie, "Limits of Uniformity in State Laws," 634.

66. Rapson, "Who Is Looking Out for the Public Interest?" 261.

67. Sostek, "Jock Trap."

68. This uniform law had been adopted by over half the states when it received an additional endorsement by the U.S. Congress, which urged the remaining states to adopt it. See "NCCUSL Press Release, December 20, 2004," http://www.nccusl.org/Update/DesktopModules/NewsDisplay.aspx?ItemID =124 (accessed June 17, 2005).

69. See "Uniform Athlete Agents Act Legislative Fact Sheet," http://www. nccusl.org/Update/uniformact_factsheets/uniformacts-fs-aaa.asp.

70. Gabriel, "Revisions of the Uniform Commercial Code: Process and Politics," 125.

71. Another major element of American business law that remains controlled largely by states is that of corporate charters. See, e.g., Romano, "State Competition for Corporate Charters," 129–54, and citations therein.

72. Stimson, "Uniform State Legislation," 25.

73. Taylor, "Uniformity of Commercial Law and State-by-State Enactments," 341.

74. Braucher, "Legislative History of the Uniform Commercial Code," 798–99.

75. Bradford Stone, *Uniform Commercial Code in a Nutshell*, p. x.

76. For a more detailed account of the early stages of the promulgation and adoption of the UCC, see Braucher, "Legislative History of the Uniform Commercial Code."

77. Louisiana's Napoleonic system of law makes it difficult for its legislature to adopt uniform laws as written.

78. As of 2001, "Articles 3, 4, 5, 8, and 9 have recently been revised, and Articles 2, 2A, and 7 are currently in the grinder" (Gabriel, "Revision of the Uniform Commercial Code—How Successful Has It Been?" 655).

79. Hisert, "Uniform Commercial Code"; Neil B. Cohen and Zaretsky, "Drafting Commercial Law for the New Millennium"; and Miller, "Is Karl's Kode Kaput?"

80. McLaughlin, "Evolving Uniform Commercial Code," 701–02.

81. Not all of the state-by-state variation in the code is problematic, however, because "even in the original UCC, a number of local options enabled individual states to choose from several alternative formulations" (Hisert, "Uniform Commercial Code," 220).

82. *Swift v. Tyson*, 41 U.S. 1 (1842).

83. Patchel, "Interest Group Politics," 93; Overby, "Modeling UCC Drafting," 651.

84. Patchel, "Interest Group Politics," 95, n. 46.

85. Ibid., 95.

86. *Erie Railroad v. Tompkins*, 304 U.S. 64 (1938).

87. Report of the Commercial Acts Section of the NCCUSL, as quoted in Taylor, "Uniformity of Commercial Law and State-by-State Enactments," 340.

88. Ibid., 340–41.

89. Patchel, "Interest Group Politics, Federalism, and the Uniform Laws Process," 97.

90. Gabriel, "Revision of the Uniform Commercial Code—How Successful Has It Been?" 653–54.

91. McLaughlin, "Evolving Uniform Commercial Code," 696.

92. Neil B. Cohen and Zaretsky, "Drafting Commercial Law for the New Millennium," 557.

93. Hillebrand, "Summary of Changes in Article 9 Relating to Consumer Secured Transactions" (Consumers Union issue brief, January 2000), http://www.consumersunion.org/finance/summwc100.htm (accessed February 21, 2008).

94. This is true for any remote sale, including catalog and telephone sales, and explains why, at the bottom of catalog order forms where one fills in the total purchase costs, one typically sees language like "Wisconsin residents add 5%." This language indicates that the firm has a physical presence in Wisconsin (a store, a warehouse, or an office) and can thus be obligated by the state to calculate, collect, and remit the sales tax.

95. Alaska, Del., Mon., N.H., and Ore. do not collect sales taxes. A sales tax is based on a percentage of an item's purchase price. A use tax is a type of excise tax imposed on a sale—regardless of where it takes place—for the use, consumption, or storage of a good or service.

96. Baudier, "Internet Sales Taxes from Borders to Amazon," par. 12.

97. Galle, "Designing Interstate Institutions," 1386.

98. *National Bellas Hess, Inc. v. Department of Revenue of Illinois*, 386 U.S. 753 (1967).

99. *Quill Corporation v. North Dakota*, 504 U.S. 298 (1992).

100. In particular, the Court's ruling in *Complete Auto Transit, Inc. v. Brady*, 430 U.S. 274 (1977), opened the door for an overruling of the *Bellas Hess* decision, as the North Dakota Supreme Court pointed out in the ruling whose appeal brought the *Quill* case to the U.S. Supreme Court.

101. The Court concluded that

although in our cases subsequent to *Bellas Hess* and concerning other types of taxes we have not adopted a similar bright line, physical presence requirement, our reasoning in those cases does not compel that we now reject the rule that *Bellas Hess* established in the area of sales and use taxes. To the contrary, the continuing value of a bright line rule in this area and the doctrine and principles of *stare decisis* indicate that the *Bellas Hess* rule remains good law. For these reasons, we disagree with the North Dakota Supreme Court's conclusion that the time has come to renounce the bright line test of *Bellas Hess*. (504 U.S. 298, quote at 317–18)

102. Ibid., 318.

103. Baudier, "Internet Sales Taxes from Borders to Amazon," para. 3.

104. *Borders Online LLC v. State Board of Equalization*, 29 Cal. Reporter 3rd, 176. See generally Tedeschi, "Web Merchants Brace for the Inevitable."

105. Graves, *Uniform State Action*, 13.

106. Chandrasekaran, "Online Sales Heating Up Tax Debate."

107. Jonathan Fried, "No Hype."

108. The ITFA (1998) was passed as part the Omnibus Appropriations Act of 1998. For a legislative history of the law, see "High-Tech Industry Cheers Enactment," pp. 21.19–21.24.

109. ITFA, sec. 1101.

110. See, e.g., Sen. George Allen, "Keeping Tolls and Tax Bureaucrats off the Information Superhighway," 18. The 2007 extension contained several provisions that state officials had sought and was seen as a victory by the NGA. See "NGA Commends Compromise on Tax Moratorium" (press release), October 30, 2007, available online via the NGA website, http://www.nga.org, under the "Press Room" section.

111. As chapter 2 notes, state officials frequently serve on federal advisory commissions. The state officials who served on ACEC were James Gilmore, the governor of Va.; Dean Andal of the California Board of Equalization; Paul Harris, a member of the Virginia House of Delegates; Michael Leavitt, the governor of Utah; Gary Locke, the governor of Wash.; and Gene LeBrun, the president of the NCCUSL. Two other members were county or city officials.

112. "High-Tech Industry Cheers Enactment," p. 21-19.

113. Houghton and Hellerstein, "State Taxation of Electronic Commerce," 16.

114. Ess, "Internet Taxation without Physical Representation?" 907–908.

115. NCSL, "The Streamlined Sales and Use Tax Agreement," http://www.ncsl.org/programs/fiscal/tctelcom.htm.

116. Gercken, Nielsen, and Dungog, "Streamlined Sates and Use Tax System," 1.

117. Galle, "Designing Interstate Institutions," 1393.

118. These labels have formal meanings defined in the March 30, 2000, agreement outlining the structure and operating rules of the SSTP. See "Streamlined Sales Tax Project, Structure and Operating Rules," http://www.geocities.com/streamlined2000/oprules.html (accessed June 17, 2005).

119. These states were Ark., Ind., Iowa, Kans., Ky., Mich., Minn., Neb., Nev., N.J., N.C., N.Dak., Okla., R.I., S.Dak., Vt., W.Va., and Wyo.

120. See, e.g., Wickline, "Panel Backs Bills on Multistate Tax Pact"; "Plugging the Internet Sales-Tax Loophole"; and Villareal, "Internet Sales Elude the Taxman."

121. U.S. House, Committee on the Judiciary, Subcommittee on Commercial and Administrative Law, *Hearing on HR 3396*, testimony of Joan Wagnon.

122. Streamlined Sales Tax Executive Committee President Joan Wagnon stated that "The rise of the Streamlined Sales Tax Project is an amazing phenomenon—45 states voluntarily coming together time after time over a period of several years to create a voluntary system to demonstrate to Congress and business that we can simplify sales taxes. The leadership exerted by the National Conferences of State Legislatures, the National Governors' Association, the Federation of Tax Administrators, and the Multistate Tax Commission was enormously helpful" (Ibid.). Testimony is available online via http://www.streamlinedsalestax.org.

123. For an overview of the competing interests in this debate, see Stan Sokul, "Internet Taxes: Challenge of the Information Age, Part 2" (National Taxpayers Union Issue Brief #121, August 14, 2001), http://www.ntu.org/main/press_release.php?PressID=192&org_name=ntu.

124. National Retail Federation, "Retailer Supports Sales Tax Simplification Bill" (press release), July 25, 2006, http://www.nrf.com/modules.php?name=News&op=viewlive&sp_id=124.

125. Tom Readmond, "The Streamlined Sales Tax Proposal: A Tax Increase Under the Radar" (Americans for Tax Reform policy brief), n.d., http://www.atr.org/content/pdf/2005/dec/120704ot_SSTPpb.pdf.

126. Ibid.

127. Garner Girthoffer (policy associate, NCSL), telephone interview, February 21, 2008.

128. Zimmerman, "Congressional Preemption During the George W. Bush Administration," 446.

129. These conditions had been met by May 2007, although not in 2005 when the bill was introduced.

130. See S 34 (introduced May 22, 2007) and HR 3396 (introduced August 3, 2007), 110th Cong., 1st sess.

131. Gramm–Leach–Bliley Act, sec. 321.

132. Posner, "Politics of Preemption," 373.

133. Neal Osten (senior committee director, NCSL), telephone interview, February 21, 2008.

134. Ess, "Internet Taxation without Physical Representation?"

135. Armstrong, *Century of Service*, 77; Gabriel, "Revision of the Uniform Commercial Code—How Successful Has It Been?" 654.

136. NCCUSL, "Statement of Policy Establishing Criteria."

137. Winning adoption of an act in these large states is also important for the purpose of generating momentum behind an act for adoption in other states (John McCabe, chief counsel of the NCCUSL, interview with the author, Chicago, Ill., January 10, 2001),

138. Miller, "Letter from the President," 1.

139. NCCUSL, *Annual Report*, 2.

140. Robinson, Cahill, and Mohammad, "Five Worst (and Five Best) American Criminal Codes," 64

141. Rehnquist, "Foreword," in Armstrong, *Century of Service*, 1.

142. Grant, "Search for Uniformity of Law," 1087. See also Sicherman, "Construction of Clause in Uniform State Laws."

143. Hoar, "Uniformity of Uniform Laws," 53.

144. Connor, "Work of the National Conference of Commissioners on Uniform State Laws," 529–30.

145. Rubin, "Uniformity, Regulation, and the Federalization of State Law," 1262.

146. McLaughlin, "Evolving Uniform Commercial Code," 696.

147. Hemphill, "Uniform Laws Craze," 60.

148. McCabe, "Foreword," 370.

149. Galle, "Designing Interstate Institutions," 1433–34.

CHAPTER 4

1. Quoted in Brooks, *When Governors Convene*, 18.

2. James L. Martin (director of State–Federal Relations, NGA), interview with the author, Washington, DC, March 12, 1997.

3. Haider, *When Governments Come to Washington*, 306.

4. See Swift, *Making of an American Senate*; Riker, "Senate and American Federalism"; and Stewart, "Responsiveness in the Upper Chamber." Prior to the Seventeenth Amendment (ratified in 1913), state legislatures rather than the

popular vote selected U.S. senators. The works just cited indicate that although that amendment formally severed the direct linkages between state legislatures and the U.S. Senate, those relationships had been attenuated long before its adoption.

5. Haider, *When Governments Come to Washington*; Cammisa, *Governments as Interest Groups*; and Dinan, "State Governmental Influence in the National Policy Process."

6. An exception to this is the work of legal scholar Larry Kramer. See "Understanding Federalism," and especially "Putting the Politics Back into the Political Safeguards of Federalism."

7. For a history of these efforts going back to the founding era, see Elazar, *American Partnership*.

8. Caminker, "State Sovereignty and Subordinacy"; Prakash, "Field Office Federalism"; and Holcombe, "States as Agents of the Nation." This point is also discussed extensively in chapter 5.

9. Conlan, *From New Federalism to Devolution*, 5–6; and Lowi, *End of the Republican Era*, 7.

10. See generally Greenblatt, "Recipe for Respect"; Nugent, "Public Officials' Associations," 518–24; David S. Arnold and Plant, *Public Official Associations and State and Local Government*; Pelissero and England, "State and Local Governments' Washington 'Reps'"; Cingranelli, "State Government Lobbies in the National Political Process"; Belkin, "For State and Local Governments, Washington Is the Place to Be"; Stanfield, "PIGs: Out of the Sty, Into Lobbying with Style"; and Hillenbrand, "Big Six."

11. Wright, *Understanding Intergovernmental Relations*, 2nd ed., 280.

12. Weissert, "National Governors' Association."

13. Ibid., 46.

14. Brooks, *When Governors Convene*, 14.

15. Weissert, "National Governors' Association," 45.

16. Brooks, *When Governors Convene*, 36.

17. See Matheson, *Out of Balance*; Brooks, *When Governors Convene*; Haider, *When Governments Come to Washington*; and Weissert, "National Governors' Association."

18. These four committees are Economic Development and Commerce; Education, Early Childhood and Workforce; Health and Human Services; and Natural Resources. For current membership of each committee, see the NGA's website at http://www.nga.org/Files/pdf/COMMITTEELIST.pdf.

19. Interview with NGA committee staff member, March 12, 1997.

20. See NGA, "Policy Positions" (under the Federal Relations section), http://www.nga.org.

21. Interview with staff member of regional governors' association, Washington, DC, October 16, 1997.

22. Hall, *New Institutions of Federalism*, 75.

23. Quote from http://www.iogcc.state.ok.us/what-we-do. For accounts of the IOGCC's recent lobbying efforts, see the organization's website, http://www.iogcc.state.ok.us/ (accessed June 20, 2008).

24. The best examinations of this topic include Zimmerman, *Interstate Relations*; and Derthick, *Between State and Nation*.

25. Perhaps the most thorough examination of an individual state's interests and efforts to influence policymaking in Washington is Liebschutz, *Bargaining under Federalism*, chap. 4. See also Morrisroe, "State of State Offices"; and Bullock, *Dollars We Deserve*. An excellent primer on the structures and functions of states offices in Washington is the NGA's *The Governor's Washington Office*.

26. A rare example of such media coverage is a *New York Times* article's mention of New York's newly elected governor's pledge to "rebuild New York's Washington Office"; however, the article said nothing else about this office or its activities (Healy, "Spitzer Visits Capitol Hill with Long List").

27. Nearly all of these offices are located in the same building—the Hall of the States, a 225,000-square-foot building located on Capitol Hill between the U.S. Capitol and Union Station. Centralizing the location of these offices in the same building with the NGA and a number of other state-based organizations is an important factor in fostering interaction among these staffers and organizations. See generally Calmes, "444 North Capitol Street."

28. Hernandez and Baker, "'Big Four' Governors Working Together to Lobby Congress."

29. Interview with the author, Washington, D.C., August 15, 1996.

30. Interview with staff member of a state office, Washington, D.C., August 15, 1996.

31. Interview with director of a state office, Washington, D.C., August 14, 1996.

32. Greenwire, "Retirement Boosts Alaska Delegation's Clout," December 7, 1995, n.p.

33. Groer, "Florida Loses Political Clout as Senior Congressmen Quit."

34. Butler, "Delaware's 'Policy Advisors' Represent State's Interest in Washington."

35. Interview with staff member of a state office, August 12, 1996.

36. Interview with a staff member of a governor's office, Washington, D.C., August 13, 1996.

37. Quoted in Calmes, "444 North Capitol Street," 18.

38. Interview with staff member of a governor's office, Washington, D.C., August 16, 1996.

39. Interview with director of a governor's office, Washington, D.C., August 15, 1996.

40. Interview with director of a southeastern state's governor's office, Washington, D.C., August 12, 1996. See also Calmes, "444 North Capitol Street," 18, on this point.

41. Haider, review of *Governments as Interest Groups*, 144.

42. Quoted in Rovner, "Welfare Reform," 21.

43. Cammisa, *Governments as Interest Groups*, 101. See also Rovner, "Welfare Reform," who notes that "Clinton seemed all but a member of Congress during consideration of the measure, traveling to or phoning Washington repeatedly" (p. 21).

44. Interview with staff member of U.S. House subcommittee, Washington, D.C., September 22, 1997.

45. Interview with NGA's director of state–federal relations, Washington, D.C., March 12, 1997.

46. Pryde, "Lobbyists for Cities and Counties Find a Niche," 3. Rhode Island has subsequently opened a Washington office.

47. James Martin, interview with the author, Washington, D.C., March 12, 1997.

48. Quoted in Calmes, "Jim Martin," 65.

49. U.S. House Committee on Government Reform and Oversight, Subcommittee on Human Resources and Intergovernmental Relations, *Federalism Debate: Why Doesn't Washington Trust the States?*, 11.

50. Interview with NGA staffer, Washington, D.C., March 12, 1997.

51. See generally Welborn, "Conjoint Federalism and Environmental Regulation in the United States."

52. Kriz, "Drinks All Around," 2862.

53. Interview with NGA lobbyist on environmental issues, Washington, D.C., March 12, 1997.

54. Interview with staff member of the Senate Environment and Public Works Committee, Washington, D.C., March 11, 1997.

55. Interview with NGA lobbyist on environmental issues, Washington, D.C., March 12, 1997. On this point see also Roberts, "New Theory for the Times"; and Brown, "Emerging Models for Environmental Management."

56. NGA, *Policy Positions*, 153–54.

57. Ibid., 154–55.

58. For details on the development of EPA rules on the reports, see Shapard, "How Safe Is Your Water?" 30.

59. Cushman, "Bill Would Give Water Customers Pollution Notice."

60. Kocheisen, "Panel Approves Drinking Water Bill," 11.

61. Interview with staff member of the Senate Environment and Public Works Committee, Washington, D.C., March 11, 1997.

62. Zimmerman, "Congressional Preemption During the George W. Bush Administration," 446.

63. According to one source, "The [1988 welfare reform] law was credited with advancing the idea that in exchange for receiving benefits, welfare recipients should take steps to improve their lives. In practice, though, JOBS

had had limited success—partly because of the economy and partly because of flaws in the program" (see "Welfare to Work Challenge," p. 7-45).

64. For a detailed exposition of the Contract with America provisions from the perspective of its supporters, see Gillespie and Schellhas, *Contract with America*. In the end, the new Republican leadership kept this promise, although little of the legislation was passed in the full form that the contract had proposed.

65. "Welfare Bill Clears under Veto Threat," p. 7-36.

66. Information on the House bill comes from "Welfare Bill Clears under Veto Threat."

67. Five Republicans voted against the bill, and nine Democrats voted for it.

68. Quoted in Broder and Barnes, "Governors Cautious on Welfare Reform Plans."

69. Ibid.

70. Quoted in United Press International, "GOP Governors Meet with Dole, Gingrich."

71. "Governors Craft Welfare Wish List."

72. Under the Byrd rule, "provisions in a budget bill can be successfully challenged on a point of order if they produce no change in revenue or spending or if such changes are 'merely incidental' to the fiscal items. It takes a three-fifths majority, or 60 votes if all senators are present, to waive the rule" (Rosenbaum, "Intricate Senate Procedure Lends a Hand to Welfare Recipients").

73. Hornbeck, "Engler Gets Front-Row Seat for Federal Budget Talks."

74. "Welfare Bill Clears Under Veto Threat," p. 7-52.

75. U.S. House Committee on Ways and Means, Subcommittee on Human Resources, *National Governors' Association Welfare Reform Proposal*, testimony of Governor Tom Carper (D-Del.), 16.

76. Lawrence, "Gubernatorial Rapprochement," 11.

77. NGA, *Policy Positions*, 113.

78. Ibid., 113–15.

79. Weaver, "Deficits and Devolution in the 104th Congress," 63. The quote refers to the statutory or state-constitutional balanced budget requirements nearly all governors face. See also Havemann, "Governors' Reform Plan Ends Welfare Guarantee."

80. U.S. House Committee on Ways and Means, Subcommittee on Human Resources, *National Governors' Association Welfare Reform Proposal*, testimony of Governor Tommy Thompson (D-Wis.), 14.

81. Havemann, "Governors Reform Plan Ends Welfare Guarantee."

82. See Rovner, "Welfare Reform."

83. "After 60 Years, Most Control Sent to States," p. 6-4.

84. Havemann, "Advocacy Groups Take on Governors' Reform Plan."

85. Carney, "Last Gasp for a Broad Reworking?"

86. Cassata, "Finale Expected to Be Short," 2445.

87. See, e.g., Stanfield, "Lots of Spin, But No Signs of Movement," 1210.

88. "After 60 Years, Most Control Sent to States," 6-6.

89. Katz, "GOP May Move to Split Medicaid, Welfare," 1762.

90. "After 60 Years, Most Control Sent to States," p. 6-11.

91. Katz, "GOP May Move to Split Medicaid, Welfare," 1762.

92. "After 60 Years, Most Control Sent to States," p. 6-12.

93. Quoted in Pear, "Republicans Finish Writing Welfare Measure." For a vivid account of this meeting from the perspective of one of its participants, see Reich, *Locked in the Cabinet*, 319–21.

94. Pear, "Republicans Finish Writing Welfare Measure."

95. Quoted in Clines, "Clinton Signs Bill Cutting Welfare."

96. See Johnson, "Governors: Republicans Endorse Turning Welfare Over to the States." For a discussion of states' requests for waivers of federal requirements, see chapter 5.

97. Quoted in "Governors Praise Congress for Reforming Welfare," 1.

98. Ibid., 2.

99. See, e.g., Pear, "Most States Find Welfare Targets Well Within Reach"; and DeParle, "Sharp Decrease in Welfare Cases Is Gathering Speed."

100. See "NGA Urges Quick Passage of Technical Corrections," 1.

101. Interview with NGA staffer, Washington, D.C., March 11, 1997.

102. Gov. John Engler (R-Mich.), quoted in "Governors Praise Congress for Reforming Welfare," 1–2.

103. Interview with NGA lobbyist, Washington, D.C., March 11, 1997.

104. Weaver, "Deficits and Devolution in the 104th Congress," 58.

105. Interview with NGA lobbyist, Washington, D.C., March 11, 1997.

106. Interview with NGA lobbyist, Washington, D.C., March 11, 1997.

107. Interview with staff member of a governor's Washington office, Washington, D.C., August 13, 1996.

108. Interview with staff member of a governor's Washington office, Washington, D.C., August 12, 1996.

109. Interview with staff member of a governor's Washington office, Washington, D.C., August 15, 1996.

110. Interview with staff member of a governor's Washington office, Washington, D.C., August 12, 1996.

111. Interview with director of a governor's Washington office, Washington, D.C., August 15, 1996.

112. Interview with director of Iowa governor's Washington office, Washington, D.C., August 15, 1996.

113. Godman, "For Flood-ravaged States, Focus Now Shifts," 5.

114. Ibid.

115. Interview with NGA lobbyist, Washington, D.C., March 11, 1997.

Chapter 5

1. Quoted in Wright, *Understanding Intergovernmental Relations*, 2nd ed., 35–36.

2. For an early discussion, see Holcombe, "States as Agents of the Nation."

3. Madison, "No. 45," in Rossiter, *Federalist Papers*, 292.

4. Alexander Hamilton, "No. 27," in Rossiter, *Federalist Papers*, 176, 177 (emphasis in original).

5. Anton, *American Federalism and Public Policy*, 44. See also Stoker, *Reluctant Partners*; DiIulio and Kettl, *Fine Print*, 16–19; and Wright, *Understanding Intergovernmental Relations*, 2nd ed., 16.

6. Stoker, *Reluctant Partners*, 11.

7. Robertson and Judd, *Development of American Public Policy*, 102–14; and David B. Walker, *Rebirth of Federalism*, 90–105.

8. For a detailed periodization scheme, see Elazar, "Opening the Third Century of American Federalism."

9. See generally Conlan, *From New Federalism to Devolution*, 307–10.

10. After holding in *Baker v. Carr*, 369 U.S. 186 (1962), that citizens in states with malapportioned state legislatures had standing to sue their state governments under the equal protection clause of the Fourteenth Amendment, the U.S. Supreme Court subsequently struck down the apportionment schemes of Alabama, New York, Maryland, Virginia, Delaware, and Colorado. The cases are, respectively, *Reynolds v. Sims*, 377 U.S. 533; *WMCA, Inc. v. Lorenzo*, 377 U.S. 633; *Maryland Committee v. Tawes*, 377 U.S. 656; *Davis v. Mann*, 377 U.S. 678; *Roman v. Sincock*, 377 U.S. 695; and *Lucas v. Colorado General Assembly*, 377 U.S. 713, all decided in 1964.

11. Chubb, "Constitution, Institutionalization, and the Development of Federalism," 280.

12. Beer, "Adoption of General Revenue Sharing," 162.

13. Ibid., 163–64. The development of state-governmental institutions through cooperation with the federal government may have much deeper roots than the Great Society programs. For the view that such collaborative efforts have strengthened state governments since the founding era, see Elazar, "States and the Nation."

14. Van Horn, "Quiet Revolution," 1. See also Stanfield, "Just Do It"; Osborne, *Laboratories of Democracy*; Nathan, "Role of the States in American Federalism"; Reeves, "States as Polities"; Beyle, "From Governor to Governors"; Beyle, "Institutionalized Powers of the Governorship"; and Bowman and Kearney, *Resurgence of the States*.

15. Quoted in Rosenbaum, "Governors' Frustration Fuels Effort on Welfare Financing."

16. See, e.g., Kurtz, Cain, and Neimi, *Institutional Change in American Politics*; Greenblatt, "Truth about Term Limits"; Basham, "Assessing the Term Limits Experiment"; and Gurwitt, "Greenhorn Government."

17. Hedge, "Political and Policy Consequences of Institutional Development, 3.

18. A similar continuum (but with four nodes) appears in Goggin et al., *Implementation Theory and Practice*, 46.

19. See generally Goggin et al., *Implementation Theory and Practice.*

20. Light, *True Size of Government*, 176–77.

21. For a discussion of this point in the area of water policy, see Gerlak, "Federalism and U.S. Water Policy."

22. Kettl, *Government by Proxy.*

23. Light, *True Size of Government*, 1.

24. U.S. Census Bureau, *Compendium of Public Employment: 2002*, 13.

25. Donahue, *Disunited States*, 11.

26. For a good discussion of how intergovernmental grants reflect the fragmented decisionmaking authority of congressional committees, see Haider, *When Governments Come to Washington*, 83–88; and Chubb, "Constitution, Institutionalization, and the Development of Federalism." Chubb notes, for example, that "categorical grants were favored by Congress because they helped get its members reelected. Categorical grants provided legislators countless opportunities to claim credit for producing discrete benefits for their districts and to help constituents with red tape and other problems that interfered with the delivery of those benefits. These forms of district aid were especially important during the 1960s and 1970s, when members of Congress were finding it increasingly necessary to rely on their own devices, instead of their parties, to get reelected" (269).

27. David B. Walker, *Rebirth of Federalism*, 268. See also Keiser, "State Governmental Interests and Policy Implementation," 3; and Derthick, "American Federalism," 68.

28. DiIulio and Kettl, *Fine Print*, 9.

29. Ibid., 64–65.

30. For a review of the literature, see Keiser, "State Governmental Interests and Policy Implementation"; and Goggin et al., *Implementation Theory and Practice.*

31. For a good discussion of how this configuration of multiple principals works in the area of environmental protection, see Scheberle, *Federalism and Environmental Policy.*

32. Deborah Stone, *Policy Paradox*, 274–75; see also Derthick, *Influence of Federal Grants*, 207–209; and Posner, "Politics of Preemption," 373.

33. See, e.g., Woods, "Primacy Implementation of Environmental Policy in the U.S. States."

34. U.S. Environmental Protection Agency, "The Plain English Guide to the Clean Air Act," under "Understanding the Clean Air Act," http://www.epa.gov/air/caa/peg/understand.html.

35. Teske, "Checks, Balances, and Thresholds," 373. See also Jeffrey S. Hill and Weissert, "Implementation and the Irony of Delegation," who note that "replacement of the agent is not always desirable or even possible when applied to the delegation of governmental authority" (345).

36. Anne Arnold (manager, Air Quality Planning Unit, EPA Region 1 office [New England]), telephone interview, May 10, 2007.

37. David Johnson (Virginia Department of Environmental Protection), interview, Richmond, Va., June 2000.

38. Anne Larason Schneider and Ingram, *Policy Design for Democracy*, 90.

39. Sharkansky, *Maligned States*, 95.

40. Many observers have pointed out the ways in which conservatives' pro-state rhetoric has often not been matched by their deeds. Barry Goldwater noted in *Conscience of a Conservative*, for example, that "in actual practice, the Republican Party, like the Democratic Party, summons the coercive power of the federal government whenever national leaders conclude that the States are not performing satisfactorily" (p. 25). See also Nagourney, "G.O.P. Right is Splintered on Schiavo Intervention"; Dao, "Red, Blue, and Angry All Over"; Broder, "So, Now Bigger is Better?"; Donn, "Making Federal Cases Out of Common Crimes"; and Grunwald, "In Legislative Tide, State Power Ebbs."

41. DiIulio and Kettl, *Fine Print*, 18. See also Nice, *Federalism*, 5; Pressman and Wildavsky, *Implementation*; and Stoker, *Reluctant Partners*.

42. For a detailed description and critique of this process, see Lowi, *End of Liberalism*.

43. This list is an abbreviated and simplified version of the rulemaking description in Kerwin, *Rulemaking*, 75–85

44. The *Federal Register* is published Monday through Friday by the U.S. Government Printing Office. According to its website, the *Register* is "the official daily publication for rules, proposed rules, and notices of Federal agencies and organizations, as well as executive orders and other presidential documents." See http://www.gpoaccess.gov/fr/about.html.

45. Pear, "Bush to Revisit Changes in Medicaid Rules."

46. Ibid.

47. Ibid.

48. Ibid.

49. Matt Salo (NGA staff member), personal communication, June 20, 2005.

50. Pear, "Governors of Both Parties Oppose Medicaid Rules."

51. NGA, "Governors Praise House Vote."

52. "U.S. Troop Readiness, Veterans' Care."

53. NGA, "Governors Reaffirm Support for Delaying."

54. Alexander, "Money Cuts Threaten Agencies."

55. "End Run on Medicaid."

56. Kerwin, *Rulemaking*, 83–84.

57. U.S. Department of Health and Human Services, "Final Rule for Temporary Assistance to Needy Families,"17722.

58. Adam Thierer, "President Clinton's Sellout of Federalism," (Heritage Foundation Executive Memorandum no. 536, June 25, 1998): 1, http://www.heritage.org/Research/PoliticalPhilosophy/EM536.cfm (accessed May 17, 2006).

59. David B. Walker, *Rebirth of Federalism*, 327.

60. Broder, "Federalism's New Framework."

61. See Derthick, *Influence of Federal Grants*, 19–23.

62. Ibid., 10.

63. Ibid., 108.

64. Derthick, "American Federalism," 68.

65. Kirk Jonas (Joint Legislative Audit and Review Commission, Commonwealth of Virginia), telephone interview, June 16, 2000.

66. Edward Myers (Disabilities Section, Department of Rehabilitation Services, Commonwealth of Virginia), interview, June 16, 2000.

67. This view of the program is not universally shared. For the view that Social Security Disability determinations are filled with discretionary and non-uniform decisionmaking, see Keiser, "State Bureaucratic Discretion," 92–93.

68. Goggins et al., *Implementation Theory and Practice*, 33.

69. Hoff, "Not All Agree on Meaning of NCLB Proficiency," 1.

70. Keiser and Soss, "With Good Cause," 1138.

71. Hoff, "Not All Agree on Meaning of NCLB Proficiency"; Ravitch, "Every State Left Behind."

72. Goggin et al., *Implementation Theory and Practice*, 35.

73. See Keiser, "State Bureaucratic Discretion."

74. See, e.g., Piven and Cloward, *Regulating the Poor*; Wagner, *What's Love Got to Do With It?*; and Soss et al., "Setting the Terms of Relief."

75. For a discussion of how states interpreted their waiver authority during this transition period, see Greenberg and Savner, "Waivers and the New Welfare Law."

76. U.S. Department of Health and Human Services Fact Sheet, "Medicaid and SCHIP Waivers: Promoting State Flexibility and Innovation," May 9, 2001, http://www.hhs.gov/news/press/2001pres/01fsmedicaid.html. See also Saundra K. Schneider, "Medicaid Section 1115 Waivers."

77. Connolly, "Thompson Cutting Medicaid Red Tape."

78. Clinton, "Remarks Following a Meeting with the Nation's Governors," 117–18.

79. See Clinton, Executive Order 12875, "Enhancing the Intergovernmental Partnership," October 26, 1993. This order notes that "the cost, complexity, and

delay in applying for and receiving waivers from Federal requirements in appropriate cases have hindered State, local, and tribal governments from tailoring Federal programs to meet the specific or unique needs of their communities. These governments should have more flexibility to design solutions to the problems faced by citizens in this country without excessive micro management and unnecessary regulation from the Federal Government." More generally, see Walters, "Walking in a Waiver Wonderland"; Devroy, "President to Order Changes in Welfare"; "Reforming Welfare, State by State"; Stoil, "President Clinton and Medicaid Waivers"; Feldmann, "Clinton Encourages New Paths on Welfare"; and Richter, "Clinton Orders Easier Medicaid Rules for States."

80. For an explanation of variation in states' uses of implementation flexibility in the Children's Health Insurance Program, see Goggin, "Use of Administrative Discretion in Implementing," especially pp. 44–51.

81. For a discussion of the "moral hazards" rhetoric underlying welfare reform, see Epstein, *Welfare in America*, chaps. 2 and 4.

82. For example, the Medicaid section 1115 waiver program "has contributed to wide variability across the states in terms of program coverage, delivery, and financing" (Saundra K. Schneider, "Medicaid Section 1115 Waivers," 109).

83. Welch, "Shifting Welfare to the States." Specifically, "at least 29 states limit how long someone can receive benefits. . . . At least 20 states are trying to discourage single welfare mothers from having more children by denying benefits for additional births. . . . At least 27 states are encouraging teen welfare mothers to stay in school by offering bonuses or reducing benefits if they drop out." See also Besharov, "State Waivers Change Welfare as We Know It."

84. Some observers at the time noted that the assortment of waivers under which states were running their welfare programs were no substitute for a full-scale reform bill. Ohio Gov. (and future U.S. Sen.) George Voinovich noted that the time-consuming approval process indicated that "the waiver process cannot be used to end welfare as we know it" ("Waiting for Waivers"). See also Besharov, who notes that "there is also a down side to using such an informal policy instrument to make these momentous changes: Many important issues go unaddressed or are hidden from public view" ("State Waivers Change Welfare as We Know It").

85. Dean, "New Rules and Roles for States," 183.

86. Ibid.

87. Pressman and Wildavsky, *Implementation*; and Lipsky, *Street-Level Bureaucracy*.

88. Keiser and Soss, "With Good Cause," 1138.

89. Ibid.

90. Kelderman, "States' Rebellion at REAL ID Echoes in Congress."

91. Kelderman, "Two States Lead Revolt against REAL ID"; Kelderman, "States' Rebellion at REAL ID Echoes in Congress."

92. Jeffrey S. Hill and Weissert, "Implementation and the Irony of Delegation."

93. Ravitz, "Utahns Cheer as Guv Signs NCLB Protest." Also see Dobbs, "NEA, States Challenge 'No Child' Program."

94. Under Congress's 1994 reauthorization of the Elementary and Secondary Education Act, states were required to develop and implement assessment regimes in at least mathematics and language arts once during grades three to five, six to nine, and ten to twelve.

95. By one estimate, the federal Department of Education makes about 50 percent of the rules but provides only about 7 percent of funding for U.S. public education. See Antle, "Leaving No Child Left Behind."

96. The passage of NCLB, with its provisions that work against states' legalistic and administrative interests, indicates the limits of intergovernmental lobbying as a safeguard of federalism. The law did, however, come with additional federal funding attached, so it promoted states' fiscal interests.

97. For a full summary of the law, see "Landmark Education Bill Signed."

98. A state's starting point was based on the performance of its lowest-scoring school district or demographic group, whichever was higher.

99. U.S. Department of Education, "New No Child Left Behind Flexibility: Highly Qualified Teachers" (fact sheet), March 2004, http://www.ed.gov/nclb/methods/teachers/hqtflexibility.html.

100. U.S. Department of Education, "No Child Left Behind: A Toolkit for Teachers," 6, http://www.ed.gov/teachers/nclbguide/toolkit_pg6.html.

101. Rod Paige (Secretary of Education) letter to Chief State School Officers, March 31, 2004, http://www.ed.gov/policy/elsec/guid/secletter/040331.html.

102. Margaret Spellings (Secretary of Education) letter to Chief State School Officers, October 21, 2005, http://www.ed.gov/policy/elsec/guid/secletter/051021.html.

103. Education Trust, "Telling the Whole Truth."

104. Ibid., 2.

105. See, e.g., the listing of state criteria for paraprofessionals on the Education Commission of the States' website, http://mb2.ecs.org/reports/Report.aspx?id=1052.

106. Commission on No Child Left Behind, *Beyond NCLB*, 35.

107. Ibid., 53.

108. NGA, CCSSO, and NASBE, "Joint Statement on Reauthorization of the No Child Left Behind Act (NCLB)" (April 5, 2007), 2–3, http://www.nga.org/Files/pdf/0704nclbstatement.pdf.

109. Margaret Spellings (U.S. Secretary of Education) letter to Chief State School Officers, September 5, 2006, http://www.ed.gov/policy/elsec/guid/secletter/060905.html.

110. American Federation of Teachers, "Eight Misconceptions about the No Child Left Behind Act's (NCLB) Adequate Yearly Progress (AYP) Provisions," http://www.aft.org/topics/nclb/downloads/8Misconceptions.pdf.

111. See Nick Anderson, "Bush Administration Grants Leeway."

112. Maggi, "State Lobbies to Preserve its Reform."

113. Dillon, "States Are Relaxing Education Standards."

114. U.S. Department of Education, "Secretary Spellings Announces Growth Model Pilot, Addresses Chief State School Officers' Annual Policy Forum in Richmond" (press release), November 18, 2005, http://www.ed.gov/news/pressreleases/2005/11/11182005.html; Nick Anderson, "Bush Administration Grants Leeway."

115. Schemo, "20 States Ask for Flexibility in School Law"; and Olson, "3 States Get OK to Use Growth Model."

116. Hoff, "Chiefs: Ed. Dept. Getting Stingier"; and "Doing the Waive."

117. Commission on No Child Left Behind, *Beyond NCLB*, 71–72.

118. See, e.g., testimony at the April 27, 2007, field hearing ("Improving the No Child Left Behind Act's Accountability System") in California of the Early Childhood, Elementary and Secondary Education Subcommittee, http://edworkforce.house.gov/hearings/ecese042707.shtml.

119. NGA, CCSSO, and NASBE, "Joint Statement on Reauthorization" (see note 108 above), p. 1. The statement also included each organization's lengthier set of principles and policy recommendations for NCLB reauthorization.

120. Dillon, "Battle Grows over Renewing Landmark Education Law."

121. Neuman, "Rules Loosened for No Child Left Behind Law."

122. See Commission on No Child Left Behind, "Growth Models: An Examination within the Context of NCLB" (commission staff research report), August 2006, http://www.aspeninstitue.org.

123. One commentator suggested that this might be an outcome of the pilot program. See West, "No Child Left Behind," 6.

124. Antle, "Leaving No Child Left Behind."

125. According to the Environmental Council of the States' website, "As of 2001, over 75% of the federal environmental programs that can be delegated have been delegated to the States. Most federal environmental programs were intended to be administered by the States" (http://www.ecos.org/section/states/enviro_actlist, accessed April 8, 2007).

126. See generally Kamieniecki and Ferrall, "Intergovernmental Relations and Clean-Air Policy in California."

127. For a table showing the status of states' primacy in each area of Clean Air Act enforcement, see the Environmental Council of the States' website at http://www.ecos.org/section/states/enviro_actlist/states_enviro_actlist_caa.

128. U.S. Environmental Protection Agency, *Plain English Guide to the Clean Air Act*, 3. The EPA's exhaustive official guide to the SIP process, the "Online State Implementation Plan Processing Manual," can be found at http://icode.pes.com/sipman/.

129. Zimmerman, "Nature and Political Significance of Preemption," 361.

130. For a description of the federal–regional–state structure of environmental protection agencies in this country, see Scheberle, *Federalism and Environmental Policy*, especially chaps. 1 and 5.

131. Adapted from the EPA's SIP timeline available online at http://www.epa.gov/region1/topics/air/sips/Revised2_SIP_TIMELINE.pdf.

132. Anne Arnold (manager, Air Quality Planning Unit, EPA New England [Region 1]), telephone interview, May 10, 2007.

133. Connecticut Department of Environmental Protection, "Proposed Revision to Connecticut's State Implementation Plan: Meeting the Interstate Air Pollution Transport Requirements of Clean Air Act Section 110(a)(2)(D)(i)," December 22, 2006, E1, http://www.ct.gov/dep/lib/dep/air/regulations/proposed_and_reports/sec110transportsip.pdf.

134. Ibid., E1.

135. Ibid., 26–27.

136. Merrily A. Gere (environmental analyst, CTDEP, Bureau of Air Management), telephone interview, May 17, 2007.

137. CTDEP, "Proposed Revision to Connecticut's State Implementation Plan" (see note 133), 30.

138. Ibid.

139. Ibid., 5.

140. For another example how Connecticut has challenged the EPA's use of scientific evidence, see David Wackter et al., "Connecticut's Response to the EPA 9-Factor Analysis for PM2.5 Designations," Connecticut Department of Environmental Protection, August 2004 (available at http://www.ct.gov/dep/lib/dep/air/particulate_matter/pm25planning/rebuttaldoc.pdf), which notes, "CTDEP has reviewed EPA's 9-Factor Analysis and believes that some of the conclusions made by the EPA are not scientifically justified. Additional data have become available to further support CTDEP's conclusion. This document will review the nine factors presented by the EPA and show that the conclusion reached is untenable" (p. 1).

141. Environmental Protection Agency, "Approval and Promulgation of Air Quality Implementation Plans" [proposed rule], 62420.

142. Merrily A. Gere (environmental analyst, CTDEP), personal communication, February 25, 2008.

143. Environmental Protection Agency, "Approval and Promulgation of Air Quality Implementation Plans" [final rule].

144. McCarthy, "Clean Air Act Issues in the 106th Congress."

145. Chapter 3's discussion of the uniform-laws process, however, indicates that states' passage of high-quality public policy may be a safeguard of federalism in itself to the extent that it keeps the federal government from legislating in policy areas traditionally the purview of the states.

146. As explained in a policy position adopted by the NGA several years ago, "The Clean Air Act Amendments contain numerous deadlines for federal and state actions. The ability of states to meet deadlines under the act, however, is often dependent on the issuance of federal rules, models, guidance, and timely state implementation plan review by EPA. When EPA fails to meet a deadline, it is impossible for states to make up the lost time and meet their deadlines. A chain reaction then begins in which industry misses its deadlines, sanctions go into place, clean air goals are not met, and everyone loses" (NGA 2000, http://www.nga.org/Pubs/Policies/NR/nr07.asp). The federal government's failure to provide states with funding to carry out enforcement efforts also constitutes shirking by the principal. See Arrandale, "Tigers No More."

147. Keiser, "State Governmental Interests and Policy Implementation"; Stoker, *Reluctant Partners*.

148. Stoker, *Reluctant Partners*, 51.

149. Beer, *To Make a Nation*, 21. James Madison made the same point in *The Federalist*, noting that "the federal and State governments are in fact but different agents and trustees of the people, constituted with different powers and designed for different purposes" ("No. 46," in Rossiter, *Federalist Papers*, 294). This view was endorsed in Justice Kennedy's concurring opinion in *U.S. Term Limits, Inc. v. Thornton*, 514 U.S. 779 (1995): "Federalism was our Nation's own discovery. The Framers split the atom of sovereignty. It was the genius of their idea that our citizens would have two political capacities, one state and one federal, each protected from incursion by the other" (p. 838).

CHAPTER 6

1. Harkness, "'Shift-and-Shaft' Federalism," 610.

2. Lindblom, "Market as Prison."

3. Sullivan, "From States' Rights Blues to Blue States' Rights," 799.

4. Brutus, "Essay VI," 138. For a more general historical review of such fears, see Weinberg, "Fear and Federalism."

5. Richard Cohen, "Always the National News." See also Hess, "Federalism and News," noting that "the stepchild of government [news] coverage has always been the state"; and Gurwitt, "Comes the Devolution."

6. For details of an effort to make political and governmental news regarding each of the 50 states more readily available online, see Stelter, "Plan to Offer 50

Sites." The website Stateline.org is a gateway to state-by-state political and governmental news as well.

7. This is not always the case, however, as the SSTP aims to convince Congress to endorse states' collection of sales tax on online sales.

8. I am grateful to an anonymous reviewer for suggesting this point.

9. See generally Gilens, *Why Americans Hate Welfare*.

10. Paul E. Peterson, *Price of Federalism*, notes that "the powers of state and local governments have been used too often by a tyrannical majority to trample the rights of religious, racial, and political minorities" (p. 9).

11. Sharkansky, *Maligned States*, 7.

12. Ibid.

13. Ford, "New Blue Federalists." See also Barron, "Progressive Federalism"; and the essays in Katz and Tarr (eds.), *Federalism and Rights*.

14. For a discussion of this phenomenon during the Bush presidency, see Krane, "Middle Tier in American Federalism." For specific examples, see Faye Bowers, "States Preempt U.S. on Immigration"; Uchitelle, "Raising the Floor on Pay"; Hakim, "Battle Lines Set as New York Acts to Cut Emissions"; Teske, "Checks, Balances, and Thresholds"; and Potoski, "Clean Air Federalism."

15. The seminal work on this issue is Tiebout, "Pure Theory of Local Public Expenditures."

16. See, e.g., Revesz, "Federalism and Environmental Protection."

17. See, e.g., Volden, "Entrusting the States with Welfare Reform."

18. Anne Larason Schneider and Ingram, *Policy Design for Democracy*, especially chaps. 4 and 5.

19. Volden, "Entrusting the States with Welfare Reform," 94.

20. Robertson, "American Federalism and the Politics of Regulation," 83.

21. For a good summary of the evidence supporting this argument, see Wagner, *What's Love Got to Do with It?*

22. See generally Alan Rosenthal, *Third House*, who concludes that moneyed interests at the state level enjoy the same sorts of organizational advantages as their national counterparts, but that money is "by no means the only or the most important resource" (p. 224). For a much less sanguine view, see Renzulli, *Capitol Offenders*.

23. For examples, see the works cited in note 14 above.

24. Rubin, "Puppy Federalism and the Blessings of America," 49.

25. Galle, "Designing Interstate Institutions," 1383.

26. Schlesinger, *Imperial Presidency*, 13.

27. Whittington, *Constitutional Construction: Divided Powers and Constitutional Meaning* (Cambridge: Harvard University Press, 1999), 4–5.

28. Ferejohn and Weingast, "Politics of the New Federalism," 160.

29. David B. Walker's *Rebirth of Federalism*, chap. 11, and "Advent of an Ambiguous Federalism."

30. This insight is informed by the analysis in Peabody, "Nonjudicial Constitutional Interpretation," especially pp. 70–71.

31. Madison famously noted that "the accumulation of all powers, legislative, executive, and judiciary, in the same hands . . . may justly be pronounced the very definition of tyranny" ("No. 47," in Rossiter, *Federalist Papers*, 301).

32. See, e.g., Van Alstyne, "Second Death of Federalism."

Appendix

1. I am indebted to Ross K. Baker of Rutgers University for mentioning this to me in a very brief conversation in the hallway at the Midwest Political Science Association convention. His comment essentially prompted a dissertation and, eventually, this book.

2. Madison, "No. 51," in Rossiter, *Federalist Papers*, 321.

3. Fenno, "Observation, Context, and Sequence in the Study of Politics," 14.

4. National Governors' Association, "Federal Relations," http://www.nga.org/.

5. See U.S Advisory Commission on Intergovernmental Relations, *Regulatory Federalism*.

6. Hamel, *Case Study Methods*, 34.

7. See Yin, *Case Study Research*, 38.

8. Ibid., ix.

9. Posner, "Politics of Preemption," 372.

Bibliography

ABA Task Force on Federalization of Criminal Law. *The Federalization of Criminal Law.* Chicago: American Bar Association, 1998.

"After 60 Years, Most Control Sent to States." In *1996 CQ Almanac,* 6-3–6-24. Washington, D.C.: Congressional Quarterly, 1997.

Ailshie, James. "Limits of Uniformity in State Laws." *American Bar Association Journal* 13 (1927): 633*ff.*

Alexander, Lex. "Money Cuts Threaten Agencies." *Greensboro (N.C.) News & Record,* June 8, 2008.

Allen, George. "Keeping Tolls and Tax Bureaucrats off the Information Superhighway." *The Hill,* February 9, 2006, 18.

Allen, Mike. "Bush Signs Repeal of Ergonomics Rules; Administration Promises Business-Friendly Workplace Safety Regulations." *Washington Post,* March 21, 2001.

Allen, Mike, and Juliet Eilperin. "Bush Aides Say Iraq War Needs No Hill Vote: Some See Such Support as Politically Helpful." *Washington Post,* August 26, 2002.

Allen, Scott. "If We Can't Bury Nuclear Waste in Nevada, Where Can We?" *Boston Globe,* May 17, 1993.

Alonso-Zaldivar, Ricardo. "50 Governors United against Federal Cuts to Medicaid." *Los Angeles Times,* June 16, 2005.

Amar, Akhil Reed. "Of Sovereignty and Federalism." *Yale Law Journal* 96 (June 1987): 1425–1520.

Anderson, James E. *Public Policymaking: An Introduction.* 6th ed. Boston: Houghton Mifflin, 2006.

Anderson, Nick. "Bush Administration Grants Leeway on 'No Child' Rules." *Washington Post*, November 22, 2005.

Anderson, William. *The Nation and the States, Rivals or Partners?* Minneapolis: University of Minnesota Press, 1955.

Antle, W. James. "Leaving No Child Left Behind." *The American Conservative*, August 1, 2005, http://www.amconmag.com/2005_08_01/article.html.

Anton, Thomas J. *American Federalism and Public Policy: How the System Works.* New York: Random House, 1989.

Armstrong, Jr., Walter P. *A Century of Service: The Centennial History of the National Conference of Commissioners on Uniform State Laws.* St. Paul, Minn.: West, 1992.

Arnold, David S., and Jeremy F. Plant. *Public Official Associations and State and Local Government: A Bridge across One Hundred Years.* Fairfax, Va.: George Mason University Press, 1994.

Arnold, R. Douglas. *The Logic of Congressional Action.* New Haven, Conn.: Yale University Press, 1990.

Arrandale, Tom. "Tigers No More." *Governing*, April 2006, http://www.governing.com/articles/4env.htm.

Associated Press State and Local Wire. "Katz Resigns as Head of Alaska's Washington, D.C. Office." November 19, 2002.

Associated Press. "Study: States Ignore Special Ed Law." January 23, 2000.

Ayres, Jr., B. Drummond. "Political Briefing: Feeling the Long Arm of the White House." *New York Times*, April 22, 2001, sec. 1.

Baldwin, Simeon E. "The Progressive Unfolding of the Powers of the United States." *American Political Science Review* 6 (February 1912): 1–16.

Balz, Dan. "GOP Governors Seek Shift in Power: Freedom from Federal Mandates Urged." *Washington Post*, November 20, 1994.

———. "GOP Governors Want a Seat at the Table." *Washington Post*, November 22, 2004.

Barnes, Robert. "Supreme Court Strikes Down State's Law to Diminish Tobacco Sales to Teens." *Washington Post*, February 21, 2008.

Barrett, Katherine, and Richard Greene. "Staying Stable." *Governing*, January 2008, http://www.governing.com/articles/0801taxrev.htm.

Barron, David J. "Progressive Federalism." *Dissent*, Spring 2005, http://www.dissentmagazine.org/article/?article=249.

Barton, Paul. "Voinovich Giving Governors a Voice." *Cincinnati (Ohio) Enquirer*, February 5, 1996.

Basham, Patrick. "Assessing the Term Limits Experiment: California and Beyond." In *Policy Analysis* (no. 413), 1–28. Washington, D.C.: Cato Institute, August 31, 2001.

Baudier, Walter J. "Internet Sales Taxes from Borders to Amazon: How Long before All of Your Purchases Are Taxed?" *Duke Law and Technology Review*, no. 5 (2006). http://www.law.duke.edu/journals/dltr/articles/PDF/ 2006 DLTR0005.pdf.

Baybeck, Brady, and William Lowry. "Federalism Outcomes and Ideological Preferences: The U.S. Supreme Court and Preemption Cases." *Publius: The Journal of Federalism* 30 (Summer 2000): 73–97.

Beer, Samuel H. "The Adoption of General Revenue Sharing: A Case Study in Public Sector Politics." *Public Policy* 24 (1976): 127–195.

———. *To Make a Nation: The Rediscovery of American Federalism*. Cambridge, Mass.: Belknap Press, 1993.

Belkin, Lisa B. "For State and Local Governments, Washington Is the Place to Be." *National Journal*, September 6, 1980, 1485–87.

Belluck, Pam. "Governors Unite in Medicaid Fight." *New York Times*, December 26, 2004.

Bennett, Walter Hartwell. *American Theories of Federalism*. University, Ala.: University of Alabama Press, 1964.

Benton, J. Edwin. "Economic Considerations and Reagan's New Federalism Swap Proposals." *Publius: The Journal of Federalism* 16 (Spring 1986): 17–32.

Berger, Raoul. *Federalism: The Founders' Design*. Norman: University of Oklahoma Press, 1987.

Besharov, Douglas J. "State Waivers Change Welfare as We Know It." *Detroit (Mich.) News*, June 23, 1996.

Bessette, Joseph M. *The Mild Voice of Reason: Deliberative Democracy and American National Government*. Chicago: University of Chicago Press, 1994

Bessette, Joseph M., and Jeffrey Tulis, eds. *The Presidency in the Constitutional Order*. Baton Rouge: Louisiana State University Press, 1981.

Beyle, Thad L. "From Governor to Governors." In *The State of the States*, edited by Carl E. Van Horn, 33–68. Washington, D.C.: Congressional Quarterly, 1989.

———. "The Institutionalized Powers of the Governorship: 1965–1985." In *State Government: CQ's Guide to Current Issues and Activities, 1988–89*, edited by Thad L. Beyle, 119–24. Washington, D.C.: Congressional Quarterly, 1988.

Biskupic, Joan. "Hill Republicans Target 'Judicial Activism'; Conservatives Block Nominees, Threaten Impeachment and Term Limits." *Washington Post*, September 14, 1997.

———. "States' Role at Issue in Rape Suit." *Washington Post*, January 10, 2000.

Bledsoe, W. Craig. "Presidential Commissions." In *Cabinets and Counselors: The President and the Executive Branch*. Washington, D.C.: Congressional Quarterly, 1997.

Blumenthal, Les. "National Guard Control Argued: States Oppose President's New Power to Deploy Units in Emergencies." *Tacoma (Wash.) News Tribune*, April 25, 2007.

Bowers, Faye. "States Preempt U.S. on Immigration." *Christian Science Monitor*, June 15, 2007.

Bowers, Matthew. "Virginia is the Last Holdout for Federal Goals 2000 Money." *Virginian-Pilot Norfolk*, November 24, 1996.

Bowman, Ann O'M., and Richard C. Kearney. *The Resurgence of the States.* Englewood Cliffs, N.J.: Prentice-Hall, 1986.

Bragaw, Stephen G. "Federalism's Legal Defense Fund: The Intergovernmental Lobby and the U.S. Supreme Court, 1982–1997." Paper presented at the annual meeting of the Midwest Political Science Association, Chicago, Ill., April 15, 1999.

Braucher, Robert. "The Legislative History of the Uniform Commercial Code." *Columbia Law Review* 58 (1958): 798–99.

Broder, David S. "Federalism's New Framework: Revised Order Satisfies State and Local Officials." *Washington Post*, August 5, 1999.

———. "So, Now Bigger Is Better?" *Washington Post*, January 12, 2003.

Broder, David S., and Robert Barnes. "Governors Cautious on Welfare Reform Plans." *Washington Post*, July 30, 1995.

Brooks, Glenn E. *When Governors Convene: The Governors' Conference and National Politics.* Baltimore: Johns Hopkins University Press, 1961.

Brown, R. Steven. "Emerging Models for Environmental Management." In Vol. 30, *The Book of the States, 1994–95*, edited by Robert A. Silvanik, 539–43. Lexington, Ky.: Council of State Governments, 1994.

Bruno, Michael. "Defense Policy Bill Outlines Major National Guard Changes." *Aerospace Daily & Defense Report*, December 12, 2007, 2.

Brutus. "Essay VI." In *The Anti-Federalist: Writings by the Opponents of the Constitution*, edited by Herbert J. Storing, selected by Murray Dry, 138–145. Chicago: University of Chicago Press, 1981.

Bryce, James. *The American Commonwealth.* Vol. 1, 3rd ed. New York: Macmillan, 1901.

Bullock, Bob. *Dollars We Deserve: How Texas Is Short-Changed of Our Fair Share of Federal Money.* Austin: Texas Office of the Comptroller, 1990.

Bumiller, Elisabeth. "Bush Signs Trade Bill, Restoring Broad Presidential Authority." *New York Times*, August 7, 2002.

Burgess, Susan R. *Contest for Constitutional Authority: The Abortion and War Power Debates.* Lawrence: University Press of Kansas, 1992.

Bustillo, Miguel. "States Sue EPA over Mercury Emissions." *Los Angeles Times*, March 30, 2005.

Butler, LaCrisha. "Delaware's 'Policy Advisors' Represent State's Interest in Washington." Gannett News Service, May 9, 1996.

Bybee, Jay S. "Ulysses at the Mast: Democracy, Federalism, and the Sirens' Song of the Seventeenth Amendment." *Northwestern University Law Review* 91 (Winter 1997): 500–69.

"California Asks Justice Department to Investigate Energy Prices." *St. Louis (Mo.) Post-Dispatch*, Dec. 17, 2000.

Calmes, Jacqueline. "444 North Capitol Street: Where State Lobbyists Are Learning Coalition Politics." *Governing*, February 1988, 17–21.

———. "Jim Martin: The Governors' Man." *Governing*, November 1989, 64–68.

Caminker, Evan. "State Sovereignty and Subordinance: May Congress Commandeer State Officers to Implement Federal Law?" *Columbia Law Review* 95 (1995): 1001–1089.

Cammisa, Anne Marie. *Governments as Interest Groups: Intergovernmental Lobbying and the Federal System*. Westport, Conn.: Praeger, 1995.

Campbell, Julie. "Is There a Conflict between E-Sign and UETA?" Unpublished manuscript, Chicago Kent Law School, July 1, 2001.

"Capitol Bloat" (editorial). *Washington Post*, January 22, 2004.

Carney, Eliza Newlin. "Last Gasp for a Broad Reworking?" *National Journal*, March 9, 1996, 537–538.

Carr, Rebecca. "Some in GOP Say Bush Abuses Powers: Congress Marginalized, Former Officials Complain." *Atlanta Journal-Constitution*, July 30, 2006.

Cassata, Donna. "Finale Expected to Be Short, but not Necessarily Sweet." *Congressional Quarterly Weekly Report* 54 (August 31, 1996): 2418–55.

Cauchon, Dennis. "For Great Lakes, A Future with Less Industry." *USA Today*, December 4, 2007.

Chandrasekaran, Rajiv. "Online Sales Heating Up Tax Debate." *Washington Post*, December 13, 1999.

Chang, Alicia. "States Rush to Build Spaceports—Again." MSNBC.com, May 13, 2006. http://www.msnbc.msn.com/ID/12746930.

Chapman, Steve. "Welcoming the Return of Divided Government." *Baltimore Sun*, November 13, 2006.

Choper, Jesse H. *Judicial Review and the National Political Process*. Chicago: University of Chicago Press, 1980.

Chubb, John E. "The Constitution, Institutionalization, and the Development of Federalism." In *The Constitution and American Political Development*, edited by Peter F. Nardulli, 262–89. Urbana: University of Illinois Press, 1992.

———. "The Political Economy of Federalism." *American Political Science Review* 79 (December 1985): 994–1015.

Cingranelli, David L. "State Government Lobbies in the National Political Process." *State Government* 56 (1983): 122–27.

Clark, Bradford R. "Putting the Safeguards Back Into the Political Safeguards of Federalism." *Texas Law Review* 80 (December 2001): 327–42.

Clayton, Cornell W., and J. Mitchell Pickerill. "Guess What Happened on the Way to the Revolution: Precursors to the Supreme Court's Federalism Revolution." *Publius: The Journal of Federalism* 34, no. 3 (Summer 2004): 85–114.

Clean Air Act of 1970. Public Law 91-604. Codified at 42 *U.S. Code*, sec. 7401. Amended in 1990 by Public Law 101-549.

Clines, Francis X. "Clinton Signs Bill Cutting Welfare; States in New Role." *New York Times*, August 23, 1996.

Clinton, William Jefferson. Executive Order no. 12875. "Enhancing the Intergovernmental Partnership." *Federal Register* 58, no. 207 (October 28, 1998): 58093.

———. Executive Order no. 13083. "Federalism, Executive Order 13083." *Federal Register* 63, no. 96 (May 14, 1998): 27651.

———. Executive Order no. 13095. "Suspension of Executive Order 13083." *Federal Register* 63, no. 152 (August 5, 1998): 42565.

———. Executive Order no. 13132. "Federalism, Executive Order 13132." *Code of Federal Regulations,* title 3 (1999): 206.

———. "Remarks Following a Meeting with the Nation's Governors." *Weekly Compilation of Presidential Documents* 29, no. 5 (February 8, 1993): 117–18.

Cobb, Roger W., and Charles D. Elder. *Participation in American Politics.* Baltimore: Johns Hopkins University Press, 1983.

Cohen, Neil B., and Barry L. Zaretsky. "Drafting Commercial Law for the New Millennium: Will the Current Process Suffice?" *Loyola of Los Angeles Law Review* 26 (April 1993): 551–62.

Cohen, Richard. "Always the National News." *Washington Post*, May 2, 1995.

Collins, Jr., Paul M. "Towards an Integrated Model of the U.S. Supreme Court's Federalism Decision Making." *Publius: The Journal of Federalism* 37 (Fall 2007): 505–31.

Commission on Intergovernmental Relations. *A Report to the President for Transmittal to the Congress.* Washington, D.C.: Government Printing Office, 1955.

Commission on No Child Left Behind. *Beyond NCLB: Fulfilling the Promise to Our Nation's Children.* Washington, D.C.: Aspen Institute, 2007.

Congressional Budget Office. *CBO's Activities under the Unfunded Mandates Reform Act, 1996–2000.* Washington, D.C.: CBO, 2001.

Congressional Review Act of 1996. Public Law 104-121, sec. 251. Codified at 5 *U.S. Code* sec. 801–808.

Conlan, Timothy. *From New Federalism to Devolution: Twenty-Five Years of Intergovernmental Reform.* Washington, D.C.: Brookings Institution, 1998.

Connolly, Ceci. "Thompson Cutting Medicaid Red Tape." *Washington Post*, July 10, 2001.

Corley, Pamela C., Robert M. Howard, and David C. Nixon. "The Supreme Court and Opinion Content: The Use of the *Federalist Papers.*" *Political Research Quarterly* 58 (June 2005): 329–40.

Cornell, Tim. "President Made Plea for Studds to Run Again." *Boston Herald*, October 30, 1995.

Corwin, Edward S. "Constitution v. Constitutional Theory: The Question of the States v. the Nation." *American Political Science Review* 19 (1925): 290–304

———. "The Passing of Dual Federalism." *Virginia Law Review* 36 (1950): 1–24.

Crabb, Jr., Cecil V., and Pat M. Holt. *Invitation to Struggle: Congress, the President, and Foreign Policy.* Washington, D.C.: CQ Press, 1992.

Crook, Sara Brandes, and John R. Hibbing. "A Not-So-Distant Mirror: The Seventeenth Amendment and Congressional Change." *American Political Science Review* 91 (December 1997): 845–53.

Cross, Frank B. "Realism about Federalism." *New York University Law Review* 74 (November 1999): 1304–1335.

Cushman, Jr., John H. "Bill Would Give Water Customers Pollution Notice." *New York Times*, June 23, 1996, sec. 1.

———. "Virginia Seen as Undercutting U.S. Environmental Rules." *New York Times*, January 19, 1997, sec. 1.

Cutcheon, Sullivan M. "Uniform State Laws." *Michigan Law Journal* 2 (March 1893): 86–92.

Cyphers, Christopher J. "Testing the Limits of Federalism: The National Civic Federation and the Campaign for Uniform State Laws." Paper presented at the annual meeting of the Social Science History Association, Fort Worth, Tex., November 14, 1999.

Danitz, Tiffany. "State School Chiefs Concerned about Details of Education Bill." Stateline.org, June 22, 2001, http://www.stateline.org/story.cfm?storyid=134105.

Dao, James. "Red, Blue, and Angry All Over." *New York Times*, January 16, 2005, sec. 4.

Dean, Howard M. "New Rules and Roles for States." *Health Affairs*, Spring 1993, 183–84.

DeParle, Jason. "A Sharp Decrease in Welfare Cases Is Gathering Speed: Windfall for the States." *New York Times*, February 2, 1997.

Derthick, Martha. "American Federalism: Madison's Middle Ground in the 1980s." *Public Administration Review* 47 (January/February 1987): 66–74.

———. *Between State and Nation: Regional Organizations of the United States.* Washington, D.C.: Brookings Institute, 1974.

———. *The Influence of Federal Grants: Public Assistance in Massachusetts.* Cambridge, Mass.: Harvard University Press, 1970.

de Tocqueville, Alexis. *Democracy in America.* Edited by J. P. Mayer. Translated by George Lawrence. New York: Doubleday, 1969. First published 1835.

Devroy, Ann. "President to Order Changes in Welfare; Food Stamp Rules, State Waivers Addressed." *Washington Post*, July 31, 1995.

Dewar, Helen. "President, Senate Reach Pact on Judicial Nominations; Bush Vows He Won't Use Recess Appointments." *Washington Post*, May 19, 2004.

DiIulio, Jr., John J., and Donald F. Kettl. *Fine Print: The Contract with America, Devolution, and the Administrative Realities of American Federalism.* Washington, D.C.: Brookings Institution, 1995.

Dillon, Sam. "Battle Grows over Renewing Landmark Education Law." *New York Times*, April 7, 2007.

———. "Facing State Protests, U.S. Offers More Flexibility on School Rules." *New York Times*, April 8, 2005.

———. "New U.S. Secretary Showing Flexibility on 'No Child' Act." *New York Times*, February 14, 2005.

———. "Report Faults Bush Initiative on Education." *New York Times*, February 24, 2005.

———. "Some School Districts Challenging Bush's Signature Education Law." *New York Times*, January 2, 2004.

———. "States Are Relaxing Education Standards to Avoid Sanctions from Federal Law." *New York Times*, May 22, 2003.

———. "Utah Delays a Challenge to Federal Law." *New York Times*, March 2, 2005.

Dinan, John. "State Governmental Influence in the National Policy Process: Lessons from the 104th Congress." *Publius: The Journal of Federalism* 27 (Spring 1997): 129–142.

Dobbs, Michael. "NEA, States Challenge 'No Child' Program." *Washington Post*, April 21, 2005.

———. "New Rules for 'No Child' Law Planned." *Washington Post*, April 7, 2005.

"Doing the Waive" (editorial). *Education Week*, April 18, 2007, 19.

Donahue, John D. *Disunited States*. New York: Basic Books, 1997.

Donn, Jeff. "Making Federal Cases Out of Common Crimes." *Los Angeles Times*, January 18, 2004.

Donnay, Patrick. "Politicians and Professionals: The Demand for Participation in the Intergovernmental Lobby." PhD diss., University of Iowa, 1991.

Donnelly, John M. "House Reverses Course on Martial Law." *CQ Today*, October 19, 2007. http://public.cq.com/docs/cqt/news110-000002609356.html.

Downs, Anthony. "Up and Down with Ecology: The 'Issue–Attention Cycle.'" *The Public Interest* 28 (Spring 1972): 38–50.

Drake, Frederick C., and Lynn R. Nelson. *States' Rights and American Federalism: A Documentary History*. Westport, Conn.: Greenwood Press, 1999.

Ducayet, James W. "Publius and Federalism: On the Use and Abuse of *The Federalist* in Constitutional Interpretation." *New York University Law Review* 68 (October 1993): 821–69.

Dunham, Allison. "A History of the National Conference of Commissioners on Uniform State Laws." *Law and Contemporary Problems* 30 (Spring 1965): 233–249.

DuPont, Pete. "Federalism in the Twenty-first Century: Will States Exist?" *Harvard Journal of Law and Public Policy* 16 (1993): 137–48.

Dye, Thomas R. *American Federalism: Competition among Governments*. Lexington, Mass.: Lexington Books, 1990.

————. *Politics in States and Communities*. 9th ed. Upper Saddle River, N.J.: Prentice Hall, 1997.

Eaton, Amasa M. "Uniformity of Legislation. An Address Delivered Before the State Bar Association of Missouri, at St. Louis, September 23, 1904," n.p., n.d.

The Education Trust. "Telling the Whole Truth (Or Not) about Highly Qualified Teachers: New State Data," December 2003, http://www2.edtrust.org/NR/rdonlyres/C638111D-04E3-4C0D-9F68-20E7009498A6/0/tellingthe truth teachers.pdf.

Ehrlich, Susan. "The Increasing Federalization of Crime." *Arizona State Law Journal* 32 (Fall 2000): 825–42.

Eilperin, Juliet. "EPA Chief Denies Calif. Limit on Auto Emissions." *Washington Post*, December 20, 2007.

Eisenhower, Dwight D. "Address to the 1957 Governors' Conference, Williamsburg, Va." Reprinted in *Politics of American Federalism*, edited by Daniel J. Elazar, 188–193. Lexington, Mass.: D.C. Heath, 1969.

Elazar, Daniel J. *American Federalism: A View from the States*. 3rd ed. New York: Harper and Row, 1984.

————. *The American Partnership: Intergovernmental Co-operation in the Nineteenth-Century United States*. Chicago: University of Chicago Press, 1962.

————. "Opening the Third Century of American Federalism: Issues and Prospects." *Annals of the American Academy of Political and Social Sciences* 509 (May 1990): 11–21.

————. "The States and the Nation." In *Politics in the American States*, edited by Herbert Jacob and Kenneth N. Vines, 449–78. Boston: Little, Brown, 1965.

Ely, John Hart. *War and Responsibility: Constitutional Lessons of Vietnam and Its Aftermath*. Princeton, N.J.: Princeton University Press, 1995.

"End Run on Medicaid" (editorial). *New York Times*, May 28, 2008.

Environmental Protection Agency. "Approval and Promulgation of Air Quality Implementation Plans; Connecticut; Interstate Transport of Pollution" [proposed rule]. *Federal Register* 72 (November 5, 2007): 62420–22

————. "Approval and Promulgation of Air Quality Implementation Plans; Connecticut; Interstate Transport of Pollution" [final rule]. *Federal Register* 73 (May 7, 2008): 25516–18

Epstein, William M. *Welfare in America: How Social Science Fails the Poor*. Madison: University of Wisconsin Press, 1997.

Ess, Eric A. "Internet Taxation without Physical Representation? States Seek Solution to Stop E-Commerce Sales Tax Shortfall." *Saint Louis University Law Journal* 50 (Spring 2006): 893–924.

Farkas, Suzanne. *Urban Lobbying*. New York: New York University Press, 1970.

Farrier, Jasmine. *Passing the Buck: Congress, the Budget, and Deficits*. Lexington: University Press of Kentucky, 2004.

"Federalism, Political Accountability, and the Spending Clause." *Harvard Law Review* 107 (1994): 1419–36.

"Feds Give California Stern Warning." *The Special Educator*, 13 (August 1, 1997).

Feigenbaum, Edward D. "Introduction." In Vol. 46, *Suggested State Legislation*, edited by Council of State Governments, p. iv. Lexington, Ky.: Council of State Governments, 1987.

Feldmann, Linda. "Clinton Encourages New Paths on Welfare." *Christian Science Monitor*, August 23, 1993.

Fenno, Jr., Richard F. *Congressmen in Committee*. Boston: Little, Brown, 1973.

———. *Home Style: House Members in their Districts*. New York: Scott Foresman, 1978.

———. "Observation, Context, and Sequence in the Study of Politics." *American Political Science Review* 80, no. 1 (March 1986): 3–15.

Ferejohn, John A., and Barry R. Weingast. "The Politics of the New Federalism." In *The New Federalism: Can the States Be Trusted?* edited by John Ferejohn and Barry R. Weingast, 157–63. Stanford, Calif.: Hoover Institution Press, 1997.

Field, David Dudley. "Centralization in the Federal Government." *North American Review* 294 (May 1881): 407–26.

Fisher, Louis. *The Politics of Shared Power: Congress and the Executive*. Washington, D.C.: Congressional Quarterly Press, 1993.

Flitner, Jr., David. *The Politics of Presidential Advisory Commissions: A Public Policy Perspective*. Dobbs Ferry, N.Y.: Transnational, 1986.

Ford, Richard Thompson. "The New Blue Federalists: The Case for Liberal Federalism." Slate.com, January 6, 2005. http://slate.msn.com/id/ 2111942/.

"Frequent Flier." *Detroit (Mich.) News*, January 26, 1997.

Fried, Charles. "How to Make the President Talk to the Local Pol." *New York Times*, November 11, 2000.

Fried, Jonathan. "No Hype: Four Web Tools that Work and Save Money." *New York Times*, June 13, 2001.

Gabriel, Henry D. "The Revision of the Uniform Commercial Code—How Successful Has It Been?" *Hastings Law Review* 52 (March 2001): 653–665.

———. "The Revisions of the Uniform Commercial Code: Process and Politics." *Journal of Law and Commerce* 19 (Fall 1999): 125–136.

Galle, Brian. "Designing Interstate Institutions: The Example of the Streamlined Sales and Use Tax Agreement." *U.C. Davis Law Review* 40 (April 2007): 1381–1435.

Gant, Scott E. "Judicial Supremacy and Nonjudicial Interpretation of the Constitution." *Hastings Constitutional Law Quarterly* 24 (1997): 359–440.

Gardbaum, Stephen. "Rethinking Constitutional Federalism." *Texas Law Review* 74 (1996): 795–838.

Garrett, Elizabeth. "States in a Federal System: Enhancing the Political Safeguards of Federalism? The Unfunded Mandates Reform Act of 1995." *Kansas Law Review* 45 (July 1997): 1113–1183.

Gercken, Keith R., Richard E. Nielsen, and Marsha-laine F. Dungog. "Stream-lined Sales and Use Tax System: Adoption of Landmark Multistate Agree-ment." *Pillsbury Winthrop LLP States and Local Tax Bulletin*, November 2002, 1–5, http://www.pmstax.com/ftp/state/bull0211.pdf.

Gerlak, Andrea K. "Federalism and U.S. Water Policy: Lessons for the Twenty-First Century." *Publius: The Journal of Federalism* 36, no. 2 (Spring 2006): 231–57.

Gerrard, Michael B. *Whose Backyard, Whose Risk? Fear and Fairness in Toxic and Nuclear Waste Siting.* Cambridge, Mass.: MIT Press, 1994.

Gilens, Martin. *Why Americans Hate Welfare: Race, Media, and the Politics of Anti-Poverty Programs.* Chicago: University of Chicago Press, 2000.

Gillespie, Ed, and Bob Schellhas, eds. *Contract with America.* New York: Times Books, 1996.

Ginsberg, Benjamin, and Martin Shefter. *Politics by Other Means: Politicians, Prosecutors, and the Press from Watergate to Whitewater.* 3rd ed. New York: W.W. Norton, 2002.

Glennon, Robert Jerome. "Federalism as a Regional Issue: 'Get Out! And Give Us More Money.'" *Arizona Law Review* 38 (1996): 829–42.

Godman, T. R. "For Flood-Ravaged States, Focus Now Shifts to Making Sure Federal Aid Gets Back Home." *Legal Times*, August, 16, 1993, 5.

Goggin, Malcolm L. "The Use of Administrative Discretion in Implementing the State Children's Health Insurance Program." *Publius: The Journal of Federalism* 29 (Spring 1999): 35–52.

Goggin, Malcolm L., Ann O'M. Bowman, James P. Lester, and Laurence J. O'Toole, Jr. *Implementation Theory and Practice: Toward a Third Generation.* Glenview, Ill.: Scott, Foresman, 1990.

Goldstein, Leslie Friedman. "State Resistance to Authority in Federal Unions: The Early United States (1790–1860) and the European Community (1958–94)." *Studies in American Political Development* 11 (Spring 1997): 159–66.

Goldwater, Barry. *The Conscience of a Conservative.* Shepherdsville, Ky.: Victor, 1960.

Goldwin, Robert A., and Art Kaufman, eds. *Separation of Powers—Does It Still Work?* Washington, D.C.: American Enterprise Institute, 1986.

"Governors Craft Welfare Wish List." *National Journal's CongressDaily*, Septem-ber 27, 1995, n.p.

"Governors Praise Congress for Reforming Welfare." *Governors' Bulletin*, August 5, 1996, 1.

Graber, Mark A. "The Nonmajoritarian Difficulty: Legislative Deference to the Judiciary." *Studies in American Political Development* 7 (Spring 1993): 35–73.

Graebner, William. "Federalism in the Progressive Era: A Structural Interpre-tation." *Journal of American History* 64 (September 1977): 331–49.

Gramm–Leach–Bliley Act of 1999. Public Law 106-102. Codified at 15 *U.S. Code* sec. 6801–6809.

Grant, J. A. C. "The Search for Uniformity of Law." *American Political Science Review* 32 (December 1938): 1082–1098.

Graves, W. Brooke. *American Intergovernmental Relations: Their Origins, Historical Development, and Current Status*. New York: Charles Scribner's Sons, 1964.

———. *Uniform State Action: A Possible Substitute for Centralization*. Chapel Hill: University of North Carolina Press, 1934.

Gray, Virginia. "Innovation in the States: A Diffusion Study." *American Political Science Review* 67 (1973): 1174–85.

Greenberg, Mark, and Steve Savner. "Waivers and the New Welfare Law: Initial Approaches in State Plans." Washington, D.C.: Center for Law and Social Policy, November 1996, http://www.clasp.org/publications/newwelf.html.

Greenblatt, Alan. "Recipe for Respect." *Governing*, February 2008, http://www.governing.com/articles/0802federal.htm.

———. "The Truth about Term Limits." *Governing*, January 2006, http://www.governing.com/articles/0601term.htm.

Greve, Michael S. *Real Federalism: Why It Matters, How It Could Happen*. Washington, D.C.: American Enterprise Institute, 1999.

Grey, Betsy J. "Make Congress Speak Clearly: Federal Preemption of State Tort Remedies." *Boston University Law Review* 77 (June 1997): 559–67.

Grodzins, Morton. *The American System: A New View of Government in the United States*. Edited by Daniel J. Elazar. Chicago: Rand McNally, 1966.

———. "Federal System." In *Goals for Americans*, 268–82. New York: Prentice Hall, 1960.

Groer, Anne. "Florida Loses Political Clout as Senior Congressmen Quit." *Orlando (Fla.) Sentinel*, June 14, 1992.

Grunwald, Michael. "In Legislative Tide, State Power Ebbs; Federalization Has Few Friends but Many Votes." *Washington Post*, October 24, 1999.

Gulick, Luther C. "Reorganization of the State." *Civil Engineering* 3 (August 1933): 420–421.

Gurwitt, Rob. "Comes the Devolution: Power to the States! But Are the Media Ready?" *Columbia Journalism Review* 35, no. 1 (May/June 1996): 52–54.

———. "Greenhorn Government." *Governing*, February 1996, 15–19.

Haider, Donald H. "Review of *Governments as Interest Groups: Intergovernmental Lobbying and the Federal System*, by Anne Marie Cammisa." *Publius: The Journal of Federalism* 26, no. 2 (Spring 1996): 144.

———. *When Governments Come to Washington: Governors, Mayors, and Intergovernmental Lobbying*. New York: Free Press, 1974.

Hakim, Danny. "Battle Lines Set as New York Acts to Cut Emissions." *New York Times*, November 26, 2005.

————. "10 States Sue E.P.A. on Emissions." *New York Times*, April 28, 2006.

Hall, William K. *The New Institutions of Federalism: The Politics of Intergovernmental Relations, 1960–1985.* New York: Peter Lang, 1986.

Hamel, Jacques. *Case Study Methods.* With Stephane Dufour and Dominic Fortin. Newbury Park, Calif.: Sage, 1993.

Hamilton, Marci A. "The Elusive Safeguards of Federalism." *Annals of the American Academy of Political and Social Science* 574 (March 2001): 93–103.

Hampel, Paul. "Is Your Poker Game Legal? Probably Not, But with Differing State Laws and Poker's Popularity, Bars and Charities Try to Play It Straight." *St. Louis (Mo.) Post-Dispatch*, March 20, 2005.

Handberg, Roger, and Joan Johnson-Freese. "State Spaceport Initiatives: Economic and Political Innovation in an Intergovernmental Context." *Publius: The Journal of Federalism* 28 (Winter 1998): 91–110.

Harkness, Peter. "'Shift-and-Shaft' Federalism." *CQ Weekly* 66, no. 10 (March 2008): 610.

Havemann, Joel, Rochelle L. Stanfield, and Neal R. Pierce. "Federal Spending: The North's Loss Is the Sunbelt's Gain." *National Journal*, June 26, 1976, 878–91.

Havemann, Judith. "Advocacy Groups Take On Governors' Reform Plan." *Washington Post*, February 29, 1996.

————. "Governors' Reform Plan Ends Welfare Guarantee." *Washington Post*, February 7, 1996.

Healy, Patrick. "Spitzer Visits Capitol Hill with Long List." *New York Times*, December 6, 2006, New York and Region section.

Hedge, David M. "The Political and Policy Consequences of Institutional Development: The View from the States." Paper presented at the annual meeting of the Midwest Political Science Association, Chicago, Ill., April 10–12, 1996.

Hemphill, John. "The Uniform Laws Craze." *The American Mercury*, May 1925, 60.

Hendren, John. "50 States' Rules Regulating Pharmacists Are a Confusing Patchwork." *St. Louis (Mo.) Post-Dispatch*, February 13, 2000.

Hernandez, Raymond, and Al Baker. "'Big Four' Governors Working Together to Lobby Congress." *New York Times*, July 20, 2004.

Hess, Stephen. "Federalism and News." *Brookings Review* 18 (Winter 2000): 28–31.

"High-Tech Industry Cheers Enactment of Moratorium on New Internet Taxes." *1998 CQ Almanac*, 21-19–21-24.

Hill, Alfred. "Opinion: The Shutdowns and the Constitution." *Political Science Quarterly* 115 (Summer 2000): 273–282.

Hill, Jeffrey S., and Carol S. Weissert. "Implementation and the Irony of Delegation: The Politics of Low-Level Radioactive Waste Disposal." *Journal of Politics* 57 (May 1995), 344–69.

Hill, Jr., C. William. *The Political Theory of John Taylor of Caroline*. Cranbury, N.J.: Associated University Presses, 1977.

Hill, Kim Quaile, and Patricia A. Hurley. "Uniform State Law Adoptions in the American States: An Explanatory Analysis." *Publius: The Journal of Federalism* 18 (Winter 1988): 117–126.

Hillenbrand, Bernard F. "The Big Six—A New Force on the Washington Scene." *Public Management*, December 1971, 3–5.

Hills, Jr., Roderick M. "Federalism in Constitutional Context." *Harvard Journal of Law and Public Policy* 22 (Fall 1998): 186–90.

Hisert, George. "Uniform Commercial Code: Does One Size Fit All?" *Loyola of Los Angeles Law Review* 28 (November 1994): 219–33.

Hoar, Roger Sherman. "The Uniformity of Uniform Laws." *American Bar Association Journal* 14 (1928): 53*ff*.

Hoebeke, C. H. *The Road to Mass Democracy: Original Intent and the Seventeenth Amendment*. New Brunswick, N.J.: Transaction, 1995.

Hoff, David J. "Chiefs: Ed. Dept. Getting Stingier on NCLB Flexibility." *Education Week*, December 13, 2006, 19.

———. "Not All Agree on Meaning of NCLB Proficiency." *Education Week*, April 18, 2007, 1.

Holcombe, A. N. "The States as Agents of the Nation." *Southwestern Political Science Quarterly* 1 (1921): 307–27.

Hornbeck, Mark. "Engler Gets Front-Row Seat for Federal Budget Talks." *Detroit (Mich.) News*, November 22, 1995.

Horowitz, Tony. *Confederates in the Attic: Dispatches from the Unfinished Civil War*. New York: Vintage, 1999.

Houghton, Kendall L., and Walter Hellerstein. "State Taxation of Electronic Commerce: Perspectives on Proposals for Change and Their Constitutionality." *Brigham Young University Law Review* (2000), 9–76.

Internet Tax Freedom Act of 1998. Title XI of *Omnibus Appropriations Act of 1998*, Public Law 105-277. Codified at 47 U.S. Code (1998), sec. 151.

Jackson, Vicki C. "Federalism and the Uses and Limits of the Law: *Printz* and Principle." *Harvard Law Review* 111 (1998): 2181–2259.

Johnson, Dirk. "The Governors: Republicans Endorse Turning Welfare Over to the States." *New York Times*, August 1, 1996.

Jones, Charles O. *The Presidency in a Separated System*. Washington, D.C.: Brookings Institution, 1994.

Kamieniecki, Sheldon, and Michael R. Ferrall. "Intergovernmental Relations and Clean-Air Policy in California." *Publius: The Journal of Federalism* 21 (Summer 1991): 143–54.

Katz, Ellis, and G. Alan Tarr, eds. *Federalism and Rights*. Lanham, Md.: Rowman & Littlefield, 1996.

Katz, Jeffrey L. "GOP May Move to Split Medicaid, Welfare." *Congressional Quarterly Weekly Report*, June 22, 1996, 1762.

Kaufman, Marc. "If New Mexico Builds It, Will Space Travelers Come?" *Washington Post*, March 27, 2007.

Keiser, Lael R. "State Bureaucratic Discretion and the Administration of Social Welfare Programs: The Case of Social Security Disability." *Journal of Public Administration Research and Theory* 9, no. 1 (January 1999): 87–106.

———. "State Governmental Interests and Policy Implementation: Gate-Keeping in the Social Security Disability Program." Paper presented at the annual meeting of the Midwest Political Science Association, Chicago, Ill., April 2000.

Keiser, Lael R., and Joe Soss. "With Good Cause: Bureaucratic Discretion and the Politics of Child Support Enforcement." *American Journal of Political Science* 42 (October 1998): 1133–1156.

Kelderman, Eric. "States' Rebellion at REAL ID Echoes in Congress." Stateline.org, May 9, 2007, http://www.stateline.org/live/details/story?contentId=206433.

———. "Two States Lead Revolt against REAL ID." Stateline.org, April 18, 2007, http://www.stateline.org/live/details/story?contentId=199732.

Kerwin, Cornelius M. *Rulemaking: How Government Agencies Write Law and Make Policy*. 2nd ed. Washington, D.C.: Congressional Quarterly Press, 1999.

Ketcham, Ralph, ed. *The Anti-Federalist Papers and the Constitutional Convention Debates*. New York: Mentor, 1986.

Kettl, Donald F. *Government by Proxy: (Mis?)Managing Federal Programs*. Washington, D.C.: Congressional Quarterly Press, 1988.

———. "Senator Warner's Posse." *Governing*, February 2007, http://www.governing.com/articles/0702poto.htm.

Kilpatrick, James Jackson. "The Case for 'States' Rights.'" In *A Nation of States: Essays on the American Federal System*, edited by Robert A. Goldwin, 88–105. Chicago: Rand McNally, 1961.

Kingdon, John W. *Agendas, Alternatives, and Public Policies*. 2nd ed. New York: Longman, 1995.

———. *Congressmens' Voting Decisions*. 3rd ed. Ann Arbor: University of Michigan Press, 1989.

Knight, Barbara B., ed. *Separation of Powers in the American Political System*. Fairfax, Va.: George Mason University Press, 1989.

Kocheisen, Carol. "Panel Approves Drinking Water Bill with Several Pluses for Cities." *Nation's Cities*, June 17, 1996, 11.

Kramer, Larry D. "But When Exactly Was Judicially Enforced Federalism 'Born' in the First Place?" *Harvard Journal of Law and Public Policy* 22 (Fall 1998): 123–37.

———. "Putting the Politics Back into the Political Safeguards of Federalism." *Columbia Law Review* 100 (January 2000): 215–293.

———. "Understanding Federalism." *Vanderbilt Law Review* 47 (October 1994): 1485–1561.

Krane, Dale. "The Middle Tier in American Federalism: State Government Policy Activism During the Bush Presidency." *Publius: The Journal of Federalism* 37 (Summer 2007): 453–77.

Krasner, Stephen D. *Sovereignty: Organized Hypocrisy*. Princeton, N.J.: Princeton University Press, 1999.

Kriz, Margaret. "Drinks All Around." *National Journal*, November 18, 1995, 2862.

Krotoszynski, Ronald J. "Listening to the 'Sounds of Sovereignty' but Missing the Beat: Does the New Federalism Really Matter?" *Indiana Law Review* 32 (1998): 11–25.

Kurtz, Karl T., Bruce E. Cain, and Richard A. Neimi, eds. *Institutional Change in American Politics: The Case of Term Limits*. Ann Arbor: University of Michigan Press, 2007.

"Landmark Education Bill Signed." In *2001 Congressional Quarterly Almanac*, 8-3–8-10. Washington, D.C.: Congressional Quarterly Press, 2001.

Lapp, John A. "Uniform State Legislation." *American Political Science Review* 4 (November 1910): 576–581.

Lardner, Jr., George. "Bill Aimed at Reversing Bush Order on Records." *Washington Post*, April 11, 2002.

———. "Bush Seeks Secrecy for Pardon Discussions." *Washington Post*, August 27, 2002.

Laski, Harold J. "The Obsolescence of Federalism." *New Republic*, May 3, 1939, 367–69.

Lav, Iris J., and Phillip Oliff. "Federal Grants to States and Localities Cut Deeply in Fiscal Year 2009 Federal Budget." Center for Budget and Policy Priorities issue brief, February 4, 2008, http://www.cbpp.org/2-4-08sfp.htm.

Lawrence, Jill. "Gubernatorial Rapprochement." *Governing*, April 1996, 11.

Lazare, Daniel. *The Frozen Republic: How the Constitution Is Paralyzing Democracy*. New York: Harcourt Brace, 1996.

Lee, Frances E., and Bruce I. Oppenheimer. *Sizing Up the Senate: The Unequal Consequences of Equal Representation*. Chicago: University of Chicago Press, 1999.

Lehne, Richard. "Benefits in State–National Relations." *Publius: The Journal of Federalism* 2 (Fall 1972): 75–93.

"Let's Try 'No State Left Behind'" (editorial). *Los Angeles Times*, February 24, 2005.

Lewin, Tamar. "At Core of Adoption Dispute Is Crazy Quilt of State Laws." *New York Times*, January 19, 2001.

Liebschutz, Sarah F. *Bargaining under Federalism: Contemporary New York*. Albany, N.Y.: SUNY Press, 1991.

Light, Paul C. *The True Size of Government*. Washington, D.C.: Brookings Institution, 1999.

Lindblom, Charles. "The Market as Prison." *Journal of Politics* 44 (1982): 324–36.

Lipsky, Michael. *Street-Level Bureaucracy: Dilemmas of the Individual in Public Services.* New York: Russell Sage Foundation, 1980.

Lochhead, Carolyn. "Small Engine Smog Rules Snuffed: Senate Rider Supersedes New State Limits." *San Francisco Chronicle*, November 13, 2003.

Lowi, Theodore J. *The End of Liberalism: The Second Republic of the United States.* 2nd ed. New York: W.W. Norton, 1979.

———. *The End of the Republican Era.* Norman, Okla.: University of Oklahoma Press, 1995.

Luton, Larry S. *The Politics of Garbage: A Community Perspective on Solid Waste Policy Making.* Pittsburgh, Pa.: University of Pittsburgh Press, 1996.

Lutz, Donald S. "Toward a Theory of Constitutional Amendment." In *Responding to Imperfection: The Theory and Practice of Constitutional Amendment*, edited by Sanford Levinson, 237–74. Princeton, N.J.: Princeton University Press, 1995.

Lutz, James M. "Regional Leadership Patterns in the Diffusion of Public Policies." *American Politics Quarterly* (1987): 387–98.

Maass, Arthur. *Congress and the Common Good.* New York: Basic Books, 1983.

Maggi, Laura. "State Lobbies to Preserve its Reform of the Schools." *New Orleans Times-Picayune*, November 22, 2002.

Magleby, David B. "Governing by Initiative: Let the Voters Decide? An Assessment of the Initiative and Referendum Process." *Colorado Law Review* 66 (1995): 13–46.

Manuel, Paul Christopher, and Anne Marie Cammisa. *Checks and Balances? How a Parliamentary System Could Change American Politics.* Boulder, Colo.: Westview Press, 1999.

March, James G., and Johan P. Olsen. *Rediscovering Institutions: The Organizational Basis of Politics.* New York: Free Press, 1989.

Marks, Alexandra. "More States Try to Model N.Y.'s Passenger Bill of Rights." *Christian Science Monitor*, January 8, 2008.

Martin, Jil L. "*United States v. Morrison*: Federalism against the Will of the States." *Loyola University Chicago Law Review* 32 (Fall 2000): 243–333.

Matheson, Scott M. *Out of Balance.* With James Edwin Kee. Salt Lake City, Utah: Peregraine Smith Books, 1986.

Mayhew, David R. *Congress: The Electoral Connection.* New Haven, Conn.: Yale University Press, 1974.

McCabe, John M. "Foreword." *Alabama Law Review* 42 (1991): 367–71.

McCarthy, James E. "Clean Air Act Issues in the 106th Congress." Congressional Research Service Issue Brief, November 14, 2000.

McClay, Wilfred M. "The Soul of Man under Federalism." *First Things* 64 (June/July 1996): 21–26.

McCloskey, Robert G. *The American Supreme Court.* Revised by Sanford Levinson. Chicago: University of Chicago Press, 1994.

McCoy, Thomas R., and Barry Friedman. "Conditional Spending: Federalism's Trojan Horse." *Supreme Court Review* 1988 (1988): 85–127.

McLaughlin, Gerald T. "The Evolving Uniform Commercial Code: From Infancy to Maturity to Old Age." *Loyola of Los Angeles Law Review* 26 (April 1993): 691–702.

Melnick, Shep. "Deregulating the States: Federalism in the Rehnquist Court." In *Evolving Federalisms: The Intergovernmental Balance of Power in America and Europe,* 109–41. Syracuse, N.Y.: Maxwell School of Citizenship and Public Affairs, 2003.

Meredith, Robyn. "Tennessee Governor Talks of Revolt on E.P.A. Smog Rules." *New York Times,* March 15, 1998, sec. 1.

Mertens, Richard. "States Eye Stricter Curbs on Great Lakes Water." *Christian Science Monitor,* January 8, 2008.

Mikesell, John. "Changing State Fiscal Capacity and Tax Effort in an Era of Devolving Government, 1981–2003." *Publius: The Journal of Federalism* 37 (Fall 2007): 532–50.

Milbank, Dana. "Senate Panel Says Enron Must Detail Policy Role; Subpoenas Shift Probe to White House Contacts." *Washington Post,* March 23, 2002.

Miller, Fred H. "Letter from the President." *Uniform Activities eNewsletter* (April 2004): 1.

———. "Is Karl's Kode Kaput?" *Loyola of Los Angeles Law Review* 26 (April 1993): 703–14.

Mooney, Christopher Z. "Modeling Regional Effects on State Policy Diffusion." *Political Research Quarterly* 54 (March 2001): 103–124.

Morgan, Dan. "Funding Bill Contains Plenty of Goodies." *Washington Post,* December 26, 2003.

———. "Hastert Directs Millions to Birthplace; Earmarked Money Skirts Procedures." *Washington Post,* May 29, 2005.

Morrisroe, Darby A. "The State of 'State Offices' in Washington: A Critical Assessment." Paper presented at the annual meeting of the American Political Science Association, Boston, Mass., September 3–6, 1998.

Murphy, Kathleen. "States Target Greenhouse Gases." Stateline.org, February 13, 2003, http://www.stateline.org/live/ViewPage.action?siteNodeID=136&languageId=1&contentId=15159.

Nagel, Robert F. *The Implosion of American Federalism.* New York: Oxford University Press, 2001.

Nagourney, Adam. "G.O.P. Right is Splintered on Schiavo Intervention." *New York Times,* March 23, 2005.

Nathan, Richard P. "The Devolution Revolution: An Overview." In *Rockefeller Institute Bulletin: Symposium on American Federalism Today,* 5–13. Albany, N.Y.: Rockefeller Institute of Government, 1996.

——. "The Role of the States in American Federalism." In *The State of the States*, edited by Carl E. Van Horn, 15–32. Washington, D.C.: Congressional Quarterly, 1989.

National Conference of Commissioners on Uniform State Laws. *Annual Report 2004–2005*. Chicago: NCCUSL, n.d. Available online at http://www.nccusl.org/nccusl/docs/AnnReport_05.pdf.

——. *Handbook of the National Conference of Commissioners on Uniform State Laws and Proceedings of the Annual Conference.* Multiple volumes. Baltimore, Md.: Lord Baltimore Press, 1920–.

——. *Proceedings of the Annual Meeting of the National Conference of Commissioners on Uniform State Laws.* 1915.

——. *Proceedings of the Fourteenth Annual Conference of the National Conference of Commissioners on Uniform State Laws.* Annual meeting of the NCCUSL, St. Louis, Mo., Sept. 22–24, 1904.

——."Statement of Policy Establishing Criteria and Procedures for Designation and Consideration of Acts, Jan. 13, 2001," http://www.nccusl.org/Update/DesktopDefault.aspx?tabindex=3&tabide=42.

National Governors' Association. "Governors Praise House Vote to Delay Implementation of Medicaid Rules" (press release, April 23, 2008). Accessed via News Room link, http://www.nga.org.

——. "Governors Reaffirm Support for Delaying Implementation of Medicaid Rules" (press release, June 5, 2008). Accessed via News Room link, http://www.nga.org.

——. *The Governor's Washington Office.* Washington, D.C.: NGA, January 1991.

——. *Policy Positions.* Washington, D.C.: NGA, February 1996.

National Governors' Conference. *Federal Roadblocks to Efficient State Government.* 2nd printing. Washington, D.C.: NGC, February 1977.

"A National Highway Priority" (editorial). *Boston Globe*, July, 2, 1995.

National Retail Federation. "Retailer Supports Sales Tax Simplification Bill" (press release). NRF.com, July 25, 2006, http://www.nrf.com/modules.php?name=News&op=viewlive&sp_id=124.

National Voter Registration Act of 1993. Public Law 103-31. Codified at 42 *U.S. Code* sec. 1973.

Neuman, Johanna. "Rules Loosened for No Child Left Behind Law." *Los Angeles Times*, April 8, 2005.

"NGA Urges Quick Passage of Technical Corrections." *Governors' Bulletin*, March 10, 1997.

Nice, David C. *Federalism: The Politics of Intergovernmental Relations.* New York: St. Martin's Press, 1987.

Noonan, Jr., John T. *Narrowing the Nation's Power: The Supreme Court Sides with the States.* Berkeley: University of California Press, 2002.

Nugent, John D. "Public Officials' Associations." In *Federalism in America: An Encyclopedia*, vol. 2, edited by Joseph R. Marbach, Ellis Katz, and Troy E. Smith, 518–24. Westport, Conn.: Greenwood Press, 2006.

Olson, Lynn. "3 States Get OK to Use Growth Model to Gauge AYP." *Education Week*, November 15, 2006, 24.

Osborne, David. *Laboratories of Democracy: A New Breed of Governor Creates Models for National Growth*. Boston: Harvard Business School Press, 1990.

Overby, A. Brooke. "Modeling UCC Drafting." *Loyola of Los Angeles Law Review* 29 (January 1996): 645–711.

Patchel, Kathleen. "Interest Group Politics, Federalism, and the Uniform Laws Process: Some Lessons from the Uniform Commercial Code." *Minnesota Law Review* 78 (1993): 83–164.

Peabody, Bruce G. "Book Review: Coordinate Construction, Constitutional Thickness, and Remembering the Lyre of Orpheus." Review of *Taking the Constitution away from the Courts*, by Mark Tushnet. *University of Pennsylvania Journal of Constitutional Law* 2 (Fall 2000): 662–75.

———. "Congressional Constitutional Interpretation and the Courts: A Preliminary Inquiry into Legislative Attitudes, 1959–2001." *Law and Social Inquiry* 29 (2004): 127–71.

———. "Nonjudicial Constitutional Interpretation, Authoritative Settlement, and a New Agenda for Research." *Constitutional Commentary* 16 (Spring 1999): 63–90.

Peabody, Bruce G., and John D. Nugent. "Toward a Unifying Theory of the Separation of Powers." *American University Law Review* 53 (October 2003): 1–64.

Pear, Robert. "Bush to Revisit Changes in Medicaid Rules." *New York Times*, February 24, 2004.

———. "Governors of Both Parties Oppose Medicaid Rules." *New York Times*, February 24, 2008, sec. 1.

———. "Governors and Officials Step Up Talks on Medicaid." *New York Times*, March 2, 2005.

———. "House G.O.P. Softens Bush Welfare Plan." *New York Times*, April 10, 2002.

———. "Most States Find Welfare Targets Well Within Reach." *New York Times*, September 23, 1996.

———. "Republicans Finish Writing Welfare Measure." *New York Times*, July 31, 1996.

———. "States Criticized on Lax Lead Tests for Poor Youths." *New York Times*, August 21, 1999, sec. 1.

———. "States Resist Bush's Appeal for Fast Deal on Medicaid." *New York Times*, March 1, 2005.

———. "Study by Governors Calls Bush Welfare Plan Unworkable." *New York Times*, April 4, 2002.

———. "U.S. Recommending Strict New Rules at Nursing Homes." *New York Times*, July 23, 2000.

Pelissero, John P., and Robert E. England. "State and Local Governments' Washington 'Reps'—Lobbying Strategies and President Reagan's New Federalism." *State and Local Government Review* 19 (Spring 1987), 68–72.

Perlman, Ellen. "The Preemption Beast: The Gorilla that Swallows State Laws." *Governing* 7 (August 1994): 46–51.

Personal Responsibility and Work Opportunity Reconciliation Act of 1996. Public Law 104-193. Codified at 42 *U.S. Code* sec. 1305.

Peters, B. Guy. *American Public Policy: Promise and Performance*. 5th ed. Chappaqua, N.Y.: Chatham House, 1999.

Petersen, John E. "The Check Is in the Mail." *Governing*, January 2007, http://www.governing.com/articles/0701fin.htm.

Peterson, Kavan. "Governors Lose in Power Struggle over National Guard." Stateline.org, January 12, 2007, http://www.stateline.org/live/details/story?contentId=170453.

Peterson, Paul E. "The Changing Politics of Federalism." In *Evolving Federalisms: The Intergovernmental Balance of Power in America and Europe*, 25–41. Syracuse, N.Y.: Maxwell School of Citizenship and Public Affairs, 2003.

———. *The Price of Federalism*. Washington, D.C.: Brookings Institution, 1995.

Pickerill, J. Mitchell, and Cornell W. Clayton. "The Rehnquist Court and the Political Dynamics of Federalism." *Perspectives on Politics* 2 (June 2004): 233–48.

Pickerill, J. Mitchell, and Paul Chen. "Medical Marijuana Policy and the Virtues of Federalism." *Publius: The Journal of Federalism* 38 (Winter 2008): 22–55.

Pittenger, John C. "Garcia and the Political Safeguards of Federalism: Is There a Better Solution to the Conundrum of the Tenth Amendment?" *Publius: The Journal of Federalism* 22 (Winter 1992): 1–19.

Piven, Frances Fox, and Richard A. Cloward. *Regulating the Poor: The Functions of Public Welfare*. New York: Vintage, 1971.

"Plugging the Internet Sales-Tax Loophole." *Seattle Times*, January 23, 2007.

Posner, Paul L. "The Politics of Preemption: Prospects for the States." *PS: Political Science & Politics*, July 2005, 371–74.

———. *The Politics of Unfunded Mandates: Whither Federalism?* Washington, D.C.: Georgetown University Press, 1998.

Potoski, Matthew. "Clean Air Federalism: Do States Race to the Bottom?" *Public Administration Review* 61, no. 3 (May/June 2001): 335–43.

Prah, Pamela M. "Budget Picture Dominates Govs' Speeches." Stateline.org, January 28, 2008, http://www.stateline.org/live/details/story?contentId=275354.

Prakash, Saikrishna B. "Field Office Federalism." *Virginia Law Review* 79 (1993): 1957–2037.

Prakash, Saikrishna B., and John C. Yoo. "The Puzzling Persistence of Process-Based Federalism Theories." *Texas Law Review* 79 (May 2001): 1459–1523.

Pressman, Jeffrey L., and Aaron Wildavsky. *Implementation: How Great Expectations in Washington Are Dashed in Oakland.* 3rd ed. Berkeley: University of California Press, 1984.

Pryde, Joan. "Lobbyists for Cities and Counties Find a Niche That Other Washington Players Just Can't Fill." *The Bond Buyer*, January 14, 1993, 3.

Raeker-Jordan, Susan. "The Pre-Emption Presumption That Never Was: Pre-emption Doctrine Swallows the Rule." *Arizona Law Review* 40 (Winter 1998): 1379–1468.

Rapaczynski, Andrzej. "From Sovereignty to Process: The Jurisprudence of Federalism after *Garcia.*" *Supreme Court Review* 8 (1985): 341–419.

Rapson, Donald J. "Who Is Looking Out for the Public Interest? Thoughts about the UCC Revision Process in the Light (and Shadows) of Professor Rubin's Observations." *Loyola of Los Angeles Law Review* 28 (November 1994): 249–285.

Rauch, Jonathan. *Government's End.* New York: Public Affairs, 1999.

Ravitch, Diane. "Every State Left Behind." *New York Times*, November 7, 2005.

Ravitz, Jessica. "Utahns Cheer as Guv Signs NCLB Protest." *Salt Lake Tribune*, May 3, 2005.

Readmond, Tom. "The Streamlined Sales Tax Proposal: A Tax Increase under the Radar." Americans for Tax Reform Policy Brief, n.d., http://www.atr.org/content/pdf/2005/dec/120704ot_SSTPpb.pdf.

Reagan, Michael. *The New Federalism.* New York: Oxford University Press, 1972.

Reagan, Ronald. Executive Order no. 12372. "Intergovernmental Review of Federal Programs, Executive Order 12372." *Code of Federal Regulations*, title 3 (1982): 197.

———. Executive Order no. 12612. "Federalism, Executive Order 12612." *Code of Federal Regulations*, title 3 (1987): 252.

"The REAL ID Revolt" (editorial). *Wall Street Journal*, May 8, 2007.

Reeves, Mavis Mann. *The Question of State Government Capability.* Washington, D.C.: Advisory Commission on Intergovernmental Relations, 1985.

———. "The States as Polities: Reformed, Reinvigorated, Resourceful." *Annals of the American Academy of Political and Social Science* 509 (1990): 83–93.

"Reforming Welfare, State by State" (editorial). *Washington Post*, December 18, 1994.

Rehnquist, William H. "Foreword." In Armstrong, *Century of Service*, 1–2.

———. "2004 Year-End Report on the Federal Judiciary." *The Third Branch* 37 (January 2005). http://www.uscourts.gov/ttb/jan05ttb/2004/index.html.

Reich, Robert B. *Locked in the Cabinet.* New York: Alfred A. Knopf, 1997.

Reinsch, Paul S. *American Legislatures and Legislative Methods.* New York: Century, 1913.

Renzulli, Diane. *Capitol Offenders: How Private Interests Govern Our States.* Washington, D.C.: Public Integrity Books, 2002.

Revesz, Richard L. "Federalism and Environmental Protection: A Normative Critique." In *The New Federalism: Can the States be Trusted?* edited by John Ferejohn and Barry R. Weingast, 97–128. Stanford, Calif.: Hoover Institution Press, 1997.

Richter, Paul. "Clinton Orders Easier Medicaid Rules for States." *Los Angeles Times,* February 2, 1993.

Riker, William. "The Senate and American Federalism." *American Political Science Review* 49 (1955): 452–69.

Rivlin, Alice. *Reviving the American Dream: The Economy, the States, and the Federal Government.* Washington, D.C.: Brookings Institution, 1992.

Ring, Carlyle C. "The UCC Process: Consensus and Balance." *Loyola of Los Angeles Law Review* 28 (November 1994): 287–307.

Roberts, Robert E. "A New Theory for the Times." *State Government News,* August 1996, 25–27.

Robertson, David B. "American Federalism and the Politics of Regulation." In *Evolving Federalisms: The Intergovernmental Balance of Power in America and Europe,* 63–86. Syracuse, N.Y.: Maxwell School of Citizenship and Public Affairs, 2003.

Robertson, David B., and Dennis R. Judd. *The Development of American Public Policy: The Structure of Policy Restraint.* Glenview, Ill.: Scott, Foresman, 1989.

Robinson, Paul H., Michael T. Cahill, and Usman Mohammad. "The Five Worst (and Five Best) American Criminal Codes." *Northwestern University Law Review* 95 (Fall 2000): 1–89.

Rockefeller, Nelson A. *The Future of Federalism.* Cambridge, Mass.: Harvard University Press, 1962.

Rogers, Henry Wade. "The Constitution and the New Federalism." *North American Review* 634 (September 1908): 321–35.

Romano, Roberta. "State Competition for Corporate Charters." In *The New Federalism: Can the States be Trusted?* edited by John Ferejohn and Barry R. Weingast, 129–54. Stanford, Calif.: Hoover Institution Press, 1997.

Rosenbaum, David E. "Gephardt Says He Will Resist Bush on Trade." *New York Times,* October 5, 2001.

———. "Governors' Frustration Fuels Effort on Welfare Financing." *New York Times,* March 21, 1996.

———. "An Intricate Senate Procedure Lends a Hand to Welfare Recipients." *New York Times,* November 1, 1995.

Rosenthal, Alan. *Governors and Legislatures: Contending Powers.* Washington, D.C.: Congressional Quarterly Press, 1990.

———. *The Third House: Lobbyists and Lobbying in the States.* Washington, D.C.: Congressional Quarterly Press, 1993.

Rosenthal, Albert J. "Conditional Federal Spending as a Regulatory Device." *San Diego Law Review* 26 (1989): 277–88.

Rossiter, Clinton, ed. *The Federalist Papers.* New York: Mentor, 1961. First published as *The Federalist* in 1788 by J. and A. McLean.

Rovner, Julie. "Welfare Reform: The Issue That Bubbled Up from the States to Capitol Hill." *Governing* 1 (December 1988): 17–21.

Rubin, Edward L. "Puppy Federalism and the Blessings of America." *Annals of the American Academy of Political and Social Science* 574 (March 2001): 37–51.

———. "Uniformity, Regulation, and the Federalization of State Law: Some Lessons from the Payment System." *Ohio State Law Journal* 49 (1989): 1251–76.

———. "Uniform State Laws: A Discussion Focused on Revision of the Uniform Commercial Code, Moderated by Albert J. Rosenthal." *Oklahoma City University Law Review* 22 (Spring 1997): 257–335.

Sack, Kevin. "States Expecting to Lose Billions from Repeal of U.S. Estate Tax." *New York Times,* June 21, 2001.

Safe Drinking Water Act of 1974. Public Law 93-523 (December 16, 1974).

Sager, Lawrence. *Justice in Plainclothes: A Theory of American Constitutional Practice.* New Haven, Conn.: Yale University Press, 2004.

Sanford, Terry. *Storm over the States.* New York: McGraw-Hill, 1967.

Saulny, Susan, and Jim Rutenberg. "Kansas Tornado Renews Debate on Guard at War." *New York Times,* May 9, 2007.

Savage, Charlie. "Hearing Set on Signing Statements: Senate Panel Will Probe Rationale for Bush Actions." *Boston Globe,* June 22, 2006.

Savage, Robert L. "Diffusion Research Traditions and the Spread of Policy Innovations in a Federal System." *Publius: The Journal of Federalism* 15 (Fall 1985): 1–27.

Schattschneider, E. E. *The Semi-Sovereign People.* Hinsdale, Ill.: Dryden Press, 1960.

Scheberle, Denise. *Federalism and Environmental Policy: Trust and the Politics of Implementation.* Washington, D.C.: Georgetown University Press, 1997.

Schemo, Diana Jean. "Effort by Bush on Education Hits Obstacles." *New York Times,* August 18, 2004.

———. "States' End Run Dilutes Burden for Special Ed." *New York Times,* June 7, 2004.

———. "States Get Federal Warning on School Standards." *New York Times,* October 24, 2002.

———. "20 States Ask for Flexibility in School Law." *New York Times,* February 22, 2006.

Schlesinger, Jr., Arthur M. *The Imperial Presidency.* Boston: Houghton Mifflin, 1973.

Schmitt, Richard B. "For Schiavo, Republicans Invite Federal Activism." *Los Angeles Times,* March 24, 2005.

Schneider, Anne Larason, and Helen Ingram. *Policy Design for Democracy.* Lawrence: University Press of Kansas, 1997.

Schneider, Greg, and Eric Pianin. "Nuclear Dump's Foes Hopeful; Reid, Now No. 2 Senate Leader, Organizes against Yucca Mountain." *Washington Post*, June 13, 2001.

Schneider, Saundra K. "Medicaid Section 1115 Waivers: Shifting Health Care Reform to the States." *Publius: The Journal of Federalism* 27 (Spring 1997): 89–109.

Schofield, William. "Uniformity of Law in the Several States as an American Ideal." *Harvard Law Review* 21 (May 1908): 583–94.

Schweitzer, Bryan. "Montana Governor on 'REAL ID' Act." By Melissa Block (host). National Public Radio's *All Things Considered* (March 7, 2008): n.p. (Transcript was accessed online via Lexis-Nexis.)

Shanahan, Eileen. "The Sudden Rise in Statehouse Status." *Governing* 9 (September 1996): 15.

Shapard, Rob. "How Safe Is Your Water?" *American City & County*, June 1997. http://www.americancityandcounty.com/mag/government_safe_water_congress/.

Sharkansky, Ira. *The Maligned States: Policy Accomplishments, Problems, and Opportunities.* 2nd ed. New York: McGraw-Hill, 1978.

Shenon, Philip. "House Votes to Issue Contempt Citations." *New York Times*, February 15, 2008.

Shepsle, Kenneth A. "Studying Institutions: Some Lessons from the Rational Choice Approach." *Journal of Theoretical Politics* 1 (1989): 131–47.

Sicherman, Jacob. "Construction of Clause in Uniform State Laws Providing for Uniformity of Interpretation." *American Bar Association Journal* 2 (1916): 60–78.

Skocpol, Theda. "Bringing the State Back In: Strategies of Analysis in Current Research." In *Bringing the State Back In*, edited by Peter B. Evans, Dietrich Rueschemeyer, and Theda Skocpol, 3–43. New York: Cambridge University Press, 1985.

Skowronek, Stephen. "Order and Change." *Polity* 28 (Fall 1995): 91–96.

Smith, Melancton. "Speech Delivered in the Course of Debate by the Convention of the State of New York on the Adoption of the Federal Constitution, June 20, 1778." In *The Anti-Federalist: Writings by the Opponents of the Constitution*, edited by Herbert J. Storing, selected by Murray Dry, 332–38. Chicago: University of Chicago Press, 1981.

Smith, Rogers M. "If Politics Matters: Implications for a 'New Institutionalism.'" *Studies in American Political Development* 6 (Spring 1992): 1–36.

Smith, Troy E. "What Safeguards of Federalism? The Exceptions' Rule." Paper presented at the annual meeting of the American Political Science Association, Washington, D.C., August 29–September 3, 2000.

Smith, Walter George. *Uniform Marriage and Divorce Laws. An Address by Hon. Walter George Smith at the Thirtieth Annual Meeting of the Ohio State Bar Association, Put-In-Bay, July 7, 1909.* Columbus, Ohio: Berlin Printing, 1909.

Smylie, Robert E. "Difficulties of a Small State in the Federal System." *State Government* 37 (1964).

"Social Policy." *Congressional Quarterly* (August 31, 1996): 2445.

Soss, Joe, Sanford F. Schram, Thomas P. Vartanian, and Erin O'Brien. "Setting the Terms of Relief: Explaining State Policy Choices in the Devolution Revolution." *American Journal of Political Science* 45 (April 2001): 378–95.

Sostek, Anya. "Jock Trap." *Governing*, June 2002, 42–44.

Stanfield, Rochelle. "Just Do It." *National Journal*, March 30, 1996, 692–702.

———. "Lots of Spin, But No Signs of Movement." *National Journal*, June 1, 1996, 1210.

———. "The PIGs: Out of the Sty, Into Lobbying with Style." *National Journal*, August 14, 1976, 1134–39.

"The States Milk Medicaid" (editorial). *Washington Post*, September 8, 2000.

Steinbeck, John. *Grapes of Wrath*. New York: Penguin Books, 1939.

Steinhauer, Jennifer. "51 Governors Resist Shifting Authority Over Guard." *New York Times*, August 15, 2006.

———. "States Prove Unpredictable in Aiding Uninsured Children." *New York Times*, September 28, 2000.

Stelter, Brian. "A Plan to Offer 50 Sites on Politics in 50 States." *New York Times*, February 18, 2008.

Stewart III, Charles. "Responsiveness in the Upper Chamber: The Constitution and the Institutional Development of the Senate." In *The Constitution and American Political Development*, edited by Peter F. Nardulli, 63–96. Urbana: University of Illinois Press, 1992.

Stimson, Frederic Jesup. "Uniform State Legislation." *Annals of the American Academy of Political and Social Science* 5 (May 1895): 1–36.

Stoil, Michael J. "President Clinton and Medicaid Waivers: Full Speed Ahead?" *Nursing Homes*, July–August 1994. http://www.findarticles.com/p/articles/mi_m3830/is_n6_v43ai_15728953.

Stoker, Robert P. *Reluctant Partners: Implementing Federal Policy*. Pittsburgh, Penn.: University of Pittsburgh Press, 1991.

Stolberg, Sheryl Gay. "The Revolution That Wasn't." *New York Times*, February 13, 2005, sec. 4.

Stone, Bradford. *Uniform Commercial Code in a Nutshell*. St. Paul, Minn.: West Publishing, 1995.

Stone, Deborah. *Policy Paradox: The Art of Political Decision Making*. New York: W.W. Norton, 1997.

Storing, Herbert J., ed. *The Anti-Federalist: Writings by the Opponents of the Constitution*. Selected by Murray Dry. Chicago: University of Chicago Press, 1981.

———, ed. *The Complete Anti-Federalist*. Vol. 6. Chicago: University of Chicago Press, 1981.

Stout, David. "Appeals Court Backs Cheney in Secrecy Case." *New York Times*, May 11, 2005.

Stovall, A. T. "Standards Proposed by United States Commission on Uniform Laws." In supplement, *Annals of the American Academy of Political and Social Science*, July 1911, 17–23.

Sullivan, Kathleen M. "From States' Rights Blues to Blue States' Rights: Federalism after the Rehnquist Court." *Fordham Law Review* 75 (November 2006): 799–813.

Sundquist, James L. *Constitutional Reform and Effective Government*. Rev. ed. Washington, D.C.: Brookings Institution, 1992.

Swift, Elaine K. *The Making of an American Senate: Reconstitutive Change in Congress, 1787–1841*. Ann Arbor: University of Michigan Press, 1996.

Taylor, Jr., E. Hunter. "Uniformity of Commercial Law and State-by-State Enactments: A Confluence of Contradictions." *Hastings Law Journal* 30 (November 1978), 337*ff*.

Tedeschi, Bob. "Web Merchants Brace for the Inevitable." *New York Times*, June 27, 2005.

Teske, Paul. "Checks, Balances, and Thresholds: State Regulatory Re-enforcement and Federal Preemption." *PS: Political Science & Politics*, July 2005, 367–70.

Thierer, Adam D. *The Delicate Balance: Federalism, Interstate Commerce, and Economic Freedom in the Technological Age*. Washington, D.C.: Heritage Foundation, 1999.

———. "President Clinton's Sellout of Federalism." Heritage Foundation executive memorandum no. 536, June 25, 1998, 1. http://www.heritage.org/Research/PoliticalPhilosophy/EM536.cfm.

Thoreau, Henry David. *Walden and Civil Disobedience: Authoritative Texts, Background, Reviews and Essays in Criticism*. Edited by Owen Thomas. New York: W.W. Norton, 1966.

Tiebout, Charles. "A Pure Theory of Local Public Expenditures." *Journal of Political Economy* 64 (1956): 416–24.

Toner, Robin. "Demands of Partisanship Bring Change to the Senate." *New York Times*, May 20, 2005.

Toppo, Greg. "States Warned about Medicaid Numbers." Associated Press, July 27, 2000.

Trade Act of 2002. Public Law 107-210, sec. 2103. Codified at 19 *U.S. Code* (2002), sec. 3801.

Truman, David B. "Federalism and the Party System." In *The Politics of American Federalism*, edited by Daniel J. Elazar, 40–51. Lexington, Mass.: Heath, 1969.

Tulis, Jeffrey L. *The Rhetorical Presidency*. Princeton, N.J.: Princeton University Press, 1987.

Turner, Frederick Jackson. *The Significance of Sections in American History*. New York: Henry Holt, 1932.

Tushnet, Mark. "The Constitution and the Nationalization of American Politics." In *A Workable Government? The Constitution After 200 Years*, edited by Burke Marshall, 154–166. New York: W.W. Norton, 1987.

———. *Taking the Constitution Away from the Courts*. Princeton, N.J.: Princeton University Press, 2000.

Uchitelle, Louis. "Raising the Floor on Pay: States Leap Ahead of Congress in Acting on Minimum Wage." *New York Times*, December 20, 2006.

Unfunded Mandates Reform Act of 1995. Public Law 104-4. Codified at 2 *U.S. Code* sec. 658–658g and 2 *U.S. Code* 1501–1571.

United Press International. "GOP Governors Meet with Dole, Gingrich." September 13, 1995.

U.S. Advisory Commission on Intergovernmental Relations. *Federal Statutory Preemption of State and Local Authority: History, Inventory, and Issues*. Washington, D.C.: ACIR, 1992.

———. *Regulatory Federalism: Policy, Process, Impact and Reform*. Washington, D.C.: ACIR, February 1984.

U.S. Census Bureau. *Compendium of Public Employment: 2002*. Vol. 3, *2002 Census of Governments*. Washington, D.C.: U.S. Census Bureau, September 2004.

U.S. Congress. *Congressional Record*. 106th Cong., 2nd sess., Sept. 19, 2000. Vol. 146, no. 111.

U.S. Department of Energy, Office of Civilian Radioactive Waste Management. *Yucca Mountain Science and Engineering Report: Technical Information Supporting Site Recommendation Consideration*. Document DOE/RW-0539. Washington, D.C.: U.S. Department of Energy, May 2001.

U.S. Department of Health and Human Services. "Final Rule for Temporary Assistance to Needy Families." *Federal Register* 64, no. 69 (April 12, 1999): 17720–931. Also available at http://www.acf.dhhs.gov/programs/ofa/tanfru1.htm (accessed May 17, 2006).

U.S. Environmental Protection Agency. *The Plain English Guide to the Clean Air Act*. Research Triangle Park, N.C.: Office of Air Quality Planning and Standards, April 2007.

U.S. House. Committee on Government Reform, Subcommittee on Energy Policy, Natural Resources, and Regulatory Affairs and the House Rules Subcommittee on Technology. *Unfunded Mandates: A Five-Year Review and Recommendations for Change*. 107th Cong., 1st sess., May 24, 2001.

———. Committee on Government Reform and Oversight, Subcommittee on Human Resources and Intergovernmental Relations. *The Federalism Debate: Why Doesn't Washington Trust the States?* 104th Cong., 1st sess., July 20, 1995.

————. Committee on the Judiciary, Subcommittee on Commercial and Administrative Law. *Hearing on HR 3396, the "Sales Tax Fairness and Simplification Act."* 110th Cong., 1st sess., December 6, 2007.

————. Committee on Ways and Means, Subcommittee on Human Resources. *The National Governors' Association Welfare Reform Proposal.* 104th Cong., 2nd sess., February 20, 1996.

U.S. Office of Management and Budget. *Budget Information for States.* Washington, D.C.: Government Printing Office, 2002.

U.S. Troop Readiness, Veterans' Care, Katrina Recovery, and Iraq Accountability Appropriations Act of 2007. Public Law 110-28, sec. 7002 (May 25, 2007).

Van Alstyne, William W. "The Second Death of Federalism." *Michigan Law Review* 83 (June 1985): 1709–33.

Van Horn, Carl E. "The Quiet Revolution." In *The State of the States,* edited by Carl E. Van Horn, 1–14. Washington, D.C.: Congressional Quarterly, 1989.

Verhovek, Sam Howe. "Drill, Say Alaskans, Who Know Their Pockets Are Lined with Oil." *New York Times,* March 18, 2001, sec. 1.

Villareal, Sandi. "Internet Sales Elude the Taxman." *St. Louis (Mo.) Post-Dispatch,* April 12, 2006.

Virginia Commission on Constitutional Government. *We the States: An Anthology of Historic Documents and Commentaries Thereon, Expounding the State and Federal Relationship.* Richmond, Va.: William Byrd Press, 1964.

Vobejda, Barbara. "Welfare Bill Glides through Senate; Approval Sends Overhaul to White House for Clinton Signature." *Washington Post,* August 2, 1996.

Volden, Craig. "Entrusting the States with Welfare Reform." In *The New Federalism: Can the States Be Trusted?* edited by John Ferejohn and Barry R. Weingast, 65–96. Stanford, Calif.: Hoover Institution Press, 1997.

Vu, Pauline. "Behind Scenes, Groups Shape State Policy." Stateline.org, June 8, 2005, http://www.stateline.org/live/ViewPage.action?siteNodeId=136&languageId=1&contentId=36188.

Waggoner, Lawrence W. "Symposium: One Hundred Years of Uniform State Laws." *Michigan Law Review* 89 (August 1991), 2079–2080.

Wagner, David. *What's Love Got to Do With It? A Critical Look at American Charity.* New York: New Press, 2000.

"Waiting for Waivers" (editorial). *The Cleveland Plain Dealer,* February 7, 1996.

Walker, David B. "The Advent of an Ambiguous Federalism and the Emergence of New Federalism III." *Public Administration Review* 56 (May/June 1996): 271–80.

————. *The Rebirth of Federalism: Slouching toward Washington.* 2nd ed. New York: Chatham House, 2000.

Walker, Jack L. "The Diffusion of Innovation among the American States." *American Political Science Review* 63 (Sept. 1969), 880–99.

Wallace, John William. *The Want of Uniformity in the Commercial Law between the Different States of Our Union. A Discourse Delivered before the Law Academy of Philadelphia, November 26th, 1851* (pamphlet). Philadelphia: L.R. Bailey, Printer, n.d.

Wallsten, Peter, and Tom Hamburger. "Bush Says Faith Should Figure in Charity Jobs." *Los Angeles Times*, March 2, 2005.

Waltenberg, Eric N., and Bill Swinford. *Litigating Federalism: The States before the U.S. Supreme Court.* Westport, Conn.: Greenwood Press, 1999.

Walters, Jonathan. "'Save Us From the States!'" *Governing* 14 (June 2001): 20–27.

———. "Walking in a Waiver Wonderland." *Governing*, October 1995, 13–14.

Watson, Traci. "EPA Is Slammed on Dirty Water: Agency, States Fail to Track Many Pollution Sources, Inspector Says." *USA Today*, August 23, 2001.

Weaver, R. Kent. "Deficits and Devolution in the 104th Congress." *Publius: The Journal of Federalism* 26 (1996): 45–85.

Wechsler, Herbert. "The Political Safeguards of Federalism: The Role of the States in the Composition and Selection of the National Government." *Columbia Law Review* 54 (1954): 543–560.

Weidner, Edward W. "Decision-Making in a Federal System." In *Federalism Mature and Emergent*, edited by Arthur W. Macmahon, 363–383. Garden City, N.Y.: Doubleday, 1955.

Weinberg, Louise. "Fear and Federalism." *Ohio Northern University Law Review* 23 (1997): 1295–1342.

Weissert, Carol S. "The National Governors' Association: 1908–1983." *State Government* 56 (1983): 44–52.

Welborn, David M. "Conjoint Federalism and Environmental Regulation in the United States." *Publius: The Journal of Federalism* 18 (Winter 1988): 27–43.

Welch, William M. "Shifting Welfare to the States: Is Innovation or Economic Boom Behind Change?" *USA Today*, May 29, 1996.

"Welfare Bill Clears Under Veto Threat." In *1995 CQ Almanac* 7-36–7-52. Washington, D.C.: Congressional Quarterly, 1996.

"Welfare to Work Challenge: How Many Jobs?" In *1995 CQ Almanac*, 7–45. Washington, D.C.: Congressional Quarterly, 1996.

West, Martin R. *No Child Left Behind: How to Give it a Passing Grade.* Brookings Institution Policy Brief no. 149, December 2005.

Weston, Liz Pulliam. "Estate Tax Repeal to Hurt State Finances." *Los Angeles Times*, May 31, 2001, part 3.

White, James J. "Ex Proprio Vigore." *Michigan Law Review* 89 (August 1991): 2106–28.

White, Leonard D. *The States and the Nation.* Baton Rouge: Louisiana State University, 1953.

Whittington, Keith E. *Constitutional Construction: Divided Powers and Constitutional Meaning.* Cambridge, Mass.: Harvard University Press, 1999.

———. "Crossing Over: Citation of Public Law Faculty in Law Reviews." *Law and Courts* (newsletter of the Law and Courts section of the American Political Science Association) 14 (Spring 2004): 5–10.

———. "Dismantling the Modern State? The Changing Structural Foundations of Federalism." *Hastings Constitutional Law Quarterly* 25 (Summer 1998): 483–527.

———. "Extrajudicial Constitutional Interpretation: Three Objections and Responses." *North Carolina Law Review* 80 (2002): 773–851.

Wickline, Michael R. "Panel Backs Bills on Multistate Tax Pact." *Arkansas Democrat-Gazette*, Feb. 15, 2007.

Wigfield, Mark. "Bush May Bypass Congress, Fill FTC Posts During Recess." *Wall Street Journal*, July 23, 2004.

Wilkins, David E. "Tribal–State Affairs: The American States as 'Disclaiming' Sovereigns." *Publius: The Journal of Federalism* 28 (Fall 1998): 55–81.

Williamson, Richard S. *Reagan's Federalism: His Efforts to Decentralize Government.* Lanham, Md.: University Press of America, 1990.

Wilson, Woodrow. *Constitutional Government in the United States.* New York: Columbia University Press, 1908.

Wise, Charles R. "The Supreme Court's New Constitutional Federalism: Implications for Public Administration." *Public Administration Review* 61 (May/June 2001): 343–58.

Woods, Neal D. "Primacy Implementation of Environmental Policy in the U.S. States." *Publius: The Journal of Federalism* 36, no. 2 (2006): 259–76.

Wright, Deil S. *Understanding Intergovernmental Relations.* 2nd ed. Monterey, Calif.: Brooks/Cole, 1982.

———. *Understanding Intergovernmental Relations.* 3rd ed. Pacific Grove, Calif.: Brooks/Cole, 1988.

Yin, Robert K. *Case Study Research: Design and Methods.* 3rd ed. Thousand Oaks, Calif.: Sage Publications, 2003.

Yoo, John C. "The Judicial Safeguards of Federalism." *Southern California Law Review* 70 (July 1997): 1311–1405.

Zagarri, Rosemarie. *The Politics of Size: Representation in the United States, 1776–1850.* Ithaca, N.Y.: Cornell University Press, 1987.

Zekan, Julianna J. "Uniform State Laws: A Discussion Focused on Revision of the Uniform Commercial Code." *Oklahoma City University Law Review* 22 (Spring 1997): 257–335.

Zimmerman, Joseph F. "Congressional Preemption During the George W. Bush Administration." *Publius: The Journal of Federalism* 37 (Spring 2007): 432–52.

———. *Congressional Preemption: Regulatory Federalism.* Albany: State University of New York Press, 2005.

———. "Congressional Preemption: Removal of State Regulatory Powers." *PS: Political Science & Politics*, July 2005, 375–78.

———. *Interstate Relations: The Neglected Dimension of Federalism*. Westport, Conn.: Praeger, 1996.

———. "The Nature and Political Significance of Preemption." *PS: Political Science & Politics*, July 2005, 359–62.

———. "Preemption in the U.S. Federal System." *Publius: The Journal of Federalism* 23 (Fall 1993): 1–14.

INDEX